MW00834889

GAME ON

GAME

ON

How Sports Media Grew Up, Sold Out,
and Got Personal with Billions of Fans

DAVID BOCKINO

University of Nebraska Press / Lincoln

The University of Nebraska Press is part of a land-grant institution with campuses and programs on the past, present, and future homelands of the Pawnee, Ponca, Otoe-Missouria, Omaha, Dakota, Lakota, Kaw, Cheyenne, and Arapaho Peoples, as well as those of the relocated Ho-Chunk, Sac and Fox, and Iowa Peoples.

Library of Congress Cataloging-in-Publication Data
Names: Bockino, David, author.
Title: Game on: how sports media grew up, sold out, and got personal with billions of fans / David Bockino.
Description: Lincoln: University of Nebraska Press, [2024] | Includes bibliographical references and index.
Identifiers: LCCN 2023028986
ISBN 9781496233172 (hardback)
ISBN 9781496239358 (epub)
ISBN 9781496239365 (pdf)
Subjects: LCSH: Mass media and sports. | Sports—Social aspects. | Mass media and culture. | BISAC: SPORTS & RECREATION / History | LANGUAGE ARTS & DISCIPLINES / Journalism
Classification: LCC GV742 .B627 2024 | DDC 796—dc23/eng/20231026
LC record available at https://lccn.loc.gov/2023028986

Set in Questa by A. Shahan.

To Matthew, Mary, and Lou

Contents

Acknowledgments

My own sports media origin story involves the 2006 Bassmaster Classic, an ESPN legend named Bruce Kalfus, and Disney's Wilderness Lodge. I think Scott Paciello was there too. That gig turned into a job with the ESPN Ad Sales Research Dream Team: Pete Leimbach, Dave Coletti, Christian DeBonville, Sara Corcoran, and Emily Gargula. From there I met dozens of people all over the world—from Australia to India to Argentina—all of whom contributed to this narrative in their own way. But I won't list them all; this book is long enough.

Many thanks to everyone at Elon University who helped with both funding and support, including the staff at Belk Library; the entire School of Communications; and my home team, the Department of Sport Management. Jonah Straus and Alec MacDonald were instrumental in putting a shape to the manuscript and finding it a home. Three more key contributors: Matthew, who always tells me what I'm doing wrong; Mary, who always tells me what I'm doing right; and Lou, who doesn't care about any of it and just wants to play cars.

GAME ON

Prologue

Unparalleled Absurdity:
Jose Canseco vs. Billy Football (2021)

In early 2021 former professional baseball player Jose Canseco agreed to a boxing match against Billy Football, a twenty-one-year-old intern for the digital media platform Barstool Sports. Canseco had been hoping to fight one of the Paul brothers (Logan or Jake), both of whom had become famous as social media influencers and one of whom had dated Canseco's daughter. But they ignored his challenge, confident that they could secure better opponents on the celebrity boxing circuit. Canseco moved on, reverting to an old beef with Dan Katz (a.k.a. Big Cat), co-host of the popular Barstool podcast *Pardon My Take.* On Twitter Canseco threw the first jab: "The only person that dodges more than the Paul boys is @BarstoolBigCat."[1] Billy Football, an intern who worked with Katz, responded: "O you have crossed the line raisin balled fuck."[2] Then Barstool president Dave Portnoy chimed in: "Jose Canceso [*sic*] vs. Billy Football. 100k to winner."[3] Both fighters quickly agreed. And suddenly Jose Canseco, once one of the most famous baseball players in the world, was scheduled to fight a Barstool Sports intern in a three-round exhibition boxing match.

Not that Jose Canseco's life had ever been normal. As an outfielder for the Oakland Athletics in the 1980s, Canseco was about as popular as any baseball player can be. He won an MVP award, made it into an episode of *The Simpsons*, and dated Madonna. He was comically strong, had cool hair, and drove around California in a Porsche 911. Canseco was the perfect caricature of a specific era in baseball history—an era ruled by performance-enhancing drugs—only nobody realized it at the time. Everyone just thought he was the man. Then he got outed as a steroid user, wrote a book accusing a bunch of fellow players of doing the same, and became a baseball pariah. As the years went on, Canseco began lingering on social media, starting illogical beefs with famous people. It was only natural that these social media tirades would eventually lead to Barstool, whose fans eat such stuff up.

Jose Canseco vs. Billy Football was scheduled for February 5, 2021, the main event for Rough N' Rowdy 13, an amateur boxing competition that Barstool had purchased in 2017. The affair was pitched as a night of "unparalleled absurdity," complete with scantily clad ring girls and an undercard of amateur fighters "throwing haymakers." The ongoing pandemic meant there'd be no live audience. Instead the fight would be exclusively streamed on the internet by Barstool for $19.95, quite a deal for "an experience worth roughly a gazillion dollars." Even better news: Stoolies, the loyal devotees of the Barstool empire, could win upwards of $25,000 by correctly choosing the night's winners. All they had to do was download the official Barstool mobile app and make their picks.[4]

There was significant pre-match chatter within the Barstool community: debate about betting odds, conversation about fitness regimes, lots of trash talking. In the days leading up to the fight Billy Football told the celebrity gossip website TMZ he was confident he'd come out on top: "I think I'm gonna shock Jose. . . . He's gonna end up respecting me and hopefully at the end of it, we can go hunting Big Foot together."[5] Then, as fight day approached, Canseco ramped up his Twitter usage. On January 14 he wrote, "Retweet if you're tired of @barstoolsports being on the internet."[6] A week later it was, "15 days until I knock @Billyhottakes senseless."[7] Then there were some tweets about cryptocurrency, a "RIP" for baseball legend Hank Aaron, who had just passed away, and a promotion for a company that makes honey. On fight day Canseco penned a tweet with his own name listed twenty times, followed by "1st ROUND KNOCKOUT."[8] Then a few more tweets and one final pitch: "20 minutes until showtime. It's only $19.99 to have the Friday night you've had this year [sic]. Don't miss this."[9]

It would have been easy to miss. Although the buildup had lasted weeks, the actual fight lasted less than fifteen seconds. After the bell the fighters shuffled to the middle of the ring. Billy Football threw a right; Canseco, a left. Both men started swinging wildly until Canseco moved in for a clinch, stumbled to the ground, and ended up in a corner. Billy Football hovered over him, connected on a couple of shots to the head, and the ref blew the whistle. Canseco winced in pain and tapped out. The fight was over.

Over the next few days Jose Canseco would claim that he had hurt his shoulder. Portnoy tweeted that this was nonsense, that Canseco had taken a dive and had swindled Barstool out of a million dollars. The Barstool Sportsbook account sent out a tweet saying that anybody who had bet on Jose Canseco would get their money back. Canseco was more than happy to engage with this post-match discourse: "You and your Barstool minions need to put down the marijuana and focus on your failing business #CrumblingEmpire."[10] Eventually Portnoy and Canseco moved on. The Stoolies, too, found some other piece of absurdity to occupy their time.

Not me. While it'd be easy to dismiss this fight as another pointless internet occurrence—such occurrences happen all the time, every minute of every day—something about this particular event stayed with me. I couldn't stop thinking about it: the participants, the consumers, the promotion. There were a few reasons why. One: I grew up a big Jose Canseco fan. I had books filled with Canseco baseball cards, a drawer filled with Canseco T-shirts, and walls covered with Canseco posters. It was disorienting and kind of sad to see my childhood idol reduced to a punching bag in a hastily prepared Barstool pay-per-view. Two: I talk about Barstool Sports often. Many of my students at Elon University are part of the loyal Barstool contingent, and I've found that teaching them the intricacies of the sports media industry becomes much easier if I throw some Barstool anecdotes into the mix. And three: as someone who has spent his entire life immersed within sports media—first as a fan, then as an employee at ESPN, and now as a college professor—I couldn't help but notice that this match occurred almost exactly one hundred years after a particularly notable fight, Jack Dempsey vs. Georges Carpentier. As one of the first sporting events to be broadcast over the radio, Dempsey/

Carpentier is considered a watershed moment in the evolution of mass communication (it's often included in introductory media textbooks) and is sometimes referred to as the beginning of the modern-day sports media industry.

A hundred years; two fights; different in almost every way. The first was between a draft dodger and a fighter pilot, was attended by thousands of people wearing suits, and was relayed by antenna into theaters equipped with radios so that those not in attendance could gather and listen to the action live. The second was between a disgraced baseball player and an intern for a digital media brand, was attended by nobody because of lingering fears from an ongoing global pandemic, and was made available to stream exclusively via pay-per-view. As someone who spends a lot of time thinking about both sports *and* media for a living, I couldn't help but feel that these two events were bookends to a narrative that hadn't yet been properly told. How did we go from Dempsey vs. Carpentier to Jose Canseco vs. Billy Football? What had happened in between to link these two events? And what does this evolutionary arc—a maturation that contains its fair share of unparalleled absurdity—tell us about ourselves as sports fans—or even as human beings?

Those questions are the genesis of this book, a history of the sports media industry from 1921 to 2021. From the radio broadcast of the Dempsey/Carpentier match in 1921, the launch of *Sports Illustrated* (*SI*) in 1954, and the emergence of ESPN in 1979 to the rise of talk radio in the 1980s, the explosion of the sports blogosphere (and Barstool) in the mid-2000s, and the onset of legal online sports wagering in the 2010s, the following chapters tell the story of how and why the sports media industry grew to become one of the most important and profitable components of the global entertainment landscape.

Woven throughout these stories is an equally important tale about purpose, about why we read about, listen to, and watch sports in the first place. In the early chapters we'll see how sports media had the unique power to bring people together, be it nationally through broadcasts of the World Cup and the Olympic Games, or regionally, with telecasts of a local baseball or football team. The importance given these broadcasts led to more people getting involved: politicians, who saw it as their duty to determine who should be and who shouldn't be allowed to see certain games, and corporations, which embarked on a quest to wring every last dollar from the seemingly insatiable sports fan. This increased interest led to more innovation and more options—cable television and talk radio and the internet. Some fans, presented with a multitude of choices, began to show deep loyalties to certain brands or personalities (like the Stoolies), sometimes in place of their loyalties to individual teams or players. And today, as the market rapidly shifts and expands, we see a seismic transformation that stands in stark contrast to the industry's origins, a move toward the personalization of sports content, where broadcasters and content creators focus on the demands of individual consumers, often at the expense of the collective experience. If there was ever a time to take stock of what's happened in the sports media industry over the last hundred years, that time is now, before online streaming and social media and advanced technology and gambling change the industry forever.

It's also just a really good story. Some parts are rather dramatic; others, kind of funny. Like in any good tale, there are plenty of subplots: Black vs. white, man vs. woman, socialist vs. capitalist. Memorable personalities pop up at every turn. A snobby wrestler accompanied by a butler plays a significant role. So does a Filipino dictator, Crocodile Dundee, Shaquille O'Neal, the president of Argentina, and Mike Francesca (if he ever reads this book, he'll like that he's in the prologue). The story also covers some ground: a trip to Germany, a stopover in Australia, a rendezvous in the United Kingdom, a detour down to South America, brief forays into India and China. But the star of the show is money. Lots and lots of money. It's the main character, although it doesn't get too many lines until a few chapters in. But when it arrives, boy does it arrive! An absolute scene stealer.

Anyway we already have an ending: a former professional baseball player writhing on the ground, grabbing his shoulder in pain while a bunch of miffed Barstool bros post angry social media messages. What we need now is a beginning.

Part 1 / Origin

Origin stories are convenient. They allow us to look back in time and say, "Well, that's where it all began, huh?" But origin stories are often inaccurate, a mishmash of useful omission and purposeful misdirection for the sake of a succinct, singular narrative.

In some ways the modern sports media industry has its own origin story: the radio broadcast of a 1921 boxing match between Jack Dempsey and Georges Carpentier. The fight is often discussed as one of the first times thousands of people in different locations—some in their homes, others in movie theaters—were brought together by technology to experience the same event right as it happened. From this match, or so the story goes, emerged an insatiable demand for sports on the radio. Broadcast television came next, then cable, satellite, the internet, social media . . .

Alas, it's not quite that simple. Over the next few decades crucial details about Dempsey vs. Carpentier would be embellished and exaggerated. The fight's importance would be somewhat misconstrued. But it remains a compelling yarn nonetheless, and the (mostly retroactive) significance assigned to the match makes it as good a place to start as any, an appropriate introduction to the complex and often disjointed history of the sports media industry.

The full story, however, begins not in 1921, when the match took place, but several years earlier, with Thomas Edison and Times Square and with yet another boxing spectacle that similarly took on a life of its own.

The Fight of the Century

1

Jack Dempsey vs. Georges Carpentier (1921)

The matchup was hailed as the "Fight of the Century," one of many "fights of the century" that would take place over the next century: Jack Johnson, a Black man, was set to defend his heavyweight boxing championship against Jim Jeffries, a white man, on July 4, 1910, in Reno, Nevada. For years Jeffries, who had retired as an undefeated champion in 1905, had refused to fight Johnson (who subsequently won the title in 1908) because he did not want to cross the "color line." Before he retired, Jeffries told the press, "Don't think I am afraid of a negro. I'm not. They can be licked just as easily as anybody else. I simply have promised myself that I would fight only white men, and I won't break my word."[1] But the dearth of talented contenders, combined with Johnson's prodigious dominance, left the (white) public clamoring for someone who could take the belt away from this seemingly unbeatable Black man. Jeffries eventually succumbed to the pressure, not least because he was broke, and agreed to end his retirement so he could face Johnson for the title.

Famous American writer, boxing enthusiast, and *New York Herald* correspondent Jack London planned on going and couldn't have been more excited: "Surely, there is a money price that would keep me away from the fight, but the attempt to calculate the amount would be very fatiguing." The matchup, London continued, was a once-in-a-lifetime event: "Viewed from every possible angle, there has never been anything like it in the history of the ring, and there is no chance for anything like it to occur in the future, at least within the lifetime of those alive today."[2] Excitement for the fight extended well beyond sports fans. While some saw Johnson-Jeffries as simply the next great championship bout, others viewed it as a referendum on racial superiority. An editorial in the *Chicago Tribune* published the morning of the match put it as follows: "It is now only a matter of hours before the absorbing question of whether a white man or a negro shall be supreme in the world of fisticuffs, which means in this instance the world at large, is answered."[3]

Oh, it was answered all right. Johnson dominated from the opening bell, leaving no doubt as to which boxer was the true heavyweight champion of the world and which had recently been resting happily at home tending his alfalfa farm. In the fifteenth round Johnson knocked the "great white hope" down for the third and final time, putting an end to a battle that was never really one to begin with. "Scarcely ever has there been a championship contest that was so one-sided," wrote former champion John L. Sullivan in the *New York Times* the next day. Granted, it was the outcome Sullivan said he had predicted, even if he had refused to write it in the paper or say it to Johnson himself because of his "well-known antipathy to [Johnson's] race."[4]

Newspaper headlines the next day affirmed that this match was as much about "Black vs. white" as it was about "Johnson vs. Jeffries." The *San Francisco Examiner* alone published several articles alluding to race: "Black Is Faster and Cleverer: Hits Harder, Cleaner, Oftener"; "Jeffries Mastered—Whipped by Grinning, Jeering Negro"; "White Man as Helpless as a Baby in Hands of the Giant Black."[5] Like Sullivan, many of these columnists and editors also made it clear for whom they had been rooting, reluctantly giving Johnson his due while doling out a series of backhanded racist half-compliments. Syndicated columnist and novelist Rex Beach wrote that Johnson "demonstrated further that his race has acquired full stature as men; whether they will ever breed brains to match his muscles is yet to be proven."[6]

To Johnson, though, the fight was less a testament to his mental capacity and physical prowess than it was a "straight business proposition."[7] And what a business it was. The battle in Reno would bring in an unprecedented $270,775 from attendees (around $7 million in today's dollars), almost \$100,000 more than from all five games of the 1910 World Series combined.[8] An article in *Harper's Weekly* published prior to the bout, meanwhile, explained just how lucrative the opportunity was for the fighters themselves, suggesting that the fight's \$101,000 purse—the money that would be distributed between the winner and loser—was "but the appetizer which introduces the golden feast."[9] First, there were the \$10,000 bonuses given out to each boxer to secure the match, a down payment of sorts. Next, there were the hundreds of thousands of dollars to be gained from appearances post-match, "jaunts around the world" where attendees could gawk at two of the most famous sportsmen on the planet.

But most exciting among all these opportunities was boxing's latest revenue stream: the production and distribution of the fight film. Ever since Thomas Edison, a boxing fan, had introduced the world to his kinetoscope in early 1894—a coin-operated machine with a peephole that allowed individuals to view short motion pictures—people had clamored for more content. One early company dedicated to producing short kinetoscope films, the Kinetoscope Exhibiting Company, decided that boxing, with its limited footprint and tidy round-by-round structure, was the perfect foil for this new technology. After having success filming and distributing a match between two lesser-known pugilists in June 1894, the company set its sights higher, arranging a fight a few months later between Gentleman Jim Corbett, the country's most popular heavyweight, and a challenger named Pete Courtney.

It was a fabricated affair. To maximize excitement (and revenue) for the film, the producers determined that the fight would last only six one-minute rounds and that it would conclude with Corbett knocking out his opponent.[10] In the limited footage that remains Corbett can actually be seen chuckling as he prances around the ring.[11] Still, the public ate it up: Corbett-Courtney became one of the highest grossing films of its era, and Gentleman Jim himself made over \$20,000 from royalties.[12] Because Corbett's victory was preordained, Terry Ramsaye, an early film historian, argues that this footage exists as "the ancestor of dramatic construction for the motion picture . . . the first step toward having things happen for the camera rather than merely photographing events ordained by other forces."[13] In some ways, then, this contrived contest should also be seen as the precursor to the pregame show, the commercial break, and the sideline interview—one of the earliest realizations, for better or for worse, that sporting events could be *produced* rather than just filmed.

By the time Johnson-Jeffries came around, motion picture technology had improved to the point that films could be projected onto a screen. Boxing remained a popular draw and *Harper's* estimated that the Johnson-Jeffries film, which would be shown in theaters in the weeks after the fight, could bring in an unprecedented $1 million (about $27 million today), almost four times as much as the gate. There was one catch: that kind of haul was believed possible only if Jeffries won. If Johnson prevailed, it was thought that white viewers would be less inclined to spend their money reliving a battle in which their chosen racial representative came out a loser. In short, *Harper's* estimated that beating Jeffries would cost Johnson around $200,000 in film-related revenue.

But the magazine failed to account for an even more ominous possibility: that a dominant Johnson performance would lead not only to subdued interest in the film, but also to violent public backlash. In fact, much of the news reported the day after the fight wasn't really about the fight at all. It was about the fallout from Johnson's win, the reverberations from a Black man's securing a no-doubt-about-it victory over a beloved white champion. On the front page of the *New York Times*, opposite an article detailing the results of the fight, was a dire account of what had transpired around the country following the match: "Riots between negroes and white men, attacks upon the former by the latter, and in many instances upon the whites by the blacks, occurred in all parts of the country yesterday evening as a result of Johnson's victory over Jeffries."[14]

It's unclear how many lives were lost in the riots following Johnson's win; one source reported at least twenty-one deaths and over three hundred injuries.[15] Regardless of the actual count, the chaos was further proof to many Americans that boxing had to go. By 1910 the sport was already banned in many cities and states, although the specific legislation varied and was often either circumvented or outright ignored. Cries from reform-minded organizations such as the United Society for Christian Endeavor followed various scripts. Some said the sport was too violent; others claimed it attracted crooks and gamblers and that it corrupted the youth. The Johnson-Jeffries fallout provided an additional argument, evidence that boxing intensified racial tensions.

When the reformers learned that banning the sport itself was futile, they decided to go in a different direction: prevent distribution of the fight films. John W. Nicely, a pastor in Chicago, was quoted in the local paper as saying, "The effect of the pictures on the young is worse than the occurrence of the prizefight itself, because they present the entire thing with all the revolting details."[16] The governor of Connecticut offered another justification: "In my opinion the public exhibition in the state of moving pictures of [a] prizefight would be much more objectionable than the fight itself, because it would reach and demoralize a much larger class of individuals, including children."[17] The mayor of Louisville blamed the public for the outcry, arguing that although Johnson-Jeffries was in no way a test of "superiority between the races," he understood that "the ignorant find excuse to array themselves in violent antagonism and the result is crime."[18] Because of that, he said, the fight film would be banned in his city.

As Johnson continued to dominate in the ring, the movement to ban fight films gained momentum. In 1912 two members of Congress, Representative Seaborn A. Roddenbery of Georgia and Senator Furnifold Simmons of North Carolina, introduced bills that would ban the transportation of the films across state lines. Unlike many politicians at the time, who justified their support for the ban by playing the "public interest" card, Roddenbery made it clear this was a race issue. He refused to mask his disdain for Johnson, or Black people in general, and referred to the champion as an "African biped beast."[19] Nonetheless, this was the Jim Crow era, a time when that sort of commentary from elected officials was common and bigotry was reason enough for legislation. So despite its inherent racist underpinnings, and partly *because* of its inherent racist underpinnings, the bill—named the Sims Act, after Senator Thetus Sims, who co-sponsored the legislation—was passed into law by both houses in late July.

While fight films could still be distributed throughout the state in which they had been filmed, the Sims Act signified the end of a brief but important era in media history. As far as the motion picture industry was concerned, the law meant that it was time to move on to other more profitable and less regulated endeavors. But for those interested in sports, fight films were evidence that people were interested in watching competition, and perhaps paying money to do so, even when they couldn't attend the actual event. There also seemed to be a formula for generating interest: provide viewers with a compelling narrative, ideally built around athletes or teams with whom they could identify (say, a white boxer vs. a Black boxer). To that end a catchy slogan never hurts; with constant references to "the great white hope," it was easy for the public to understand what Johnson-Jeffries was all about. And to many members of society, especially those in the government, fight films were the first indication that sporting events distributed through new technology had the unique potential to bottle the passion and energy once reserved for inside the stadium and the arena and unleash it among a wider swath of the public. That was a potentially lucrative, and perhaps dangerous, proposition. Many people took notice—politicians, certainly, but also a legion of new entrepreneurs ready to take advantage of whatever technology was coming next.

In those days newspapers still held an iron grip on the distribution of sports content. They had even figured out how to go live, complementing their traditional print coverage with a more immersive as-it-happened experience. In New York City a reported thirty thousand people packed into Times Square to watch the results of the Jack Johnson–Jim Jeffries battle unfold on giant bulletin boards set up on the facades of the *New York Times* office. There was no audio and no video. Just words. And yet the crowd, which was clearly pro-Jeffries, "equaled in number the mighty throngs that have congregated there on election nights in the past, and it was every bit as noisy and must have been ten times as excited." When Jeffries went on the offensive in the fourth round ("Jeff gets first blood" read the board), the mostly white audience whooped and hollered, and "boys danced and chattered like so many monkeys." Alas, the excitement died down as Johnson took the momentum back. And when the final report was put up—"Johnson wins in the fifteenth"—the crowd "began to move away sadly."[20]

The *Times* had a more intricate system than its competitors. One 1911 article spoke proudly of the bulletin boards' complexity: "Here one can only point out a few salient features of this most delicate and ingenious device."[21] These boards, the precursors to the electronic news ticker and the "bottom line" that crawls across television broadcasts delivering scores of other games, were designed to cater to the public's demand for immediate news. They were a way to be *there*, if not necessarily there. It worked, making Times Square a popular gathering space for standing around and looking up (which, of course, it still is).

In that same article the *Times* also took the opportunity to push back against the idea that news and information would soon become more audio-based: "In one of H. G. Wells's prophetic romances he tells of the newspapers of the future bellowing forth through phonographs the news." But our bulletin, said the *Times*, "makes possible exactly the same wide dissemination of information of interest with just as much efficiency and infinitely greater comfort to all concerned." Written as a boast, this statement was more likely a preemptive strike because regardless of how proud the newspaper personnel were of their bulletin board service, they knew it was only a matter of time until their near monopoly on human attention would be challenged. And they no doubt saw one particular piece of technology—one that could deliver live events not only to a crowd on a street, but also to people's homes—as the greatest potential threat.

There is no year that radio was invented. There is also no single inventor of the radio. The device, at least as we recognize it today, emerged from years of incremental progress: a small addition here, a slight modification there, and eventually, voila, radio. It began with dots and dashes, as people figured out how to transmit Morse code without wires. The ocean served as a useful testing ground; ships were decked out with the latest instruments. In 1899 the *New York Herald* used Morse code to get results from that year's America's Cup yacht race off the coast of New Jersey.[22]

Next came actual audio, voices and music, with the first broadcasts sent over small distances. By 1912 there's evidence to suggest that researchers at the University of Minnesota were able to broadcast the first football game over the airwaves, although it's doubtful many (if any) people heard the actual broadcast. A few years later another person who probably deserves to be on radio's birth certificate, Russian immigrant and future president of the Radio Corporation of America (RCA) David Sarnoff, proposed the idea of having radio function as a household utility, like "the piano or phonograph," so that people could sit at home and listen to music.[23] But Sarnoff's vision was premature: the technology wasn't quite ready. And when World War I arrived, the U.S. government took control of all radio stations, putting a temporary halt to further developments in the wireless industry. Sarnoff's idea would have to wait.

When the war ended in 1919, three important plot lines emerged. One, the U.S. government ceded control of the airwaves back to the public, paving the way for continued innovation in radio technology. Two, the heavyweight title was now in the hands of a white man, Jack Dempsey, who had beaten another white man, Jess Willard, who had beaten Jack Johnson. That was a crucial development. The Johnson-Jeffries matchup had demonstrated how sports could simultaneously unite and divide large groups of people—white people cheered for the white boxer and Black people cheered for the Black boxer, but everybody paid attention—and how new viewing options, such as fight films and bulletin boards, could build upon the already substantial print coverage to exacerbate that unity and division. The precursor to that unity and division was a good story, something that would get people riled up and separated into different cheering sections. With the boxing world no longer focused on "the great white hope," the time was ripe for a new narrative, perhaps one that wasn't so racially charged, to propel the sport forward. And three, because of the war, emotions remained high, with people across the world ready and willing to channel their energy into something (anything!) else.

The stage was set, then, for a larger-than-life event that could combine these things into one coherent, promotion-friendly narrative. And nobody of the era knew how to craft that kind of script better than the architect behind the Johnson-Jeffries fight: George Lewis "Tex" Rickard. Condensing Rickard's rollicking life into a single paragraph is a fool's errand. Nevertheless, here goes. He was born on January 2, 1871 (or maybe 1870), in a Missouri (or possibly Kansas) cabin during a shootout between the famous outlaw Jesse James, who was a neighbor, and two dozen of the town's policemen. (The chaos into which Rickard was born, his mother would later say, muddied the details of his birth.) By the age of eleven Rickard was out of the house, driving cattle herds and hanging out with men twice his age. At twenty-three he became city marshal of the small Texas town to which his family had moved, helping grandmas, kissing babies, and fighting bad guys with names like "Pete the Pest." A year later he resigned his post to follow the crowd up to Alaska for the great Klondike gold rush. Once there he realized he was better at making money off the people who were looking for gold than looking for gold himself. He got a job in a gambling house, bartending and dealing cards. When he was gifted his own place to run, he lost it in a bet two weeks later and went back to his old job. Rickard alternated between success and failure (as most gamblers do) for years, eventually cashing in his chips and moving back south. He found himself in Seattle, where a convicted prisoner told him about a secret unexplored diamond mine in South Africa. They sailed to South Africa. There was no diamond mine. Ever the optimist, ("it was a wonderful trip," he said of the transatlantic journey), Rickard returned to the United States and established a gambling house in Goldfield, Nevada.[24] It was there that the former cattle herder/marshal/gold miner/explorer finally settled into the rest of his life, building up his business and using it as a launching pad to become the promoter for a series of high-profile prizefights, including the Johnson-Jeffries "Fight of the Century" in 1910.

By 1919 Rickard was the most famous fight promoter in the United States, always looking for his next big bout. So it was only natural for him to team up with that era's most famous fighter: a hard-hitting brute by the name of Jack Dempsey. There were no forays to Alaska or Africa in Dempsey's early life, but it was still quite eventful. Born in Manassa, Colorado, as one of eleven children and forced to work in the mines by his mid-teens, Dempsey's childhood was a struggle. He took to fighting early, learning from his older brothers. His earliest tussles were against friends and co-workers and guys like One-Punch Hancock and Boston Bearcat. He won them all. From there Dempsey lived as if he was pilot-testing the archetypal Hollywood boxing movie: he had a cool nickname, "the Manassa Mauler"; he met his manager in a barroom brawl; the manager went by the name of "Doc"; he married a prostitute who played piano in a saloon; they had a messy divorce; she tried to ruin his life. And on it went. The most intriguing plot twist to the Dempsey story, however, was the exemption he received from the U.S. government during World War I to skip his military service and to instead continue his boxing career. The release, granted because he claimed to be the sole breadwinner for several members of his family, didn't go down so well in the court of American public opinion. It would haunt him for years.

Then, as if from central casting, there emerged an ideal contender to challenge Dempsey for the belt. His name was Georges Carpentier, and he was perfect: handsome, refined, and French. He lived in an apartment in Paris; he socialized with actors and musicians; he wore beautiful clothing. And, oh yeah, he was also a distinguished fighter pilot, having been awarded two of France's most important military honors while fighting the Germans in World War I. Women swooned when they met him; men wanted to be him. The press described him as a "Greek God" and gave him elegant nicknames like "Gorgeous Georges" and "the Orchid Man." Here was Rickard's next narrative, almost too good to be true: rough-and-tumble American draft dodger vs. refined French war hero.

There was much wrangling and plenty of negotiation, but Rickard finally got the two men to sign on for a fight at a custom-built outdoor arena in Jersey City on July 2, 1921. Dempsey, dutifully fulfilling his "everyman" role, set up his training camp among the casinos and saloons of Atlantic City. Carpentier opted for a more polished environment, setting up on the ritzy north shore of Long Island. With both fighters hunkered down and fight day approaching, it was time for members of the press to do their thing. And they did, almost overwhelmingly so, covering the fight from every conceivable angle. There was an article detailing how Dempsey had sent his mother a cow capable of producing "seven gallons of milk a day and twenty-one pounds of butter a week."[25] There were also reports that Dempsey was growing a beard, with the stubble meant as a kind of "armor" for his jaw.[26] One newspaper in Ohio devoted an entire article to the fact that Carpentier's eight-year-old neighbor had lit a candle in his honor and another to explain how the Frenchman had garnered the support of two women who shared the title of "prettiest pair of legs in the world."[27]

And there was endless debate about the fighters' mental and physical fitness. The two men were even asked to take something called the "Woodsworth and Wells test for attention," which required them to quickly work through a series of mental riddles. Here's one part of the exam, presented verbatim: "Write any letter except 'g' just after this comma . . . , and then write no if 2 times 5 are 10. . . . Now, if Tuesday comes after Monday, make two crosses here . . . ; but if not, make a circle here . . . or else a square here." In the end Carpentier completed the test faster and made fewer mistakes than Dempsey, leading the doctor overseeing the event to declare, "The European contender is fifteen per cent faster in his mental processes than the American contender."[28]

This matchup—and it almost didn't have to be said, but it was, many times over—was "the Fight of the Century." Everybody chose a side. Most followed the prepared script: war hero vs. draft dodger. Many Americans, high off the emotion of World War I, were actually pulling for the Frenchman. One group of veterans in San Diego even sent Carpentier a telegram that read, "Make Dempsey crawl behind a woman's skirts or shipyard fence again and hundreds of veterans here will cheer."[29] Others took a more superficial route toward picking a side. In one newspaper article (headline: "What of Women? Easy! Georges Is an Adonis"), Miss Marion Stroble is described as "a loyal American, but challenges any woman to remain a true patriot after looking at Carpentier's face." Another woman told the reporter, "Of course, I'm for Carpentier. I met him in France during the war and I'm enchanted with him but Oh-o-o. . . . Oh-o-o, I'd hate to see Carpentier's face smashed."[30]

With so much interest in the fight it was all hands on deck to get the news to the public as soon as it happened. In France arrangements were made for "six high-powered army airplanes" to fly over the city, flashing red lights if Carpentier won and white lights if he lost.[31] In London crowds were set to gather in theaters where results would be announced from the stage as soon as they came in on the telegraph. And across the United States newspapers prepared to offer their usual bulletin board services, with frequent ads touting their setups in the days leading up to the bout. "Keep Up with the Fight, Be in the Crowd!" read one notice in the *Arkansas Daily Gazette*. "Third street is long and wide; there will be room for all."[32]

Planes, theaters, hordes of people crowding into the street—there had to be an easier way. And there was. Three months before the bout somebody approached Tex Rickard and suggested that it might be a good idea to broadcast the fight using the latest radio technology. Whose idea it was exactly has become a matter of great debate. Many signs, including an article in *Wireless Age* magazine in August 1921, point to a man named Julius Hopp, a colleague of Rickard's at Madison Square Garden (which Rickard operated at the time).[33] But at least two other men, David Sarnoff, the "household utility" guy and a big player in the early radio industry, and J. Andrew White, editor of *Wireless Age* and the fight's play-by-play broadcaster, would both claim credit for the idea as the years went on.

Regardless of where it came from, Rickard was intrigued with the proposal and agreed to give it a shot. But how? None of the infrastructure was in place. The arena hadn't been designed to accommodate a live radio broadcast. There was no tower, no transmitter. And it wasn't as though millions of people had radios sitting in their homes, anxiously tuned to a local station and waiting for the opening bell. Even if Rickard's team was somehow able to send the signal out, it still needed to figure out a way for people to hear it.

It became a team effort. To generate some funding for the initiative, Andrew White (who was acting president of the National Amateur Wireless Association [NAWA] at the time), reached out to Sarnoff, who correctly believed that more sports broadcasts would lead to more people wanting radios. Then another member of NAWA secured the use of a transmitter, one built by General Electric and earmarked for use by the U.S. Navy. There was no place to put it at the arena, so it was installed two and a half miles away, at a railway terminal in Hoboken, New Jersey. Next, a telephone line was strung from ringside to the transmitter with the goal of having the broadcast read into a telephone handset, have it travel the two-plus miles to the transmitter, and then for the transmitter to send the signal out across a two-hundred-mile radius.

But to whom? At the time, only about sixty thousand American homes (one out of every four hundred) had a radio.[34] Not all these households were in the fight's broadcast range, and of those that were, many weren't savvy enough to pick up the signal. The next step, then, was to enlist amateur radio enthusiasts to help equip theaters and halls with the technology needed in order to receive the broadcast. There was no budget for these installations. Instead many of the amateurs who signed up had to pay for them out of their own pockets. They did it anyway, eager to test radio's capabilities and, just maybe, be a part of history. Dozens of halls were decked out—such as the Majestic Theatre in Williamsport, Pennsylvania, and the Mozart Theatre in Elmira, New York—and they were advertised as gathering spots for the fight, a way to experience the event with other fans as it unfolded. Admission would be charged, of course, but most of the proceeds would go to two charities: the American Committee for Devastated France and the Navy Club.

The day of the fight came. It rained a bit and then stopped. Upwards of ninety thousand people piled into the arena, including dozens of politicians, seven hundred sportswriters, and thousands of women (a new and potentially lucrative demographic for the boxing industry). The preliminary fights were fought. And then, just before three o'clock, it was time for the main event. Carpentier entered the ring; Dempsey followed. The ring announcer went over to the "Manassa Mauler" and introduced him as "the champion, Jack Dempsey, on whom every redblooded American pins his hopes this day" (a claim, as noted above, that was not true). The announcer then found Carpentier, introducing him as "the heavyweight champion of the Old World, the idol of his people, and a soldier of France."[35] The fight began. Carpentier, considered a significant underdog by those in the know, came out swinging. But it wouldn't be enough to subdue the talented Dempsey, who gamely endured the Frenchman's best efforts and knocked Carpentier out in the fourth.

The radio listeners heard it all, live as it happened. In the theaters and halls, crowds were mostly in the hundreds. There were also the amateur radio enthusiasts, able to find the broadcast on their own devices and happy to voluntarily contribute a few dollars to the effort. A New Jersey man, W. Harold Warren, attached a radio to a "roller chair" and provided the fight to people along the Asbury Park boardwalk. He noted that the reception was great, "notwithstanding the fact that we were but 100 feet from the noise of the breaking surf." He ended up sending a check for thirteen dollars for the charities. Others hosted small gatherings at their homes, such as A. E. Jackson of Smithtown, New York, who "entertained a few friends" and sent along $1.80.[36]

As happens with so many historic events, details about the broadcast would become distorted as time went by. Thirty-four years after the bout

J. Andrew White published an essay in *Reader's Digest* describing the events of the day.[37] In it contradictions and hyperbole abound. White claimed, for instance, that "the audience that awaited our broadcast that sticky afternoon numbered between 200,000 and 300,000, and it was located in some 200 theatres and halls, ballrooms and barns throughout the eastern United States." But White himself told a reporter in 1924 that of the original 250 amateurs who had agreed to help set up the infrastructure to broadcast the fight in theaters, by the day of the event "our loyal band had shrunk to about ninety."[38] Nor is there any concrete proof that the fight was heard by hundreds of thousands of people; at least one source uses information distributed by White's own magazine, *Wireless Age*, to estimate an audience closer to fifty thousand.[39] And what about White's claim that "on the outcome of the broadcast hung the future of a whole new industry"?[40] Silly. If the broadcast of Dempsey-Carpentier hadn't gone well, there's no reason to believe that radio innovation, which had had been going on for close to three decades at that point, would have simply ground to a halt.

White also overstates the initial enthusiasm around the broadcast. The essay's final paragraphs detail how, after the bout, an exhausted White and Sarnoff were approached by a newspaper wire service manager who told them, "You gave us a world-wide newspaper story. We scooped everyone into London and Paris with the news of the world's first real broadcast!"[41] While that encounter may very well have happened, the articles published over the next few days concerning the radio broadcast were nothing more than small blurbs, noting a few details of the broadcast but mentioning little about how "the era of radio for the millions had begun," as White stated in his essay. The *Scranton Republican* was one of the few newspapers to mention the wireless coverage on its front page, declaring that "for the first time in the history of the city, Scranton received news of a championship boxing bout by way of the wireless telephone"; it then listed the names and (for some reason) the home addresses of Scranton citizens who received the fight on their radios.[42] The *Boston Globe* also found the broadcast worthy of a mention but buried the news on the bottom of page four with a forty-four-word article about Robert Parker Jr. (of North Belfast Ave. in Augusta, Maine), who received a report of the fight through his "high tension wireless outfit."[43] The *New York Times* pushed the news back even further, reporting on page six that "it was the first time in the history of boxing matches that wireless telephony had been used to spread broadcast [sic] the details of a bout." The brief article concluded with the news that "the phones at the ringside were operated by J. N. White, David Saranoff and H. L. Welter"; this means that the *Times* managed to misspell the names of all three men involved (it's J. A. White, Sarnoff, and Welker).[44]

But perhaps we'll let White have his historic moment because regardless of how many people listened to Dempsey-Carpentier, the broadcast was undoubtedly important, less for what it achieved that particular day than for what it ultimately meant going forward. As mentioned above, at the time of Dempsey-Carpentier, only about sixty thousand American homes had a radio. But by 1928, according to one of the first media audience reports ever produced, that number had ballooned to over a third of all households and close to forty million potential listeners. Four out of five of these homes listened to the radio every day, and almost a quarter said that they listened for four hours or more. Programming preferences varied. Urbanites preferred "classical music" and "grand opera" while those in the country listened to "crops and market reports" and "religious service." "Athletic reports" were listed as a favorite by just under a quarter of the total households.[45]

In 1926, with radio sales booming, Dempsey lost the title to "the Fighting Marine," Gene Tunney. A year later, with Tex Rickard once again manning the promotional helm, Dempsey and Tunney fought in a highly anticipated rematch at Soldier Field in Chicago. The numbers were big, even for Rickard, with the *Chicago Tribune* reporting an audience of 145,000 and a gate of around $2.8 million.[46] And how many people listened on the radio? Again that's a matter of debate. The day after the fight the *Tribune* reported a "conservative" estimate of 15 million potential listeners within hearing range of the broadcast and noted that "a number of them probably listened in."[47] Over the years that number would go up. Articles celebrating the fight's anniversary in 1987 in *Sports Illustrated* and the *Los Angeles Times* estimated the audience at 40 and 50 million respectively.[48]

The truth is that nobody will ever know how many people listened to either Dempsey-Carpentier or Dempsey-Tunney. Does it matter? Of course not. If anything, the inflated audience numbers for both fights are symbolic, accepted distortions meant to represent the growing power and ubiquity of a mass communication device the likes of which society had never before seen. While the power of the narrative—Black vs. white, draft dodger vs. war hero—would continue to reign supreme, the method by which that narrative could now be distributed had been changed forever. And the 1912 Sims Act, the U.S. government's attempt to quell the influence of sports (and the influence of a powerful Black man, Jack Johnson) by banning the interstate distribution of fight films, would become a mere historical footnote, a feeble and unsuccessful attempt to slow down an industry that was just getting going.

By the end of the 1920s radio was firmly entrenched in the cultural psyche. It was evocative, immediate, and increasingly accessible, a remarkable tool that allowed dispersed groups of people to coalesce around a single mega-event. The age of mass media had finally begun.

Part 2 / Purpose

Once technology became capable of bottling up a great event and distributing it to thousands (soon to be millions) of people around the country (soon to be the world), an important question arose: what exactly should society do with this newfound power?

The question was posed in legislative chambers. It was discussed in boardrooms and in war rooms. It made it into the notebooks of Nazis and onto the desks of Communists and was even considered by a wrestler who wore fancy robes, had a butler, and made money by belittling the people who paid tickets to see him perform.

The purpose of sports media, specifically, sparked a furious debate. On one side were the optimists and the philosophers, those who saw these games as a potential antidote to so many of society's problems. The invention of radio kickstarted much of this talk. The emergence of television, the growth of national magazines, and the promise of satellite technology, especially in a world weary of global conflict, would supercharge this idealism: "If only we could all read about or listen to or watch the same match or game together . . ." But by the end of the 1960s this idealism would be mostly forgotten. And sports media would become a pawn within an even larger industry, one that would influence so much of what we do, how we act, and who we aspire to be.

A Dangerous Precedent

2

Berlin Summer Olympics (1936)

In 1926 Tex Rickard offered the radio broadcast rights of the first battle between Jack Dempsey and Gene Tunney to the highest bidder. He even threw out a number: $35,000.[1] Nobody bit. With just five days to go before the bout, there were still no takers. Yet Rickard held his ground, declaring that regardless of whether anybody purchased the rights, print reporters would be forbidden to wire blow-by-blow reports of the fight back to their newspaper offices, something they had been doing for years: "This is a 'private show' and I have a perfect right to say who can and who can't broadcast. . . . The broadcasting privileges will go to whoever gets my contract."[2]

Finally, with just three days left, Rickard's team announced that the rights had been purchased by the Royal Typewriter Company.[3] For a discounted rate of $15,000 the company was granted full radio privileges and planned to cobble together a network of stations across the United States in order to air the fight to millions of potential listeners. It even relaxed Rickard's stance on exclusivity, allowing newspapers to continue their traditional bulletin board broadcasts. Why did a typewriter company buy the rights to the radio broadcast of a boxing match? To sell more typewriters, of course. In the days leading up to the match the company purchased ads touting its investment in the fight, a promotional tactic that would become standard in the years to come.

Following the match, a debate ensued about whether this kind of advertiser-supported model was good or bad for the radio industry. One article in *Radio Broadcast* magazine decried the arrangement as a "dangerous precedent," suggesting that since boxing had been helped rather than hindered by the emergence of radio, the sport's promoters showed "ingratitude" by choosing to profit directly from a broadcast from which they were, in fact, already profiting.[4] Others disagreed. An opposing editorial argued that this model should be celebrated, mostly because the alternative was the ceaseless mediocrity currently swamping the airwaves: "One thing is certain: no advertiser is going to pay to broadcast anything which isn't good and desired by the listeners. It wouldn't pay him to do so."[5]

It was a very optimistic statement. It was also very wrong; advertisers over the next hundred years would come to care far more about reaching the right people—young men, prospective car buyers, stay-at-home parents—than about the content with which those people were engaging (exhibit number one: the internet). Nevertheless, these types of articles were emblematic of the larger discussion concerning radio taking place across the world in the 1920s and early 1930s. And central to that discussion were two fundamental questions: what's the purpose of radio and who's going to pay for it?

The two questions were intertwined, mostly because of the larger political, social, and cultural environment into which radio arrived. A major war had just ended, killing tens of millions of people and upending the lives of hundreds of millions more. Many rightfully feared what the next decade would bring (the answer was economic catastrophe). Continued industrialization had upended so much of what people held dear. It seemed like everything and everyone was being torn apart, both physically and mentally. And yet here was radio, a curious thing, a box you could put in your living room and hear the world come to life as thousands, or even millions, of others did the exact same thing. As two researchers would suggest in the 1930s, "Radio is perhaps our chief potential bulwark of social solidarity. It stems the tide of disrupting influences, and strengthens the ties that are socially binding."[6] Or at least that was the idea.

In the United States the two questions permeated newspapers and magazines. American radio in the early to mid-1920s was a bit of a free-for-all, with many players and little regulation. Content creators—some in fancy studios, others in their basements—often jockeyed for the same frequencies. Some of the content was great: world class musicians, storytellers, and comedians. But a lot of it was terrible, meant only to fill the hours in the day. Everybody was looking for answers, a way to fix this obviously broken structure. In 1924, around the time Rickard was debating the pros and cons of having radio at his own events, *Radio Broadcast* magazine threw the predicament out to its readers, offering a prize of $500 to whoever came up with a "workable plan which shall take into account the problems in present radio broadcasting and propose a solution."[7] A panel of judges, one of whom was J. Andrew White, the announcer from the Dempsey-Carpentier fight and one of the world's first true sports broadcasters, would ultimately decide the best plan. Around eight hundred proposals were submitted.[8]

In March 1925 the winner was announced as H. D. Kellogg Jr. of Haverford, Pennsylvania, who proposed "a federal stamp tax on crystals and tubes, with revenues distributed to the various broadcasting stations by the government."[9] In an overview of his plan Kellogg argued that radio was most effective if it could provide "the best entertainment possible, untrammeled by any commercialism or advertising."[10] To ensure this kind of quality content the medium needed some sort of admission charge, such as theaters had, which placed the financial burden on the consumer rather than an advertiser. A tax on crystals and tubes, the technology that determines both the life and the range of the radio, would create a tiered system that reflected how often listeners listened and what programming they were able to access through their particular device. With some back-of-the-napkin math Kellogg suggested that his model would generate around $18 million in total revenue (about $270 million today), money that could then be dispersed across dozens of legitimate radio stations.

Zeh Bouck, a contest judge and noted radio industry expert, offered tepid approval of the plan: "Certainly, did it not possess considerable merit it would not have won." But Bouck found several weaknesses in the design, not the least of which was Kellogg's insistence on getting the government involved. "This is not socialism, anarchy, or Bolshevism," wrote Bouck, before suggesting that governmental control of the radio coffers could lead to "an odious censorship comparable to that we are told now exists in Russia." Bouck quoted Herbert Hoover, secretary of commerce and future president of the United States, who added his own thoughts on the plan's un-Americanness: "I do not believe that your prize-winning plan is feasible under conditions as they exist in this country, however well it may work elsewhere."[11]

Hoover was right; nothing close to Kellogg's plan ever came to fruition. In 1927 the U.S. government acknowledged the importance of radio to the national psyche by creating the Federal Radio Commission, an entity tasked with granting licenses to stations based on "public convenience, interest or necessity." Still most of the particulars, such as what would air and when, were left in the hands of the almighty market. Over the next decade the American radio industry would evolve into a mostly advertising-based, mostly national model. Two powerful networks emerged, NBC and CBS, entities that strung together regional stations in order to air the same programming and, of course, the same ads. These networks held sway, controlling the vast majority of what Americans heard through their sets. And in 1932, when the U.S. Olympic Committee demanded $100,000 for the right to air the Summer Games from Los Angeles, the two networks had a unified response: "Absolutely not." The networks argued that a radio broadcast of the Olympic Games was of vital national importance and airing the games was no different than, say, airing a politician's speech (for which, of course, they would never pay). In the end there was no agreement, and coverage of the 1932 Olympics was limited to recaps and reports.[12]

As all this unfolded, as the American radio industry innovated and stumbled and consolidated, the British watched intently and asked the same questions: what's the purpose of radio and who's going to pay for it? In one British magazine there was even a column called "The Way They Have in America," which documented journalist Hamilton Fyfe's thoughts on American radio as he traveled through the United States. In one column Fyfe goes to the Chicago Radio Exhibition, where he meets the "Champion Woman Listener," a lady who had listened to over three hundred radio stations.[13] In another column Fyfe describes the newfound joy of American housewives, who listened to radio as they performed their mundane household chores: "Tuesdays we all do our ironing and it used to be pretty tough to get through a big basketful of laundry. Now it's a pleasure."[14] A third column discusses the American system of broadcasting football games. While Fyfe is perplexed by the sport itself—"for most of the time the players are piled up in writhing, wriggling heaps"—he's nonetheless intrigued by the broadcast: "So the man in the box spoke. He spoke as if he was telephoning. He was telephoning, but in the box was a microphone, and his voice, when it reached the radio station in Chicago, was broadcast into hundreds of thousands of homes all over the country."[15]

Fyfe was hardly an unbiased source. The magazine in which these columns appeared, *Radio Times*, was an extension of the British Broadcasting Corporation (BBC), the country's lone radio broadcaster. Founded in 1922, the BBC began as a private company but became a government-supported entity five years later. There would be no advertising on the BBC; rather, households would pay for an annual license, a system that continues to this day. And the BBC's charge, laid out in a royal charter, was to act as a "public utility service" where programming was "developed and exploited to the best advantage and in the national interest."[16]

Sports were seen as a natural component of this mission. Just weeks after becoming a public utility, the BBC aired its first athletic event, a rugby match between England and Wales. More rugby matches, a few partial soccer games, boat racing, and some scattered cricket commentary would follow in the months to come.[17] Similar to what was happening in the United States, not everyone supported these new sports broadcasts. Part of the concern came from the fact that the BBC, which, like NBC and CBS had done with the Olympics, steadfastly maintained that its "running commentaries" were no different than newspapers' recaps and refused to pay for the right to air matches. The BBC's offer to donate £100 to a charity chosen by the Football Association (FA)—a "fair sporting offer," according to an article in one newspaper—in order to air the 1930 FA Cup Final didn't do much to move the needle.[18]

Yet another concern came from soccer club owners, who believed that radio broadcasts would keep people away from the stadiums. The next year *Radio Times* responded with an editorial titled "The Attack on Broadcast Football Is Based on a Fallacy." In it the author suggested that "broadcasting is, and will probably continue to be, a convenient whipping-boy for the less successful impresarios in all walks of life." For one thing, attendance was higher on the day of a radio broadcast compared to days without, at least according to a string of anecdotal evidence offered up by the magazine. For another, people still liked going to matches—"Britain is not yet a nation of armchair loafers"—so providing a radio broadcast should have no real effect on the gate. Moreover, the broadcasts had opened up the national pastime to entirely new demographics: the blind and the bedridden and the elderly. The article even included some letters from listeners to support this point: "I have been bedridden for nearly thirteen years, so you can realize what a boon wireless is to me" and "I am a blinded soldier, and up to losing my sight was a keen follower of Soccer matches. . . . You make the game become very real to us who cannot see the actual play."[19]

Over in Germany it was more of the same: what's the purpose of radio and who's going to pay for it? In the 1920s and early 1930s German radio was, for the most part, controlled by private companies and paid for by private money.[20] Content was meant to be educational and entertaining. While some programs were designed for national appeal, others were distinctly regional. Most content avoided overt political topics. Music was popular. But with the arrival of the Nazis the German radio industry underwent a drastic and intentional transformation. Radio, it was thought, was too powerful to be left in the hands of private entities. Instead it was to become a mouthpiece of the Reich, ingrained with the Nazi agenda, and infused with direct and persistent propaganda.

Much of this strategy is laid out in a manuscript written by Nazi Radio Program Chief Eugen Hadamovsky called *Propaganda and National Power*. The book is no masterpiece. It's wordy and rambling, the hubristic musings of a person who thinks he's come up with something remarkable by rehashing a few elementary albeit important truisms of the human condition. For example: people like to be part of a group. Or: information is more effective in the absence of a rebuttal. And of course: repetition is an effective persuasion tool. Nevertheless, Hadamovsky lays bare exactly what the new regime thought the purpose of radio should be (to support the Nazis) and how it should be paid for (by the Nazis). In a section dedicated entirely to the medium, Hadamovsky writes that "for the first time in history we now have in radio a medium which enables us to mold nations of many millions by daily and hourly influence. Old and young people, workers and farmers, soldiers and officials, men and women sit listening in front of their radios."[21] These listeners are inherently vulnerable to manipulation, as they have a desire "to be one of a crowd of people who think, feel, and react the same way."[22] The purpose of this new technology, then, is to harness those emotions as a means to "form the will of the nation."[23]

But how? First, the regime needed to ensure absolute control of this powerful new device. Beginning in 1933–34 German radio was brought under the jurisdiction of the Ministry for Public Enlightenment and Propaganda, a national entity led by one of Hitler's favorite henchmen, Josef Goebbels. Next, the Nazis had to make sure everybody had a way to hear what they were going to say. By subsidizing the production and distribution of a cheaper device, the Volksempfänger (the "people's receiver"), the Nazis made radio immediately accessible to many of those who had previously been priced out. And finally, there were substantial programming changes, including the addition of more national events—such as political rallies and speeches—in order to inculcate all listeners under one big loud German umbrella. Politics, once largely absent from the airwaves, became a regularly scheduled program. As Hadamovsky wrote in his missive: "It is disgraceful that for so many years political considerations were never given priority in the proposals for the reform of radio. . . . Radio must be political. Or, better, radio must only know one kind of politics, that of the political leader."[24]

If the goal is to spread unapologetic nationalism, blatant political rhetoric from the country's leader certainly does the trick. But even the most ardent nationalist needs an occasional break from the endless prattle of a xenophobic demagogue. For that, one option is sports, a malleable, multipurpose pastime through which, as one historian has noted, "the individual, even the one who only cheers, becomes a symbol of his nation himself."[25] And no event encapsulates such an opportunity more than the Olympic Games, the ancient tradition of separating the world into teams and having these teams run as fast as they can, lift heavy stuff, and do somersaults on elevated beams in order to determine which country, among all the countries, is the best country.

Adolf Hitler, who up to that point hadn't really thought much about the connection between sports and national identity, came to see the 1936 Olympic Games in Berlin as the ultimate propaganda tool, a way to not only tell Germans how great Germany was, but also to tell other countries how great Germany was. Radio would be the primary, although not only, medium through which this message would be sent. To accomplish their goal Hitler and his regime spared no expense, constructing the most sophisticated radio broadcasting operation the world had ever seen.[26] Four years earlier the organizers of the 1932 Los Angeles Olympic Games had put together a system with 270 circuits and two miles of cable. The operation in Berlin dwarfed these numbers, with an estimated ten thousand circuits and four thousand miles of cable. The beating heart of it all was a control room dubbed the 40-Nations Switchboard, from which German engineers could produce broadcasts in different languages and send them all over the planet. Nobody paid for the right to air the games; the Germans subsidized everything. And foreign reporters were treated almost as visiting royalty, paired with handlers who drove them around, arranged their schedules, and brought them people to interview.

A key component of the Nazi media machine was the use of new shortwave radio technology, which allowed for broadcasts to be sent over much farther distances. These transmitters—and in 1936 the Germans had more of them than anybody—were used not only by foreign broadcasters to get their signals back home, but also by the Germans, who employed multilingual broadcasters to send unfiltered Nazi propaganda straight into houses all over the world. American stations, for one, were encouraged to pick up the shortwave German broadcasts and convert them for use on their own frequencies. This led to a situation where some listeners (such as those in New York) had the choice of three or four—NBC, CBS, BBC, German—Olympic broadcasts from which to choose. Said one *Philadelphia Inquirer* reporter upon hearing one of these German shortwave broadcasts, "Some evening, any evening, turn your dial there . . . where you will hear music, usually gay and happy music that's gay and happy so it'll attract well the international audiences. . . . Everything's so wonderfully clear."[27]

Not content with limiting their Olympic propaganda campaign to radio, the Nazis also attempted the first-ever comprehensive live television sports broadcast. It was a complex method that included the use of a telecine, a device that transforms film, such as that used in movie theaters, into video. Twenty-five receiving rooms with specially constructed screens were set up across Berlin and transmission from arena-to-screen was reportedly completed in less than a minute. This was groundbreaking stuff, barely believable to some Americans. In the *Los Angeles Times* one columnist wrote that the Germans "have made arrangements to transmit the full program by television to various auditoriums in Berlin" before adding, "No, I'm not kidding."[28]

Alas, the television broadcast was a disaster. An American reporter who watched the U.S. gold medal victory in the 4 x 100–meter relay wrote that "it was clearly evident that the boys were running fast, but Jesse Owens looked pale and Frank Wyckoff's legs wobbled. The stadium's spectators in the background sort of melted together, and the whole scene shook like jelly."[29] An article in the *Baltimore Sun* with the headline "Flop" described interest in the broadcast as "extremely tepid" and attendance as "very meagre." The reporter even noted that the "disappointing transmission is deemed to have hampered progress of television here. General feeling is that commercially-practical television is still several years off."[30]

Despite the television missteps many scholars have come to see the 1936 Berlin Olympics as a success, at least as far as the Nazi push to be seen as powerful and competent was concerned. One researcher has described the games as a "propaganda coup," writing that they were "magnificently organized" and "in every sense of the word, spectacular."[31] Another writer has said, "The German people liked their Olympic Games. This was the way Germans liked to see themselves: open to the world, tolerant, splendid hosts, perfect organizers."[32] Stadiums sold out; the opening ceremony alone welcomed more people than the entire 1932 Winter Games in Lake Placid, New York. It didn't hurt that German athletes won eighty-nine medals, over thirty more than the nearest competitor, the United States. And the near-constant radio coverage—updates on victories, interviews with athletes, commentary on upcoming events—no doubt contributed to this feeling of national pride.

Of course in order to successfully stage the Olympics Games, an event meant to emphasize fair competition, sportsmanship, and inclusivity, the Nazi regime had to literally ignore everything it stood for. Hitler's ideal Olympics would have involved a splendid in-person experience (check), a technologically sophisticated media operation (check), and every gold medal won by a German of "Aryan" descent (not a check). But that's the thing about sports; it often veers from the desired narrative. And when the Black American sprinter Jesse Owens became the games' breakout star, winning four gold medals and breaking three world records, the German press was told to refrain from derogatory commentary that might damage the carefully constructed, media-enhanced sheen of German hospitality and inclusivity. In other words, the members of the press were told specifically not to be Nazis, just for a few more days, until all these reporters and athletes went back to their home countries, taking the global spotlight off Germany. Then they could be Nazis again.

Before the games began, as the *New York Times* crowed about the technological might of Germany's 40-Nations Switchboard, the paper wondered "whether the Olympic Games are likely to do much to unite a disunited world."[33] The answer was that they would do nothing of the sort. The worldwide audience for the games was undeniably big. Many sources peg the number of radio listeners at around three hundred million, although that's just an estimate. But the more intelligent listeners, the ones who were carefully paying attention, saw through what the Nazis were trying to do. Their heinous agenda had never disappeared; it was just pushed aside for a few weeks so that the regime could preen and show off. Over the next few years, Hitler would unleash this agenda, kill over six million people, and plunge the world into the greatest conflict of the twentieth century. Sports and sports media became an afterthought. Rightly so.

But when it was all over, when people decided it was time to move forward, to start forgetting the horrors of the war, a new device adept at providing highly immersive daily distractions began showing up in living rooms. The rollout was slow at first but gathered steam, finding a niche with the legions of baseball fans scattered around the United States. And playing a big role in it all was the unlikeliest protagonist, a man who had no interest in baseball whatsoever. Instead he described himself as gorgeous and strutted through arenas as if he owned them. His name was George.

3 Made for Television

*New York Yankees vs. Brooklyn
Dodgers World Series (1947)*

When George Wagner of Harrisburg, Texas, moved to New York in the mid-1930s to pursue a career in wrestling, he was often introduced at events as "George Wagner of Germany." Wagner hadn't been born in Germany. He had never even been to Germany. And he didn't speak German. But the promoters needed storylines, something to sell tickets, and using the wrestling ring as a proxy for larger ethnic or racial conflicts was standard operating procedure. So "George Wagner of Germany" was put in the ring against "Abe Goldstein" or "Sammy Stein," and the crowd would whoop and holler and wonder if the German would beat the Jew. George was fine with it. He used his time in New York to hone his skill, to perfect his holds and his takedowns and his rope maneuvers. Most of all he learned an important lesson. As his biographer John Capouya explains, George realized that "who you actually are isn't paramount—it's who you *seem to be*, the image you project, that people respond to."[1]

From New York George bounced around the country, wrestling for whatever promoter would have him. The length of the matches and the results, as they are now, were often determined beforehand. Because of that the most popular wrestlers weren't necessarily the best athletes but rather the ones who put on the best show. George ended up in Oregon, where he met a woman named Betty. They got married, and she joined him on the road—to Los Angeles, over to Ohio, down to Arizona, back to Oregon. As the years went on, George decided to inject some life into his act by switching his persona from good guy (or "babyface") to bad guy (or "heel"). The changeup required a gimmick, something that could provoke the audience. Together with his wife George came up with the idea for an arrogant character who reveled in excess. To test the new act Betty stitched together an elaborate satin robe with silver sequins. One night George put it on and sashayed into the ring. It worked; the crowd erupted, mostly in disgust. More elements were added: carefully coiffed hair, a manservant who sprayed the ring with perfume, the song "Pomp and Circumstance." George would call the crowd "peasants" and talk about how he was "the greatest." And at some point the character was given a name, one that had been used before (such as by the French boxer Georges Carpentier) but one that was so perfect for this particular situation that it simply had to be used again: Gorgeous George.

Wagner's re-brand came at a fortuitous time. A few years after George became Gorgeous, television began fulfilling its decades-long promise (or threat, some would say) to become the centerpiece in every American home. While numbers vary greatly from source to source, there were probably only a few thousand sets in operation in the United States at the beginning of the 1940s. Five years later, at the conclusion of World War II, that number had risen to around fifty thousand. Two years after that it was over a million. And by the beginning of the 1950s it was over ten million.[2] The increase in potential viewers meant networks were desperate to fill the hours of the day with content people wanted to see. Luckily for George, wrestling checked all the boxes. For one thing, filming was a breeze. Similar to how Edison saw boxing as ideal for kinetoscope experiments, television executives found wrestling and its static setup conducive to the era's still-developing camera technology. It was also cheap: set up a camera, get an announcer, and you're good to go. And then there was the malleability of it all, entirely scripted and never a threat to end too early, because of something like a quick knockout, or too late, because of overtime or extra innings. Put it all together, and the sport was a programmer's dream, with all the big networks airing wrestling at least once a week in the late 1940s and early 1950s.

Gorgeous George was the undisputed star. And to some, especially the traditional sports scribes, he was nothing short of appalling. The esteemed sportswriter and future Pulitzer Prize winner Red Smith went as far as calling George's schtick "wife beating by proxy." Here's how he explained it: "George's golden coiffure and flabby white hide give him, of course, a womanish appearance. This impression of watching a man beat up a female may account for his popularity in Hollywood. In Hollywood, it is understood, authorities disapprove of husbands kicking their loved ones in the mouth. They have to enjoy that hobby vicariously."[3] Jimmy Cannon, another sports writing legend, was equally unimpressed. In a column for the *New York Post*, one so entertaining that the newspaper reprinted it decades later, Cannon wrote, "There is nothing original about any of it. It is repetitious and graceless. The comedy of the wrestlers is depressing." He went on: "It is an insult to the human family even to suspect that anyone would give a night of a lifetime to watching this."[4]

But, oh boy, did they watch. People loved Gorgeous George. Or, more accurately, people loved to hate Gorgeous George. Exactly why is a matter of debate. Perhaps it's because George represented everything Americans in the mid-1940s had been told not to be. After several years of careful war rationing—with food, clothing, gasoline—is it at all surprising that people got worked up about a wrestler who so brazenly flaunted his showy wardrobe and expensive haircuts and snazzily dressed servants? Or maybe, as Capouya has suggested, it was the complete opposite, a bit of a "they-hate-him-because-they-want-to-be-him" complex, a theory that is often used to explain the success of modern-day celebrities like the Kardashians. Whatever it was, George knew that he had struck a chord with the "Gorgeous" act. He also knew that television had amplified his message beyond what he had ever thought was possible. "I don't know if I was made for television," he once said, "or television was made for me."[5]

After the endless debate about the purpose of radio, about public service and education and civic responsibility, the question has to be asked: was this really the kind of content Philo Farnsworth, a man often credited as the father of television, had in mind when he was dreaming up his device in the 1920s? In one interview Farnsworth told a journalist that he thought television could "play an important part in halting the current trend toward the break-up of the family unit."[6] And who knows? Perhaps having the whole gang hurling vitriol at Gorgeous George did indeed have significant bonding benefits.

But Farnsworth almost certainly had other uses in mind for an invention that began, or so the story goes, when he was cultivating a potato field on his family's Idaho farm. It's been said that Philo (he would soon go by just "Phil") saw how the field was being plowed, line by line, and surmised that it might be possible to project pictures onto a screen using a similar method. The young genius sketched out his idea, calling it an "image dissector," and scrounged up some seed money. In 1927 he applied for his first four patents. After Farnsworth had put together a successful prototype and given a few demonstrations for the press, word got out about what he was doing. The excitement grew. In 1931 David Sarnoff, the head of RCA and someone who believed that all media innovation needed to go through him and him alone, visited Farnsworth's lab and offered to buy everything for $100,000 (nearly $2 million today). Farnsworth said no. Sarnoff seethed.

Then came the lawyers. For the next several years Farnsworth and RCA would bicker about patents, about who invented what and when. It was classic Sarnoff, a maneuver the ruthless mogul liked to employ to slow down his competition. But Farnsworth had no intention of ceding control of his invention to a company that already had a near monopoly on the radio industry. In 1934 Farnsworth unveiled the latest iteration of his invention to the public at the Franklin Institute of Philadelphia. People were floored. The next day the *New York Times* reported that the technology was "capable of broadcasting not only close-ups but entire football and baseball games and tennis matches."[7] That same year, desperate to generate cash from all his work, Farnsworth licensed some of his technology to the British for $50,000. A year later he made a similar deal with a German company, providing the Nazis with the infrastructure needed to attempt their television exhibition during the 1936 Berlin Olympics.

Despite Farnsworth's success RCA and Sarnoff never let up. They were intent on taking control of the television industry before it had even begun. In 1936 RCA used its NBC network to put together some experimental television broadcasts in its studios at Rockefeller Center. Three years later Farnsworth and RCA agreed on a patent-licensing deal, one of the first times that the powerful RCA had been forced to succumb to a competitor. Over the next ten years Farnsworth's influence in the television industry would wane. There were many reasons: the onset of World War II, the expiration of some important patents in 1947, a devastating fire at the Farnsworth home, the inventor's health. Farnsworth also seemed to be following the script laid down by some of the world's greatest inventors: a jilting of his first true love (television) in order to pursue another infatuation (nuclear fusion).

That Farnsworth was growing preoccupied with a new obsession mattered little to David Sarnoff; on the contrary, the RCA mogul was quite content to take over control of the burgeoning industry. In 1939, the same year RCA and Farnsworth agreed to a patent deal, Sarnoff went to the World's Fair in Queens, New York, grabbed a microphone, and announced the beginning of commercial television in the United States. In typical Sarnoff fashion the speech dripped with platitudes: "It is with a feeling of humbleness that I come to this moment of announcing the birth in this country of a new art so important in its implications that it is bound to affect all society. It is an art which shines like a torch of hope in a troubled world. It is a creative force which we must learn to utilize for the benefit of all mankind."[8]

Two years later, in 1941, the Federal Communications Commission (FCC) finalized its technical standards for television broadcasting and began issuing commercial licenses. Previously those in the television business had made most of their money by selling actual television sets. Now it was possible to supplement that income with advertising. After two decades of innovation it seemed that everything was coming together. It was the dawn of the television age, the greatest gold rush in media history, the moment Farnsworth and Sarnoff had dreamt about, and then . . . Pearl Harbor. America's entrance into World War II. And television's coming-out party was temporarily put on hold.

Once the war ended, the party came, quickly and with Gorgeous George as the unexpected host. It may have taken a couple of decades, an economic crisis, and a second horrific conflict, but the television era had finally arrived, ready to change the living room forever. Growing interest meant content was needed, cheap and easily produced material that could generate advertising interest. Sure, wrestling could fill part of the schedule. And big audiences meant brands were willing to pay to get their messages next to celebrities like George and his ilk. But there was another sport, a real one with legitimate winners and losers, equally suited to this new medium. It was a sport that provided content on a consistent basis for multiple hours each day and one with storylines that stretched for months, maybe years, no writer's room necessary. This particular sport would become so essential to the initial development of Farnsworth's invention, in fact, that authors James R. Walker and Robert V. Bellamy have suggested that "Television did not create baseball, but baseball helped to create television."[9]

Of course the average American was no stranger to baseball from the living room couch; the sport had been a mainstay on radio since the 1930s. It had not arrived without a fight. As had happened with Rickard and boxing or in England with soccer, some baseball owners had been concerned that radio broadcasts would keep fans at home, threatening their primary source of revenue. Others disagreed and saw radio as an ally, a way to keep their fans interested so that they'd want to attend a game down the road. The latter group would eventually win this battle, especially as radio fees from networks and sponsors, although still relatively small, became another way for teams to make money.

And yet even as individual clubs began to embrace the medium (by 1939 every team had some sort of radio presence), there was a separate conversation being had about the World Series. Nobody was too concerned about attendance—the series was going to sell out regardless of whether it was on radio or not. But as advertising became the manner by which radio subsisted, there was talk that the World Series should never be burdened with a sponsor, that it was too important of an event to leave in the hands of some faceless corporate brand. The commissioner at that time, Kenesaw Mountain Landis, had even told the networks that there would be "no commercial sponsorship of the Series or any individual game."[10] Niles Trammell, an executive at NBC, agreed, arguing that "base ball [sic] is such a part of American life [the World Series] should be carried on a non-commercial basis and should be made available to all radio stations regardless of whether they were networks stations or not."[11]

Money, the undefeated champion of anything and everything, would eventually win out. In 1934 Landis reached a $100,000 deal with Ford

Motor Company for the first-ever broadcast sponsorship of the World Series. It was a big deal, both literally and figuratively, and sparked a mad scramble to figure out what World Series broadcasts would look like going forward. Would the series eventually find an exclusive home on a single network? Would it be smarter for the networks to bid for the rights themselves and then go out and find a sponsor? And how much, exactly, was sponsoring or securing an event like the World Series worth? Was $100,000 too much? Was it too little? Nobody knew. Regardless, it was clear that Ford's sponsorship of the 1934 World Series signified the end of one era and the beginning of another. As Walker has written, "[Landis's] contract with Ford made the World Series too important to be unsponsored. There would be no turning back. The era of sports as public-service programming faded to silence."[12]

In May 1939 baseball made the leap from radio to television when NBC aired what is often referred to as the first-ever televised game, a matchup between Columbia and Princeton. In August that same year came the first televised professional baseball game from Brooklyn's Ebbets Field, with the Reds playing the home-team Dodgers. The early 1940s (the war years) saw additional experimentation, including a broadcast of the first night game and weekly airings for hospitalized war veterans. By 1947, with television ownership increasing, ten out of sixteen teams were broadcasting at least some of their home games. Baseball was an integral component of programming lineups, so much so that a brief examination of the schedules by one magazine found that the sport made up nearly half of all programming in June and July.

That same year baseball's new commissioner, A. B. (Happy) Chandler, indicated that the World Series would be televised for the first time ever. All he needed was a sponsor willing to pony up the asking price: $100,000.[13] In early September, with a Brooklyn Dodgers–New York Yankees matchup all but assured, Chandler received an offer from Liebmann Breweries of Brooklyn.[14] The commissioner said no thanks, suggesting that the World Series was too important, too sacred, too family-friendly, to be sponsored by an alcoholic beverage. It was a curious decision; a journalist at the time said it had a "most peculiar aroma."[15] And in retrospect it seems Chandler's decision was probably based more on currying favor with Kentucky voters, a state where half the counties were "dry" and where the commissioner harbored future political ambitions, than it was about protecting baseball's integrity. Nevertheless, with just a week to go before the all–New York matchup, there was still a question as to whether the series would be on television or not.

As all these negotiations played out, television companies flooded newspapers with ads using the "maybe/maybe not" World Series as bait. A newspaper in Delaware ran the following ad for an RCA Victor set: "See the batting practice, the fielding workouts; stand with the crowd as they sing the National Anthem; sit tight on the edge of your chair as the umpire calls 'play ball'; jump up and cheer as hits crack off the bats of DiMaggio, or Dixie Walker, or Jackie Robinson."[16] And a paper in New Jersey ran this one for a Philco set: "How many times have you said, 'Boy! How I would love to see the World Series.' Well! You can see it NOW! Not only see one of the games but the entire series . . . and see it in comfort, right in your own home." It's likely that only the most discerning readers noticed the asterisk at the bottom of the ad that noted, "Although the telecast rights have not as yet been sold for the World Series it is almost a certainty that they will be. . . . If not . . . [you'll] still want to rent a set for the opening of all the major college football games—the rodeo at Madison Square Garden and numerous other special attractions."[17]

Facing pressure from the industry, Chandler knew he had to make a move. With just a few days before the series was set to start, Chandler agreed to a sponsorship deal with Ford and Gillette for $65,000.[18] The price was significantly lower than the offer from the brewing company, but the commissioner saw Ford and Gillette as two brands that wouldn't tarnish the (contrived) image of America's pastime. The telecast would be limited to just four markets—New York City, Philadelphia, Washington DC, and Schenectady, New York—and production duties would be farmed out to three New York stations, with each deploying its own play-by-play man for their respective games.

Television drama aside, New York was fired up for this matchup. It was a big one. The Yankees, led by Joe DiMaggio, had won seven of the last fifteen titles. But the Dodgers were a legitimate contender, with Pee Wee Reese and Ralph Branca leading the team to ninety-four wins and a National League pennant. The Dodgers also held claim to the best story of the year: in April they had called up Jackie Robinson, the first Black player in major league history. Robinson would go on to win the league's inaugural Rookie of the Year award. Could he now lead the Dodgers to their first ever championship? Or would the Yankees, the clear favorites, take home another title? The city buzzed. On the eve of the first game the *Brooklyn Daily Eagle* reported that "Brooklyn patriotism was running so high" that one restaurant temporarily took "Yankee bean soup" off its menu.[19] Another article mentioned that a trial was temporarily halted so that the jurors could watch the game on television.[20]

The Yankees began by protecting their home-field advantage, winning the first two games in front of sellout crowds at Yankee Stadium in the Bronx. For Game 3 the series shifted to Brooklyn's Ebbets Field, and the Dodgers rushed out to a 6–0 lead. The Yankees fought back, with home runs by DiMaggio and Yogi Berra, but the Dodgers held on to win 9–8. Game 4, called "the craziest, most wonderful baseball game in history" by one observer, saw the Dodgers go nearly the entire game without a hit before pinch hitter Cookie Lavagetto went up to bat with two outs in the bottom of the ninth and laced a two-run double off the wall in right field to even the series at two apiece.[21] The Yankees would take Game 5, also in Brooklyn, before losing Game 6 at home. In Game 7 the Dodgers ran out to a 2–0 lead before the Yankees scored five runs, to take both the game and the championship.

After the series newspaper columnist H. I. Phillips summarized what he had just witnessed: "Television came in with a bang through the World Series. There were television sets everywhere, in homes, clubs, saloons, shops, offices and even on railroads and ships at sea. All of which was wonderful. But it marks the beginning of the dehydration of man's imagination." Phillips goes on to ponder the at-home postgame experience—"You are immediately back in a humdrum world, with no after glow, no high blood pressure, no laughter, no hot arguments, no discovery somebody has your watch"—and cautioned that "all the things that used to call for effort, gusto and a few grunts will become a matter of electrical impulses and a little box with a screen attached." This future, he suggests, is bleak: "Reality will disappear. Man will witness the complete procession of human events and never see an actor in the flesh, hurry across the street from a ball park [*sic*] for a quick beer or denounce somebody for stepping on his corns."[22]

Phillips wasn't the only one to raise this kind of alarm. Many commentators regarded the emergence of television as evidence of a new, disconnected society, one in which the joys of communal life—and baseball games were undoubtedly one of those joys—were replaced by people holed up inside their living rooms staring at a flickering screen. But try as people like Phillips might, there was no stopping this new trend. The World Series had been on television and would be on television every year until 1994, when contentious labor negotiations between owners and players, precipitated in part by, yes, rising television revenues, forced the cancellation of baseball's postseason.

In 1948, with the Boston Braves and Cleveland Indians meeting in the World Series, there was an attempt to extend the broadcast beyond the big East Coast cities. A young inventor named Charles "Chili" Nobles came up with the idea—he called it "Stratovision"—to use a specially equipped B-29 bomber to bridge a five-hundred-mile divide.[23] During the broadcast the plane would fly somewhere over western Pennsylvania. The signal would be beamed up from a station in Baltimore, get picked up by the plane, and then get beamed down to a station in Cleveland. The setup required good weather, minimal interference, and perfect plane positioning. It worked, kind of. *Broadcasting* magazine reported that the crew waiting in Cleveland "got a picture, but not a good one. Worse yet, they couldn't hold it."[24] Still people were intrigued with the technology. After an earlier Stratovision experiment, one columnist asked: "Will several video-sound and several more FM programs some day be broadcast to 80% of the population via 12 planes droning at 30,000 feet?"[25] The answer was no, but it wasn't a bad question. Satellites, of course, would eventually do something quite similar.

By 1951 the B-29 bomber setup had run its course. AT&T had completed a wired relay system that could deliver the first ever coast-to-coast World Series broadcast. Expanded coverage brought more viewers; more viewers brought higher sponsorship costs. In 1949 Gillette paid $200,000 for the rights to televise the World Series; a year later the company anted up $800,000; and a year after that it signed a six-year, $6 million contract.[26] The company then turned around and granted exclusive broadcast rights to NBC, which the network maintained for nearly three decades.

Gorgeous George probably saw all this hoopla and fanfare and money being generated by baseball and thought: "I can beat that." And in some ways he did. At most the World Series took center stage for seven days out of the year. But Gorgeous George was a constant, on television several times per week, all year long. He continued to cash in. In 1952 the *Los Angeles Times* reported that George had collected $160,000 for 277 performances the previous year (and another $128,000 from his side hustle: raising turkeys).[27] He was making other people rich as well, with many pundits arguing that wrestling and Gorgeous George were just as responsible for moving television sets off the shelves as baseball. Still it was a schtick, and schticks are fleeting. As the years went on, George lost his youthful vigor and started drinking more. He got divorced, which led to even more drinking. Meanwhile, the networks began to look for more upscale programming, eager to attach higher prices to their advertising inventory. By the mid-1950s wrestling was no longer a mainstay on network television, and the Gorgeous George phenomenon had ground to a halt. Health problems would force George to retire in 1962 at the age of forty-seven. He would die of a heart attack a year later.

Unlike George, who had embraced and subsequently profited from everything that television offered, baseball's leaders stepped into the television era with great skepticism. While many had been scared of what radio would do to their business, most were downright terrified of television. (There were exceptions, however, such as Phil Wrigley of the Chicago Cubs, who reportedly supported television broadcasts because it meant he wouldn't have to leave his house to watch the games.) Many of these owners were live-event folks, used to bringing in money from the gate and uncomfortable with the idea that fans could now watch games from their couches. They saw baseball as a zero-sum business—a fan at home meant one less fan at the ballpark.

But as the owners would soon learn, baseball was not a zero-sum game. There was more money to be had. A lot more. And with the United States slowly emerging from World War II, where everybody was asked to sacrifice time and money for the collective good, the coffers were about to be swung wide open. Radio broadcasts didn't kill baseball; television broadcasts wouldn't either. On the contrary, they would do more to shape the trajectory of the sports industry than any other invention in history.

Gee Whiz

4

The Launch of Sports Illustrated *(1954)*

With the telecast of Game 7 of the 1947 World Series limited to a handful of markets and with outlets like ESPN and YouTube still decades away, most baseball fans woke up on the morning of October 7 and did what they had always done to see who had won the big game: they opened the newspaper.

In Georgia the fan who grabbed a copy of the *Atlanta Constitution* would have found a detailed play-by-play recap written by none other than sixty-six-year-old Grantland Rice, the most famous American sportswriter of the early twentieth century. "It couldn't go on forever," wrote Rice about the historic matchup. "In a series that broke almost every known record, good and bad, the Yankees beat the Dodgers 5 to 2 in the seventh game to become the 1947 champions of baseball's world." The series was a mess, explained Rice, "the worst pitched series ever known," but it was captivating, exciting until the very last out.[1]

In Alabama the fan who grabbed a copy of the *Birmingham News* would have also discovered a piece penned by the legendary Grantland Rice. Tucked between two articles about college football—this was Alabama after all—was an analysis of how the Yankees had prevailed because of their superior rotation. "Pitching, supposed to be the final measurement between success and failure, usually dominates a World Series," explained Rice. The Yankees had three world-class hurlers, capable of throwing strikes and pitching deep into games. The Dodgers' pitchers, on the other hand, "had no vague idea of where the home plate was located."[2]

In Pennsylvania the fan who grabbed a copy of the *Harrisburg Telegraph* would have found World Series content from—can you believe it?—esteemed American sports scribe Grantland Rice. This particular piece was neither a recap nor an analysis but rather a broad commentary on the value of hard work and determination: "While watching the Brooklyn Dodgers run wild on the bases during the world series, the thought came to me just what hustle means, and how much it is needed in baseball as well as other sports." Rice and his buddies—"a group of old-timers"—then perform one of the great baseball fan traditions, the compilation of an imaginary lineup based on specific criteria. This made-up squad consisted of only those players who "give all they have to pull out the game," and it was anointed the "all-time hustling team."[3]

And finally, in Massachusetts, the fan who grabbed a copy of the *Boston Globe* would have found—surprise!—the thoughts of the immortal Grantland Rice. Unlike the editors in Atlanta, Birmingham, and Harrisburg, the *Globe* team thought it appropriate to honor the conclusion of a historic World Series with one of Rice's patented poems. It was called "The Call of the Curfew." The first few lines were as follows:

New York's sun was slowly setting over the flats and far away,
Filling all the land with beauty at the close of one big day.
And the low rays, now descending, fell upon the Yankee team—
Stirnweiss, Henrich and Rizzuto—looking to a golden dream.[4]

That Grantland Rice, known to his friends and colleagues as "Granny," had four pieces published in four newspapers across four separate states at the age of sixty-six is a testament to the writer's legendary proficiency. In his autobiography Rice estimated that he wrote over sixty-seven million words during his fifty-three-year career, an achievement that would have required the writer to pen an average of thirty-five hundred words every single day of his life.[5] That seems unlikely, a seemingly innocent exaggeration, until you realize that Rice was still churning out several thousand words a day in 1947, thirty years or so after becoming the best-paid sportswriter in the country and during a time when television was threatening to usurp both radio and print as the most dominant medium in the world. And yet that was just Granny being Granny, a man whose life revolved around competition and whose career both contributed to and benefitted from the country's increased interest in spectator sports during the first half of the twentieth century.

Born in 1880 in a small town in Tennessee, Grantland Rice was a solid if unspectacular athlete, playing both baseball and football, first in high school and then at Vanderbilt University. After college Rice found work writing about sports for a local paper. His columns, sprinkled with odd poetic diversions, were well received, and he quickly moved up the newspaper ranks. He took a job in Atlanta, then a better paying one in Cleveland, and then an even better paying one in Tennessee. In 1911 Rice decided to go big time, agreeing to terms with a paper in the country's media hub: New York City. There his profile grew, and he was soon hired to write for the *New York Tribune* and the *Tribune* syndicate, where his column would be printed in papers all over the country. By this time Rice's reputation was so great that the *Tribune* published a full-page story with quotes from over three dozen "big men" touting his arrival. "Any paper that could get the services of such a sterling writer is to be congratulated, and I am glad to add my compliments to those of the rest," wrote the coach of the Columbia University crew team.[6]

Rice would step away from writing to serve his country in World War I. When he returned, he found out that the lawyer with whom he had left most of his savings had lost the money (close to $1 million in today's dollars) and committed suicide. Rice wasn't mad. Instead he blamed himself "for that poor fellow's death," saying that he "shouldn't have put that much temptation in his way."[7] Back at his job with the *Tribune* Rice quickly reestablished himself as the country's most eminent sports pundit. He became a multimedia star, augmenting his syndicated newspaper columns with magazine gigs, frequent radio appearances, and a production house that put together small films. By the mid-1920s Granny was as famous as the people about whom he was writing. He played golf with the president of the United States. He was friends with Babe Ruth, Jack Dempsey, and Bobby Jones. And he was rich, pulling in enough money to maintain both a place in Manhattan and an estate in the Hamptons with its own pitch-and-putt golf course.

Rice's rapid career trajectory was primarily the product of two things: everybody liked Grantland Rice, and Grantland Rice liked everybody. He strolled through life as an eternal half-glass-full type of guy; his writing was mostly devoid of critical commentary. In time Rice would become the poster boy for what would be called the "gee whiz!" style of sports journalism, an oft-chided, bloated technique, where athletes played the role of mythical heroes and where fans, of which Grantland was the biggest, were the fortunate onlookers. All that was fine with Rice, though, who liked what he did and had fun doing it.

In his autobiography Rice demonstrates this "gee whiz!" style through a series of brief anecdotes about New York Yankees legend Babe Ruth. In the first story Rice writes of a morning when Ruth asked to be picked up for their scheduled round of golf because he had gotten drunk and wrecked his car the previous night. In the second story Rice recounts an incident where Ruth punched a policeman in the face after the cop pulled him over to ask if he'd been drinking. And in a third story Rice describes being in the car when Ruth decided to drive the wrong way down a one-way street. Yet again a cop showed up, only to relent once he found out the identity of the perpetrator. And what was Grantland Rice's reaction to all this worrying behavior? "And so it went," he concludes; nothing to see here, just Babe being Babe! Perhaps Rice's most useful trait, then, was not his geniality but rather his selective memory, such as when he ends the Babe Ruth chapter by writing, "For the 30 years I knew Babe—until cancer killed him in 1948—I never saw Ruth really sore at anybody," even though he had just, mere pages ago, rehashed an anecdote about Babe Ruth punching a cop in the face.[8]

Nowhere was Rice's elevation of athletes to mythical status more apparent than in his most famous column, a recap of a Notre Dame–Army football game in 1924. The article begins with a description of Notre Dame's backfield: "Outlined against a blue-gray October sky, the Four Horsemen rode again. In dramatic lore they are known as Famine, Pestilence, Destruction and Death. These are only aliases. Their real names are Stuhldreher, Miller, Crowley and Layden." Rice claims that the idea for the Four Horsemen analogy had come to him the previous year after he had noticed that the Notre Dame backfield resembled a "wild horse stampede." Other sources give credit to a Notre Dame public relations assistant named George Strickler for planting the idea in Rice's head. Either way, the "Four Horsemen" introduction is perhaps the most famous piece of sports writing of all time. After the notable beginning the piece meanders for another two thousand metaphor-laden words, with Rice comparing the athletes to cyclones, African buffaloes, and military tanks that move at the speed of motorcycles. Gee whiz! indeed.[9]

While many of Rice's contemporaries were employing similar narrative techniques, others were trying to provide alternatives to this hyperbolic prose. A little over a week after Rice's story appeared in newspapers, a relatively new magazine named *Time* provided its own recap of the Notre Dame–Army matchup. Relegated to a ninety-five-word snippet on page twenty-two, the game was treated as a bit of an afterthought.[10] It wasn't even the lead story in the magazine's skimpy "Sport" department—that went to the thirty-ninth annual show of the Horse Association of America. And yet even in such limited space the recap still managed to cross the ethical line, at least in a journalistic sense, reporting that the Notre Dame backfield had run "like the Four Horsemen." While the phrase was put in quotes, it included zero attribution, no indication that the description came not from the *Time* editorial team but rather from the country's most famous sportswriter (or, if the story is true, George Strickler).

A brief recap in an easily digestible format with information culled from other sources; it was classic *Time*, through and through. The magazine had launched a year earlier, in 1923, the brainchild of two recent Yale University graduates named Henry "Harry" Luce and Briton "Brit" Hadden. As they worked their way up the Yale literary and journalistic ladders, Luce and Hadden arrived at the conclusion that the average American had neither time nor interest in reading the era's sensationalized and overly verbose newspapers. What the country needed was an alternative, a pithy news source that could keep hard-working folks, those scurrying from one important engagement to another, updated on national and international affairs.

Upon graduation Luce and Hadden got to work creating this very publication, tapping their Ivy League connections for startup money and laying out a general editorial framework. Their first idea for a title, *Facts*, was soon replaced by *Time*, a name the founders saw suitable for a magazine that aspired to keep readers informed in a quick and efficient manner. The magazine would have minimal reporting and no bylines; instead writers would pull information from newspapers, distilling it down into a compact summary. All the content would be written in a similar style, a lively format so distinct that it would eventually be referred to, often mockingly, as "Timese." The magazine would include about a hundred articles per week, and none would be more than four hundred words.

Time magazine launched in 1923. Although the magazine struggled financially for the first few years, the theory upon which it was built—that young and affluent Americans of the 1920s needed and wanted an easier way to stay informed—soon came to fruition, with the magazine's growing upscale audience attracting the kind of advertisers the publication needed to stay afloat. America, it turned out, really loved *Time*. And *Time* really loved America. In just a few short years the magazine would become, according to Luce's biographer Alan Brinkley, a "familiar and predictable experience" that was "both a response to the nationalization of American culture—and eventually a contributor to that nationalization."[11]

In 1929 Brit Hadden developed a serious strep infection and died at the age of thirty-one. With his co-founder gone, Luce was now sole proprietor of the Time, Inc. empire, a position he would embrace to become one of the most powerful media executives on the planet. Over the next few years the company would launch a business magazine called *Fortune*, which was a hit, and a photography-driven periodical called *Life*, which was a phenomenon. Success bred ambition, and Luce began mentally wandering outside the magazine bubble, becoming one of the first, but hardly the last, media mogul to ponder life's big questions. In particular he became obsessed with what the United States *was*, what it was meant to do, and what role he was meant to play in all of it. He came to believe that his magazines were more than just magazines, once telling his team that "our publications have been outstanding, and often pioneers, in showing to Americans what American life is like."[12] But he explicitly wanted to go further (and thought he needed to, although nobody was really asking), to build a coherent argument and strategy based off of these middle-aged philosophical musings.

In February 1941 Luce published what would become the most famous thing he would ever write, an article for *Life* called "The American Century." In it he pleads for the United States to take a more prominent role on the global stage, to become "the dynamic center of ever-widening spheres of enterprise, America as the training center of the skillful servants of mankind, America as the Good Samaritan, really believing again that it is more blessed to give than to receive, and America as the powerhouse of the ideals of Freedom and Justice." Indirectly patting himself on the back—"The American people are by far the best informed people in the history of the world"—and railing against isolationists, Luce argued for the emergence of a world shaped and molded by American ideals and values, by "our Bill of Rights, our Declaration of Independence, our Constitution, our magnificent industrial products, our technical skills."[13] Only then would the country fulfill its global responsibility, its inherent duty to promote success, innovation, and, above all, happiness.

During the war, and then after it, Luce continued to harp on about America and its purpose. While he did, the magazine industry exploded. From the launch of *Time* in 1923 to the publication of Luce's famous essay in 1941, magazine advertising had gone from $110 million to around $168 million. That's healthy, if unspectacular, growth, stymied by the lean years of the Great Depression. But by 1950 advertisers had increased their spending in magazines to over $400 million. By 1955 they were spending over $600 million.[14]

The confidence advertisers placed in magazines was buoyed by the industry's unique ability to deliver highly targeted niche audiences. There are few metrics that advertising executives value more than efficiency, firm knowledge that an ad is being seen by the people for which it was intended. As the magazine industry expanded, brands would figure out what consumer segment they wanted to reach and then pick the publication most applicable to that segment. If you wanted to reach housewives, you advertised in *Good Housekeeping*. If you wanted to reach car fanatics, you went with *Popular Mechanics*. And if you wanted to reach parents, it didn't get any more efficient than *Parents' Magazine*.

One group missing from this list of postwar consumer segments was "the sports fan," mostly because the concept of "the sports fan" at the time didn't really exist as it does now. Sure, there were sport participants, people who golfed or hunted or cycled. There were also sport spectators, boxing and baseball and football fans. But it was generally assumed that there was little that bound these disparate groups together, no common thread around which a big-time magazine could find—and, more importantly, maintain—success. In 1946 Macfadden Publications (best known for its founder, Bernarr Macfadden, who claimed that humans could live to the age of 125 if only they followed the advice offered in his health and fitness magazines) decided to give it a shot, establishing a monthly magazine called *Sport*. With a focus on players and a touch of Grantland Rice's "gee whiz!" writing, the magazine found some success, generating a circulation base of around a half million by the mid-1950s.

It was around that time that Harry Luce decided to get in on the game. It wasn't because he needed the money; on the contrary, his company was thriving. From 1941 to 1955 *Time*'s circulation more than doubled, to nearly two million. *Life* was even more popular, with a circulation of almost six million and with each issue pulling in over $2 million in advertising. Still moguls are gonna mogul, and with World War II slowly fading into history, Luce brought his team together to brainstorm on how to best expand his empire. One idea, a true crime periodical called *Murder*, didn't get enough traction. Neither did an idea centered around short fiction. But then someone brought up the idea of a weekly sports magazine. Luce was intrigued, partly because he was able to mentally cram the idea into his larger purpose-driven ideology. In Luce's mind America stood for freedom, which in turn meant the pursuit of happiness. Happiness is pursued through leisure. And leisure, a newfound American focus due to a postwar increase in both free time and disposable income, often takes the form of sports. It made too much sense; it had to be done.

A team was put together to tackle the project, one with a noticeable lack of sports experience or knowledge. It included an editor from *Life*, an advertising director from *Time*, and a former publicist for the wrestler Gorgeous George. During the initial meetings a new phrase was coined—"the wonderful world of sport"—that would serve as something akin to the magazine's guiding light. (It helped, of course, that Luce was the one who coined it.) Luce hoped to name the magazine *Sport*, an obvious fit in the *Time*, *Life*, and *Fortune* family. But Macfadden's asking price was too high, and the team settled for *Sports Illustrated*, a title that had been previously attached to two short-lived, unsuccessful publications. As the date of the first issue neared, there was strong interest from potential subscribers—the magazine would start with 350,000 subscribers—but a more tepid reaction from advertisers. The initial thought was that this magazine could tap into the country club crowd, that it could attract high-end brands by attracting upper class readers. But the "dummy" issues put together to drum up interest didn't necessarily reflect that. One advertising executive reacted to a prototype by saying that the magazine "covers too much ground. It's a hybrid. Do baseball and boxing fans mingle with fox hunters in pink coats?"[15]

Probably not, but it was too late to change course. And so *Sports Illustrated* barreled forward, releasing its first issue in August 1954. Not surprisingly, it was a confusing mess, devoid of any coherent strategy. The issue had articles about boxing and baseball cards. It also had articles about beavers, boomerangs, and poison ivy. One article discussed how to best prepare a dog for hunting season. Another piece shared tips on how to pick out a puppy: "Look for the one that is alert and has bright eyes. Beware the wallflower who sits with his head bent and quivers when you go near." And one column, called "Soundtrack," zigged and zagged so much that it was almost as if it had been written by a team of people who were specifically told not to collaborate in any way but then, at the very last moment, asked to take what they had written and put it together into one final essay. The article began with a report about the first ascent of K2, the second highest mountain in the world, before moving into an examination of the amoeba, "the simplest of living things," and then segueing into a discussion about kittens: "The theory that kittens play at chasing spools so that one day they may be expert at chasing mice is easy and may even be true."[16]

Thus began a rough couple of years for the country's first weekly sports magazine. Advertising sales sputtered along; staff morale dropped. Nobody could quite pinpoint what *Sports Illustrated* was supposed to be. Was it a magazine for highly literate sport participants? Affluent elites? Baseball fans from the local bar? It wasn't clear. One reader complained that there were "too many safaris, bullfights, birds and fashion." Employees were equally confused about the mix of content, with one writer remembering that "there were so many goddamn people covering yachting."[17] To add to the confusion famous authors were occasionally brought in and asked to write about sports. Here, for example, was William Faulkner's description of ice hockey: "To the innocent, who had never seen hockey before, it seemed discorded and inconsequent, bizarre and paradoxical, like the frantic darting of the weightless bugs which run on the surface of stagnant pools."[18]

Had *Sports Illustrated* been the invention of two young, cash-strapped entrepreneurs, like *Time* had been, it may have very well folded after the first year. But as the youngest sibling in the Time, Inc. family, the magazine got away with stuff the others couldn't—namely, losing money for the first decade of its life. It also had a father who wanted it to succeed, both because he wanted to grow his media portfolio and because he thought it was an important part of the American soul. And every so often there was tangible evidence that the magazine was indeed the product of Harry Luce and his purpose-driven ideology. In an article naming track star Rafer Johnson the Sportsman of the Year of 1958, *Sports Illustrated* had this to say about Johnson's accomplishments: "Any year *Sports Illustrated* might well have had a different Sportsman. But this year it could not have had a better. For he represents an attitude toward life and self that reaches far beyond the playing field into American character. It is an attitude which *Sports Illustrated* respects in Rafer Johnson, in sport and in America."[19] In other words, if we were all a little more like the great American sprinter Rafer Johnson, the world would be a better place.

In 1960 Harry Luce installed a heavy-drinking French journalist named André Laguerre as the new managing editor. Laguerre would give the magazine a complete makeover, changing what kind of sports were being covered, encouraging more color photography, and beginning the deeply reported, long-form pieces for which the magazine would become known. Coverage of participatory sports was pushed aside to make room for more coverage of spectator sports; according to historian Michael MacCambridge, the number of articles the magazine ran about professional football and college basketball nearly tripled from 1955 to 1965. Laguerre also hired some of the writers that would make the magazine a household name, people like Frank Deford, Dan Jenkins, and John Underwood. In 1964, after tens of millions of dollars of losses, *Sports Illustrated* finally turned a profit.

There will never not be a time when somebody, somewhere, is writing about sports. What that writing will look like largely depends on the era in which it appears. It's impossible to talk about Grantland Rice without talking about the 1920s and 1930s, about the limited media options and the acceptance of sports figures as mythical heroes as the world lurched from a war to a boom to a depression to another war. If Rice had been born a hundred years later, writing sappy poems about baseball players, he'd have been laughed at, and his columns would have been turned into memes. Yet in the 1920s that kind of stuff made him the most read and highest-paid sportswriter in the country. It's also impossible to talk about *Sports Illustrated* without talking about the rise of the American middle class and the rapid adoption of television, a medium that turned out to be the magazine's greatest ally. As Americans began watching more sports, they began wondering more about the players and the coaches and the teams. *Sports Illustrated* would provide some context to these events, turning viewers into fans and proving, almost definitively, that the sports media industry was not a zero-sum game but rather an untapped depository of ancillary opportunities. If fans were willing to watch four baseball games a week from their couches and then spend several hours reading about the players from those baseball games, what else would they be willing to do? And how much more money was there to be had tapping into that interest?

The answer, of course, was a lot, way more than even the most optimistic media mogul of the 1950s could have ever imagined.

5   The Greatest Game Ever Played

The Sports Broadcasting Act (1961)

An important thing to remember about Pete Rozelle, the commissioner of the National Football League (NFL) for nearly three decades (1960–89), is that he was trained in the art of public relations. He even had his own personal origin story, often telling interviewers that the most influential moment of his life had come at the age of ten, when a camp counselor pontificated on the meaning of reputation. Or maybe it was a high school coach, not a camp counselor; the circumstances of the incident were actually a bit fluid from telling to telling. Regardless, it was one of Rozelle's favorite anecdotes. Here's what he said he learned from the encounter with the counselor during one interview with the *New York Times*: "Character is what you *are*. Reputation is what people *think* you are. But if your reputation is bad, you might as well have bad character—the one is useless without the other."[1]

In 1946 a twenty-year-old Pete Rozelle got the chance to put his favorite lesson into practice when he was hired to create game day programs for the NFL's Los Angeles Rams. Five years later, after enrolling at the University of San Francisco (USF) and taking a job as the school's sports news director, Rozelle traveled to New York City for a USF-Fordham football game at Yankee Stadium. He spent his visit hyping up the school to local newspaper reporters and accompanied Grantland Rice to the game, no doubt hoping for good publicity in Rice's syndicated column the next day. Rozelle completed his undergraduate degree and bounced from job to job, first as the publicity director for the Rams, then as a partner at a public relations firm in San Francisco, and finally back to the Rams to serve as the team's general manager in 1957. Two years later NFL commissioner Bert Bell was at a game when he suffered a heart attack and died. Forced to pick a replacement, the league's owners struggled to come to a consensus. After a week and a half of negotiations Rams' owner Dan Reeves suggested his general manager as a possibility. Rozelle was young but had a pristine reputation. "I was the only candidate who hadn't already alienated most of the people in that meeting," Rozelle would say later.[2] The owners decided that was good enough, voting to install the thirty-three-year-old as the NFL's next leader.

By the time Rozelle became commissioner in 1960, the NFL had just celebrated its fortieth birthday. It had been a rocky ride. The league's early years were filled with experiments and missteps. Owners lost money. Rules changed. Franchises came and went. The matchups of the early years were often between teams long forgotten—the Hammond Pros, the Staten Island Stapletons, the Duluth Eskimos—and more familiar franchises such as the Green Bay Packers, New York Giants, and Chicago Bears. By the end of the 1930s the frenetic turnover had slowed, and the NFL was beginning to establish a small yet devoted fan base.

The onset of World War II was both tumultuous and fortuitous for the league. As the war sapped resources and took players away from the field, owners were forced to improvise in order to stay afloat. In 1943 the Philadelphia Eagles and Pittsburgh Steelers combined to form a single squad unofficially referred to as the "Steagles." The next year the Steelers left their partnership with the Eagles in order to merge operations with the Chicago Cardinals and form a team known as "Card-Pitt." Yet despite these desperate measures optimism for professional football remained high. Three new leagues were proposed during the war years. While two of them never got off the ground, the third, the All-America Football Conference (AAFC), successfully launched in 1946 with eight teams. The AAFC's founding sparked an intense battle for relevancy between the two competing leagues. After four contentious years the NFL and AAFC came to a truce, with three franchises—the Cleveland Browns, San Francisco 49ers, and Baltimore

Colts—absorbed into the new thirteen-team NFL for the 1950 season. The rest of the AAFC packed up shop and went home.

Here's one version of what happened next. Over the next decade the perpetually disjointed and financially precarious National Football League evolved to become the all-powerful and stunningly wealthy (*cue* NFL *Films background music, cue the immortal voice of John Facenda, cue shots of a snowy Lambeau and a rowdy Arrowhead*) NATIONAL. FOOTBALL. LEAGUE. Central to this epic transformation was the 1958 NFL Championship Game between the Baltimore Colts and New York Giants. Played at Yankee Stadium in front of sixty-four thousand raucous fans, the game featured what one author has called the "greatest concentration of football talent ever assembled for a single game."[3] There was Colts quarterback Johnny Unitas, a Tom Brady before Tom Brady, a late round, afterthought draft pick who would go on to win multiple NFL titles and establish himself as one of the greatest players in league history. The Giants had their own collection of stars, two of whom—running back Frank Gifford and kicker Pat Summerall—became even more famous, and made the league even more famous, when they stopped playing and entered the broadcasting booth. On the sidelines were a group of men who would go down in history as some of the league's most innovative coaches: Weeb Ewbank, head coach of the Colts; Vince Lombardi, who directed the Giants' offense and became head coach of the Packers in 1959; and Tom Landry, who directed the Giants' defense and became head coach of the Cowboys in 1960.

Despite this elite collection of talent, the game was a mess. The teams combined for seven total turnovers; the Giants alone fumbled six times, losing four of them. And yet it's easy to forget the mundane set list when you're blessed with an unforgettable encore. With the score tied 17–17 at the end of regulation, the teams were told that they'd be participating in the first sudden death overtime in championship game history. Many players were surprised; some had even left the field to go into the locker room, thinking the game had ended in a draw. In the extra time the Giants won the coin toss and chose to receive the ball. They couldn't do much and were forced to punt, handing Johnny Unitas the opportunity to lead the Colts on an 80-yard touchdown drive to seal both the win and the league title. In a recap the following week Tex Maule of *Sports Illustrated* tried to put the game into perspective: "Never has there been a game like this one. When there are so many high points, it is not easy to pick the highest. . . . With each team playing as well as it was possible for it to play, the better team finally won."[4] The title of the article, "The Best Game Ever Played," probably isn't the most appropriate way to describe a contest that included so many miscues. Over the next few decades the 1958 NFL Championship Game would settle for a different nickname: "The Greatest Game Ever Played."

The Colts-Giants game would come to represent a symbolic turning point for the league, a time-stamped delineator between an era of when the NFL was *nothing* and an era of when the NFL was *everything*. Rehashing the game has become something of a cottage industry, with dozens of books, articles, podcasts, and documentaries all detailing the exploits of Unitas and Gifford and Landry and Lombardi. Even author Mark Bowden, of *Black Hawk Down* fame, has written about the game, finding time among his investigations of Pablo Escobar and Osama bin Laden to publish a book titled (in an obvious ode to the SI article) *The Best Game Ever: Giants vs. Colts, 1958, and the Birth of the Modern NFL*. The league has been more than happy to play along with all this revelry. In 2019, as the NFL celebrated its hundred-year anniversary, the 1958 championship was unsurprisingly ranked as the greatest game of all time (beholden to a widely used nickname, the list makers probably didn't have much of a choice here). Eager to project a fantastical aura around the contest, the NFL tapped storyteller extraordinaire George R. R. Martin, creator of the *Game of Thrones* universe and self-proclaimed fan of both the New York Jets and New York Giants, to say a few words. In a video posted to the NFL website Martin toes the company line, explaining that the Colts-Giants game "transformed the NFL into a national passion."[5]

An important component to this frequently repeated story is that the game was broadcast on national television and was watched by a can-you-believe-it forty-five-million Americans. Bowden has written that "an estimated forty-five million people, the largest crowd to ever witness a football game, saw spectral players battling in shades of white and gray against a stark black backdrop."[6] A *Washington Post* article describes the television audience as a "a record-shattering 45 million."[7] And in *The League: How Five Rivals Created the NFL and Launched a*

Sports Empire, John Eisenberg wrote: "Ratings experts would estimate that 40 million people had watched the Colts and Giants on NBC. Forty million! That was roughly one-fifth of the country's population."[8]

While forty (or forty-five) million people is indeed a lot, a single data point is meaningless without context. For instance, the *Washington Post* article is wrong: nothing about this audience was record-shattering. In fact, according to television ratings published in *Broadcasting* magazine a few weeks after the game, two college football games (the Rose Bowl and the Sugar Bowl) generated significantly larger audiences that very same week.[9] Also, while forty or forty-five million sounds like a lot—and today's broadcast networks, forced to compete against cable television and streaming services, would certainly be thrilled with a number like that—the top television audiences in the late 1950s were generally pretty big. That's what happens when you have an exciting new medium and only a couple of options from which to choose. During the two-week period in which it aired, the NFL title game actually ranked just ninth in total reach (that is, how many people viewed at least some of the broadcast) across all networks, behind not just the Rose Bowl and Sugar Bowl, but also behind regularly scheduled programs like *Wagon Train* and the *Perry Como Show*. And finally, although the game was celebrated as a monumental turning point, the audience for the 1958 NFL Championship Game was actually *lower* than the audience for the previous year's championship game (Lions vs. Browns) and *higher* than the audience for the following year's matchup (a rematch of Colts vs. Giants).[10] All of this is to say that while the television audience for the 1958 NFL championship was good, it was also kind of what should have been expected if anybody had been paying attention.

This brings us to the second version of this story, an alternate explanation of how the NFL became the most powerful component of the American sports industry. While there are some similarities between the two stories—for instance, television plays a key role in both—this version is admittedly not as fun as the previous account. It doesn't begin and end in a couple of hours (it lasts decades actually). The incredible ensemble cast is exchanged for a roster of typecast supporting roles: legendary Indianapolis Colts quarterback Johnny Unitas is replaced by a longtime congressman from Brooklyn, and New

York Giants running back/celebrity Frank Gifford becomes a judge in eastern Pennsylvania. The script also takes a hit, with the thrilling climax of sudden death overtime substituted for the drawn-out tedium of antitrust hearings. And one historic, supposedly record-shattering nationally televised game is swapped for games that aren't televised at all. So, yeah, this version is admittedly nowhere near as exciting. But it's definitely worth telling, because it's a far more accurate assessment of how the NFL became what it is today rather than how people think the NFL became what it is today—you know, that whole character vs. reputation thing.

A good place to start this version is in 1953, when the U.S. Department of Justice filed a civil suit against the NFL, alleging that the league's policy concerning radio and television broadcasts was illegal. The league had put in place a system of strict rules, a strategic plan that forbade the television broadcast of home games within a seventy-five-mile radius of the stadium, the broadcast of other league games in a region where a team was playing at home, and even the broadcast of other league games when an in-market team was playing an away game. All these rules were explicitly designed to maintain the only real revenue stream the league had at that time: the gate.

The government suggested that these policies restricted trade and were therefore in violation of American antitrust rules. The argument was that the system not only deprived the public of games it had a right to see, but it also had a negative impact on television stations that desperately needed audience-friendly content in order to survive. The NFL, on the other hand, argued that the rules were essential to its own survival, that they were a "reasonable restriction" necessary for the league to create and build a sustainable business. In its attempt to dismiss the case the NFL suggested that television was uniquely positioned to chip away at its established business model: "More than any other sport except perhaps boxing, the telecasting of football games affords a viewer a spectacle as attractive as that which he sees when he visits the stadium, minus the discomfort of the trip. The viewer of a football game on television has a view of the game not from the 50-yard line but as if he were in the backfield." Allowing fans to have unfettered access to games on television would therefore lead to a "devastating and ruinous decrease in attendance."[11]

Judge Alan K. Grim's ruling came down on November 12, 1953. There were several components. For one thing, Grim decided that the league was indeed allowed to prevent the broadcasts of outside games in markets where a team was hosting a game. "Professional football is a unique type of business," Grim wrote in his decision. "Like other professional sports which are organized on a league basis it has problems which no other business has."[12] Blacking out home games within a certain region was understandable; it forced fans to pony up for a ticket. Blacking out the games of other teams when the in-market team was playing at home was also a perfectly reasonable business maneuver as it dissuaded fans from staying home to watch another team on television. Grim also decided, however, that the league couldn't extend this exception to radio or to instances when the in-market team was playing an away game. And he believed that the NFL commissioner should never hold unilateral power over these broadcasting decisions. That, Grim noted, was illegal and needed to be changed.

Paying close attention to this legal skirmish was U.S. Congressman Emanuel Celler. Born in Brooklyn to a well-off family and elected to the House of Representatives as a Democrat in 1922, Celler vowed to serve as a guard against the increased consolidation of American wealth and power. He believed that monopolies went against everything the United States stood for: opportunity, equality, pursuit of happiness. Celler vowed to untangle the economic quagmire, to give power back to the people not through increased government control—that would be communism, and Celler needed people to understand that he wasn't a Communist—but by making sure the markets were as open and as competitive as possible. In 1949 he was put in charge of a subcommittee approved by President Harry S. Truman to investigate the growth of monopoly power. He dove into the inquiry with gusto. And the average American would surely support him, right? As Celler wrote in his 1953 autobiography, "Didn't [monopoly power] concern the laborer whose job opportunities were confined to fewer and fewer corporations, with the labor policy of corporations determined by fewer and fewer men?"[13]

No, it didn't. "I was wrong," Celler wrote about the public reaction to his new inquiries. "No man has ever been more wrong. I had hit the most sensitive nerve of American pride—its bigness in business."

His 1951 investigation into whether Major League Baseball, which had been granted an antitrust exemption in 1922, operated as a monopoly infuriated a broad segment of his constituents. Many believed Celler was out to destroy America's favorite pastime: "Never had such controversy raged. Never had so many columns been filled with torrents of words."[14] In the end, while the committee found significant evidence that baseball did indeed operate as something close to a monopoly, it declined to pass legislation to address the issue. And Major League Baseball, with no real competitors, continued to operate as is.

Still Celler's obsession with monopoly continued. The 1958 NFL Championship Game came and went. In 1960 public relations connoisseur Pete Rozelle finally entered the picture as the new NFL commissioner. And then, a sight for Celler to behold: a new competitor rose up to challenge the growing power of the NFL. Following in the tradition of jilted rich guys starting their own leagues after being rejected by the NFL, Lamar Hunt, heir to a Texas oil fortune, launched the American Football League (AFL) in 1960. This was good, thought Celler. The AFL meant competition for the NFL. And competition was the lifeblood of the American economy. The system was working!

In June 1960 the AFL signed its first television deal, a five-year, $10.6 million package with ABC.[15] The deal was unique in that it was negotiated by the league office and gave the network the exclusive rights to all regular-season games. Rozelle took notice. Up until that point each NFL team had negotiated its own television deal, a system that led to teams in bigger markets getting more money than teams in smaller markets. In 1960, for example, the Los Angeles Rams pulled in nearly three times as much television revenue as the Green Bay Packers ($300,000 vs. $105,000).[16]

The following year Pete Rozelle and the NFL followed the lead of the AFL and signed their own exclusive broadcasting deal, a two-year $9.3 million package with CBS for the rights to their entire regular-season schedule.[17] The revenue would be distributed equally across the fourteen-team league, with each franchise receiving $332,000 in both 1961 and 1962 (compared to an average of less than $200,000 in 1960). But in July Judge Grim would nix the deal, saying that the agreement violated a clause in his 1953 ruling that barred the league, rather than individual teams, from making unilateral decisions regarding when and where certain games could be blacked out. The NFL was incensed. So was the AFL. Believing that his own agreement would be nullified next, AFL commissioner Joe Ross argued that football and television were now one and the same: "Pro football survived without television, but the sport's period of expansion, solvency and growth is directly equated to its entrance into the field of television."[18]

Emanuel Celler, competition's biggest cheerleader, needed the AFL to survive. And if pooled broadcasting rights were the key to survival, then pooled broadcasting rights it would be. A few weeks after Grim nullified the CBS-NFL pact, Celler proposed a bill that would exempt professional sports leagues from the antitrust rules invalidating their exclusive television arrangements. Debate ensued. Vincent Waskilewski, vice president of the National Association of Broadcasters, was adamant that the bill should be rejected: "We believe that no blank check should be given to professional sports which allow them to arbitrarily black out from the airwaves, through concerted activity, the telecasting and broadcasting of games which have such great public appeal."[19]

Pete Rozelle disagreed, suggesting that in order to provide a product with "such great public appeal," the NFL needed to pool its resources as a way to ensure that teams in the smallest markets, like the Packers, could compete against teams in the larger markets. "One of the key things that a sports league needs is unity of purpose," he would be quoted as often saying. "When we stay together on something, we're normally successful and we grow. When we're going to splinter off, we're not as successful."[20] This kind of strategy wasn't necessarily Rozelle's idea. For decades NFL owners had pursued policies explicitly designed to benefit the league as a whole rather than individual teams. In the 1930s the owners had agreed to institute a college draft, where the worst teams from the previous year would get the highest picks. Team executives had also agreed to a policy whereby a home team shared the gate revenue with the away team, thus ensuring that teams with more robust attendance figures didn't have an outright financial advantage. Rozelle's goal with his tenure was to supercharge this corporate harmony, to reshape the league into "a single entity [similar to] Sears or McDonald's."[21]

In October 1961 President John F. Kennedy officially signed a bill allowing professional sports leagues to pool their broadcasting rights.

It would become known as the Sports Broadcasting Act. A few months after the law went into effect, CBS agreed to the same deal that had been rejected the year before: a two-year, $9.3 million exclusive package for regular-season NFL games. From there the money would go up. And up. And up. In 1964 it was a two-year deal with CBS for $28.2 million. In 1966, another two-year deal: $36.6 million. And in 1968, yet another two-year pact: over $50 million.

While the AFL and NFL were cashing their television checks, they found time to deliver the ultimate slap in the face to one of their supposed government allies: Emanuel Celler. In 1966 the leagues agreed to join forces, creating a single entity with two separate conferences. The merger was complete by 1970, after which the newly invigorated NFL signed television deals worth $142 million over four years. The growth would continue, unabated and exponential, dispersed equally to all NFL teams. And just like that, all Celler's hard work to maintain the survival of a competitive professional football market had led to the complete opposite: the strengthening of what would become the most financially dominant professional sports league in the country.

So that's the second version of the story of how the NFL became king of American sports. In some ways it's a simple tale about supply and demand. Buoyed by an "all-for-one, one-for-all" company culture, the NFL deftly navigated the complex American legal and legislative landscape in order to meticulously control the way the public received its product. Forced to support the hometown team and given the opportunity to do so only once a week, Americans developed highly synchronized, rabid regional allegiances. Sunday afternoons became synonymous with professional football, a time when people in Cleveland cheered for the Browns and people in Philadelphia cheered for the Eagles. Audiences grew, television networks drooled, and advertisers opened their wallets. One football historian has argued that "Pro football succeeded ultimately because it struck a resonant chord in the American psyche. In a time of increasing alienation and urban flight, when a sense of community was dissipating, it unified cities in ways that other civic enterprises could not."[22] That's probably true. But pro football also succeeded because it followed a series of classic tried-and-true corporate strategies: limit supply, maximize demand, carve out a niche, build loyalty, diversify revenue.

And what's the final step to all that ruthless corporate maneuvering? Hide the backroom shenanigans as best you can. For that the league needed a mirage, an exciting anecdote to which it could refer on its website, at employee retreats, or during client meetings and say, "See? There's Unitas and Gifford and the first championship overtime. That's when it happened; that's when we became the apple in America's eye." And while reputational guru Pete Rozelle never came out directly and said it, he undoubtedly knew that the "Greatest Game Ever Played" could provide the league with the narrative it needed, an origin story worthy of the country's new favorite pastime.

Remember that *Sports Illustrated* story by Tex Maule that came out the week after the championship game calling Colts-Giants "the best football game ever played"? Well, Maule had previously been the publicity director for two NFL teams, including the Los Angeles Rams, and good friend of, yep, Pete Rozelle. And guess who penned the introduction to John Steadman's *The Greatest Game Ever Played*, a 1988 book detailing the events of December 28, 1958? Pete Rozelle. He begins it as follows: "The 1958 National Football League championship escalated the popularity of professional football far greater than any single player, coach or owner ever has."[23]

According to the official version, then, the NFL didn't become the country's favorite league because of legal battles and government lobbying and an effective television strategy that limited supply and maximized demand. It became the country's favorite league because once there was a game starring all these great players and that game went into overtime and Johnny Unitas and Frank Gifford and Vince Lombardi and Tom Landry were all there, and it was quite simply the greatest game ever played. And, oh yeah, didn't you hear? It was watched by *forty-five million people* on television.

Amazing.

Our World

6

FIFA *World Cup (1966)*

In the early 1920s, as the original NFL owners experimented with different rules and new formats for their struggling professional league, politicians from all over the world got together and talked about something far more important: how to prevent a massive global conflict from ever happening again. One of the conclusions they came up with was to form a bunch of committees, collections of people grouped together under generic names easily abbreviated by short acronyms. One of those groups was the "International Committee on Intellectual Cooperation" (ICIC). According to historian Suzanne Lommers, the ICIC was made up of some of Europe's most distinguished thinkers and was charged with developing "international synergy via standardization in fields like academia, the arts, and the sciences."[1] This synergy, it was thought, could get everybody on the same page. Peace would follow.

A few years went by; the committee made little progress. In 1929 it was decided that a new committee should be formed to study the effectiveness of the old committee. This group was called the "Committee of Enquiry to Study the Programme, Work and Organisation of the International Committee on Intellectual Cooperation and the Institute." The recommendation of this committee was to expand the scope of the initial group by turning it into an organization, which is how the "Intellectual Cooperation Organization" (OCI) was born.[2]

Undeterred by the inertia of its predecessor, the OCI thought big right from the start. As Lommers has explained, members of the organization "imagined a world in which all citizens would feel acknowledged: east, west, from every nation, from every local community, and every group."[3] Radio would be key in executing the OCI's agenda, the primary medium through which its ideas would be distributed.

Formed around the same time as these committees and organizations was yet another collection of like-minded people: the International Broadcasting Union (IBU). Unlike the previous groups, which were primarily made up of policy wonks, the IBU was a multinational consortium of broadcasting services. One objective of the IBU was to determine the best way to divvy up radio frequencies, a major issue in a continent like Europe, where nations were plentiful but space was limited. To tackle this issue the IBU put together a "Gentleman's Agreement," a nonbinding pact that discouraged nations from broadcasting potentially inflammatory propaganda. At first the agreement seemed to work. In 1927 one of the members of the IBU remarked that "One of the best results, from a moral point of view, obtained by a mutual entente between the members of the International Broadcasting Union, has been the suppression of all transmissions of an offensive nature to another country."[4]

All these committees, organizations, and unions had a few things in common. They all recognized that World War I had been awful and wanted to prevent something similar from happening in the future. They also realized that new mediums like radio, depending on how they were used, had great potential to both bring the world closer together *and* break it further apart. And they had come to the conclusion that they needed to work collectively not only for moral and ethical reasons, but also because these new technologies were quite complex, oblivious to the often arbitrary borders laid down by national governments. The work they set out to do, then, was as much about infrastructure and policy as it was about saving the world from itself.

For the most part they failed. The 1930s brought Hitler and Mussolini; then came World War II. As we saw in chapter 2, propaganda from all sides infiltrated the European airwaves. Any attempt to corral these new mediums into doing something positive and collaborative was transformed into stopping a vile coalition from taking over the world. And yet there was also a recognition that these technologies—radio and the much newer television—weren't going away once the war ended. They were increasingly as much a part of household life as the sofa or the kitchen table, even if their overall influence was still a bit unclear. Because of that, there remained a desire in many circles to use broadcasting not as an agent of war but rather as a way to encourage peace and understanding. A 1944 article in the magazine *Wireless World*, for instance, laid out a proposal for a "European Broadcasting Alliance" and suggested that "many problems would be resolved if every European could be made conscious of his status as a European—a member of a nation within a group of nations."[5] Everybody listening to or watching the same programs at the same time might help make that vision a reality.

While that specific proposal went nowhere, the hope for collaboration lingered as the war died down. It had to contend with obvious global fissures. By the beginning of the 1950s the IBU had splintered into two cold-war delineated organizations: the European Broadcasting Union (EBU), which consisted of countries in Western Europe, and the International Radio and Television Network (OIR), which consisted of countries in Eastern Europe. Initially, and with television adoption rapidly increasing, the EBU's primary focus was on infrastructure and policy: making sure all those wires and cables and frequencies were set up correctly and working as they were supposed to work. But then a Swiss representative suggested creating some sort of multinational program depositary to save costs. The suggestion was buoyed by the successful 1953 broadcast of Queen Elizabeth II's coronation, televised live in multiple countries across continental Europe to a rousing reception. One newspaper even reported that French viewers "jostled for a good view" of televisions set up in the windows of shops and newspaper offices.[6] Broadcasters took note, and because there are few things a network executive desires more than quality content at a cheap price, plans were put in place to make this type of content-sharing system permanent. Hundreds of miles of cables were laid; towers were installed to push signals over water and mountains. And a British journalist gave the system a name: Eurovision.[7]

By 1956 Eurovision was humming along. A columnist at the time called it "a complex, smooth-running system by which programs are exchanged without fuss or red tape."[8] Much of the content was pretty standard: music, arts, news. Other programs were a bit unorthodox, however, leaving some commercial networks hesitant to participate. As one opinion writer explained, "Consider the feelings of a detergent manufacturer, when, before his 'spot' at 9 o'clock, he finds that for what he has paid he gets not the Tiller Girls from London [a popular dance group] but peasants dancing on the ramparts of Dubrovnik."[9] Regardless, what was happening in Europe with Eurovision was unprecedented. The continent was, at least occasionally, being treated as a monolithic audience, similar to how Americans on the East Coast often watched the same network-driven content as Americans on the West Coast. As the president of the EBU said at the time, "No one now thinks it surprising for New Yorkers to watch a baseball game in San Francisco, and physically there is no difference in our watching in this island [Great Britain] his Holiness the Pope blessing the crowd before St. Peter's in Rome."[10]

Sports were big for Eurovision, making up two-thirds of all programming in the late 1950s and early 1960s.[11] This made sense from both a demand perspective, since similar sports were played across many European countries, and a technical perspective, since audio commentary in local languages could be easily swapped in and out. Soccer, the most popular sport of all, was a programming staple. In 1958 Eurovision paid close to $300,000 for the rights to broadcast approximately twenty hours of live footage from the FIFA (Fédération Internationale de Football Association) World Cup in Sweden.[12] Eurovision also began airing footage of the new European Cup, the precursor to the UEFA (Union of European Football Associations) Champions League and a tournament of the continent's best club teams. In 1960, in what is often remembered as one of the greatest matchups of all time, Eurovision aired the final between Spain's Real Madrid and Germany's Eintracht Frankfurt. The match, in which Real Madrid took home its fifth consecutive title, took place in Glasgow, Scotland, and was broadcast to at least a dozen countries across Europe. By the end of the decade, with Eurovision supplementing the ample coverage dedicated to soccer in individual countries, television had fundamentally reshaped the continent's relationship to its favorite sport. As the historian David Goldblatt explains in his seminal book, the medium was creating "moments of collective experience that outstripped anything achieved in earlier eras."[13]

Eurovision also provided soccer fans with something they didn't really need: a new reason to complain about their favorite teams. In Britain particularly, coverage of foreign teams left fans demanding more from their own clubs. One English columnist wrote that many supporters "have become sharper and more outspoken critics now that their eyes have been opened by Eurovision and by the visits to the shores of certain overseas teams."[14] With a new global perspective soccer enthusiasts were arguing "not only the merits of Manchester United, Arsenal or Crew Alexandra, but also the differences of British, Continental and South American techniques."[15] Anger and frustration with the staid performance of the national teams became more pronounced, more visible. After the broadcast of the 1960 European Cup final, for example, one Scottish columnist published the following "I told you so!" rant: "For more than a decade I have returned from across the Channel annually preaching the gospel of Continental football. I have been repeatedly accused of exaggerating the skill, the artistry, the virtues of the foreigners. Club officials and legislators have told me, in blunt fashion, that I was bletherin'. Now the fans know the truth, and they will no longer be content with a standard of play that is the result of outdated ideas."[16]

The 1966 World Cup, set to take place in England, would be a good litmus test for the hosts. Although it was England's fifth World Cup, the team had never advanced past the quarterfinals. In its 1950 debut England had failed to get out of the group stage, mostly because of an embarrassing 1–0 loss to a ragtag American team. Four years later England made it to the quarterfinals but lost to the defending champion, Uruguay. In the 1958 tournament in Sweden England again failed to make it out of the group stage. Four years after that the team lost to the eventual champion, Brazil, in Chile. For a country that considered itself the inventor of the sport, these performances were rather disappointing.

The 1966 World Cup would be different, both on and off the field. Various innovations had converged to produce the greatest and biggest stage the tournament had ever seen; it was the year, as one scholar has written, that "football went global."[17] The world's first commercial satellite, Early Bird, had launched in 1965, and live broadcasts could now be beamed much further than cables and radio towers had ever allowed. The coverage itself had changed as well. Floodlights allowed for night games, embedding an element of what one writer called "a theatrical intensity."[18] Slow-motion instant replay was making its first appearance. Broadcasters also began supplementing games with ancillary content: panels and experts and additional hours of analysis. For the first time the stadiums in which the tournament would take place were chosen partly due to their ability to satisfy press and television requirements. And kickoff times were adjusted to maximize the amount of televised content, to make sure people didn't stay home to watch a different, more exciting matchup. All of this meant media coverage, and television in particular was no longer an afterthought but rather an integral part of the World Cup experience.

Some critics became skeptical of the medium's increasingly prominent role. In an article for *The Times* published less than two months before the tournament, a columnist asked: "Is there too much sport on television? And is it presented in the best possible manner?" The writer expressed dismay with all the hoopla and technology, suggesting that these so-called advancements were just inconveniences that took away from the game itself. And what about the future? What would that bring? More inanity, little of which was meaningful: "Shall we next year be joining the players after their morning shave? Perhaps it might be an idea if they were given a little more privacy and the viewer less irrelevant information."[19]

The criticism fell on deaf ears; the BBC, for one, promised to go all out in its World Cup coverage. And it did: the British broadcaster delivered preview shows, highlight shows, pregames, and postgames. And while coverage from the host country was undoubtedly the most substantial, a record seventy-five countries joined in on the party, airing at least part of the 1966 World Cup. Myriad delivery systems were used to send the games around the world. Eurovision, with help from the BBC, sent coverage to members of the EBU. Intervision, the Communist version of Eurovision, provided footage to Eastern bloc countries such as the USSR, Hungary, and Czechoslovakia. And a combination of satellite and videotape brought the tournament ever further abroad, to such far-flung locales as Australia, Venezuela, and Hong Kong.[20]

The tournament itself kicked off on July 11 with a 0–0 draw between England and the two-time World Cup champion, Uruguay. Subsequent 2–0 victories against Mexico and France brought England into the quarterfinals against Argentina. Brazil, the tournament favorite, wasn't so lucky, bowing out early after surprising losses to both Hungary and Portugal in the group stage. Things were falling into place for the hosts. In the quarterfinals England beat Argentina 1–0 and advanced to a semifinal round that included Portugal, West Germany, and the Soviet Union. England then got two goals by Bobby Charlton, considered one of the greatest players in English history, to beat the upstart Portuguese 2–1. That set up a final match against West Germany, which had defeated the Russians in the other semifinal.

The 1966 World Cup Final would become the most watched British television program of all time, with over thirty million viewers tuning in to watch the hosts win their first and, to date, only World Cup trophy.[21] All it took was a hat trick by striker Geoff Hurts, two goals in extra time, and a major controversy, with some insisting even today that England's third goal never fully made it over the line. What the 4–2 victory over West Germany meant for England and for Britain overall has been discussed, debated, and analyzed ever since. The writer Tony Mason has argued that the entire tournament, and the final game in particular, "have become part of the collective memory of the English."[22] But Mason also cautions against the simple conclusion that it was equally important to the other countries that make up the United Kingdom: Scotland, Wales, and Northern Ireland. He brings up the example of one Scottish newspaper the next day, which devoted as much time to a university golf tournament as it did to the World Cup final. And what about countries even further away? Was there any joy in, say, Peru or Tunisia? Doubtful.

Such points lead back to an important question, one that had been endlessly discussed by the committees, organizations, and unions mentioned above: do globally televised multinational sporting events, such as the World Cup or the Olympics or the UEFA Champions League, actually bring people closer together? The answer is debatable. Some sociologists might argue that millions of people simultaneously participating in a shared visual experience undoubtedly create a sense of unity, an understanding, however fleeting or superficial or subconscious, that "we are all here right now and we all care about the same thing." But those same sociologists might also advance the counterargument that despite this element of unity, sporting events have clear lines of inherent demarcation. Different groups of viewers root for different outcomes. So while it's true that these televised mega-events allow millions of viewers in disparate locations to watch the same thing at the same time, it's also true that these events perpetuate a distinct "us vs. them" delineation. Television brings this dichotomy to a whole new level, providing each group with a clearer picture (literally) of its opponent than print or radio ever did. It's pretty hard to boo a newspaper article; it's a bit easier to boo a radio program; it's quite easy to boo a television broadcast.

At least one scholar, in fact, German professor Christian Henrich-Franke, has argued that the EBU and Eurovision did very little to foster a united Europe. In one article Henrich-Franke writes that even though the EBU "allowed people across Europe to watch the same images, there was no creation of transnationality," a concept that he loosely defined as a "shared culture" or a "sense of community."[23] Instead, because many of the programs sent across borders, such as the soccer tournaments discussed above, were localized with national languages and broadcast within national contexts, it was the differences among countries that became the most pronounced, a counterproductive outcome that most likely promoted unity *within* countries more than *across* countries. As Henrich-Franke wrote: "The EBU did not automatically contribute to a better understanding among the nations and people of Europe. On the contrary, sports events like international football matches or the Eurovision Song Contest [for which Eurovision is now primarily known] let the people of Europe experience their (imagined) national differences."[24]

Still the visionaries kept at it. In 1967 the EBU doubled down on global unity, organizing an ambitious feel-good satellite extravaganza designed to bring the world together through the magic of satellite technology. Unlike the World Cup, which was broadcast from a single country, *Our World* would be the most complicated production ever attempted, with live content being fed in from close to twenty different nations and with a potential audience of half a billion. While both politicians and commercials were explicitly forbidden, global politics nonetheless reared its ugly head. A few days before the broadcast was set to go live, five countries, led by the Soviet Union, pulled out. Citing ongoing unrest in the Middle East, a representative for the bloc argued that "the television transmission has thus lost its original humanitarian idea."[25]

Despite the disruption the show went on as scheduled (with one clever writer noting that the program should have been called *Our Capitalist World* instead).[26] After a brief introduction by the announcer, the program began with the singing of "Our World" in several different languages, a discussion of the technology behind the broadcast, and some graphics detailing the planet's expanding population. All of that was followed by live shots of newborn babies in four different countries—Japan, Denmark, Mexico, and Canada—with full play-by-play of the births: "The parents are very happy because the child is perfectly normal and robust, as you can see." The host then takes viewers to a steel factory in Linz, Austria, before providing an aerial shot of traffic patterns in Paris, France, and a street shot of a market in Tunis, Tunisia: "See the Muslims, going through the narrow streets, on the way to the mosque. This is a souk. Girl walking through the streets as girls have walked through the streets for centuries now."[27]

The technology was groundbreaking. The content? Not so much. One television critic wrote that he was "reminded of the melancholy truism that modern man has at his disposal fantastic power of communication and very little to say."[28] Fortunately the pace would pick up as the program went on, memorably concluding with the Beatles' first-ever performance of their iconic song "All You Need Is Love." In the end it was generally agreed that *Our World* was a success, especially from a technical standpoint, if not an outright phenomenon.

Over in the United States the program seemed like it would have fit nicely into the programming lineup of the country's newest national network, ABC. Although ABC was a distant third to the two broadcast heavyweights, NBC and CBS, one of its marquee programs had a goal similar to what *Our World* was trying to achieve. Described by long-time ABC executive Roone Arledge as the "most influential sports program in history," ABC's *Wide World of Sports*, airing on Saturday afternoons beginning in 1961, was a ninety-minute, year-round show that famously promised to "span the globe" in order to bring viewers "the thrill of victory" and the "agony of defeat."[29] With a mission to, as one ABC executive put it, "mirror sports as the international language whereby people all over the world could better know and understand each other," the program would go on to broadcast nearly five thousand different events from fifty-three countries.[30] Both viewers and critics adored it; over the years the show would win close to a dozen prime time Emmy awards.

When the opportunity came to piggyback on this success with an exclusive airing of the most ambitious global television spectacle of all time, executives at ABC would surely jump at the chance to participate, wouldn't they? Not quite. ABC turned down *Our World*. So did NBC and CBS. The program was ultimately picked up and aired in the United States by the noncommercial National Educational Television, the predecessor to the Public Broadcasting Service (PBS). When it aired, it would compete for viewers with the regularly scheduled programming from the big three networks. In New York *Our World* went up against games involving both hometown baseball teams, the Mets and the Yankees. In Pittsburgh baseball was on at least three different networks at the time. And in California *Our World* was forced to jockey for ratings against bowling, golf, and the big in-state professional baseball rivalry, Giants vs. Dodgers.

In his autobiography Roone Arledge, the president of ABC Sports at the time, gives a succinct explanation for why his network passed on a once-in-a-lifetime television event like *Our World*: "Television networks, not being charities, judge success in dollars and cents."[31] With commercials forbidden, the financial incentive to air the program had been taken away. In its place was some wishy-washy incentive that promised to help bring the world closer together.

How are you supposed to make any money doing that?

Part 3 / Spectacle

As the 1970s began, many questions about the purpose of sports media had been settled. The discussion regarding the industry as a vehicle through which people across countries, continents, or even the world could be brought together in order to fulfill some sort of grand vision, for better or for worse, had been mostly pushed aside. Instead media executives had bombarded viewers, bamboozled politicians, and seduced advertisers in order to transform the industry into a closely guarded, profit-minded machine.

Much of the talk was now about scale. In an era of limited distribution outlets the biggest and the loudest brought the most attention, which brought the most people, which brought the most money. Because of that, sports media executives learned to embrace the spectacle.

Three events in the 1970s would epitomize this new landscape: a tennis match between a man and woman, a boxing match hosted by a brutal dictator, and an upstart global cricket competition—a circus, many called it—that had the potential to disrupt generations of sporting tradition.

Libber vs. Lobber

Billie Jean King vs. Bobby Riggs (1973)

7

It has to be asked: where are all the women? It's a good question. Pick any aspect of the sports media industry in the middle of the twentieth century—amount of coverage, quality of coverage, employment opportunities, leadership roles—and in all of them women were being ignored, stereotyped, marginalized, and discriminated against. In short, the sports media industry was a man's world, through and through.

As proof, consider what was happening in the country's most popular sports magazine. In 1956 just over 4 percent of all articles in *Sports Illustrated* were about women.[1] Twenty years later that number had barely increased, to just under 7 percent. Some of the coverage that did exist was downright offensive, such as the following 1960 description of the Canadian gymnast Ernie Russell. (Oh wait! It's actually "*luscious* Ernie Russell," at least according to the article's subheading): "Her name is Ernestine Jean Russell; she is 22 years old, exactly five feet tall, and her 110 pounds are becomingly distributed over a marvelously supple body—dimensions 35-24-34. The record proves that she is the best woman gymnast in North America, and it may well be that she is the prettiest woman athlete in competition anywhere." And here's the lead paragraph to a 1969 article about French skier Annie Famose: "She would have been a beautiful world champion, little Annie. She had all of it: the gamin look, the turned-up personality and nose to match; that catch-me-come-kiss-me haircut. The walk of a lady panther."[2]

Embarrassing stuff. So embarrassing, in fact, that four years after this article came out, *Sports Illustrated* owned up to its poor treatment of female athletes. The magazine's mea culpa came via an eleven-page spread called "Sport Is Unfair to Women." It began as follows: "There may be worse (more socially serious) forms of prejudice in the United States, but there is no sharper example of discrimination today than that which operates against girls and women who take part in competitive sports, wish to take part, or might wish to if society did not scorn such endeavors." The article goes on to paint a picture of a sports world built for and catering only to men. Nobody was off limits, including si's own editorial team: "Rather than describing how well or badly the athlete performed or even how the contest turned out, writers tend to concentrate on the color of the hair and eyes, and the shape of the legs or the busts of the women."[3] It was a remarkable and sudden about-face. How had si gone from "catch-me-come-kiss-me haircut" to "no sharper example of discrimination today" in just four years? What had happened?

Well, women had happened. The social winds were shifting, change was in the air, and the second wave of the women's liberation movement, begun in the 1960s, was accelerating. In 1972 Gloria Steinem and Dorothy Pittman Hughes launched *Ms.*, the country's first monthly magazine dedicated to feminism. Its first stand-alone issue had a picture of Wonder Woman on the cover and articles about abortion, voting, and double standards ("Body Hair: The Last Frontier"). That same year a game-changing federal law called Title IX was passed, ensuring that "No person in the United States shall, on the basis of sex, be excluded from participation in, be denied the benefits of, or be subjected to discrimination under any educational program or activity receiving federal assistance." While the law wasn't meant to be specifically about sports, it nonetheless became almost synonymous with the industry, doing more to provide opportunities—facilities, scholarships, equipment—for both girls and women than any other piece of legislation or event in American history. In the next year, 1973, came Roe v. Wade, the landmark U.S. Supreme Court case that guaranteed American women the right to have abortions (although the case would be overturned nearly fifty years later).

Nine months later, in September 1973, came another momentous event: part carnival, part television extravaganza, part tennis match. Rarely has a sporting event fit so appropriately into the larger cultural narrative of its era. And rarely has a sporting event delivered an outcome so socially relevant, so worthy of celebration, that it would be hailed decades later, at least according to one author, as "the match that changed everything."[4] While the story of the match has been rehashed dozens of times over the years, it's worth telling again, if only to properly place the match within the larger evolutionary arc of the modern sports media industry.

First, we have the protagonist, the great female tennis champion Billie Jean Moffitt, turned Billie Jean King. Born in Long Beach, California, King grew up playing sports. She played basketball and football and baseball and was good at all of them. But her father, a traditionalist, preferred that his daughter switch to a sport more appropriate for a proper young lady. That was tennis. King excelled at that too and began playing competitively in the 1950s. She began winning everything. In 1961 she took home her first major championship, the women's doubles title at Wimbledon in London.

The win brought neither fame nor wealth. At the time the major tennis championships were reserved for amateurs; payouts were limited to expenses and per diem, often delivered under the table to protect the "amateur" ideal. The system even had a name: "shamateurism." The title didn't even get King a scholarship to play tennis in college. Only men got those. So she enrolled at Los Angeles State College, joined the tennis team, and met a guy named Larry. They got engaged and Larry, who would go on to enjoy a lucrative career highlighting the accomplishments of other people, became her biggest fan. In 1964 King was invited to Australia to train with some of the best players and coaches in the world. Larry encouraged her to go, telling King that she'd regret it if she didn't pursue her dream. She quit college, left her fiancé, and traveled across the world. The gamble paid off. In 1966 King won her first major single's championship at Wimbledon, the first of three consecutive titles. By the end of the decade Billie Jean King was a no-doubt-about-it tennis superstar, the number one player in the world. Yet because there was no such thing as professional women's tennis, she was still relatively poor.

Next up in the story we have the opponent, Bobby Riggs. Born in 1918 as the youngest of seven children, Riggs, like King, was a good athlete even at an early age. Short and skinny, he competed against his older brothers in all kinds of events: running races, basketball, ping-pong. Riggs eventually gravitated to tennis, a sport conducive to his diminutive stature. He dominated the amateur circuit, winning Wimbledon at the age of twenty-one before the tournament shut down for World War II. By the time it returned, in 1946, Riggs had decided to cash in by joining the men's-only professional circuit. After several years of touring Riggs retired from the grind and tried to settle down. He got married (for the second time) and worked a regular job. Bad idea. Bobby Riggs wasn't cut out for domesticity, saying once, "I doubt very much whether I really matured past the stage of a teenager, or a young twenty probably at best."[5] At the heart of this immaturity was a love of gambling. That's worth saying again: Bobby Riggs loved gambling. He was an addict, tethering a wager to pretty much everything he did. His need for action—any action in any activity against anybody—made a normal family-oriented lifestyle all but impossible.

In 1968 the tennis world finally did the inevitable, opening the biggest tournaments in the sport to both amateurs and professionals. The new system, combined with the emergence of television, brought bigger purses to tennis than ever before. Billie Jean King was initially thrilled and teamed up with three other women players to join a group of men on a professional tour. But when she realized that the prize money still disproportionately favored the men, King and eight other women broke away and started their own tour, buoyed by a sponsorship from the cigarette manufacturer Philip Morris. The Virginia Slims Circuit kicked off in 1971, made it to nineteen cities, and was a success, distributing over $300,000 to its players. Billie Jean King herself pulled in over $100,000, the first female tennis player to hit the six-figure milestone. Two years later total prize money on tour was up to half a million. The next year it was nearly $800,000. In 1972 King was named co-sportsperson of the year by *Sports Illustrated*. (She shared the honor with UCLA basketball coach John Wooden.)

Soon Billie Jean King was being discussed as a leader in the women's liberation movement. She embraced the role carefully; King was hesitant to use words like "feminist" and "feminism" because of how polarizing they were across much of society. As she recounts in her autobiography, "My goal was to win hearts and minds. My intent was to make transformational, long-lasting change. To do that, I knew we had to bring men along with us to help us, not drive them away."[6] Regardless, things were happening, good things: "It felt like a new world was bursting open at the seams, and sometimes all we had to do was say the word and a first was spoken into existence."[7]

As all this unfolded and as the prize money in tennis went up and up, Bobby Riggs wanted in on the action. (As noted, he always wanted in on the action.) Unsatisfied with his domestic lifestyle and eager to return to the spotlight, he began playing in senior tournaments. He beat everybody. Soon he too had some financial complaints, realizing that the payouts he was getting on the senior tour paled in comparison both to the payouts to younger men, which was fine, and payouts to the women, which absolutely was not. The same went for exposure: why was everybody paying attention to Billie Jean King? He wanted in on that action too.

Recently divorced and in the thick of a midlife crisis, Riggs came up with a plan. He knew nothing about the women's liberation movement. Regardless, he argued vehemently against it. By doing so, he became one of the first media personalities (but hardly the last) to generate attention by passionately arguing for something that he really didn't care too much about. His commitment to the belief that a male tennis player of any age could beat a female tennis player of any age became his calling card, and he relished the attention he received for all his chauvinistic bloviating. Riggs became a living soundbite, a constant headline generator, and he wore shirts that said stuff like "WORMS: World Organization for the Retention of Male Supremacy." He was playing a role. And he played it to perfection.

There was only one way to settle the issue. In 1971 Riggs challenged King to a match. She said no. He continued asking. The answer was always no; King was busy and had nothing to prove. So he went to the second name on his list, Margaret Court, one of King's main rivals and one of the best women players of all time. She said yes, mostly because she'd receive $10,000 for just showing up. Riggs and Court played on Mother's Day, 1973. Court had no idea what to expect, hadn't prepared, and made tons of mistakes. Riggs knew exactly what to expect, executed his plan perfectly, and won convincingly. The press lapped it up, calling it "The Mother's Day Massacre."

After the match Riggs repeated his desire to play the outspoken King. This time she had no choice. It had to be done. The match was scheduled for Thursday, September 20, 1973, at the state-of-the-art Houston Astrodome, and it would have a winner-take-all $100,000 prize. At least that's how it was pitched. In reality each player had a guaranteed payday. But what fun is that?

While Riggs built much of the hype for the match by just being obnoxious, an event of this size requires the deft hands of a professional publicist. Enter Jerry Perenchio: future billionaire, future collector of Cézanne and Picasso originals, and future occupant of the mansion featured in the television hit *The Beverly Hillbillies*. Perenchio was a serial entrepreneur, seemingly successful at whatever he did. As an undergraduate student at UCLA in the 1940s, he turned a side hustle of booking bands for fraternity parties into a lucrative catering business in California. Upon graduation and after a few years in the Air Force, Perenchio joined up with the talent agency MCA. When that company's talent division was deemed too powerful by the U.S. Justice Department in the 1960s, Perenchio started his own agency. Adept at wooing celebrities, his client list soon included such luminaries as Elizabeth Taylor, Glen Campbell, and Andy Williams.

In 1971 Perenchio got into the boxing business, orchestrating the next iteration of the "Fight of the Century," this one between Muhammad Ali and Joe Frazier at Madison Square Garden (more about that in chapter 8). At the time *Sports Illustrated* described Perenchio as an "instant Tex Rickard," despite Perenchio's admitting that "[he didn't] know the first thing about boxing."[8] That didn't matter. Both Rickard and Perenchio knew that one of the most effective promotional strategies is to provide an audience with an easy-to-grasp, easy-to-identify-with narrative. For Rickard a fight between Jack Johnson and Jim Jeffries was most marketable when transformed into "Black boxer vs. white boxer." With the King-Riggs event Perenchio knew that the match could cast an even wider net, one that hadn't yet been properly exploited within the sports industry and one that could take advantage of the burgeoning television market. As one of Perenchio's best friends would say, "He took the most basic conflict in the world, which is man versus woman, and he took that conflict and used tennis as the metaphor and created the match. And therefore the whole world became interested."[9] Executives at the Roone Arledge–led ABC certainly did; the network paid around $700,000 for the broadcast rights to the match and subsequently sold all fifteen minutes of allotted commercial time mere hours after signing the contract.

Sportswriters took it from there, transforming the "man vs. woman" storyline into a headline-friendly alliterative concoction: The Libber (Billie Jean King) vs. the Lobber (Bobby Riggs). Coverage of the match, also referred to as the "Battle of the Sexes," appeared weeks in advance, much of it coming from a cantankerous consortium of disgruntled men. The journalist Nancy Woodhull, who would go on to become a staunch advocate of newsroom diversity and a founding editor of USA Today, commented that "the match has brought all the aging, insecure sportswriters of America out from under their dusty typewriters. Their pre-match coverage has finally revealed sport pages and sportswriters for what they really have been all along: dumb, hopelessly biased, incapable of telling the truth about anything that might suggest that there is more to manliness than sweat, hair and muscle."[10]

One didn't have to search far for evidence to support Woodhull's observation. George Puscas, a middle-aged male sportswriter for the *Detroit Free Press*, lamented that the match was upending the traditional American household, mostly because of "headstrong dames who lie in wait to zing their man any chance they get."[11] Dan Nelson, a middle-aged male sportswriter for the *Bismarck Tribune*, explained that he wanted to bet his wife $500 that Riggs would win but that he dared not, knowing she'd probably "blow it on groceries or a new lamp."[12] Most of these writers predicted a Riggs victory, owing to the observation that women were emotionally fragile. Vince DiPaolo, a middle-aged male sportswriter for the *Belvidere Daily Republican*, expected King to wilt under the lights: "Billie Jean wants to beat Riggs so badly, that her emotions, stirred by Riggs' psyche job, will work against her and she will choke. She will try too hard and make mistakes."[13] And Edwin Pope, a middle-aged male sportswriter for the *Miami Herald*, agreed, believing that the whole charade was meaningless: "It won't prove anything except what a con man Riggs is and that women are more sensitive than men, especially when they're taking a physical beating, and what else is new?"[14]

The day of the match finally (thankfully) arrived. Thirty thousand people showed up to the Astrodome to watch it live while millions at home tuned their televisions to ABC. The telecast began with a version of the show tune "Anything You Can Do (I Can Do Better)," rewritten with lyrics appropriate for the event—"Any ball you can hit, I can hit faster"—followed by a roll call of the night's sponsors. Howard Cosell, the most famous sports personality in the country, took it from there. He wore a tuxedo, used the same phrases over and over (probably because he knew little about tennis), and dutifully played up the spectacle, fawning over the size of the crowd and comparing the atmosphere to a big-time college football game. Cosell was joined in the broadcasting booth by female tennis star Rosie Casals, who picked King to win in a straight set victory, and male tennis star Gene Scott, who said Rosie had the score right but that Riggs would win, not King.

Sitting courtside were the celebrities, flown in on a private jet by Perenchio and noticeably buzzed from a long day of drinking. Wandering through the aisles was football-player-turned-television-personality Frank Gifford, who stuck his microphone in people's faces and asked them what they thought of the match. Actor Andy Williams said, "It was the best thing to happen to tennis in a long, long time" and called Riggs "a great entertainer." Model Claudine Longet, who was married to Williams at the time, proclaimed her allegiance to King and noted that Riggs "looked like a rabbit." There were shots of cheerleaders, a waiter delivering drinks, a marching band.[15]

It was a circus. And then suddenly it wasn't, with King's impressive early play changing the mood entirely. Riggs began sweating; he looked rattled. In the first set, with the score tied 4–4, Cosell reflected on the new atmosphere: "Funny, this match, I suppose we all expected to have some high humor involved in it. Instead it seems to have become a very, very serious thing because the comedy has gone out of Bobby Riggs." Unlike Margaret Court, who had made a bunch of unforced errors, King was beating Bobby at his own game: dinking and dunking, playing the angles, forcing the wily veteran to drag his aging body around the court. King's growing confidence energized Rosie Casals, who relished in her role as part cheerleader, part women's lib representative. When Scott called Riggs a good athlete, Casals replied, "I don't think Bobby's a good athlete. I wouldn't consider someone who walks like a duck a good athlete." Riggs continued to fade. Casals continued to gloat. Cosell continued to interrupt. Scott grew quiet. By the end of the second set it was clear that a King victory was all but inevitable. "Looks like I'm gonna make some money on this match," Casals quipped.

With the final game tied at deuce Bobby Riggs double-faulted, giving King a chance to break his serve and wrap things up. On match point Riggs faulted again. Then he lobbed a serve, King hit a return, and Riggs slammed the ball directly into the net. It was a straight-set victory, Libber over Lobber: 6–4, 6–3, 6–3. The crowd roared. King threw her hands in the air. Riggs hopped over the net and the two opponents shook hands. ABC put up a graphic with the final score, Cosell gave Cadillac one last mention ("America's #1 luxury car"), and then it was over.

But really it was just beginning. Over the years and decades to follow the match would be dissected and discussed and talked about so much that it's almost as if those two hours of tennis on an otherwise normal Thursday evening in September were a mere prelude to what was to come. Conversations about the match permeated all corners of society, and everybody involved would be asked to rehash the details many times over. Riggs became depressed, concerned that his battle with King would be the most famous thing he ever did. (It was.) Even those not directly involved have attempted to assess and measure the match's importance, as evidenced by the countless movies and books and documentaries made about the "Battle of the Sexes" since. It might be helpful, then, to sort things out a bit, to figure out what exactly this tennis match between Billie Jean King and Bobby Riggs *was* and *did* (or, just as important, *was not* and *did not do*), particularly as it relates to the primary subject of this book, the sports media industry.

First, the match *was* unequivocally a television success, at least in the United States. Rather than being a distraction, the prematch hullabaloo was an integral part of the equation. All the hot takes, all the chest thumping, all the soundbites and headlines and interviews contributed to the massive publicity blitz orchestrated by Jerry Perenchio. That blitz generated attention; that attention brought viewers. In the end the match was watched by an average audience of somewhere between forty-five and fifty million people. That made it the third most-viewed telecast of the week, just behind the popular movie

Bonnie and Clyde—which CBS aired at the same time in an effort to siphon viewers off from ABC—and an episode of *All in the Family* and just ahead of episodes of *Hawaii Five-O* and *Sanford and Son*.[16] While hardly earth-shattering, the result was enough to make King-Riggs the most viewed tennis match of all time.

That said and despite many reports to the contrary, the match *was not* a global phenomenon. In fact, there seems to be zero evidence that it drew anywhere near the "ninety million worldwide viewers" so often cited (including multiple times in King's autobiography and on her website).[17] No, this was an American affair, with American athletes and American viewers. The president of the company who had purchased the international broadcast rights said as much in the days following the match: "Overseas, the thing is a bust. It's an absolute floppo."[18] In fact, the only country besides the United States to air the match live was Venezuela. A subsequent survey showed that the million or so Venezuelans who tuned into the event knew little about the sport and watched mostly because "a shapely woman was playing a 55-year-old-man."[19]

The match *did* energize the already growing market for tennis. In 1974 *Sports Illustrated* published a long article about the sport's booming popularity. The magazine claimed that tennis was "growing five times faster than golf" and that it could stake its claim as the "passion sport of the '70s."[20] More courts were built. Rackets and clothing flew off shelves. And, perhaps most pertinent to this story, more tennis was being shown on television than ever before. According to Herbert Warren Wind, of all the sports content shown on the three national television networks in 1971, only 2 percent involved tennis. Five years later that number had ballooned to 13 percent. Wind also says that by the end of the 1970s, more hours of tennis were being televised on some Sundays than had been televised in *entire years* before the boom.[21] How influential was the "Battle of the Sexes" to this growth? It's impossible to say. But it undoubtedly played a role.

In terms of opportunities off the court, King's victory *did* coincide with, if not directly cause, a trickle of new roles for women within the sports media industry. In 1973 ABC named Eleanor Sanger Keys the first female producer in the history of American network sports. Sanger Keys went on to produce nine Olympics and over forty college football games, collecting seven Emmy awards along the way.[22] Around the same time CBS hired longtime sports reporter Jane Chastain, making her the country's first regular woman sportscaster. With close to thirteen years of experience Chastain was thrust into a variety of roles, including as a commentator during the network's high profile NFL games.

Unfortunately for Sanger Keys and Chastain and the millions of others who followed their lead, the match *did not* eliminate the systematic misogyny within the industry. Not that anybody thought it would. Chastain, for one, lasted only a few years at CBS. During that time the network jerked her around, not having any idea what to do when a woman—gasp!—was brought into the broadcast booth. During one football game Chastain was specifically told to talk not about the action on the field but rather about "the hats the ladies were wearing."[23] Another time, after an NBA game, a producer asked Chastain to conduct a postgame interview and suggested that perhaps she could "act impressed with how tall the guy [was]".[24] This new world was apparently tough sledding for the old-timers, the guys who had been working in sports their whole lives *without* women. To be fair, some did their best to adapt. Longtime ABC Sports producer Doug Wilson has written that "we men had to learn quickly that a woman at work was to be considered a colleague. Not a female colleague, simply a colleague, gender neutral." This meant new rules, many of which were difficult to stomach: "We were not to acknowledge a woman's attractiveness or how she dressed or behaved, even if she *seemed* to be inviting attention."[25]

Entrenched misogyny notwithstanding, the match *did* generate some initial optimism around increased coverage of women's sports. Billie Jean King and her husband, Larry, played a substantial role here, investing a good chunk of their money into a new magazine called *womenSports*. It was an important project for King, one she started as a way to provide more coverage of female athletes: "*Sports Illustrated* was not covering us properly and it covered us on looks too much, not just on our performances and our accomplishments."[26] The next year Sanger Keys produced a program called "Colgate's Women in Sports," an hour-long special that aired on ABC and was dedicated to the growing influence of women in the sports industry. Hosted by entertainer Dinah Shore, the program featured Soviet gymnast Olga Korbut, jockey Robyn Smith, and, of course, Billie Jean King. "Even a year ago, nobody would have spent this kind of money for a sports show," Sanger Keys told the *New York Times*. "There's a whole new self-awareness among women, and the idea of learning to use your body in a nonsexual way, plus the excitement of women's sports, has changed the whole atmosphere."[27]

But despite these efforts the match *did not* lead to a prolonged increase in the coverage of women's sports. This isn't just conjecture; nearly every single piece of available evidence supports this conclusion. Some research even suggests that despite a surge in female sports participation in the 1970s and 1980s (largely due to Title IX), the coverage of women athletes across the media landscape—for example, in *Sports Illustrated* or on network news—either remained flat or went down. Why? One group of researchers who has studied the issue has argued that it all begins at the top: "There is no reason to believe that this trend will reverse itself . . . unless producers decide that it is in their interests to do so."[28]

If only the sports media industry had more producers like ABC executive Roone Arledge, the famed media pioneer who had bought the rights to the "Battle of the Sexes" match between Billie Jean King and Bobby Riggs, right? Well, not quite. For Arledge it would seem that King-Riggs had little to do with women's liberation or a commitment to women's sports programming and everything to do with money. The match was mentioned only once in Arledge's autobiography, during a section that included the line referenced in the last chapter: "Television networks, not being charities, judge success in dollars and cents." And as if to hammer that point home, the lone mention of the most famous tennis match of all time is almost directly followed by the following sentence: "My personal life was also taking a substantial turn for the better with Ann Fowler, a sports-savvy former Miss Alabama, who'd been my secretary."[29] In other words, "I helped produce this great event that furthered the cause of the women's liberation movement, but actually it was really only about the money and, more important, did you hear that I started sleeping with my smoking-hot secretary who likes sports?"

One step forward; two steps back.

Another Fight of the Century   **8**

Muhammad Ali vs. Joe Frazier (1975)

In the United States the 1966 FIFA World Cup Final, in which England beat West Germany 4–2 for the country's first and only World Cup title, aired on a two-hour tape-delay on NBC. It was watched by an average audience of 2.4 million people, about half of what a typical regular season baseball game would pull in at the time and about twenty times less than what "the Battle of the Sexes" would pull in seven years later.[1] The response by the American public was so underwhelming that all three major broadcast networks (ABC, CBS, NBC) turned down the chance to air the next World Cup in 1970. In an era of limited viewing options, where the goal was to maximize advertising revenue by all means necessary, network executives simply couldn't afford to waste two or three broadcast hours on niche programming. What they wanted were hits, sports spectacles like Riggs vs. King and shows like *Bonanza* and *Gunsmoke*. Hits brought big audiences. Big audiences brought big advertisers and their big money. A one-off soccer match between England and West Germany held little appeal. As Rene Anselmo, president of Magnaverde Productions, the company that held the U.S. World Cup broadcast rights at the time, explained: "The networks aren't going to go out on a limb to show the games unless they have backing. Their advertisers just aren't interested in a sport without a proven public."[2]

So Anselmo went in a different direction, renting out movie theaters and larger venues, such as sports arenas, across the United States and airing World Cup matches on closed-circuit television. Revenue came from attendees rather than advertisers, with each fan buying a ticket to enter. In 1970, the World Cup Final between Italy and Brazil was shown in two dozen cities and viewed by a quarter million people.[3] For the 1974 World Cup Anselmo organized viewings in nearly forty cities across both the United States and Canada, drawing about half a million attendees.[4] While many fans were appalled by the exorbitant price—it cost between ten and twenty dollars for a ticket to the final, at a time when a regular movie ticket was about two dollars—others found the experience more than worth the price of admission. One fan who watched the 1974 final at Madison Square Garden commented, "The atmosphere in the Garden is great, thousands of people around, screaming their heads off. It's much better than sitting home and watching a game by yourself."[5]

Boxing fans already knew this. By the 1970s they'd been regularly gathering to watch big fights on screens outside their homes for over two decades. Profit margin, rather than audience, was the culprit here, as promoters realized they could make more from selling rights to theaters and charging admission than by selling a one-off package to one of the big networks. The first major exclusive closed-circuit telecast was the June 1951 Joe Louis–Lee Savold fight at Madison Square Garden. Unable to secure a check from any of the three major networks for the requested $100,000, the promoters shifted gears, signing up nine theaters to show the fight and drawing close to forty thousand paying customers.[6] The match didn't disappoint, as Joe Louis, in one of his last fights before retirement, knocked out the man known as the "Battling Bartender" with a flurry of punches in the sixth round. Results of the closed-circuit experiment were equally impressive. Boxing promoters saw the numbers and gasped; theater owners were similarly enthralled. "Nothing since the introduction of sound has stirred more general excitement among exhibitors than the drawing power of the Joe Louis–Lee Savold pictures," observed one trade publication.[7]

A few weeks later came another fight, Jake LaMotta vs. Bob Murphy at Yankee Stadium. This time the matchup was more akin to a brawl and by the seventh round LaMotta had taken so many punches that a doctor ordered the fight stopped, giving Murphy the victory. But the real winners were the theater owners. Building off the momentum from the Louis-Savold experiment, the fight was screened across eleven theaters and drew more paying customers (thirty-five thousand) than the number who witnessed it in person (twenty-one thousand).[8] By then it was clear: boxing had a new business model.

Beyond the financial repercussions the appearance of these closed-circuit broadcasts had cultural implications as well. Overlapping with the emergence of the American civil rights movement, the shift of boxing to theater television (as it was then called) provided an intimate gathering space for predominantly Black communities to celebrate a sport often discussed through race-related narratives. No longer were boxing fans who were unable to afford a ticket to the fight confined to their homes. They were now let loose, encouraged to congregate and celebrate together. As one scholar who has studied the era has written, "The momentous occasion of a heavyweight championship bout in the theater was a collective, live experience in which the excitement of a night on the town fused with the act of participating in what was, and always had been, a racially politicized event."[9] It was also a lot of fun. A 1970 *Sports Illustrated* article described a closed-circuit broadcast as a rollicking good time, ideal for the boxing fanatic: "The price is right—six bucks, ringside, just enough to keep out the tourists. The atmosphere is fraternal. . . . And there is the pleasure of shared knowledge. Everyone howls when a fighter hits on the break. Yeah, I saw it, I saw it. And, mind you, no commercials."[10]

By the time the 1964 Cassius Clay–Sonny Liston fight came around, closed-circuit broadcasting was boxing's primary moneymaker. While Louis-Savold had been available in a paltry nine theaters, Clay-Liston was available in a record 355 across the United States and Canada.[11] Perhaps because of this massive reach, the fight was also a political lightning rod, with both fighters instigating battles beyond the ropes. In one corner was Sonny Liston, who used his leverage to demand that the fight be shown only in desegregated theaters: "I feel that the color of my people's money is the same as anyone else's. They should get the same seats. If not, I don't want those places to have the fight."[12] His ultimatum worked; two theaters in New Orleans refused to accommodate Liston's request and were denied access to the fight.

In the other corner was Cassius Clay. At the time Clay was not yet a champion but had nonetheless become one of the most famous and polarizing athletes the world had ever seen. Much of the appeal surrounding the fight, in fact, stemmed from Clay himself. As one reporter observed, "His flair for publicity, his enthusiasm, his physical attractiveness, his youth and his torrent of words have elevated him to Tuesday's admirable, if precarious, position. The publicity men and promoters who slave behind the scenes for any big fight could not have asked for a richer, more cooperative subject."[13] Theater television had provided boxing with a grand stage, and Cassius Clay had arrived just in time to become the feature presentation.

Yet he was still an underdog as far as the fight was concerned. At the time Liston was considered a lock, an overwhelming favorite to defeat the loquacious upstart. Few experts gave Cassius Clay much of a chance at all; in fact, only three of the forty-six sportswriters covering the fight predicted that Clay would emerge with the belt. But from the minute the bell rang, Clay impressed, dancing and bobbing around the ring—you know, "Float like a butterfly" and all that— before delivering a right hand to Liston's jaw in the sixth that opened a cut on the champion's face. That injury, combined with an ailing shoulder, forced Liston to throw in the towel just before the seventh round, making Cassius Clay the heavyweight champion of the world.

But this victory, of course, was merely the beginning of a much longer story. Shortly after the match Clay would proclaim his allegiance to the Nation of Islam and unveil his new name: Muhammad Ali. Just over a year later, in January 1966, Ali would announce the birth of a new company, Main Bout, Inc., responsible for managing the rights to his fights going forward. Two months after that Ali announced that he would refuse conscription into the U.S. military, a controversial declaration that both captivated and infuriated large swaths of the American public. After Ali's decision booking fights for him on U.S. soil became impossible as local governments spurned the pleas of promoters to bring the most famous boxer in the world to their city or state. Main Bout took Ali's matches to Canada and then Europe. Purses dipped at first and then rebounded; Ali was simply too interesting and too good to ignore.

He also knew how to stir the pot. One pre-fight event in December 1966 ended with Ali repeatedly calling his upcoming opponent, Ernie Terrell, an "Uncle Tom" when Terrell insisted on calling him Cassius Clay. The event generated headlines, the headlines generated interest, and the interest generated revenue: the closed-circuit broadcasts for the February 1967 fight pulled in approximately $1 million. Ali received a similar amount for his victory. But a few months later everything came crashing down. In April Ali refused to step forward when his name was called for induction into the army. And in June he was convicted of draft evasion charges, sentenced to five years in prison, and fined $10,000. Ali wouldn't fight again for three years.

As Muhammad Ali built a name for himself in the ring, television executives were fighting a battle of their own. Shortly after the closed-circuit system emerged in the early 1950s, a group of industry leaders assembled what they called the "Fair Television Practices Committee," imploring the government to do what it could to protect the nascent television business. One committee member questioned the underlying legality (and, in some ways, the morality) of for-profit, closed-circuit broadcasting, arguing that "it had generally been recognized that the purchase of a television receiver carried with it the implied right to receive all programs free of charge."[14] But the television folks would lose this battle. By the mid-1960s none of the major networks would have a regularly scheduled boxing broadcast; most of the biggest fights were reserved for closed-circuit distribution, while the smaller fights, similar to what had happened with the FIFA World Cup, were passed over because they couldn't generate a large enough audience.

But while fans of soccer and boxing dutifully flocked to local theaters to watch their favorite athletes, some of the world's greatest minds were hard at work trying to figure out the most effective way to bring that kind of niche programming into the home. One of these men was J. C. R. Licklider, a genius of a man with a resume to match. From a fellowship at Harvard and a professorship at MIT to important positions at both IBM and the U.S. Department of Defense, "Lick," as he liked to be called, never shied away from a technological challenge. In 1962, while tens of millions of Americans sat glued to their television sets watching *The Beverly Hillbillies*, the highest-rated show of the year, Licklider was busy sketching out the parameters of an "Intergalactic Computer

Network," an idea that would eventually contribute to the birth of the modern internet. He later articulated some of these ideas in a paper that was, at the time, a rather radical prognosis: "In a few years, men will be able to communicate more effectively through a machine than face to face. That is a rather startling thing to say, but it is our conclusion."[15]

Not one to be restricted by a single, world-changing prophecy, Licklider also foretold the emergence of another important, if not a bit less exciting, medium: cable television. In a 1967 essay Licklider put forth the notion of "narrowcasting," a concept meant to "emphasize the rejection or dissolution of the constraints imposed by commitment to a monolithic mass-appeal, broadcast approach." With narrowcasting those large network audiences would be broken up into smaller groups of viewers, and tailored content would be provided to those groups through "a multiplicity of channels."[16] With this framework in place broadcast time would no longer be considered a hotly contested scarce resource. Instead there'd be sufficient room (and hopefully appetite) to air such maligned programs as mid-level boxing and the FIFA World Cup.

Patrick Parsons, a professor at Penn State University and author of *Blue Skies: A History of Cable Television*, has suggested that three interlocking components were needed to make this "narrowcasting" vision a reality: cable-connected homes, satellite technology, and a consistent stream of new programming. Cable came first. As mentioned in chapter 3, the end of World War II led to a television buying bonanza in the United States, even in regions that couldn't be reached by a local station. One source estimates that of the eight hundred thousand television sets sold by the end of 1948, fifty thousand were located in cities that couldn't receive adequate broadcasts. Ingenuity soon followed. Shopkeepers who sold televisions in these areas learned that they could receive a signal if they connected cables to the antennas on nearby mountains and ran them down to their shops. Some even redirected these wires to provide signals to their own houses or to a handful of friends and family. "Cable," in this sense, was merely a redirection of the traditional broadcast signal.

Once proven to work, these systems began popping up everywhere, and nowhere more so than in the hilly coal mining region of eastern Pennsylvania. Nestled deep within the ridges of the surrounding mountains, small towns in this area were unable to receive the signals originating from nearby Philadelphia. Sensing the beginnings of a lucrative new business, a crew of local entrepreneurs went to work, running cables down the mountains into people's homes for a small fee. In Lansford it was Marty Malarkey, owner of the local music store, who wired the town. An hour away in Easton it was a Taiwanese immigrant named Bark Lee Yee.

Years later an appliance dealer by the name of John Walson from Mahanoy City would claim to have been the first of this resourceful group. In one interview Walson explained the difficulty of selling televisions in a city with no television reception. When customers would arrive in his shop, Walson would be forced to "drive those people to the top of this mountaintop and demonstrate the TV set and make sure the TV set was working." Eventually Walson got the idea to run a cable from the antenna to his shop so that customers could see the televisions in action. And once he did, the citizens of Mahanoy City couldn't get enough: "The television sets were displayed in the window, and the three channels with speakers outside allowed people to listen to one channel at a time. . . . The old people stood right in front of the store, and they used to stay there until 12 o'clock, until the stations went off the air."[17]

This, Walson claimed, was the origin of cable television. A 2007 article in Allentown's *Morning Call* (headline: "Cable TV Invented in Mahanoy City") would repeat this boast, profiling Walson as an underappreciated paradigm-shifting visionary.[18] But while Walson was certainly *one* of the first to run cables down from a mountain, he almost certainly wasn't *the* first. In fact, Parsons suggests Walson only got the idea for his business because of the ingenuity of another Mahanoy City citizen, Ed "Peanuts" Trusky, who put up a tower on a local mountain and ran cables into his poolroom for the enjoyment of his patrons.

Moreover, the "cable" component was only one part of the trifecta needed to execute Licklider's vision of what would eventually be called cable television. Equally important were the increased use of satellite technology and the creation of new programming. The limited use of satellite, discussed in chapter 6, was adequate for the biggest events. But what the industry really needed was a more sustainable model, one that could be adapted for a variety of audiences, both big and small. At the time direct-to-home (DTH) satellites, similar to what DirecTV and Dish TV would eventually offer, were simply untenable; they were too costly for the average consumer, and their development was limited by a bureaucratic structure designed to protect the heavy hitters of the television industry. A more realistic path forward was the merging of cable and satellite technology, whereby cable providers would receive satellite signals from networks and subsequently distribute those signals via cable to their subscribers.

But here the industry faced a problem. Although technology in the 1970s had improved to the point that a satellite built to receive these signals (also called an "earth station") could be had for a reasonable price, cable providers were still unwilling to invest in the system unless they were guaranteed a consistent stream of programming for which their subscribers would pay. Content providers, meanwhile, hesitated to invest in the development of new programming until they knew cable providers would be willing to sign up for their service.

The industry needed somebody to fill in the third piece of the narrowcasting puzzle. Into the picture stepped Charles "Chuck" Dolan, future owner of the New York Knicks and New York Rangers. Born in Cleveland, Dolan moved to New York to pursue a career in the media industry. Reserved yet competent, Dolan was not the type of person who craved the front page of the newspaper. One writer would later describe him as "utterly lacking in the little-boy bombast and self-promoting razzamatazz which makes CNN's Ted Turner a media star."[19] But once in New York, Dolan proved his mettle and found a job with Sterling Information Services, a company that, among other things, produced content (both printed and video) for New York City tourists. A few years later Dolan was instrumental in getting the company one of the first permits to run cable lines through Manhattan. To complete this massive undertaking he then secured a significant investment from Time Life, Inc., the parent company of *Sports Illustrated*. While the cash infusion helped, maintaining a cable system through the jumbled grid of New York City wasn't cheap; at one point Sterling had spent $2 million and wired only four hundred homes.[20] The company desperately needed a new revenue stream.

Dolan was intrigued by the possibility of live sports. In a speech given around this time he suggested, "In the future of professional and amateur sports, we see the development of cable television becoming, in effect, a way to enlarge the seating capacity of New York arenas and stadiums. The economics of cable television will permit teams to telecast home games to fans who either can't get a ticket or can't attend every game."[21] Then in 1971, or so the legend goes, Dolan was on vacation lounging on a European ocean liner when he had the brilliant idea to launch a new cable network, one based around live sports and movies and one for which people would have to pay extra. He initially named it "the Green Channel." The name was soon changed to Home Box Office (HBO).

Time Life, which by then had taken control of Sterling's cable business, bought into the idea. So did John Walson, the self-proclaimed founder of cable television mentioned above. In November 1972 HBO launched its service to 365 of Walson's cable subscribers in Wilkes-Barre, Pennsylvania. The program was broadcast via microwave, which required the strategic placement of antennas that could transmit signals as long as the line between each station was clear. The first HBO telecast was a hockey game between the New York Rangers and the Vancouver Canucks. The first original HBO production came a few months later: the Pennsylvania Polka Festival from Allentown. Subscribers were intrigued but hesitant. Many would sign up for the new service, try it for a bit, and then bail. To maintain subscribers HBO needed a more consistent stream of programming. For that it needed revenue. And for that it needed scale, which meant the network needed to be available to as many people as possible. Microwave technology was workable but cumbersome and expensive; the obvious answer was satellite. But if HBO was going to make this transition, it couldn't just wade in slowly. It needed to make a splash, one that would ripple throughout the media industry.

Around the time Chuck Dolan lay on his cruise ship bunk sketching out the parameters of the idea that would eventually become HBO, Muhammad Ali was settling into the second act of his boxing career. In 1970, while his legal case was working its way through the system, Ali and his promoters took advantage of the absence of a state athletic commission in Georgia (and therefore the mechanisms by which the administration could prevent Ali from fighting), as well as the support of a few important businessmen, to secure a fight against Jerry Quarry in Atlanta. More good news came from New York, where a judge ruled that the state couldn't legally ban Ali from fighting even though his case was still pending. Ali's boxing license was restored, and in December 1970 Ali fought and defeated Oscar Bonavena at Madison Square Garden.

But those fights were just the appetizers. In March 1971 Muhammad Ali agreed to return to the Garden to fight Joe Frazier in a matchup that would determine the heavyweight champion of the world. The buildup to what was anointed the "Fight of the Century" was colossal, with Ali and Frazier (but mostly Ali) trading verbal beatdowns to the delight of a giddy press corps. According to journalist Mark Kram, who covered the boxer for decades, Ali called Frazier "a little old nigger boy who ain't been anywhere 'cept Philly, never done anything for nobody 'cept rich people that back him and politician crooks, never had a thought in his dumb head 'cept for himself." And Frazier countered by saying, "He's no martyr. The heroes are them kids with their pieces of body all over Vietnam, a lot of poor blacks. I don't care about his draft thing. His politics. His religion. But he ain't no leader of anything. He stop the war? How do people buy his shit?"[22] Tact and civility aside, this stuff sold papers.

Boxing fans lined up in droves. Before the match one of the fight's promoters told reporters that he expected the live gate to bring in approximately $1.25 million while the closed-circuit broadcasts would command upward of $15 million.[23] Because of the demand each fighter was guaranteed $2.5 million, a record purse emphasized in a *Time* magazine cover story in early March: "Never before has the public been willing to spend so much to see two men whack away at each other in a ring."[24] When fight night arrived, the Garden quivered with anticipation. Elvis was there. So were the Beatles and Salvador Dali and Frank Sinatra, who was for some odd reason taking pictures for *Life* magazine. Incredibly, the fight lived up to expectations. It was brutal, intense, constant. At the end of fifteen rounds, with both fighters near collapse, Frazier won by unanimous decision. He then spent nearly a month in the hospital recovering.

In June 1971 the U.S. Supreme Court reversed the conviction against Muhammad Ali, allowing him to fight wherever and whenever he wanted. Over the next few years both fighters stayed busy, with Frazier losing his title to the hard-hitting George Foreman. In January 1974 Ali and Frazier would reconnect at Madison Square Garden for the title-less sequel. Ali won by decision, then beat George Foreman in Zaire ("the Rumble in the Jungle") to regain the world heavyweight belt. A rubber match with Frazier was all but inevitable.

While it's a bit unclear how the 1975 finale of the Ali-Frazier trilogy ended up in the Philippines, there's little doubt that some bureaucratic chicanery was involved. The two men who helped arrange the fight, Bob Arum and Don King, tell slightly different stories. Arum speaks of a chance meeting with a member of the Malaysian armed forces who put him in touch with the head of the Filipino games and amusement board. But King's story is even more interesting: Ferdinand Marcos, the president of the Philippines from 1965 to 1986, asked him to become a global ambassador for Filipino sugar. "That deal never materialized," said King, "but the fight did. We got the word that Marcos wanted to have an event there, the way Zaire did with the Ali-Foreman fight the year before. . . . Marcos never got any cash out of the fight. He just wanted the fight to show the world his government's stability."[25]

This was not Ferdinand Marcos's first foray into international public relations. Nearly a decade before Ali-Frazier III and five years before *Time* published a cover story on "The Fight of the Century," a journalist from the magazine would arrive in Manila to profile Marcos as he began his reign. After describing the issues facing the Philippines—crime, social inequality, government corruption—the author then submits the following, an improbable sequence of words that reads more like satire than reporting: "It would take a hero to rule so complex a society, and the hardest thing to accept about Ferdinand E. Marcos is that any mortal could have tucked into 49 years as much action, adventure, heroism, devotion to duty, romance, singleness of purpose and accomplishment as he has." He then heaps praise on Marcos's ability as an athlete, notes that the president set the national record for the bar exam (98.01 percent), and details how Marcos was one of the country's "most effective" soldiers in World War II: "Singlehanded, he stood off a 50-man Japanese patrol; when his submachine-gun fire drove them off, Marcos pursued them alone for two miles—despite the fact that he had taken a bullet in the leg."[26] Decades later much better journalists would uncover documents that showed Marcos's war heroics to be exaggerations at best and outright lies at worst.[27] It seemed that many early biographers, such as the *Time* correspondent, simply relied on the word of Ferdinand Marcos himself rather than doing the legwork necessary to confirm these absurd reports. Nevertheless, articles such as this helped the president achieve his desired goal: to become a national hero and an international icon.

In 1972, with power secured, the Marcos administration declared martial law, beginning a decade-plus reign of what was essentially authoritarian rule. Marcos and his wife, Imelda, ruled the country as if it was their very own country club, building lavish buildings, funneling billions of dollars into offshore accounts, and restricting the rights of the country's citizens. At some point Marcos decided that hosting an international fight with the most famous sportsman in the world might provide a stream of positive press, the same way the *Time* magazine article had shaped the (false) narrative of his own life. In an interview conducted just days before the matchup, Marcos explained his rationale: "The fight publicizes our country. Many people do not know where the Philippines are and don't know what the situation is here. They think that the military runs the government, tanks are on the streets. Have you seen any tanks?"[28]

Ferdinand Marcos wasn't the only opportunist intent on taking advantage of the media frenzy surrounding Ali-Frazier III. By 1975 Gerald "Jerry" Levin, future CEO of Time Warner, had replaced Chuck Dolan as the head of HBO. In April Levin came to a historic agreement with the cable provider UA-Columbia to feed programming via satellite to subscribers in Fort Pierce–Vero Beach, Florida. Another cable provider in Jackson, Mississippi, signed on soon after. Levin then brokered a deal with Don King Productions to secure exclusive television rights to the final chapter of the Ali-Frazier trilogy. The price was an undisclosed amount of cash and the right to use HBO's microwave facilities in New York for the closed-circuit broadcasts.[29] It would be HBO's coming-out party, an exclusive airing of the most anticipated fight of the year, combined with a demonstration of the cable-satellite union. The fact that it was taking place halfway around the world only added to the allure.

Before the fight Muhammad Ali did Muhammad Ali things. He talked about Frazier as an Uncle Tom and berated his intelligence. "What will the people in Manila think?" he asked during one training session. "We can't have a gorilla for a champ. They're gonna think, lookin' at him, that all black brothers are animals. Ignorant. Stupid. Ugly. If he's champ again, other nations will laugh at us."[30] And he famously said, "It's gonna be a thrilla, and a chilla, and a killa, when I get the gorilla in Manila."[31]

On September 30, 1975 (October 1 in Manila), HBO delivered an exclusive broadcast of the "Thrilla in Manila" via satellite to a select group of subscribers in Florida and Mississippi. The fight is often cited as the first ever pay-per-view boxing match.[32] That's not exactly true. The subscribers who received the Ali-Frazier broadcast were paying a monthly fee for HBO rather than paying a one-time fee for the fight. In that sense the fight was more of a precursor to the cable television model, in which subscribers would pay a fee for a network or a bundle of networks, than it was to the pay-per-view model, which more accurately traces its lineage to the lucrative era of closed-circuit broadcasts.

The fight was also one of the most technologically complex events ever aired. The *New York Times* detailed the transmission of the fight as follows:

> From a satellite transmitter in the Philippines the signal was bounced across the Pacific by Intelsat, the international satellite, to an earth station at Jamesburg, Calif. From there it was carried cross-country by AT&T. land lines to a telephone switching center in Manhattan's Battery, where it was routed to Home Box Office studios on 23d St., which sent it to 60 Broad St. where RCA has a technical center. There it was relayed by RCA microwave to a domestic satellite transmitter in Valley Forge, Pa., which beamed it on Western Union's Westar satellite for a short hop to an earth station at Fort Pierce. Yet another microwave link was used to deliver it to the two local cable systems.[33]

Despite this intricate design and the nine-thousand-mile gap between Florida and the Philippines, the HBO subscribers lucky enough to be involved received a near-instantaneous signal. Said one of the cable operators in an interview years later: "When you looked at the close-ups, the fighters looked like they were in the next room, the picture quality was that extraordinary."[34]

What these subscribers witnessed—an Ali victory when Frazier's camp threw in the towel after the fourteenth round—has been recounted hundreds of times. Of all the recaps Mark Kram's essay for the October 13, 1975, issue of *Sports Illustrated* is often considered not only the best of the bunch, but also one of the best pieces of sports writing ever produced. In it Kram details a vicious and memorable showdown: "Time may well erode that long morning of drama in Manila, but for anyone who was there those faces will return again and again to evoke what it was like when two of the greatest heavyweights of any era met for a third time, and left millions limp around the world."[35]

Kram knew Muhammad Ali well. He had followed the boxer for years, offering observations that often flew in the face of the standard narrative. In the introduction to his book *Ghosts of Manila*, he wrote that the work was "intended to be a corrective to the years of stenography that have produced the Ali legend. . . . Junk commentary has been slapped on it to the point that precise appreciation of just who Ali was (and is) has become obscured." Kram called Ali a "simpleton" and suggested that the boxer "was played like a harp by the Muslims, a daft cult with a long record of draft dodging." If he had been born a few decades later, in fact, Muhammad Ali would be "looked upon as a contaminant, a chronic user of hate language and a sexual profligate."[36]

But that never happened. Instead Ali understood how to shape his own narrative. "With TV," Kram wrote, "Ali had the good fortune to have a medium that seemed to be invented for him. He didn't pervade it, he invaded, demanding that you become a participant in his career, a rapt listener to his egoistic mantra." And sports journalists? Kram claimed they were nothing if not subservient, content to lap up the rhetoric and recycle it into paper-selling, ratings-generating headlines: "The Fight of the Century"; "The Rumble in the Jungle"; "The Thrilla in Manila." As Kram suggested, "Contrary to opinion, the sports press likes to fling incense, be part of the show, create stars, and to that end prints and televises a fraction of what it knows. Heroes fuel circulation and ratings: ride the star, retain access."[37]

In many ways, then, both the "Battle of the Sexes" in 1973 and the "Thrilla in Manila" in 1975—with years of manufactured hype, frenzied prematch atmosphere, and saturated postmatch analysis—were merely previews of what was to come: a sports media industry unshackled by the restraints of limited broadcast time. The fight specifically was also proof that people would be willing to pay for content that they cared about. Over the next month 40 percent of cable subscribers in Jackson, Mississippi, and 30 percent in Fort Pierce–Vero Beach would become HBO subscribers.[38] On a national level HBO would add close to ninety-five thousand subscribers per month through the end of 1975, over six times more than what it was getting in the months before the fight.[39] Imitators soon followed. Ted Turner, with his "little-boy bombast and self-promoting razzamatazz," would launch TBS in 1976. The USA Network arrived in 1977. Cable was here to stay; sports would soon be all day, every day.

With this shift wins and losses would no longer be sufficient. Instead there would have to be more stories, more context, more narratives, vacuuming up broadcast time and delivering material to a public eager to talk about sports. And Muhammad Ali, with his incessant dispersal of verbal fodder, had provided the perfect blueprint: find an angle and just keep talking.

9

An Arid Spectacle

World Series Cricket (1977–79)

As Muhammad Ali became a global icon, imitation was inevitable. In the western suburbs of Sydney, Australia, an aspiring pugilist named Paul Hogan was one of many who became enamored with both Ali's extraordinary skill and his remarkable charisma. At first Hogan tried to emulate the boxer's success in the ring. He started training and was good enough to dabble professionally as a welterweight. But paydays for a middling boxer are sporadic, and before long Hogan put down the gloves to find a better way to support his wife and three young children. He cycled through a series of odd jobs before settling in as a rigger on the Sydney Harbour Bridge.

And yet the Muhammad Ali schtick had not yet run its course. While Hogan was unable to mimic Ali's athleticism, he shared the boxer's magnetic disposition and gift of gab. With the bridge as his stage, he entertained co-workers and talked a few suicide jumpers off the literal ledge. In 1971, on a lark, Hogan sent a letter to an Australian television talent show called *New Faces*. He claimed to be the country's leading "tap-dancing knife thrower," which wasn't really a thing, just a ruse to get attention. It worked. Hogan was invited onto the Network Nine program without so much as an audition. He showed up, made fun of the judges, put a garbage can on his head, did a little jig, threw the knives on the floor, and walked off stage. The panel stared; the crowd cackled; the phone lines lit up.

Thus was born the career of the man whose role as a fictional crocodile wrangler in a series of Hollywood movies would make him the most recognizable Australian in the world. Overwhelming audience demand led to Hogan's being invited back on *New Faces*, then invited back again, and finally being offered a more permanent role as a comedic man-on-the-street correspondent for a news program on Network Nine called *A Current Affair*. One of the producers of the show, John Cornell, soon decided that the-bridge-rigger-turned-comedian needed a bigger spotlight. Together the two men pitched an idea for a travel program where Hoges (as the future Crocodile Dundee was affectionately known to Australians) would go around "meeting the locals, learning new customs and habits and generally making good-humored fun of the experience."[1]

The network was all for it and put up the money. Cornell and Hogan traveled to Singapore, where they stumbled through the production of their first episode. Then they went to London and did it all again. After that they were summoned back to the offices of Clyde Packer, the executive in charge of the program and potential heir to the Network Nine empire. When they arrived, Packer accused the men of playing loose with their production budget. Cornell took exception to this, and tensions boiled over. As Hogan explains it in his autobiography: "John grabbed Clyde by the shirt front and dragged him right across the room and shoved him hard against the wall. . . . Clyde, a rich powerful magnate, wasn't used to anyone manhandling him and didn't know what to do."[2] After the encounter Cornell and Hogan would leave the network and launch a program called *The Paul Hogan Show* for a different station. It quickly became one of the most popular shows in the country.

The incident between Clyde Packer and John Cornell was unusual. Most people didn't bully the Packer family, one of Australia's most famous lineages. On the contrary, the Packers had more or less gotten their way in Australia for the better part of the twentieth century. The family's rise began with Packer's grandfather, Robert Clyde (R. C.) Packer, who grew from a respected journalist into a respected editor into the co-owner of two "unashamedly sensationalist" Sydney-based newspapers.[3] Eager to immerse his young son, Frank, in the family business, R. C. hired the seventeen-year-old to work an undercover beat in the early 1920s. Despite a headline-grabbing story in which he bought cocaine from a local pharmacy (headline: "Boy Buys Enough to Kill 20 People"), Frank disliked the reporter lifestyle and left the paper to roam Australia as a ranch hand. A few years later, with circulation at his papers stagnant, R. C. Packer took a page from the American promotional handbook and launched a Miss Australia contest. After a winner was chosen, Packer tapped Frank to chaperone the young lady around the United States for a promotional tour. The campaign was a success on two fronts. First, it boosted subscribers for Packer's papers. And second, it reignited young Frank's interest in the media business.

Soon Frank was making his own moves. In the early 1930s Frank first threatened to launch a new publication, a threat that allowed him to secure a hefty buyout from a potential newspaper rival, and then he actually did launch a new publication, creating a magazine called *Women's Weekly*, which would become one of the most widely read periodicals in Australia. When his father passed away in 1934, Frank was put in a position to consolidate the family's media interests. Consolidate Frank did, forming a company called Consolidated Press Ltd. in 1936. The company grew, and Frank Packer became one of the most financially and politically influential people in the country. In the 1950s, as television entered the home, the government decided that Australia would have a public station, controlled by the Australian Broadcasting Commission (ABC), and a handful of licensed stations that could sell commercials. Frank Packer wanted a television license and felt he deserved one. He argued that while television programming was "going to be a very important factor in building up the character of the nation," it was also going to be costly.[4] Because of the costs only companies with the financial runway to withstand several years of losses should be granted these valuable assets. The government agreed, awarding Frank Packer a commercial television license in Sydney.

As television spread, Packer next suggested that the government assist in making the big companies even bigger, with more licenses in different cities, thus allowing for networks such as his own to sell big advertising deals for big programs with big budgets. Doing so, Packer suggested, was in the best interests of all Australians: "I don't believe people look at television for local matter. They like to be entertained.

They like to see the big events on television."[5] Frank Packer contin- ued to consolidate his empire until his death in 1974. At first the plan was for his older son, Clyde, to take control of the family business. But several incidents, including the one in which Clyde was thrown against a wall by Paul Hogan's best friend and co-worker John Cor- nell, made Clyde realize that he had no interest in becoming a media tycoon. He moved to Los Angeles, cashed out of the family empire, and wrote a book about people who had left Australia and had never gone back (like himself).

As the Clyde Packer story fades away, the story of Frank Packer's younger son, Kerry, begins. Loud, brash, and stubborn, Kerry Packer was a perfect manifestation of the archetypal business tycoon. He would further expand the company his father and grandfather had built, often through brute force and intimidation, to create one of the most powerful media conglomerates in the world. Yet while he could hold a grudge with the best of them, he was savvy enough to know when to relent, especially in those early years. By the mid-1970s tensions between John Cornell and the Packer family had thawed to the point that Network Nine was ready to bring Cornell and Hogan back on board. Although contractual obligations with another network would postpone the reunion for a few years, the lines of communication had been opened far enough for Cornell to feel comfortable pitching Packer on other ideas.

One idea in particular stood out. Having spent the last few years hobnobbing with some of the country's most famous celebrities, Cor- nell came to realize that Australian cricketers, even the most popular ones, were poorly treated and horribly paid. That's because all matters relating to logistics and competition went through the Australian Cricket Board (ACB; not to be confused with the ABC). The ACB was a group of tradition-bound bureaucrats who lived in the past and treated the athletes as if they were lucky to even be given the opportunity to play for their country. Despite performing at the highest level in their country's most popular sport, most cricketers had other jobs. One was a bank teller; another ran an antiques business. At some point in 1976—as with so many of these incidents, the details of who came up with the idea first are murky—Cornell pitched Packer on a big- money breakaway cricket competition, made up of the best players in

Australia and around the world, and available exclusively on Packer's Network Nine.

Packer was intrigued for several reasons. First, government regulations required Australian television networks to air a fixed percentage of locally produced content. Because original scripted programming was expensive, Packer viewed sports as a relatively cheap option to achieve this quota. Second, Packer's affluent upbringing had exposed him to what was going on overseas, especially in the United States, where programs like *The Battle of the Sexes* and *Monday Night Football* had transformed sporting events into spectacles, attracting huge audiences and massive advertising revenue. Third, color television had finally arrived in Australia, opening up new and exciting production techniques that could be used to hold the attention of even the most casual cricket fan. And fourth, Kerry Packer had already tried to get the rights to premier Australian cricket and had failed. In early 1976 Packer had barged into a meeting with the ACB and offered it $1.5 million over three years for exclusive television rights. The board demurred, then declined, opting to stick with tradition and sign with the ABC for a paltry three-year, $210,000 deal.[6]

Packer was incensed. So when Cornell came to his office later that year proposing a cricket competition made just for him and his network, he couldn't say yes fast enough. The first step was getting a commitment from the players. Cornell, Hogan, and a third partner, former journalist and athlete Austin Robertson, created a new company so they could represent players. Then they traveled around secretly signing up some of the best cricketers in the world. It wasn't that difficult, mostly because they had access to Kerry Packer's bank account. Dennis Lillee, already in business with Cornell and one of Australia's most effective bowlers, was one of the first to commit. After making as little as $8,000 a year playing for the national team and after famously saying that the grounds crew often pulled in more money per match than he did, Lillee was thrilled to sign a three-year, $105,000 contract. English captain Tony Greig came aboard soon after, as did Viv Richards, a fierce West Indies batsman, and Imran Khan, so revered in Pakistan that he would eventually be elected the country's prime minister. For the players it was life-changing money, even if they weren't quite sure where or how often they would be playing.

On May 10, 1977, word finally got out about what was happening. The reports were light on details (because details hadn't been sorted out yet), but the general idea was that a rich Australian media mogul named Kerry Packer had signed thirty-five of the world's best cricketers to compete in a bunch of matches set to take place during the upcoming Australian summer. The word "circus" was tossed around, as were guesses as to how Packer's ploy would alter the future of the sport. Bill O'Reilly of the *Sydney Morning Herald*, was skeptical but curious as to how the ACB would react: "The game of cricket itself has little to gain, if anything, out of this business experiment, but three hearty cheers for the opportunity it has given our administrators to show their latent skills in the hurly-burly of modern business."[7] Others saw the new development as an existential challenge to everything cricket was supposed to be and represent. John Arlott of *The Guardian* called the proposal "the most historic event in the history of the modern game" and wrote that "the possible consequences are so immense that it is difficult to believe that those responsible, on both sides, have fully understood or considered them."[8]

Much of the criticism focused on the circuit's three-team structure: a breakaway group of Australians, a breakaway English side, and a stitched together group of "world" players. One editorial suggested that "talent by itself, whether it is called 'The Rest of the World' or 'Australia' (with an unrepresentative side), cannot create the suspense of matches where national prestige is at stake."[9] Writing in *The Times*, John Woodcock, who would become one of Kerry Packer's harshest critics, agreed with this assessment, writing that "more than anything—more even than the presence of a majority of the world's best players—international cricket needs the stimulus of national pride."[10] And Ian Peebles of *The Guardian* argued that the system would eliminate the national "partisanship" or allegiance on which the sport was built: "No obviously contrived event is going to evoke [partisanship], and without it, whatever the skills, a sporting event is an arid exercise."[11]

Packer didn't care. He wanted cricket for all the reasons mentioned above and had no interest in pondering these larger philosophical questions. Packer was also prepared to win at any cost. Quite literally. When he became embroiled in a legal skirmish against the International

Cricket Conference (ICC) regarding which players would be allowed to participate, Packer shrugged it off. "I've got more money than they have," he said.[12] He was right; he did, and he ending up winning the case. When Packer was then told he couldn't use any of the traditional Australian cricket grounds, his team came up with an expensive plan to grow pitches in makeshift greenhouses and transport them to stadiums more commonly used for other sports, such as Australian rules football and horseracing. It was an imperfect solution, impossible without lots of money, but it worked.

Kerry Packer's World Series Cricket (WSC) kicked off on December 2, 1977, at VFL Park, just outside Melbourne. The match was a supertest between Australia and the West Indies, a format designed to compete with the traditional five-day test matches coordinated by the ACB and its equivalents around the world. Packer had publicly predicted that these matches would see an average of fifteen thousand attendees. John Cornell had guessed thirty thousand. Another WSC executive shot even higher: fifty thousand. But the first day saw a gate of fewer than three thousand. Low turnout continued to be a problem as the WSC season went on. The seventy-three days of WSC cricket throughout the summer saw an average attendance of just under five thousand. Such figures produced an estimated total gate of just under $1 million, not even enough to cover the bill for the players' wages—estimated to be around $1.5 million—much less all the other expenses involved in staging the competition.[13]

Was Kerry Packer flustered by what would become a supposed $3.2 million deficit? Hardly. In an interview conducted at the conclusion of the first season, a reporter from *The Age* remarked that Packer seemed to be "a happy man who is having the time of his life."[14] And when questioned about the poor attendance and mediocre television ratings, Packer was quick to bring up an American comparison: "The first time they ever played the Superbowl [sic] in the United States, they played it in front of 2,000 people, 15 or 20 years ago. Today they play it in front of 110 million people on television and over 100,000 in the stadium." The numbers were incorrect. The Super Bowl was actually an immediate success, attracting over sixty thousand attendees and over fifty million viewers in its first year. But the reference is telling, an indication that Packer wanted to usher the Australian sports media landscape into a lucrative, tradition-be-damned, American-like future, come hell or high water. Television was key, and money was no object. As he said to his players and their families during a dinner celebrating the conclusion of the first season, "There will never be a shortfall of cash."[15]

As for the actual television broadcast, a lot of ideas were thrown around. The result was an intriguing yet inconsistent first season. Some of the ideas had been good in concept *and* good in execution. Increased camera angles, the use of instant replay, and the addition of an on-screen chyron that showed scores and statistics were well-received, regarded as entertaining if perhaps superfluous innovations. Many of these production techniques came from the mind of an up-and-coming television producer named David Hill, who was just getting started on a career trajectory that involved the reinvention of both English soccer (see chapter 13) and American football (chapter 15). There were also ideas that were good in concept but bad in execution. The decision to imbed microphones on the field, for instance, was designed to immerse the viewer in the match, to provide a fresh perspective for the average cricket fan. The result was indeed fresh. As WSC director John Crilly said, "The count for the first season was something like 13 shits, 14 you bastards, three fucks and one cunt that got on the air."[16] And then there were the ideas that were simply bad in concept. When famous Australian tennis player John Newcombe stopped by the production offices to offer some advice, he suggested that the crew focus on intimate details. In a discussion about Australian legend Ian Chappell, Newcombe suggested, "The way he scratches his crutch before a ball's bowled must be a turn-on for women. Image is important, no matter what the traditionalists say and how much they hate it."[17]

Newcombe got one thing right: the traditionalists were definitely not the primary audience. Packer's goal was to make cricket accessible and enjoyable to the average Australian, not because he was an altruist, but because he needed audiences large enough to attract the kind of advertising that could offset his significant investment. In other words, he needed a spectacle. By the end of the first season the strategy seemed to be working. A winter poll conducted by *The Age* found that over half of Australians thought that Packer's experiment had "improved cricket for the general public," compared to about a quarter who thought it had a "damaging effect" on the game. (The rest were apparently still deciding.)[18] Even more important to Packer's strategy, younger fans were far more likely to see WSC as a step forward, compared to older fans. And younger fans, of course, were the ones Packer and his advertisers cared about.

The tide was clearly shifting. In April 1978 Kerry Packer was told he'd be able to use the most famous cricket stadium in the country, the Sydney Cricket Ground (SCG), for the second season. That was a huge deal, an implicit acknowledgment that WSC wasn't going away any time soon. Work quickly began on outfitting the grounds with lighting sufficient to host the competition's famous night matches. Knowing that momentum was finally going their way, Packer and his team continued their propaganda push throughout the entire offseason, aiming to keep the WSC brand at the top of minds for all Australian sports fans. A flashy documentary called *The World Series Cricket Story* aired on Network Nine and was meant to remind viewers (or maybe convince them) just how scintillating the first season had been. Traditional marketing was also ramped up. A new jingle was commissioned—the famous "C'mon Aussie, C'mon"—and T-shirts were sold with slogans such as "I'm into Cricket, Balls and All" and "Big Boys Play at Night."

The beginning of the end of Kerry Packer's circus came on November 28, 1978, when the SCG played host to a one-day match between Australia and the West Indies. It began at 2:30 p.m., paused at 6 p.m. for a dinner break, and resumed an hour later, making history as the first cricket match played under the lights at the SCG. Packer had anticipated a good crowd, around twenty thousand people. But when fans continued to pour in throughout the afternoon and early evening, the organizers threw open the gates, allowing late arrivals to jockey for standing-room-only positions. It was only right, then, that Australia took care of business, batting second and winning easily by five wickets. Dennis Lillee, the first cricketer to sign on with John Cornell and Paul Hogan, played a starring role, setting down some of the West Indies' best batsmen and eliciting a sustained chant—"Lillee! Lillee!"—from the amped-up Aussie supporters. And when Ian Davis hit the winning run, hundreds of fans rushed onto the pitch, a celebratory ending that observers pointed out rarely occurred in the drawn-out structure of test cricket. The event was a success in every conceivable way, a spectacular performance that, according to Bill O'Reilly, would give "the Australian Cricket Board and the various State associations plenty to think about as they swallow the lumps in their throats."[19]

The next day fervent Packer critic John Woodcock wrote that the match "was more like a game of American football than a cricket match," a comparison that wasn't meant as a compliment. He then suggested that perhaps the West Indies side had capitulated for the greater good and that the entire charade seemed more akin to theater than competition: "It has to be remembered that all wsc players are basically on the same side."[20] In other words, Team Kerry Packer. But the crowds didn't care; they ate it up. Packer and the players made money. And it was clear that cricket had entered a new era. Gideon Haigh, who has written the definitive account of the competition, summed it up nicely: "wsc was not against the establishment this evening. It was the establishment."[21]

The ACB came to this realization as well. Its members had been worn down, bullied and bamboozled by a boisterous outsider who wasn't going to go away until he got what he wanted. In April 1979 Network Nine won the exclusive rights to test matches played in Australia for the following three years. Another subsidiary of Packer's sprawling conglomerate won a ten-year contract to market and promote Australian cricket. That was good enough for the country's most stubborn media tycoon, who decided that the wsc experiment had accomplished what it had been designed to accomplish. There would be no third year.

As expected, protests and challenges to Packer's new dominant position in the cricket hierarchy ensued. In its 1979 annual report the ABC suggested that Australia adapt a policy similar to that of the British, whereby sporting events of great national importance are limited to the selling of only nonexclusive television rights, thus ensuring each and every person in Australia the chance to watch his or her cricketing heroes. But in December Australia's Trade Practices Commission declined to get involved, allowing the deal between Packer and the ACB to go through. Cricket had officially gone commercial; Network Nine would hold a vice grip on the television rights to home Australian test matches for the next four decades.

With the cricket situation sorted and everybody making money, John Cornell moved on to his next challenge. This time Paul Hogan was the one with the idea. He wanted to make a movie, starring himself, about a guy who was a "real outback character, someone who thought seven people was a crowd."[22] In the first iteration of the script the character's name was a mashup: Buffalo Jones (part Buffalo Bill, part Indiana Jones). After a rewrite it became Crocodile Dundee. Cornell loved it. When they were ready to pitch to investors, the men brought it to—who else?—Kerry Packer. But Australia's richest man passed; movies weren't his thing. Instead Hogan and Cornell secured investment from an array of speculators, including Australian cricket stars Greg Chappell, Dennis Lillee, and Rod Marsh. The movies, of course, were massive blockbusters, an outcome John Cornell had predicted. As he explained in the *New York Times* in 1988, the film appealed to all ages, all people, "a demographic like a double-barreled shotgun."[23]

It was a true spectacle: easy to follow, easy to understand, all laid out in a neat package, the perfect recipe for movie-making success. Cornell had now conquered television, sport, *and* Hollywood. How? By learning from the best. As he told the *Times* reporter, "I cut my teeth on Kerry Packer."[24]

Part 4 / Growth

By the end of the 1970s sports had a limited yet consistent role within the global media landscape. The spectacles certainly drew attention, even from the most casual fans. They were endlessly promoted and made big money. Network executives loved them because advertisers loved them: large groups of engaged viewers all staring at the same thing, wondering what was going to happen next—what better place to jump in and peddle a product?

The more avid sports fans soaked up what they could from the supplementary offerings. They watched highlights of their teams on their local news broadcasts, combed the newspapers to catch up on transactions, and read *Sports Illustrated* on the weekends to get the inside scoop from their favorite reporters. They had more information than ever before. What more could they want?

A lot, apparently. Over the next twenty years new technology and relaxed regulations would usher in an era of spectacular growth: more games, more discussion, more analysis, more everything. Interested in Notre Dame vs. Michigan? Sure, you could still watch that. But if you preferred Purdue vs. Northwestern? Not a problem, even in California. For media companies a massive audience was nice but unnecessary. Instead the only requirement was a group willing to stay engaged long enough to monetize the content (and even that was negotiable, as we'll see below). The "broad" in broadcasting, of course, would never go away; the spectacle would prove eternal. But the narrowcasting ideas proposed by the early cable television innovators would take hold through sports in various ways, through mid-major conference basketball tournaments and bass fishing competitions, through regional blogs and videogames.

How did it all happen? How did the sports fan go from a limited menu of sporadic options to an all-day, everyday buffet of games, discussion, analysis, and highlights? As the famous American television producer Don Ohlmeyer once told journalist Tony Kornheiser, "The answer to all of your questions is money."[1]

How to Be Rich   **10**

The Launch of ESPN *(1979)*

"Do you want to make a million? Believe me, you can—if you are
able to recognize the limitless opportunities and potentials around
you and will apply these rules and work hard. For today's alert,
ambitious and able young men, all that glitters truly *can* be gold."
—J. Paul Getty, *How To Be Rich*[1]

Follow the money they say. And so follow the money we will, all the way
back to 1915, when an alert, ambitious, and able young man named
Paul Getty secured a lease on a parcel of land in Oklahoma. Getty was
an oil wildcatter, a prospector, a speculator. He had spent close to a
year scouting the state's terrain, looking for a place to drill. When
he found one he both liked and could afford, Getty signed the lease,
assembled a team, crossed his fingers, and began drilling. A month
later gushed oil, lots of it, enough to generate upwards of a thousand
barrels a day. The young man celebrated, bought a Cadillac, and flipped
the lease for a significant profit. Using the proceeds from that sale,
Getty repeated this process several times over until he became, at the
age of twenty-three, a millionaire.

It was vindication for Getty's father, George, who had encouraged
his son to follow in his footsteps and enter the oil business. George
had even provided Paul—who had dreamt of being a writer, maybe
a diplomat—with both living expenses and the funding necessary to

drill once suitable land was procured—seed money, if you will. As Paul himself has written, "Any attempt to deny that my own seat in life was reserved for me would be ridiculous."[2] George's plan worked almost too well. After two years of leasing, drilling, and flipping, Paul Getty decided to retire. He told his dad he was done, packed up his stuff, said goodbye to his friends in Oklahoma, and moved to Los Angeles. Once there, Getty reveled in the life of a young, rich socialite. He went clubbing with Rudolph Valentino, bickered with Charlie Chaplin over women, and had sparring sessions with Jack Dempsey. As Getty remembers in his autobiography, "A man in his mid-twenties who had both time and money to spare could have scarcely hoped for more."[3] Life was good. Life was also boring.

> "A businessman must constantly seek new horizons
> and untapped or under-exploited markets."
> —J. Paul Getty, *How to Be Rich*[4]

Paul's retirement lasted only two years; he simply wasn't the retiring type. Early success in Oklahoma had whetted his appetite for more speculating, more drilling, more, more, more. Moreover, Getty recognized that the world was shifting to a lifestyle largely powered by gasoline-powered vehicles. Society was going to need more fuel. A lot more. Who better to provide it than him?

Getty started drilling again, expanding his business to California. In 1930 George Getty died, putting Paul in position to mold the family company into his own vision. Over the next few decades Paul Getty pulled off a series of prescient business maneuvers. When the market dipped during the Great Depression, Getty doubled down, speculating that the downturn would be temporary. Then he consolidated, navigating around the interests of the company's board of advisors, his competitors, and his own mother, to create a fully integrated oil conglomerate. And, finally, he expanded, securing control of a valuable piece of land in the Middle East on the assumption that the world's demand for oil would keep going up, up, up.

He was right. By the mid-1960s Getty had amassed such a fortune that the American press was calling him the world's richest man. In one interview he was asked what he thought of the moniker. His response: "It's rather bad manners. How can anybody be sure?"[5] Getty nonetheless had no qualms penning a series of essays for *Playboy* magazine on how to grow one's wealth. Those essays eventually became a book filled with motivational anecdotes and self-help truisms, many of which are sprinkled throughout this chapter. The book was aptly named: *How To Be Rich*.

And yet although Paul Getty had perfected the art of making money, he had never figured out how to be a decent human being. He was a terrible husband, an awful father, and a pathetic grandfather. He cheated on all five of his wives, screwed one son out of a decent inheritance, and famously refused to negotiate the release of his kidnapped grandson in Italy until the ransom price became more reasonable. When Paul died in 1976, he left behind a vast fortune. Nobody knew how big, least of all Paul, who was fond of explaining to reporters that millionaires could hardly be expected to keep track of their millions. Many guesses actually pegged his wealth at closer to $1 billion. Some said it could be as high as $2 billion. Other sources said four.

Where would all the money go?

"Loyalty—another important quality in executives—can only be recognized and judged after it has been demonstrated."
—J. Paul Getty, *How to Be Rich*[6]

One thing Getty fails to point out in *How To Be Rich* is that nobody gets rich on his or her own. Even the most independent entrepreneur has a team, a group of loyal lifers operating in the background, integral to the entire operation. For Paul Getty loyalty was the antecedent to joining such a team. Yet how does one demonstrate loyalty to a tycoon fundamentally disconnected from the outside world? By doing whatever one is asked to do, no questions asked, with a minimal amount of fuss. And nobody did this better than a man named Stu Evey.

Evey's first brush with the Getty fortune came through a job moving household furniture for George, Paul's oldest son. He was so good at hauling couches and tables that he was asked to stick around and help manage an entire office building. Evey excelled at this too and soon found himself as George's personal assistant, a sort of fixer, executing daily tasks of what he called "portentous and ponderous proportions."[7]

Sometimes this involved finding a place for George to do laundry or to go on vacation. Other times it involved firing employees or buying drugs. When George got divorced and sold his home, Evey negotiated a contract with the buyer, Dodgers owner Walter O'Malley, who was in the market thanks to a recent cross-country business relocation from Brooklyn. And when George Getty, drunk and strung out on drugs, locked himself in his bedroom threatening to kill himself, it was Evey who received the call and rushed to George's house. Evey broke down the door, found that his boss had stabbed himself in the stomach with a knife, and got Getty to a hospital. He then went back to the house, threw away the pill bottles, cleaned the knife, and slid it back into a drawer. The next day the *New York Times* reported that George Getty had "died of a cerebral hemorrhage."[8] There was no mention of alcohol, drugs, or a knife. Stu Evey, you see, was both very loyal *and* very good at his job.

After George's death, Evey was left to focus on his other, more official title for the Getty empire: vice president of diversified operations. The role required Evey to manage all company investments unrelated to oil. As Evey remembers, Paul once said, "Money is like manure: if you spread it around, it will make things grow."[9] That was Evey's primary task: turn lots of money into even more money. There was a hotel in Mexico, a plywood plant in Liberia, and various real estate holdings around the world. After funerals for both George (1973) and Paul (1976), Evey's motivation for the role hit a speed bump: "For five long years, I simply went through the motions of showing up for work and being alive. I drank. I disappointed myself."[10] He also took several trips to the Kona Surf Hotel in Hawaii, a hotel in which Evey was considering investing, where he "went through the motions" by golfing, sitting on the patio that overlooked the Pacific Ocean, and sipping bourbon. During one of these trips the lawyer who represented the owners of the hotel pitched Evey on a different idea. It would be the one that jolted Evey out of his supposed stupor.

"The door to the American Millionaire's Club is not locked.
Contrary to popular modern belief, it is still quite possible
for the successful individual to make his million—
and more. There will always be room for the man with

energy and imagination, the man who can successfully
implement new ideas into new products and services."
—J. Paul Getty, *How to Be Rich* [11]

Of course the most important brand in sports media history has an
origin story. How could it not? As Bill Rasmussen likes to tell it, the
idea for ESPN came while he was sitting in traffic with his son Scott
in August 1978. Bill was a seasoned entrepreneur, having formed and
cashed out of his own logistics company by the age of thirty. From
there he had embarked on what he believed would be a more fulfilling
career as a broadcaster, doing play-by-play for New England sports
on radio and then television. In 1974 Bill was named communications
director for the New England Whalers, a hockey team in the short-lived
World Hockey Association. Four years later, among significant team
and league upheavals, Bill was fired from that gig (the Whalers would
become part of the National Hockey League the following year). Out of
work at the age of forty-five, Bill Rasmussen returned to his entrepre-
neurial roots, combining everything he had learned about sports media
into a new idea: an all-sports cable station in Connecticut. He held a
series of meeting with cable companies, some of whom said, "Okay,
but have you thought about using a satellite?" Good idea, he thought,
even if he didn't really understand what that meant. Bill arranged a
meeting with a salesman at RCA, who mentioned that the Rasmussens
could lease time on one of the company's satellites for a little over a
thousand dollars a day. Bill and Scott thought about it, crunched the
numbers, and dove straight in, signing a five-year contract.

Then came the traffic jam, or so the story goes. As Bill and Scott sat
on the interstate, a more ambitious idea emerged. With the satellite
connection, why couldn't the network go national? It could. With a
national network, why should the programming focus only on New
England sports? It shouldn't. And with so many sports to choose
from, why would they limit the broadcast to five hours a night, as
was their original plan? They wouldn't. Instead Bill and Scott decided
that they'd launch the country's first national, twenty-four-hour cable
network dedicated to sports. They talked about staffing: they'd need at
least eighty people. They talked about content: the National Collegiate
Athletic Association (NCAA) had hundreds of hours of events every

year, only a small fraction of which were televised. And, of course, they talked about money. The satellite would cost about half a million dollars a year. Each production truck would set them back at least a half million each. Top line talent would command a salary of a couple hundred grand.

Money. They'd need a ton of it to get the idea off the ground. The Rasmussens' early commitment to RCA proved fortuitous here. Just weeks after their deal an article in the *Wall Street Journal* prompted a run on satellite space. Because Bill and Scott already had this part sorted, an investment firm named K. S. Sweet took interest in their fledgling company. After a couple of meetings the firm agreed to provide initial funding, create a business plan, and direct the search for big-time investors. The first two tasks proved relatively straightforward. The third, not so much. One member of the K. S. Sweet team, "a pipe-smoking, intense ex-Marine captain" named J. B. Doherty, recalls running the idea by at least a half dozen heavy hitters.[12] They all passed.

Life went on for Doherty, who, in November 1978, flew to Hawaii to help negotiate the sale of a hotel to a man representing Getty Oil. His name was Stu Evey. While the hotel deal would never materialize, Doherty took the opportunity to pitch Evey, an avid sports fan and season ticket holder for both the Los Angeles Dodgers and Oakland Raiders, on the idea of a twenty-four-hour national cable sports network. Evey was intrigued and agreed to meet Rasmussen when he got back home to Los Angeles. He then started learning as much as he could about cable television, even calling RCA at one point for confirmation that its satellite was indeed in space. The company confirmed that it was.

Evey met Rasmussen, describing him later as "a good speaker, fluid with ideas, glib, and well dressed." He became "seduced and drawn to the concept," so much so that when Rasmussen left, Evey immediately ran the idea up the Getty ladder, reporting that the investment would cost about $10 million and asking for a commitment.[13] While Rasmussen waited for an answer, he went about trying to secure more content for his proposed network. The NCAA, with its hundreds of hours of unaired sporting events, was the ideal partner. Rasmussen's pitch to the college athletics behemoth suggested that more sports on television would be a benefit to all: "The additional coverage will further enhance the Association's stated goal of advancing the overall interest of intercollegiate athletics and provide national exposure to more institutions and student athletes than ever before possible."[14]

Two big breakthroughs came in February 1979. Getty agreed to finance the project with $10 million, and the NCAA agreed to provide programming, including championships for sports like basketball and baseball. In May Anheuser-Busch signed a sponsorship deal for over $1 million, eager to pitch its products to the network's potential young male audience. In July Rasmussen finally settled on a name, changing his original idea of ESP-TV to ESPN: Entertainment and Sports Programming Network. And on September 7 ESPN went live as host Lee Leonard uttered the words that would become an integral piece of sports media lore: "If you love sports, if you really love sports, you'll think you've died and gone to sports heaven."

> "But the oil industry is by no means the only business that offers golden opportunities to the beginner today. All the potentials for an era of unprecedented business activity and prosperity are present—for those who are open-minded and imaginative enough to recognize them."
> —J. Paul Getty, *How to Be Rich* [15]

Millions of words have been written about ESPN since its launch in 1979. Stu Evey wrote a book about the network's beginning. So did Bill Rasmussen, who was chased out of the company shortly after its launch. There's an "oral" history (James Andrew Miller), an "uncensored" history (Michael Freeman), and an "institutional and cultural" history (Travis Vogan). Critics of all backgrounds and vocations— scholars, viewers, investors, competitors—love to talk about what ESPN was, what it should be, and what it's going to become. Everyone has an opinion. The conversation *about* ESPN is often as loud and as contentious as the conversations *on* ESPN. That alone is an apt signifier of the network's cultural and economic impact, proof that its launch entailed a seismic reshaping of an industry that, for sixty or so years, was rather tidy: a section in the newspapers, a few hours of broadcast time, radio, some magazines.

ESPN was the beginning of the end for that model. The network's entrance into the media landscape serves as the perfect chronological delineator, the precise moment in time when the industry and its emphasis on the spectacle began to get carved up into smaller, potentially monetizable components. Many of the network executives of the 1960s and 1970s said it couldn't be done, that only the biggest and most important sporting events could generate an audience big enough to justify air time. Bill Rasmussen saw this firsthand. He reached out to many of those executives about his ESPN idea and was laughed out of the room. These were men who abided by a few dictums: don't show too many sports; when you do, make it relevant to lots of people; listen to the advertisers because they're the boss; most important, get in and get out (and get back to *I Love Lucy*). They had stumbled upon a profitable, advertiser-centric formula and were hesitant to probe further or dig deeper, wary of upsetting their lucrative if limited business model.

This was surface-level thinking, an after-the-fact observation that makes the analogy almost too easy. Oil and sports: two products (addictions?) with seemingly insatiable demand. In the 1930s Paul Getty made his billions by betting on oil's future. He bought low and hoped that the changing nature of society and technology—more people, more cars, more planes, more everything—would provide the kind of demand needed to take advantage of his company's tremendous scale. His thought process proved prophetic; his bank accounts filled up accordingly.

It made perfect sense, then, that when ESPN was hemorrhaging money a year after its launch, much to the delight of the entrenched network executives mentioned above, Stu Evey came to the Getty board of advisors with the following plea: "Gentlemen, in early 1979, when I first proposed the ESPN project as a possible investment for the Getty Oil Company, I told you our initial exploration investigations showed that the geological surveys and seismic studies showed that we had discovered a reservoir worth tapping. . . . Not only has the reservoir been discovered, it is much, much deeper, and I need more drill pipe to reach the objective."[16]

It was a narrative these executives could understand. And what oil baron can resist the seduction of an unexplored and untapped reservoir? ESPN got its money, allowing the network to navigate through a difficult first few years. Those in charge of making decisions at ESPN would be asked to stop buying pipe, to stop drilling, when the network reached the point at which every sports fan's need had been satisfied, fulfilled, achieved.

In 1984 the Getty company was sold to Texaco. Texaco, having no interest in the media business, sold ESPN to ABC. Despite the change of ownership the drilling never stopped. Several decades later it continues unabated. Evey was right; the reservoir was massive. And lots of people, consequently, have gotten very rich.

A Classic Cartel

11

*NCAA vs. Board of Regents of the
University of Oklahoma (1984)*

Nearly seventy years after an Oklahoma oil well became the catalyst
to a fortune that would fund the most important sports media brand
of all time, the state would play host to yet another pivotal media-
related moment. In 1984 the University of Oklahoma teamed up with
the University of Georgia to challenge the almighty and all-consuming
power of the NCAA in front of the U.S. Supreme Court. The decision
that emerged solidified the role television would play in the evolution
of college football and unleashed an almost unthinkable amount of
money into the sport. Understanding where the case came from and
exactly why it's so important, however, requires a bit of a history lesson.
And there's no better place to begin the story of this earth-shattering
legal case than with the story of an equally earth-shattering football
play—a play so terribly violent, so brutal, that it was banned almost
as soon as it was invented.

   The idea for the play came from a man named Lorin F. Deland.
Before becoming one of the most influential individuals in the history
of American football, Lorin was known mostly as a "good, practical
husband," the loyal companion of famous twentieth-century novelist
Margaret Deland.[1] Lorin's own profession was a bit unclear. One report
pegged him as a roving business consultant; another said he was a
well-known advertising expert; yet another suggested that he handled

his wife's day-to-day business with editors and publishers. Everybody agreed that Lorin was quite brilliant, so it's certainly possible he did all these things and more. The one thing we know for sure, though, is that Deland was an avid military nut, enthralled with historical figures such as Napoleon Bonaparte and spending much of his free time poring over books on tactics and maneuvers.[2]

In 1891 one of Deland's friends took him to a college football game. He enjoyed it, mostly because it reminded him of his favorite subject. "It was war," he told a newspaper reporter. "Two armies were being hurled at each other, and I was in my element." Deland went to more games and decided that the sport was ripe for innovation: "So I began a long study of the application of strategy as seen in war to a game of foot ball [sic]. Days and days and weeks and weeks I spent my leisure time in working out new foot ball plays. Finally, I felt convinced that I had something that could be used on the field, and naturally I was curious to have the plays tried."[3]

Soon Deland was no longer being referred to as "Margaret's husband" but rather as a "football scientist."[4] His most famous invention was a play in which two groups of offensive players would line up on each side of the field. Before the play began, each group would run toward the middle of the field at different speeds. The opposing team, unsure as to where exactly these groups were headed, would mostly stay put, manning individual positions. Once they reached the middle of the field, the two groups would then form a wedge and turn up the field toward their opponents. With one player serving as a decoy, the ball would be given to a runner protected by the formation as the wedge was "hurled against two or three players at a rate of speed vastly greater than the defensive line."[5] At some point the wedge would open, providing a funnel through which the ball carrier could proceed to the end zone. When the "flying wedge" worked, which was often, it resulted in big yardage for the offense. But the ferocious momentum caused by the maneuver also led to mangled bodies, broken bones, and concussions. Just a year after being invented Deland's creation was permanently banned from college football.

And yet although it was prohibited on the field, the flying wedge would live on in the American psyche as a symptom of a far greater problem. At the turn of the century football was dangerous, often deadly, and banning a single play was nothing more than a band-aid for an ailment that required surgery. From 1900 to 1905 forty-five people died playing football.[6] The list of causes varied: broken necks, heart failure, concussions, and infections. Rarely a week went by without at least one newspaper reporting on some poor boy or young man who had gone out to play his favorite sport and never returned home. At the beginning of one college season the *New York Times* somberly explained to its readers what the upcoming months would bring: "Already the process of transforming healthy and weighty young men into bruised and shattered skeletons has begun. . . . No one ever saw a more magnificent set of young men than Yale's football players were last week. But from this time until the great day of public Thanksgiving their decline will be large and their falls numerous."[7]

Something had to be done. In October 1905 President Teddy Roosevelt invited a group of college football leaders to the White House for a "long and serious conference" about how to stop football players from dying.[8] Of course it was imperative that everybody understand one thing before the discussion commenced: Teddy Roosevelt was no pansy. The president loved football. He thought it built character. And he had no interest in eliminating the physicality of the sport. "I have no sympathy whatever with the overwrought sentimentality that would keep a young man in cotton wool," Roosevelt once opined, "and I have a hearty contempt for him if he counts a broken arm or collar bone as of serious consequence when balanced against the chance of showing that he possesses hardihood, physical address, and courage."[9] Football, Roosevelt thought, just needed a few tweaks, a rule change here and there, enough to keep the players breathing, if not necessarily upright.

Administrators at most colleges agreed with Roosevelt: football had become too dangerous *and* it needed to be saved. The colleges were less concerned with football as a creator of manly men than with the sport's role as a publicity tool, directing much needed attention toward the schools with the best teams. Successful football led to more admissions; more admissions led to more tuition revenue. Thus banning the sport outright was never going to happen. Instead it was agreed that schools simply needed to further collaborate, to talk about what could and couldn't be done to improve safety. In December 1905 sixty-two colleges agreed to form the Intercollegiate Athletic Association of the United States (IAAUS). Among the group's primary objectives was to come up with a set of guidelines that could reduce football injuries. The group banned questionable plays, lobbied for standardized officiating, and discussed equipment changes. In 1910 the organization changed its name to the National Collegiate Athletic Association (NCAA). It continued to tinker with the rules of football, and injuries decreased. Pleased with its success, the NCAA formed rules committees for over a dozen other sports, including basketball, volleyball, and wrestling. Its power and influence grew.

Over the next few decades college sports, and especially football, became an integral component of American life. Many saw this development as worrisome. In 1929 the Carnegie Foundation for the Advancement of Teaching issued a wide-ranging report called "American College Athletics," examining the growth and influence of college sports. The document began with a fictional European visitor, perplexed by the intimate connection between football and higher education. "How do students, devoted to study, find either the time or the money to stage so costly a performance?" this fake European visitor hypothetically asked.[10] The report then went on to criticize the current state of coaching—"the position of a coach whose tenure depends upon victory is both unfortunate and unfair"; recruiting—"the deepest shadow that darkens American college and school athletics"; and safety—"there exist serious deficiencies in the relations of the medical profession to college athletics."[11]

In one section the study described how sportswriters were partly to blame for all this madness, elevating the importance of college sports beyond what any sane society would consider acceptable. This was unique to the United States: "In no other nation of the world will a college boy find his photograph in the metropolitan paper because he plays on a college team." Embellished reporting was common, primarily because "the less intelligent reader is the more likely to be attracted by the sensational in sports writing and much of the material on certain sporting pages represents an attempt to provide such persons with the kinds of reading-matter which, because of years of carefully incited indulgence, they increasingly crave." That's not to say that all the blame should be placed on the reporters. On the contrary, many schools were eager participants: "Into this game of publicity the university of the present day enters eagerly. It desires for itself the publicity that the newspapers can supply. It wants students, it wants popularity, but above all it wants money and always more money."[12]

No school benefitted more from this publicity (and wanted more money, always more money) than the University of Notre Dame. It hadn't always been that way. The Catholic, Indiana-based football program was born from rejection, with Notre Dame having tried and failed to join the Western Conference, the precursor to the Big Ten, not once (1897), not twice (1908), but three times (1913). The conference wanted nothing to do with the school; it was too small, too insignificant, too in-the-middle-of-nowhere. Forced to forge its own path, Notre Dame turned those perceived weaknesses into its greatest strengths. Lacking a conference, it scheduled games outside its natural geographical footprint, providing the program with national exposure, as well as a recurring matchup with Army in New York City. Notre Dame football also became a unifier of disparate worshippers, an entity through which the pious Catholic fan could root for both football and Jesus, often in the same breath. At one point the president of the university even suggested that the team's success depended on how many students came to receive communion each weekend.

Beyond its national schedule and Catholic affiliation Notre Dame also had the all-important sports press in its pocket. Grantland Rice, with his penchant for turning otherwise normal athletes into mythical superheroes, was an all-too-eager participant in the creation of the Notre Dame mythology. Rice's depiction of the school's 1924 offensive backfield—the so-called "Four Horsemen"—was verbose and exaggerated and over the top. In other words, it was classic Grantland Rice, the chairman of the era's "gee whiz!" style of sports journalism and a man who, according to one writer, "spun out his hyperbolic leads and game stories, sped through his signed columns, met his deadlines, and went drinking with his favorite coaches and athletes."[13]

In the 1929 Carnegie report Notre Dame was mentioned by name only a few times; among these was a comment that it was one of the few schools in the country that could afford "squad pants made of aeroplane silk."[14] This was true: Notre Dame had money. One source notes that the football team pulled in around $4 million from the onset of World War I through the mid-1930s, enough to both keep the team well equipped and fund the construction of several buildings around campus.[15] The smartest people in South Bend, Indiana, however, knew that the only thing more valuable than money was publicity. So when radio networks came to Notre Dame in the 1930s asking if the school would be interested in selling exclusive rights for its telecasts, administrators turned them away, preferring a system where dozens of stations could broadcast their games across the entire country.

Eventually the growing dollar signs proved irresistible to even the most publicity-focused administrators. At first Notre Dame moved cautiously, signing nonexclusive radio contracts. But when the war ended and televisions came barreling into the American home, officials at Notre Dame knew they'd have to shift strategies. Giving up a few thousand dollars here and there in return for a larger broadcast footprint and a potentially bigger audience—the "Notre Dame is America's team" argument—seemed like an easy call in the 1920s and 1930s. But giving up $100,000—or more—in potential television revenue? That was different. Justifying these new lucrative agreements soon became a matter of divine intervention, with one administrator suggesting the following about exclusive television deals: "If it is from God, we can't stop it; if it is not, it will die of its own accord."[16] In 1950 God blessed the university with a bidding war among three networks. When it concluded, DuMont had secured the rights to five Notre Dame home games for an unprecedented $185,000. Hallelujah!

By the time Notre Dame signed this deal, the NCAA had grown considerably. It had nearly four hundred total members and had become far more than just an arbiter of standardized rules. Spooked by the money Notre Dame was pulling in with its new television deal, concerned that increased television exposure would lead to decreased attendance at smaller schools, and alarmed that a single member might potentially be prioritizing its own success over the success of the whole, the NCAA put together a new task force: the NCAA Television Committee. The group's charge was to figure out what the emergence of this new technology meant for college athletics and, of course, for the NCAA itself.

A study to analyze the issue was commissioned, and the results were presented the following year. The biggest takeaway was that television did indeed lead to a decrease in attendance: "If there had been no televised games in 1950 . . . attendance at college games would have been 40 percent higher."[17] But the results were far from definitive. Some researchers found significant methodological missteps in the study's design. Others pointed to variables that should have been taken into consideration, such as a decrease in overall college student enrollment. Still others pointed out typos in the final report, inferring that the investigation had been unnecessarily rushed by a biased source. Nevertheless, most NCAA members saw what they wanted to see: an increase in televised games, benefitting only a handful of big-time schools (such as Notre Dame), decreased gate receipts at most colleges. The Television Committee saw the warning signs and recommended "a moratorium on live telecasting of college football games for 1951."[18] The vote passed 161–7 (not every NCAA member voted), with Notre Dame one of the dissenters.

A full moratorium never happened. Instead the NCAA rolled out a limited schedule for the 1951 season with both national and regional windows, flexibility in case top-ranked teams faltered and others rose up, and a restriction limiting each school to two appearances, one home and one away. The money coming in would be distributed to the schools that appeared on television, with a cut also going to the NCAA. In 1952 the slate was further reduced, with fewer games and with schools allowed only a single appearance. This allowed the NCAA to distribute the television revenue among even more of its dues-paying members.

These policies didn't sit well with the country's most popular football program. As Notre Dame saw millions of dollars slip out of its grasp, the school's administrators frequently resorted to a popular retort among Americans of that era: This is socialism! After learning of a radical proposal that would divide television revenues equally among NCAA members regardless of the number of television appearances, Notre Dame president John W. Cavanaugh declared the plan "socialistic in nature and hardly to be expected of an official committee of the NCAA."[19] The school's athletic director, Edward "Moose" Krause, was equally perturbed, telling one group that the plan was "illegal, immoral, un-American, and socialistic."[20] And during the 1953 NCAA convention, Notre Dame's newly installed president, Theodore Hesburgh, presented a ten-point rebuttal to the organization's restrictive television policy. Within that rebuttal was the following rant: "We believe that any attempt to restrict and boycott what is successful in other television programs would be thought of as un-American and illegal. Any attempt to go further and to share the honest reward for any talent would be looked upon as socialistic, a removal of incentive to excellence and a premium placed on mediocrity."[21]

While the proposal of dividing television revenues equally never passed, the NCAA nonetheless withstood this anti-American rhetorical barrage to retain control of the television rights to college football. Schools that had hoped to get their own deals, such as Notre Dame, didn't have much of a choice. Faced with potential expulsion from the NCAA and a subsequent lack of opponents, these schools dropped their resistance to a unified television strategy and fell in line accordingly. It certainly helped that college football was an increasingly coveted television asset. As mentioned above, the 1960s were the beginning of the Roone Arledge era, one in which televised sports would become as much about entertainment as they were about competition. In 1960 ABC outbid NBC and became the home of college football. Over the next few years the rights bounced around from CBS (1962–63), to NBC (1964–65), and then back to ABC (1966–67). ABC would remain the exclusive network of college football for a decade and a half, even though the price kept going up. In 1968 it paid over $10 million annually for a two-year deal. When that contract expired, the network and the NCAA agreed to a deal valued at about $12 million per year. By the beginning of the 1980s ABC was paying over $30 million per year for the rights to broadcast football games among college students.

As the money poured in, college football coaches kept their ambitions in check, recognizing the need to maintain rigorous education and good behavior as the paragons of the college football ecosystem. Just kidding! What actually happened is that college football became even more of a free-for-all, more of an all-out arms race, with coaches and athletic directors doing anything they could to secure better players, more exposure, and a larger cut of the television payout. The excesses outlined in the 1929 Carnegie report never went away. Instead they became even more pronounced, with the rich getting richer and the corrupt getting corrupter.

A 1979 exposé (Sooner fans probably called it a "hit piece") in *Esquire* magazine about the University of Oklahoma (OU) and its head coach, Barry Switzer, documented many of these transgressions. The reporter, Philip Taubman, wrote: "The state is infatuated with football, and Oklahomans spare nothing for their team. They want glory and will pay any price." Taubman detailed recruiting violations, ticket-scalping conspiracies, and even "espionage schemes," where fans would sneak into the practices of OU's opponents to steal plays. He describes Switzer as "the talk and toast of the state" and "the king of Oklahoma," someone who could walk into any restaurant in Oklahoma and get his meal comped. At one point, as if to illustrate the divide between football and academics, Taubman counted the number of books in the suite of a couple of football players, deeming the fourteen titles a pathetic collection "for two guys who have been enrolled for two years each."[22]

Taubman was clear that the problems he cited weren't confined to Oklahoma. On the contrary, it was standard operating procedure: "It may do things on a bigger scale than most, but Oklahoma is part of a breed. At places like Ohio State, Alabama, Texas, Notre Dame, USC, Michigan, and Oklahoma, they've all forgotten football is just a game. It has become a big business, completely disconnected from the fundamental purposes of academic institutions." There was one goal: "All that matters is winning, moving up in the national rankings, and grabbing a bigger share of the TV dollar that comes with appearances on NCAA's game of the week on ABC." Even newly installed University of Oklahoma president William Banowsky recognized the role of football on campus, explaining to the audience on the *Barry Switzer Show* that "it's much easier to be president when we're 8 and 0. If it was the other way around, both Barry and I would be looking for other jobs."[23]

Banowsky, who had started his career as a minister before moving to higher education and then on to the business world, would be a key witness in the 1984 case against the NCAA. That came as no surprise to people who knew him; he had always relished the spotlight, saying as much in an interview with the *Los Angeles Times*: "The thing I loved about the ministry was having a soap box. . . . It was a very thrilling kind of an ego thing." Yet Banowsky was never satisfied on the pulpit: "Frankly, I was never much of a Holy Joe. I was interested in guttier opportunities."[24] In 1971 Banowsky became president of Pepperdine University, where he quickly became known as a prolific fundraiser, securing enough money to move the school to a beautiful oceanfront location in Malibu, California. Enrollment increased eightfold; Banowsky's reputation skyrocketed. In 1978, in search of a new challenge, Banowsky was named the new president of the University of Oklahoma. And it was there that he would get the opportunity to banter and preach and proselytize while embroiled in a lawsuit that would eventually reach the biggest stage of all: the U.S. Supreme Court.

By the time Banowsky took the job at Oklahoma, the college football powers—including Notre Dame, Oklahoma, Penn State, and Alabama—were becoming increasingly resentful at having to share their television bounties with the sport's minnows. They thought the whole system needed a reboot. In 1976, in an effort to lobby for greater control of television riches, approximately sixty schools came together to form the College Football Association (CFA). The group's own committee, the "CFA Television Study Committee," found (shockingly) that bigger schools (like theirs!) drove higher ratings, which drove more advertising revenue, which drove higher rights fees. This led to an obvious and self-serving conclusion: the big schools needed more of a say in how these media deals were being structured. And they needed a bigger cut of the money.

In 1982 the University of Oklahoma teamed up with the University of Georgia to file suit against the NCAA, accusing the organization of antitrust violations in its handling of college football television rights. In his testimony Banowsky claimed that the NCAA cost the University of Oklahoma "several million dollars" in annual revenue and that the organization's power was "so pervasive" and "almost dictatorial" that he lived in fear of what would happen if Oklahoma lost the case. After hearing the case, U.S. District Court judge Juan Burciaga eventually agreed with Banowsky and the plaintiffs, ruling that the NCAA had violated antitrust laws by hoarding the rights to all college football games: "Rather than letting the market operate freely, NCAA has seriously restricted free-market forces in the economics of college football television. Were it not for the NCAA controls, many more college football games would be televised. The court concludes that the NCAA controls over college football make NCAA a classic cartel."[25]

The case wound its way through the American legal system and reached the Supreme Court in early 1984. There the well-worn arguments were repeated. The NCAA claimed that its system was necessary for maintaining competitive balance, equity among its members, and robust revenue. Oklahoma and Georgia claimed that the NCAA was operating as a monopoly, that individual schools needed more autonomy, and that more televised football would have far more benefits than costs. In the witness stand as the Sooner representative was Andy Coats, the mayor of Oklahoma City, who argued that additional regional telecasts would be a boon to communities and cities around the country. By being able to watch games involving the local team week in and week out, "People in a local area would identify with the players, the team and the school and go to see the games."[26]

The ruling came down against the NCAA on June 27, 1984. The Supreme Court sided with Judge Burciaga's original opinion, meaning that television rights would now be given back to the individual schools. William Banowsky, for one, was pleased: "What we have here is deregulation at work in athletics." Still the challenges were just beginning: "They deregulated the airline industry and it brought them some headaches. We shouldn't assume that all will be downhill from here. All we really won was freedom, and freedom is risky."[27] Other administrators were similarly pessimistic, knowing that television revenues would probably go down, at least for a couple of years. Some were downright scared. "It's the worst possible thing that could have happened," said Don Canham, the athletic director at the University of Michigan.[28]

Few experts expected each college to negotiate its own television contract. That wasn't feasible on many levels, not the least of which was timing. In fact the only clear winners in the immediate aftermath of the Supreme Court decision were the television networks, which quickly realized that increased supply would lead to a buyer's market. That's exactly what happened. While members of the CFA, the Big Ten Conference, and the Pac-10 Conference negotiated television deals in 1984, all the schools involved made less money than they had the previous year. In October *Sports Illustrated* suggested it was "the year in which everybody got greedy and America got bored." There were too many games; ratings were down; viewers didn't know what to watch. Consider "Harry Homeviewer," an SI columnist explained, a moniker that represented the average American college football fan: "Harry now can see almost any number of games on Saturday. The desultory ratings, however, suggest he may be suffering from Shoppers' Confusion. Like the bewildered bloke who goes into a store, sees 10 items of equal value and walks away without buying anything, the TV fan may be freezing at the switch."[29]

Probably the only college that could have cut a national deal with a television network was the University of Notre Dame. One newspaper reported that the school had been offered $2 million per home game by Turner Broadcasting.[30] But the deal never came to fruition, and Notre Dame games remained part of the CFA coalition. Perhaps it was because Notre Dame had other issues to deal with. The early to mid-1980s hadn't been kind to Irish football, with a string of mediocre performances. In 1986 Notre Dame hired Lou Holtz as its new coach. The next year the team began to turn things around. Then came a 12–0 record and a championship in 1988, followed by a 12–1 record the following year. Notre Dame was back on top at the perfect time. In 1990 Notre Dame broke away from the CFA and sold an annual package of six home games to NBC for a total of $38 million over five years. It was the ultimate rejection from a school that had been born from rejection, a slap in the face to the CFA members who had benefitted significantly from having the Notre Dame brand in their collective television package. And it was a move that no other program could have pulled off. Said a writer at *Sports Illustrated* at the time: "Only Notre Dame could cut such a deal because, in the nearly 80 years between Rockne (as in Knute) and the Rocket (as in current star Raghib Ismail), the Irish have had eight national championship teams and seven Heisman Trophy winners, not to mention the Four Horsemen, the Gipper and various other heroes, all of which have produced a national following that is unique in sports."[31]

The assessment was correct; Notre Dame was an anomaly. Over the next three decades not a single college football superpower would copy the Irish's playbook. Instead colleges would all remain tethered to their respective conferences, content to have the legal right to sell their own television packages but with no desire to do so. It was the right move. The conference system, operating as mini versions of the NFL, would prove to be quite lucrative. And Harry Homeviewer, *Sports Illustrated*'s fictional football aficionado, would eventually realize that more college football was, in fact, exactly what he had been looking for all along.

1-800-SPORTS 12

Mike and the Mad Dog (1989)

It was a short-lived but memorable era, a brief blip in the long history of the telephone: the sudden emergence and equally swift retreat of the 1–900 number. The model, prevalent in the late 1980s and early 1990s, was simple enough. You called a number and were charged money—often two dollars for the first minute and one dollar each additional minute—for however long you stayed on the call. Whatever revenue came in was split between the phone company and the content provider. There were numbers for jokes and videogame hints and murder mysteries. Celebrities saw it as a way to boost their income, with promises of behind-the-scenes gossip and secrets. Every '80s icon had one, from Paula Abdul to Tiffany to both Coreys (Haim and Feldman). You could pay to get yelled at, with Dial-an-Insult charging people to get insulted. And you could pay to yell at someone else, with Sound Off encouraging people to air their grievances. According to an article in the *New York Times* in 1988, "People blasted boyfriends, the economy, the weather, the Pope."[1] One participant even called in to complain about Sound Off being a ripoff.

The industry grew fast. In 1989 there were fewer than three thousand 1–900 lines in existence. But by 1991 there were over ten thousand, generating close to $1 billion in revenue.[2] Sports made up a sizable chunk of this business. One journalist at the time called 1–900 numbers a "moneymaker—perhaps the biggest to hit sports since the advent of cable television."[3] Gambling tips were big, as was college recruiting gossip. One entrepreneur, Mickey Charles from Huntingdon Valley, Pennsylvania, operated a number called Dial Sports, which provided updated sports information—scores, weather, injuries—and Charles claimed he was pulling in anywhere from $10,000 to $20,000 a month.[4] Competing with upstarts like Charles were the entrenched media heavyweights, unwilling to cede control of this new moneymaker to off-the-street entrepreneurs. *Sports Illustrated* had a 1–900 number focused on breaking news. ESPN had one too, reportedly changing the information on the tape every ten minutes.[5]

Athletes, meanwhile, took their cue from Hollywood, setting up numbers where they offered no-holds-barred access. Jose Canseco, an Oakland A's outfielder and probably the most famous baseball player in the world at the time, reportedly made more than $500,000 in the two months following the launch of his number.[6] In one ad for the service Canseco, dressed entirely in white and leaning against a white Porsche 911 (it was the 1980s, after all), promised candid information about both his personal and professional life, including a tidbit about a recent arrest: "If you want to know if I use steroids, how fast I drive or about why I was carrying that gun, call 1-900-234-JOSE."[7]

What compelled these people, and these sports fans specifically, to dial? Experts had a few guesses. One executive, perhaps foretelling the imminent arrival of the internet, swore it was the public's growing impatience: "People want more forms of entertainment than they used to and they crave instant information. They're not willing to wait for the morning paper or radio news."[8] Another operator commented, "There's an intimacy to the phone that you can't get from TV or newspapers, even if it is a recording."[9] Immediacy and intimacy were certainly big drivers of this business. But so was interactivity, the idea that the fan, after years of mostly passive behavior, was increasingly interested in being part of the action.

The emergence of the 1–900 number was certainly one example of this move toward interactivity. Yet the system was all take and no give, hardly adequate for the sports fan bursting with opinions and with nobody to tell. So while some fans were content to dial Jose Canseco's number, sit back, and find out how fast he drove, other fans were dialing up their local radio stations, itching to engage someone—

anyone!—about Jose Canseco's defense or his baserunning or his loyalty to the team or his rumored relationship with Madonna: "Let me tell you something about Jose Canseco!" began most of these phone calls (probably). Yes, it was around this time, in the late 1980s and early 1990s, that sports talk radio went mainstream. And that meant the fan would never have to remain quiet again.

That's not to say sports talk radio was a brand new format. It wasn't, as versions of it had been around for decades. On March 30, 1964, NBC's flagship radio station in New York City (WNBC) launched the first-ever call-in sports show. Designed to appeal to the avid New York sports fan, the show was hosted by a Ukraine-born, Brooklyn-bred broadcaster named Bill Mazer. In an interview decades later Mazer explained how the concept "caught on like wildfire" and how it was "fueled disproportionately by teenage boys who called in seeking his opinions."[10]

In one of the few recordings that exist today Mazer can be heard having a conversation with one of these young listeners. The discussion concerns Game 2 of the 1966 World Series between the Baltimore Orioles and the Los Angeles Dodgers, a matchup in which the Dodgers committed six errors to spoil an otherwise solid start by future Hall of Famer Sandy Koufax. The exchange, part of which is transcribed below, sounds nothing like the heated diatribes that would become a staple of these shows in the years to come:

BOY: Hello, Bill?
MAZER: Yes, young man.
BOY: How did you like the Series today?
MAZER: Well, I gotta tell you something. I'm doing a pretty good job with alka seltzer today. I was a little aggravated.
BOY: I think Koufax was pitching a good game.
MAZER: Oh, he was pitching well. I don't think he was pitching as well as I've seen him because he wasn't that overpowering.[11]

And on it went, like a genteel uncle sitting on the couch with his young nephew. Of course this kind of civility was never going to last, not in the overcharged and exaggerated world of sports fandom. A better harbinger of what would become sports talk radio launched a few years later in 1969, when three men from Boston—Eddie Andelman, Jim McCarthy, and Mark Witkin—were tapped to host a show called *Sports Huddle*. Conceived as an antidote to the sterile world of sports journalism, where (or so the hosts claimed) favors and access were exchanged for favorable coverage, the *Huddle* was a place where anything and everything was fair game. The men played pranks, antagonized athletes, and ran trivia contests. During one skit they asked listeners who Florence Wishmeyer was and had to wait weeks before somebody came up with the answer: the valedictorian of Hall of Fame pitcher Bob Feller's high school graduating class. What was the point of all this? Nothing; just a couple of guys having a good laugh, talking sports, messing with each other. As Witkin would tell *Sports Illustrated*'s Herman Weiskopf: "Not only do we represent the fans, we *are* the fans."[12]

Andelman was the undisputable star: loud, brash, and always talking. He was also somewhat of a caricature, overweight and prone to exaggeration. His wife claimed he ate four foods—baloney sandwiches, hot dogs, Chinese food, and chicken soup—while Andelman himself said he was too fat for deodorant and instead smeared peanut butter under his arms before leaving the house. Most important, he was a local, through and through. Andelman was born in Boston, moved to another part of Boston when he was twelve, went to college in Boston (Boston University), pursued a graduate degree in Boston (Northeastern), and eventually began working in insurance . . . in Boston. It was only when a producer overheard Andelman, McCarthy, and Witkin talking sports one day in a bar after work—a perfect origin story if there ever was one—that radio entered the picture.

Despite his local credentials not everyone in Boston was an Andelman fan. Weiskopf, who wrote the definitive book about *Sports Huddle*, noted that when Andelman started doing commentary for a local television network, letters poured in from viewers expressing their displeasure with the choice. One wrote that Andelman was "the most disgusting, sarcastic, and insulting thing I have ever seen." Another wrote, "I am in the first grade and I bet I am smarter than you, you big ox." Still there was no ignoring Andelman's pull—for whatever reason, people wanted to talk to him and his two friends. On its worst nights *Sports Huddle* would attract six to eight thousand calls; on its best, it got over twenty thousand.[13]

With growing interest in this new interactive call-in format an all-day sports radio network was all but inevitable. In fact the first attempt to deliver 24/7 sports content through radio came from the same people who launched the first attempt to deliver 24/7 sports content through television: Bill Rasmussen and his son, Scott. After being pushed out of ESPN in 1980, the Rasmussens didn't go far, moving fifteen miles northeast of Bristol to Avon, Connecticut, to launch Enterprise Radio, the country's first all-sports radio network. Unlike ESPN Enterprise operated not as a stand-alone service but rather as a content provider, transmitting features, twice-an-hour sports updates, and a thirteen-hour overnight bloc of talk radio to affiliate stations across the United States. It would be funded through advertising. Charged with building out the network's roster was John Chanin, a free-spending veteran of ABC Radio who lured talent to the startup by promising lavish expense accounts and increased salaries. The network launched on January 1, 1981, with a recording of "Auld Lang Syne" and an introduction by future New York Yankees broadcaster John Sterling: "This is Enterprise Radio, THE sports network, the first one of its kind. And you're here—and we're here—for one significant reason: America's first love is sports, and this is the first radio network to devote itself fully, totally, completely to sports."[14]

But devotion was no substitute for competence. In April 1981 Bill Rasmussen told the *New York Times* that Enterprise would be profitable by the end of the year.[15] Whether that was blind optimism or purposeful misdirection is unknown, but the network was off the air by September, drowning in expenses and unable to continue operations. In *Jock around the Clock*, former Enterprise employee John Birchard's history of the company, those involved with the network tell stories of unpaid bills and abruptly revoked medical insurance. Jim Boeheim, longtime basketball coach at Syracuse University, recalls being offered $5,000 to help with an event and never being paid. Part of it was simple mismanagement. One employee said Chanin "spent money like a drunken sailor."[16] But the network also failed to generate enough cash from national advertising. Sterling remembers there being so few ads that most of the breaks were saturated with public service announcements: "You know McGruff the Crime Dog? Take a bite out of crime? . . . It must have aired a thousand times."[17] Although it was only on the air for less than a year, Enterprise lost an estimated $5–$7 million.[18]

Unlike what had happened at ESPN, when Getty Oil swooped in to save the fledgling yet promising cable startup, no wealthy investor came to rescue Enterprise from its financial predicament. This was partly because of the way the radio industry was structured at the time. Historically regarded as a scarce resource meant to serve the needs of a diverse public, radio had always been mired in government regulation. There were limits as to how many radio stations a single entity could own, as well as guidelines as to what kind of content could be produced. For many entrepreneurs getting involved with radio simply wasn't worth the hassle.

By the early 1980s, however, change was in the air. Around the time Enterprise was closing up shop, the free market cavalry was barging into Washington DC, bolstered by the election of Ronald Reagan and buoyed by a strong belief in a deregulation agenda. Leading the charge for the media industry was recently appointed Federal Communications Commission (FCC) chairman Mark Fowler, an avid believer in the tenets of both the First Amendment and capitalism. "I don't see any role for the government in a democratic society in controlling the information flows," he told one journalist.[19] He believed so deeply in the notion of the free market that he required employees who had the gall to suggest "collectivist ideas" to don a hat emblazoned with the red star of the People's Republic of China.

In a 1982 *Texas Law Review* article Fowler called for an overhaul of the way radio was regulated. The cumbersome laws discouraged investors, he wrote, creating "undesirable barriers to entry" and turning radio stations into "super-citizen[s], with obligations that go beyond providing goods and services that the public wants." Instead of relying on these "restrictive" policies, Fowler thought it would be best to have faith in the "broadcasters' ability to determine the wants of their audiences through the normal mechanisms of the marketplace." In a classic, by-the-book, free-market daydream, Fowler envisions a media landscape where "the public's interest, then, defines the public interest."[20]

And what did the public want? Sports, clearly. And more of it. In 1984, while the Supreme Court was paving the way for more college football to appear on television, the FCC was increasing the number of radio stations a single company could own. Changes to the guidelines on what kind of content could go out over the airwaves soon followed. And as this once heavily regulated industry became a capitalist free-for-all, aspiring media moguls began to make their moves. In 1986 Jeff Smulyan, the head of an Indiana-based company called Emmis Broadcasting, paid $53 million for three New York–based radio stations, adding them to the company's growing radio portfolio.[21] Included in the deal was an AM-based country music station, WHN 1050, which also held the broadcast rights for the Mets, the best baseball team in the city. One of those things made sense for a New York audience. The other didn't.

Smulyan and his team made the decision to jettison Dolly Parton and Willie Nelson and go all-in on sports. To lead the charge they tapped one of the only people in the country with experience in such an endeavor: John Chanin, the highly respected, free-spending executive who had been an integral part of the short-lived Enterprise experiment. Under Chanin's direction the station built out a completely redesigned programming schedule. Chanin's wife, meanwhile, provided the idea for the call letters: FAN. At 3 p.m. on July 1, 1987, WHN, New York's preeminent country music station, officially became WFAN, the country's first twenty-four-hours-a -day, seven-days-a-week sports radio station. While the first voice on Enterprise had been that of John Sterling, the first voice on WFAN was that of Sterling's future booth partner, Suzyn Waldman: "Good afternoon everybody and welcome to the first broadcast of WFAN all-sports 1050. You're sharing a part of radio history with us today."[22]

Taking a page from his time at Enterprise, Chanin targeted national names to fill WFAN's initial lineup. The early morning slot went to Greg Gumbel, who was born in New Orleans and grew up in Chicago. The mid-morning/afternoon window went to Jim Lampley, who was born in North Carolina and grew up in Florida. While both were paid handsomely (per Chanin's style), neither had any idea how to connect with the rabid New York fan base. Lampley wasn't even based in New York; because of a commitment to CBS, he was forced to broadcast the show from Los Angeles. The conversations in the first year ranged from college football to the Tour de France to Wimbledon—hardly the kind of material appropriate for a disgruntled Yankees fan from the Bronx. Ratings slumped. And as the months dragged on, it was clear Chanin's second attempt wasn't going much better than his first: the station lost an estimated $7 million in its first year and had to fire dozens of people.[23]

There were, however, some crucial differences between Enterprise and WFAN. For starters WFAN was a single station, not a network, allowing it to easily pivot when things went awry. Plus, Emmis was a diversified company, and its other divisions were doing well, providing the station with financial breathing room. Smulyan would say later that he never really considered pulling the plug on WFAN despite the rough first year; on the contrary, his management team was confident that the station was onto something big. In one interview an early WFAN executive recalls visiting the offices of Al Ries and Jack Trout, marketing gurus who popularized the concept of brand "positioning."[24] Their advice to WFAN was to go all-in on local. In other words, the station would never be all things to all sports fans. But it *could* be all New York things to New York sports fans. Howie Rose, future play-by-play man for the Mets, lifelong New Yorker, and part of the station's initial lineup with Gumbel and Lampley, had the same thought. During those early years Rose talked about how he would "refer to guys I grew up with in the schoolyard—maybe one or two guys would have heard it live and rang up another one and said, 'Hey, he was talking about you!' That kind of stuff has tentacles, you know? It reaches out to where people say, 'Hey, maybe he's going to talk about where I went to school, or at the very least that we had a rivalry with that school.'"[25]

Chanin was soon forced out, and a man named Mark Mason was brought in to reshape the station's lineup. In 1988 Emmis became the largest privately held radio group in the country when it spent $120 million to acquire five additional stations. As part of the deal Emmis became the owners of 660 AM, one of the most powerful radio signals in the United States and home of the New York Knicks, the New York Rangers, and Don Imus, host of one of the country's most popular morning shows. In October of that year WFAN slid down the dial from 1050 to 660, pairing a strong signal with an increasingly robust programming schedule.

Things were moving in the right direction. All that remained for WFAN to establish itself as the go-to station for New York sports fans was a headline-generating, nothing-on-the-air-sounds-like-it, afternoon-drive-time show. Pete Franklin, a well-known radio host from Cleveland, had been given the first crack to establish himself in this lucrative slot when WFAN launched in 1987. But his schtick, constantly berating listeners and calling them schmucks, didn't fly in New York, especially since he wasn't from the area. Within less than two years Franklin was gone, and the station was looking for a replacement.

Mike Francesa, a part-time host during the station's early years, knew just the man for the job: Mike Francesa. A native of Long Island and graduate of St. John's University, Francesa was to New York what Eddie Andelman was to Boston: a no-doubt-about-it local. But unlike Andelman, Francesa actually had media experience, having worked in production for both ESPN and CBS. Confident that his future lay in radio rather than television, Francesa parlayed some contacts at WFAN into the occasional fill-in and weekend hosting gig. Executives liked what they heard, and the frequency of the slots increased. When Franklin left the station in 1989, Francesa, who had (and still has) an ego as big as anyone in the sports media business, made it clear that he was ready to take control of the coveted afternoon timeslot.

Mark Mason had another idea. While Francesa was filling gaps in WFAN's lineup, another young New Yorker named Chris Russo was making a name for himself doing sports updates for Don Imus. Russo was Italian, like Francesa, and was from Long Island, like Francesa, but beyond that the two had little in common. Francesa was a die-hard Yankees guy; Russo liked the San Francisco Giants. While Francesa had cut his teeth in television, Russo had been around the radio block, taking low-paying gigs in both Orlando and Jacksonville before returning to New York. And while both could easily get worked up into a frenzy when they disagreed with a caller, their agitation was revealed in different ways. Francesa would get annoyed, almost disgusted, as if he couldn't believe someone could say something so dumb or misguided. Russo, meanwhile, would get physically excited, seemingly unable to control the torrent of words pouring out of his body. There would be yelling, so much yelling, to the point that it was fair to wonder if Chris Russo's normal speaking voice was simply a few decibels louder than a normal human being's. Mason saw all this and decided these two men needed to co-host a radio show: "Mike would be viewed as the more knowledgeable one, and Chris would be the uber-fan, the foil, the Everyman, the wacko."[26] When Howie Rose heard about the station's plan, his "very first reaction was, 'You got to be kidding!' And 10 seconds later I thought . . . It's fucking brilliant."[27]

It was indeed. The pairing of Mike and the Mad Dog (as Chris Russo would be anointed by *New York Daily News* media critic Bob Raissman), quickly became the highest rated radio program in its time slot for the coveted male 25–54 demographic. How? By complaining about the Knicks and their playoff woes. By arguing about the Hall of Fame credentials of Yankees players from the 1950s. And by taking calls from listeners and then telling those same listeners that they had no idea what they were talking about. One journalist wrote: "Imagine two guys in undershirts chugging Budweiser and ranting about anything to do with sports."[28] Another writer quipped: "They are the sound New York makes when it is talking to itself."[29]

Mike and the Mad Dog brought WFAN to the next level, making it a staple in the New York sports media world. Radio executives saw the money coming into the station—upwards of $70 million by the early 1990s—and began to breed copycat all-sports lineups, often scouring their areas for overlooked blue-collar talent. In 1992 executives at a newly christened AM station called "The Score" hired Mike North, owner of three local hot dog stands, to co-host a show—*Monsters of the Midday*—with retired NFL lineman Dan Jiggetts in Chicago. Rich "Da Coach" Gilgallon, meanwhile, got his first shot at radio when the general manager of a radio station discovered him working as a bartender and decided to hire him to do sports updates for a local country station. A few years later he was part of the initial lineup for Washington DC's first all-sports radio station, co-hosting a show called *Kiley and the Coach* with radio veteran Kevin Kiley. It was explained to one journalist as "radio for guys with hair on their backs."[30]

Soon stating an opinion about an industry where everybody could state an opinion became an industry unto itself. The old school print guys led the charge, ridiculing and dismissing their new competitors as no-talent hacks. Bob Ryan, longtime columnist at the *Boston Globe*, argued that sports talk radio "poisoned the atmosphere between the legitimate press and players. The athletes lump talk radio hosts, callers, and writers under a general umbrella of 'the media.' It creates a 'bigger wall.' There's no accountability. They don't have to face anyone. There's certainly no accountability for callers who disappear into the ozone."[31] Syndicated writer Bob Kravitz wrote that many of the radio personalities are "raving lunatics, their opinions transparent and contrived." What's worse, they often got in the way of *real* sports journalism: "The print guys will be gathered around an athlete and have him talking emotionally about his tortured childhood, close to tears and in the midst of some great catharsis, when some sap will approach, do exploratory nasal surgery with his boom mike and ask, 'Who's got more pressure: Dallas or Buffalo?'"[32]

Sports Illustrated columnist Rick Reilly, never one to shy away from an opinion, called sports talk "the Everybody Here in the Studio Is Cool and Everybody Else Is a Jerk school of broadcasting." To further his point he unleashed a memorable parade of quotes from sports legends such as CBS broadcaster Billy Packer, who called the industry "diarrhea of the mouth"; Penn State football coach Joe Paterno, who claimed that sports talk "has distorted all of the things that we should be getting out of sports"; and Kentucky basketball coach Rick Pitino, who described callers as "frustrated at home, can't get a date, don't do well at their jobs and are basically at the nadir of their lives."[33]

Still not everyone was waving a pitchfork. In 1996 Pamela Haag, author and self-described "feminist academic," explained her obsession with WFAN—and Mike and the Mad Dog specifically—in an article in *South Atlantic Quarterly*. While admitting that "it is undoubtedly pathetic to feel compelled to speak so seriously and redemptively about something like sports radio," she nonetheless goes on to do just that, arguing that the medium helps construct and maintain communities of people who would otherwise never know or care about one another. She opined that WFAN was "the airwave equivalent of the Department of Motor Vehicles—one of the last social melting pots where callers who abashedly confess to being physicians or lawyers when medical or legal expertise is solicited rub earlobes with those who are alienated from the economy altogether."[34] In a documentary released years after the show went off the air, Russo agreed with this sentiment, explaining that he and Francesa had a unique ability to unite a cross-section of New Yorkers: "The white-collar fan down on Wall Street loved to listen, and the blue-collar fan who was a cab driver loved to listen."[35] So while sports talk radio undoubtedly has its share of faults, Haag argued that the medium played a valuable role: "In an age when communication is expected to *do* something, sports talk demonstrates an older function of communication, that of concretizing social rather than economic communities."[36]

No doubt contributing to this sense of community was the interactive nature of sports talk radio. While most Americans knew who Howard Cosell was, they didn't have his phone number (nor did he have a 1–900 number). That wasn't the case for Mike and the Mad Dog, two guys from Long Island who were more than happy to take your calls and chat about the Mets or the Knicks or St. John's basketball. Sure, you might get ridiculed, maybe even get hung up on, but that was all part of the fun. And if you couldn't offer an appropriate take—say, if you couldn't adequately explain why John Starks shot so poorly in Game 7 of the 1994 NBA Finals—then what business did you have calling in the first place?

Those who did muster the courage to consistently call in, going toe-to-toe with Francesa and Russo, became quasi-celebrities in their own right. Longtime WFAN listeners are as familiar with Bruce in Bayside or Doris from Rego Park as they are with Mike and Dog. And then there was Joe from Saddle River (real name: Joe Benigno), who ended up calling the show so many times, and gaining the respect of multiple people inside the station, that he was offered a one-hour block to serve as host during WFAN's Listener Appreciation Day in 1994. Three other callers got the same opportunity: Eli from Westchester, Al in White Plains, and Vic in Corona. But Joe from Saddle River was the star that day, performing so admirably that he was given the chance to serve as an occasional, part-time host. Then, when the overnight window became available, WFAN producers decided that nobody was as well suited for the gig as Benigno. He was offered the role, quit his sales job, and ended up working for the station for twenty-five years.

Benigno's passage through the supposed fourth wall, his elevation from average Joe Sports Fan to salaried radio pundit, was perhaps the clearest example of how talk radio would change the sports media landscape. The renowned writer David Halberstam once suggested that sports talk radio "has almost deputized fans, giving them a voice, making teams quasi-public institutions."[37] But Benigno *was* deputized, not almost; he had been a run-of-the-mill food salesman who was abruptly handed a megaphone, one of the biggest in the country, and asked to share his thoughts on the state of New York sports. Suddenly what Benigno said mattered, maybe not to the extent that what Bob Ley or Pat Summerall said mattered, but those are impossibly high bars for someone who, before being offered the job, had been just a regular guy driving around New Jersey. And Joe from Saddle River achieved all that by doing what he'd always done: sharing his opinion; ranting and raving and screeching and sobbing; and caring—truly, deeply, passionately caring—about things like Jets quarterbacks and Mets relievers.

It was a sign of a new era, one where the fans could finally be heard, not just by their close friends and family but by a potentially much larger audience. There was only one catch: if you really wanted to make your mark, you had to stand out. Mike and the Mad Dog succeeded because, for one thing, they had a first-mover advantage and, for another, they seemed to actually care about what they were talking about. As one producer noted, "What Mike and Chris did was just talk sports. There was no phoniness to it. It wasn't like they were on stage. . . . It was two guys, really passionate about sports with really strong opinions about sports with great knowledge."[38] Benigno, with no radio experience at all, had used a similar playbook to get his own opportunity.

But there's a fine line between passion and theater, and as these hosts would come to understand, the latter is often disguised as the former. Francesa said it well: "Callers were different than listeners. Callers want to perform."[39] Not only that, callers *had* to perform; otherwise they'd be dismissed, laughed at, mocked for their unsophisticated, boring analysis. This performance mentality—and surely people like Benigno understood it as well as anyone—became a staple not only with callers, but also with the legions of sports talk hosts who arrived riding the coattails of Mike and the Mad Dog. In 1996 up-and-coming radio personality and soon-to-be syndication superstar Jim Rome explained his thought process as he tried to stand out against the legions of wannabes: "I've gotta have more balls. I've gotta ask the questions the other hosts won't ask. I need to have a take, and I can't suck."[40]

I need to have a take: it's as if Rome was introducing the next three decades of sports media.

A Whole New Ballgame　**13**

English Premier League's
Monday Night Football (1992)

Coming up with an idea for a new product is often the easy part. Promoting it, inserting the item or service into the avalanche of marketing messages that the public receives on a daily basis, that's where things can get tricky. And yet even with that caveat it's still rather shocking that the ninety-second ad announcing the 1992 launch of the English Premier League and its partnership with the network Sky Sports ever saw the light of day. The ad is both absurd and awesome, a tour de force of early 1990s nostalgia. Set to the song "Alive and Kicking" by the Scottish rock group Simple Minds, it begins in black and white, with a group of professional soccer players leaving a hotel, boarding a bus, and lining up to participate in what seems like a run-of-the-mill photo shoot. But then things go awry. First, the ad is interrupted by a shot of a woman bringing Swedish player Anders Limpar orange juice as he wakes up in bed. That's followed by a clip of English goalkeeper David Seaman playing soccer with his kids in his backyard before the video cuts to another player hovering over a sink, splashing water in his face. With the song building toward a crescendo, the commercial then takes the viewer inside a gym, where shirtless players are seen getting massages and lifting weights, before transitioning to the most bewildering part of all: a steady procession of shower scenes, highlighted by one memorable cut where towel-clad players guffaw as tough guy Vinnie Jones lifts a hairbrush to his face and pretends it's a mustache. The ad ends with a shot of players running through a tunnel before revealing the broadcaster's American-inspired slogan: "It's a whole new ball game."[1]

It was a strange (and sort of hilarious) beginning for an entity that would eventually become the most popular sports league in the world. It's also possible that the goofy tone was intentional, a deliberate breath of fresh air meant to signal a new beginning for an entity that desperately needed one. The 1980s had been a brutal decade for English soccer. Attendance had plummeted, partly due to an economic recession that had left many working-class fans unable to afford tickets. Poor attendance brought dwindling revenue, leaving owners unwilling and unable to upgrade dilapidated stadiums. Fans that did show up to the matches often misbehaved. Hooliganism ran rampant, with violent clashes between rival supporters an all-too-common occurrence. Fights that began in the streets often spilled into the stadium; fights that began in the stadium often spilled into the streets. For these individuals it was no longer enough to identify with a particular club. Instead it became fashionable to identify with a particular gang (or firm, as the gangs were known), which in turn supported a particular club.

With tottering grounds and festering violence a major disaster (or several) was all but inevitable. In March 1985, during a sixth-round FA Cup match, a battle between the supporters of Luton Town and Millwall led to dozens of injuries and a subsequent inquiry by Prime Minister Margaret Thatcher. A few weeks later a used cigarette ignited a pile of trash under the stands at Valley Parade stadium, the home of Bradford City, killing fifty-six and injuring hundreds more. And shortly after that, during the Liverpool-Juventus European Cup final at Heysel Stadium in Brussels, an aggressive charge by Liverpool fans across a barrier meant to separate the two groups of supporters led to a panic, the collapse of a concrete wall, and the deaths of thirty-nine people. Fourteen Liverpool fans ended up in jail on manslaughter charges, and English clubs were banned from European competitions for five years. (The match went on as scheduled, with Juventus winning 1–0.)

In a speech to the House of Commons after the Heysel disaster, Prime Minister Thatcher declared that "radical change is needed if football is to survive as a spectator sport and if English clubs are once more to be acceptable abroad."[2] Over the next few years Thatcher's government would advocate for increased surveillance, more policing, and a mandatory identification card for any fan who attended a live match. It was a classic law-and-order decree, designed to attack the problem from the top down rather than from the bottom up. The result was an increasingly militaristic game-day experience where fans were herded through gates, shoved into pens, and told to behave *or else*. Four years after Heysel a *New York Times* journalist compared British stadiums to the more family-friendly American environments: "Ringed by steel fences and mounted policemen in full riot gear . . . [they] look nothing like American-style bowls or stadiums, but more like ramshackle brick warehouses crowding up against the square of the playing fields."[3]

The last gasp for this version of English soccer came on April 15, 1989, the scheduled date for the FA Cup semifinal between Nottingham Forest and Liverpool. The match was sold out, with more than fifty-three thousand expected to make their way to a neutral site: Hillsborough Stadium, the home of Sheffield Wednesday. Crowd control was a priority. Liverpool fans were marshalled into one end of the stadium, where a handful of turnstiles led to four standing-room-only pens separated by high fences. Fifteen minutes before the scheduled kickoff security noticed that there were several thousand Liverpool supporters still congregating outside the turnstiles. Eight minutes before kickoff a decision was made to open an exit gate, causing a large group of fans—some with tickets, some without—to swarm into the two central pens. These late arrivals, eager to see kickoff, pushed forward, causing a barrier inside one of the pens to break and creating a powerful surge forward. Those in front of the pens were crushed, trapped under the weight of a panicked crowd. Fans who weren't incapacitated began searching for an escape route. Many climbed the fences surrounding the area, landing on the pitch even as play began. Five minutes into the match a referee noticed what was happening and blew his whistle. All in the stadium stopped what they were doing and turned their attention toward the worst tragedy in English sports history.

In the end ninety-six people died and nearly eight hundred were injured at Hillsborough. Two days after the disaster a government official, Lord Justice Peter Taylor, was tapped to lead an investigation into the incident. Taylor would release two documents: an interim report and a final report. The former focused on what had happened at Hillsborough and why, detailing a "number of factors" that had led to the pens' becoming "grossly overcrowded."[4] The final report, released months later, went further. In a scathing hundred-plus-page document Taylor admitted that "wider and deeper inquiry shows that overcrowding is only one feature amongst a number causing danger or marring football as a spectator sport. The picture revealed is of a general malaise or blight over the game due to a number of factors. Principally these are: old grounds, poor facilities, hooliganism, excessive drinking and poor leadership."[5]

In a detailed review of these factors Taylor didn't mince words. Many of the most popular grounds were old and disgusting, with fans expected to tolerate "lamentable" facilities. With bathrooms few and far between, "the practice of urinating against walls or even on the terraces has become endemic and is followed by men who would not behave that way elsewhere."[6] Meanwhile, because of the strict policies adopted to segregate fans of opposing clubs, "the ordinary law-abiding football supporter travelling away is caught up in a police operation reminiscent of a column of prisoners of war being marched and detained under guard."[7] Taylor ultimately wondered what those measures said about the national sport: "I know of no other sport or entertainment in a civilised country in which it is necessary to keep those attending from attacking each other."[8] In the end, "there is no panacea which will achieve total safety and cure all problems of behaviour and crowd control." However, "the years of patching up grounds, of having periodic disasters and narrowly avoiding many others by muddling through on a wing and a prayer must be over. A totally new approach across the whole field of football requires higher standards both in bricks and mortar and in human relationships."[9] In other words, Taylor was advocating for a whole new ball game.

The model, it seemed, was across the Atlantic. For years owners of some of the more prominent English clubs had taken notice of the similarly named but safer, glitzier, and more profitable "football" on display in the United States. David Dein, owner of the club Arsenal at the time, had commented on the differences: "Certainly, seeing an American football match, it was an entertainment. The color, the spectacle, the way it was promoted, the way it was televised. They made the most of the event."[10] And Dein no doubt saw the rewards of such an approach—namely, the *half billion dollars* a year the NFL was generating from television contracts alone. That kind of money would allow not only for the specific changes recommended by Taylor, such as eliminating standing-room-only areas and building seats, but also for the complete overhaul many claimed was sorely overdue.

And yet Dein's thought process bucked a long-standing tradition of keeping television out of professional soccer. As the journalists Joshua Robinson and Jonathan Clegg have explained, for much of English soccer history, "television wasn't merely an afterthought[;] it was considered a vile, pernicious influence on the game."[11] Many owners didn't *want* their games to air on television, believing that once fans got a taste of watching the game from their couches, nobody would ever buy a ticket again. No live league games were shown on English television for much of the 1960s and all of the 1970s. And by the time ESPN launched in the United States, providing the American sports fan with both a bounty of live events and twenty-four hours a day and seven days a week sports coverage, English soccer fans were still limited to either attending the games in person or catching highlights on the popular Saturday evening BBC program *Match of the Day*.

Things began to change in 1983. The BBC and ITV, the two main players in the English television market, agreed to pay £2.6 million annually for the right to air ten live games and highlights each season over a two-year period. Compared to what was happening in the United States, it was chump change. And because of the way English football was structured, the revenue had to be split between all ninety-two teams in the English Football League. But it was a start.

When the contract came up for renewal in 1985, the networks put together an annual offer of £4 million, a modest increase over the previous agreement. The clubs said no, citing a recently commissioned third-party analysis that valued the rights at closer to £12 million.[12] But the networks refused to budge, aware that if they raised their offer, they would essentially be bidding against themselves. This did not sit well with club owners, some of whom accused the networks of outright collusion. "BBC and ITV effectively were a cartel," said

Irving Scholar, the owner of Tottenham Hotspur at the time. "They were trying to depress the value of football on television."[13] And yet depress the value they did, all the way to zero, as there were no live games or highlights shown on television for the entire first half of the 1985–86 league season.

As the sport disappeared from television, the owners of the Big Five clubs—Arsenal, Everton, Liverpool, Manchester United, and Tottenham—considered their future. They felt weighed down by the structure of English football, an antiquated system where the most popular and successful teams were forced to share revenue with dozens of teams that drew few fans and little interest. In 1988, with television rights once again up for renewal, the clubs nearly broke off to form their own league but were eventually coaxed back into the old structure with a four-year, £44 million offer from ITV.

A year later came the Hillsborough disaster and the Taylor report. The requirements laid out by the government meant the clubs would be required to embark on an expensive reconfiguring of their grounds. That also meant reduced capacity, which in turn lowered the clubs' primary source of revenue: ticketing. This was a bad combination for nearly every owner. As one journalist wrote of English soccer at the time, "Even the glitziest of its clubs have more glamour than cash, with few managing to do much more than break even in a typical season."[14] If there was ever a time when the top clubs should and could break away to secure their own league in order to secure a bounty of untapped revenue, this was it.

On July 17, 1991, the Big Five and seventeen other clubs finally did the inevitable, signing a document that established the basic parameters by which a new, top-heavy league, called the FA Premier League, would function. The agreement allowed for this new league to negotiate its own broadcasting contracts. Whatever money came in would be shared through a new 50-25-25 system: 50 percent shared equally among all the clubs, 25 percent distributed based on the previous year's performance, and 25 percent based on number of television appearances. What kind of windfall would this new league bring? That was the big question. If the new Premier League had been forced to negotiate only with the entrenched stalwarts—the BBC and ITV—it's likely it would have still secured a contract that dwarfed the previous four-year deal signed in 1988. But add to the mix Rupert Murdoch, a man who has been called "probably the most inventive, the bravest deal-maker the world has ever known?"[15] Well, in that case, it seemed only the sky was the limit.

Murdoch was no stranger to money. His father, Keith, had been in the news business, both as a journalist and as the owner of Australia's largest newspaper chain. The company had grown to the point that Keith's family could live in what was described as the most expensive house in Melbourne.[16] When Keith passed away in 1952, a twenty-one-year-old Rupert returned from his studies in England to take control of the family business. He wasted little time in continuing his father's work, buying up newspapers and launching the country's first national daily, *The Australian*.

By the 1960s Murdoch had decided to expand his empire beyond Australia. In 1968 he bought the British tabloid *News of the World*. A year later he gained control of a "radical" and "independent" paper called *The Sun* and remade it into "a brash, unashamedly downmarket tabloid."[17] He followed a similar script in the United States by launching *Star* in 1974, seeing it as a competitor to the *National Enquirer*, and by acquiring the *New York Post* two years later. According to biographer Neil Chenoweth, Murdoch knew how to harness the potential of these tabloids and would subsequently "reap a huge financial benefit in doing what no one else would accept."[18] Scandal, gossip, and murder delivered big audiences. So Murdoch gravitated toward scandal, gossip, and murder.

There was one other topic that fit this formula: sports. In an interview with *Vanity Fair* in 1999 Murdoch said, "We've always known that sports had universal appeal. Right from the beginning, in Adelaide, we used sports to sell the papers. When I got to London with *The Sun*, we set out from day one to outsport *The Mirror*. We knew it was football, football, football. It had to be on the back page almost every day of the year."[19] And if football happened to collide with scandal, gossip, and murder? Pure gold. As hooliganism increased in England in the 1970s and 1980s, Murdoch and his tabloid brethren gleefully dove right into the morass, plastering sensational headlines—"ANIMALS!"—and shocking images of the dustups all over their newspapers. The amount of coverage allotted to hooliganism was so staggering that one

American professor commented that "Britain's daily tabloids have reported incidents of football fan misbehavior with such unabashed enthusiasm that the reader often wonders whether any other news occurred that day."[20]

In fact many suggested that the tabloids were partly responsible for stoking the fire, sensationalizing hooliganism to the point that young football fans looked up to those who became newspaper stars. One British sociologist wrote that continued coverage of hooliganism "creates a situation of confrontation, where more people than were originally involved in the deviant behaviour are drawn into it—forced to 'put up a good show' or increase the wager, up the odds. Next week's 'confrontation' will then be bigger, more staged, so will the coverage, so will the public outcry, the pressure for yet more control . . . and the press has a significant part to play in each twist of the cycle."[21] This how-low-can-you-go mentality led to passages such as the following, published in *The Mirror* in April 1977: "Another idea might be to put these people in hooligan compounds every Saturday afternoon. . . . They should be herded together preferably in a public place. That way they could be held up to ridicule and exposed for what they are—mindless morons with no respect for other people's property or wellbeing. We should make sure we treat them like animals—for their behaviour proves that's what they are."[22]

It took several years, however, for coverage of hooliganism to reach its absolute nadir, a level from which it was impossible to descend further. And it was a Murdoch-owned paper (of course) that would stoop the lowest. Four days after the Hillsborough disaster *The Sun* published an article claiming to have new details about the worst day in English soccer history. Under the boldfaced headline "The Truth" (one Murdoch employee actually remembers the media mogul banning the use of the word "reportedly"), the paper claimed that as bodies piled up inside the grounds, Liverpool supporters ran amok, sifting through the pockets of the deceased and urinating on police officers. "The fans were just acting like animals," one police officer was quoted as saying. "My men faced a double hell—the disaster and the fury of the fans who attacked us."[23] And yet none of it was true. In fact the editors involved with the article would later claim that culpable police officers fed *The Sun* these details in order to shift the narrative away from their own incompetence. Still the damage had been done.

Murdoch wasn't finished. Never afraid to fan the flames of controversy while simultaneously selling fire extinguishers, Murdoch and his minions also used the Hillsborough disaster to forcefully advocate for substantial change. An editorial published the day after the disaster in the *Sunday Times*, Murdoch's more upmarket paper, made no mention of "The Truth" but instead called for a complete overhaul of English soccer: "Despite disaster after disaster, nothing seems to shake the complacency and incompetence of those who run the country's most popular spectator sport. Soccer stadiums, and their administration, remain a disgrace. They are filthy, dangerous places that spectators only put up with because of their enthusiasm for what happens on the pitch."[24] These stadiums, the editorial would go on to say, needed to be upgraded. No more excuses. Sure, it would be expensive, but if that's the price of saving lives, then so be it.

For readers of *The Sun*, aghast at the appalling behavior of English soccer fans, and readers of the *Sunday Times*, who nodded along at the suggestion that their national sport could benefit from a complete overhaul, it was clear that what the country needed most of all was somebody willing to come in and shake up the established order—an innovator, a dealmaker, somebody willing to embark on an entirely new path. And, oh hey, look at that! If it isn't Rupert Murdoch himself riding into town to save the day. How convenient!

In reality Murdoch needed a bailout as much as anyone. In February 1989, just two months before the Hillsborough disaster, Murdoch had launched a satellite television service named Sky, one of the first true competitors to the BBC and ITV. But television proved trickier than print. Even after he had merged with his lone rival the following year (after which the company was called BSkyB), Murdoch's fledgling business continued to bleed money, unable to generate the kind of subscriber growth it needed to reach a break-even point.

Murdoch saw live sports as the answer. He knew that if he could win the television rights for the new Premier League, millions of English soccer fans would be forced to ante up for his new satellite service. ITV, however, wasn't willing to concede the rights to English soccer quite yet. After some spirited back and forth ITV submitted an offer of £262 million over five years, about five times more than what it had paid per year in 1988. And yet Murdoch came back with a bold counteroffer: £304 million over five years. Not only that, but BSkyB also vowed to give the new Premier League an NFL-style makeover: more pregames, more highlights, more analysis, more, more, more. The two offers were put to a vote. Murdoch and BSkyB won 14–6 (with two abstentions), sending a jolt through the British sports media landscape. As the *Wall Street Journal* reported a few days after Sky secured the rights, "In addition to their traditional colored scarves and raucous voices, most U.K. soccer fans soon will need an extra accessory to cheer on their favorite teams—a satellite dish."[25]

The immediate fallout was harsh. One journalist wrote: "By selling its soul to Rupert Murdoch's Sky cable network, with the BBC getting a sop of a weekend highlights package, this country's senior soccer executives have disenfranchised millions of fans."[26] *The Guardian* piled on as well: "The biggest losers are the fans. Symbolically, the announcement of the TV deal coincided with the demolition of the North Bank at Highbury [a section of stands at Arsenal's old stadium]. A lot of people who want to watch matches regularly in future are going to have to buy a bond or a dish."[27]

No component of this partnership was more emblematic of the seismic changes Murdoch would bring to English soccer than the unveiling of the American-inspired *Monday Night Football*. To many ticket holders, most of whom were used to attending their clubs' matches (and the local pubs) on Saturdays or Sundays, *Monday Night Football* was an unwanted inconvenience. Some clubs were forced to placate these fans by offering ticket refunds if their matches were moved to Mondays. "We will continue to make every effort to minimise the number of occasions we are involved on Monday evenings," Everton's chief executive declared.[28] Queens Park Rangers, meanwhile, had a different gripe. Annoyed that they were being asked to play three times in six days to accommodate the new television calendar, the team told Sky Sports that their players wouldn't be participating in postgame interviews. This both confused and angered David Hill, the head of sport at Sky, who commented on the club's apparent hypocrisy: "I can't believe a group of professional adults could act this way. I find it remarkable. . . . They have said nothing about not taking the television money. They are taking the money but not talking to us."[29]

The first *Monday Night Football* to air on Sky Sports was a match between Queens Park Rangers (QPR) and Manchester City on August 17, 1992. It was a decent matchup: City was coming off a season in which it had finished fifth in the old setup while QPR had come in eleventh. Of course the clubs' previous year's records hardly mattered. This was the dawn of a new era; the first weekend of the Premier League; and the beginning of a sparkling new, American-born, Arledge-inspired tradition. As Robinson and Clegg have pointed out, "The model for *Monday Night Football* was explicitly and shamelessly the NFL. The boxy computer animations with giant team crests, the electric-guitar power riffs . . ."[30]

And, of course, the money. The first graphic ever shown on a Premier League *Monday Night Football* telecast was a Ford logo. An introduction of the teams came next, quickly followed by a graphic for another advertiser: Foster's beer. "Mondays are changing," announced Richard Keys, as the camera focused in on the cheerleaders performing at midfield. "No longer that start of the week depression, we're into a whole new ballgame on Sky Sports—Mondays are now officially part of the weekend. That means a few smiles, some family fun—and these are the Sky Strikers about which you've heard so much."[31]

As the pregame wound down, Keys could barely hold back his laughter. At the end of one elaborate number involving dozens of dancers, fireworks, and a giant Sky Sports banner, Keys turned away from the performance, chuckled, and said to the audience, "Well that seemed to go down very well, thousands of dancers, balloons all over the place, fifteen Sky Strikers. Monday nights are going to be special." He then turned his attention back to the field: "We're expecting some parachuters very shortly, we need a match ball. . . . It's being delivered I think in a way that's never previously been delivered to a football match . . . from the skies." He then laughed again, turned back to the teleprompter, composed himself, and asked analyst Chris Waddle, "But the game is about entertainment, isn't it?" To which Waddle replied, "The public pay a lot of money to watch football and I think what service you get now is entertainment not just for the football but before the match as well."[32] And somewhere Rupert Murdoch smiled.

Some of the players didn't know what to make of it all. Paul Lake, a midfielder for Manchester City, remembers walking out of the locker room and seeing "a circus of reporters, cameramen, musicians, skydivers and dancing girls. . . . I felt like a stranger in my own backyard. It was as if the traditions of Maine Road, and football in general, were quite literally being trampled on."[33] But that was kind of the point, wasn't it? The final Taylor Report had suggested that the very foundation of English soccer had to be demolished and rebuilt from the ground up. If that meant that some of the traditions were going to be lost in the rubble, then so be it; anything to prevent another disaster such as those of Heysel or Hillsborough.

The game itself, according to Lake, was "something of a damp squib" and ended in a 1–1 draw.[34] Of more immediate importance, however, was what the average Premier League fan thought of the shiny graphics and scantily clad women. According to a survey conducted by *The Guardian* during the first few months of the season, opinions were mixed. Many fans were in favor of the enhanced technical production such as the new camera angles and a permanent time/score graphic. Other changes weren't so popular. Some thought the addition of cheerleaders and fireworks reeked of "desperation." They were "dismissed as 'razzmatazz' and 'Americanisation,' another example of the old game appearing ridiculous and undignified in its attempts to flaunt itself for the TV cameras." Respondents also raised concern that the sport "seems intent on destroying the sense of community and camaraderie which supporters feel is at the root of their devotion to the game."[35] While the formation of the Premier League and its subsequent partnership with Rupert Murdoch was seen as "an inevitable consequence of a 'money at all costs' approach," that does not exclude the culpability of both the "football authorities and the BBC," the latter of which "is seen as having a public-service responsibility to show the national game comprehensively."[36]

Of course Murdoch didn't care about any of this. He was an unabashed businessman, a free market champion who chuckled at the mere thought of soccer being a "public good." His goal was, and always would be, to grow his business and to make money. If sports could help him achieve those goals, then sports it was. And the Premier League was just the beginning. In a 1995 *New Yorker* article a friend explained that Murdoch's overarching strategy came from an understanding of "the nexus between programming and platform," the symbiotic relationship between the technology by which the content is delivered to the consumer and the content itself.[37] From a sports perspective that meant controlling not only the satellite or cable systems that carried the networks (such as BskyB), the networks themselves (like Sky Sports), or the broadcasting rights to air games on those networks, but also *all* of these things *and* the actual teams that played the games. Only then would one achieve the capitalistic pinnacle: true vertical integration.

Beginning with the Premier League/Sky deal, Murdoch would embark on a sports spending spree. In 1993, in a deal that shook up the American sports media landscape, he spent $1.58 billion for the rights to broadcast the NFL on his growing Fox network (more on that deal below). In 1995 Fox secured a five-year package of NHL rights for $155 million (more on that also below). Murdoch also bought up a handful of regional sports networks, leading to a loosely coordinated patchwork of Fox Sports affiliates spread around the United States. And, finally, he set his sights on the teams themselves. In 1997, after watching his archrival Disney take control of the Los Angeles Angels, he agreed to buy California's more popular (and more expensive) baseball team, the Los Angeles Dodgers, for $350 million. A year later, in 1998, fearful that the biggest Premier League teams would perhaps begin to negotiate their own individual broadcasting rights, Rupert Murdoch tried to buy one of the most popular clubs in the world: Manchester United. The deal was ultimately blocked by the United Kingdom's Monopolies and Mergers Commission, which ruled that the deal would give Rupert Murdoch's company too much power over the symbiotic relationship between the programming and the platform. Murdoch must have thought: "Yes. That's the point."

Although Murdoch lost that deal, he had plenty to keep himself busy. This land grab in the mid-1990s, in fact, was part of a bigger plan to stay relevant and remain profitable within the segments of the media industry he understood best: newspapers and television. Murdoch knew that the media landscape was changing. The internet was coming, and it had the potential to shake up everything from news and sports to music and movies. Murdoch wasn't blind to this reality; he just couldn't generate the enthusiasm needed to crack the code of yet another medium. One of his biographers once wrote that "Murdoch can almost single-handedly take apart and re-assemble a complex printing press, but his digital-technology acumen and interest is practically zero."[38] So it would be left to others to figure out how to best harness this thing called the internet, how to get content to the right groups of people, and how to make money doing so. It wasn't going to be easy.

Sports.com

14

ESPN vs. SportsLine (1994)

In the uncluttered early days of the internet it was common to choose a domain name that directly corresponded to the particular product or service being offered. At the time that made sense. Search engines were in their infancy, and nobody really knew how the internet worked. If somebody was looking for, say, lamps, it's possible that this person's first move would be to open up Netscape Navigator, one of the world's first internet browsers, and type "www.lamps.com." The original digital entrepreneurs sought to capitalize on this behavior. In 1998 the owner of Alan's Shoes, a trio of footwear stores in Tucson, Arizona, shrewdly set up a digital extension at Shoes.com. News.com was quickly claimed by the savvy folks at the tech-focused publisher CNET (who still uses it today to direct people to its main website). The world's biggest companies got involved too. Procter & Gamble, for one, cast its net wide, snatching up not only brand-specific domains such as Folgers.com and Downy.com, but also badbreath.com, cavities.com, cakemix.com, and cookingoil.com.[1] For some of the earliest movers the domain name game also proved to be quite lucrative. In the early 1990s, back when few people were even thinking about the internet, Charles Stack, owner of Books Stacks Unlimited, secured both Books .com, which he used to launch a company that would be sold for over $4 million, and Movies.com, which he eventually flipped to Disney.[2]

All of this leads to the strange story of Sports.com, a long-forgotten domain name seemingly tailor made for the pre-Google era. Launched in 1999 and based out of London, the site, according to its "About Us" page, was "committed to being recognized as the leading site for internet sports around the world." Early versions of the site featured front-page news about the NFL, NBA, and NCAA basketball. But the focus soon shifted to a distinct non–U.S. strategy, with information and links to European soccer, rugby, and international cricket. At the time a spokesperson for the company explained that the site hoped to become a catch-all for all kinds of fans, with extensions such as football.sports.com and France.sports.com, and with exclusive content agreements with high-profile partners like Wimbledon, St. Andrews Links, and Manchester United. Those types of agreements led to interest from financial titans such as Goldman Sachs and George Soros. Popular American athletes such as Tiger Woods, Shaquille O'Neal, and Michael Jordan chipped in with some cash as well. By the end of the decade Sports.com had attracted about $50 million in venture capital, and there was talk of taking the company public.[3]

Of course there was. In 1999 a record number of American companies made themselves available for public investment. Most of the hype was driven by internet-based firms, many of them employing a similar model: find a cool domain name, create a website, scrape together something that resembles a business plan, pitch it to investors, go public, cash in. Whether or not the business was profitable or even could be profitable was largely irrelevant. One analysis in 1999 looked at two hundred public internet companies and found a collective valuation of $450 billion and a cumulative net annual *loss* of $6.2 billion.[4] This, of course, was the retroactively named dot-com bubble, the irrational rush to become a part of the next big thing and the culmination of a frenzy that had begun over a decade earlier when the average American was first introduced to the concept of going "online." Unfortunately Sports.com never actually made it to the point where it could cash in, and by the end of 2002 the original version of Sports.com, the one that aimed to be the "leading site for internet sports around the world," no longer existed.

To understand why Sports.com faded away, it's necessary to go back to the early 1990s, a time when the only way for the average consumer to get online was through something called an online service provider. These services were the internet before the internet, software that allowed consumers to use the modems on their home computers to access an ever-evolving cache of curated content. One of the earliest players in this space was Prodigy, the brainchild of two entrenched corporate behemoths: IBM and Sears. Designed primarily as an advertising medium for niche interests, Prodigy was kind of like a magazine. Or even better, a magazine stand, one that charged a flat price for access and that stood apart from its competition by providing a graphics-based, user-friendly interface.

Sports were big for Prodigy. One ad in 1991, launched under Prodigy's "You gotta get this thing!" advertising blitz, included a man telling his companion, "You can even get the scores before the paper does!"[5] In 1993 executives announced plans for Prodigy to become a "multiple platform, multimedia system in which subscribers [would] hook cable lines to their PC's." In just a few short years, they promised, ESPN viewers "will be able to click a button and have a baseball game picture reduced to a quarter of the screen while scores of other games, batting averages or other sports information appear on the rest of the screen."[6] With an early head start and mountains of capital at its disposal, the service seemed destined for greatness. Said one Sears executive: "The issue really isn't success or failure.... We're not going to fail. It's really a question of how big the success is going to be."[7]

He was wrong; Prodigy failed. The company was soon surpassed by the growing might and marketing acumen of a new online service provider, America Online, and the increased ubiquity of a tool that would transform the entire media industry: the internet browser. The browser was the great equalizer in the battle for online relevance. It opened up the World Wide Web for both creators, who could now establish their own websites, and users, who could now browse sites and choose which best met their needs. And while Prodigy provided consumers with a well-curated, regularly scheduled supply of content, it was hardly enough for the die-hard sports fan, who saw the possibility of what the internet could offer—unlimited and instantaneous information—and immediately demanded more.

One of those fans was a Florida-based man named Michael Levy. A graduate of Georgia Tech and a devoted fan of the Miami Dolphins,

Levy was not your typical fresh-out-of-college digital entrepreneur. He was the founder of a company called SportsTech International, which delivered video editing equipment to teams such as Notre Dame, Penn State, and the Dallas Cowboys, and a former CEO of Lexicon Corporation, a pioneer in handheld electronic language translators. The beginning of Levy's next venture, or so the story goes, began with the 1994 Orange Bowl, a classic matchup that saw Heisman trophy-winning quarterback (and future New York Knicks point guard) Charlie Ward lead Florida State to a thrilling 18–16 victory over a Tommie Frazier–led Nebraska team. After watching the game, Levy remembers going online to read about what he had just seen. Disappointed with the "skimpy" recaps provided by Prodigy and America Online, Levy decided, perhaps right then and there, that what he and the world really needed was an in-depth, information-heavy sports website.[8] So he decided to create one, calling it SportsLine USA.

Drumming up support for a website in 1994 was much harder than it would be five years later, but Levy's previous success had left him well connected. Tapping into that network, he scored a meeting with Jimmy Walsh, agent for retired New York Jets quarterback Joe Namath. Intrigued by Levy's pitch for an equity stake in this groundbreaking sports website, Namath agreed to become SportsLine's first spokesperson. With Broadway Joe on board Levy was then able to get the attention of some big-time investors. His biggest catch was Kleiner Perkins Caufield & Beyers, the almost mythical venture capital firm, which agreed to sink over $5 million into the idea. Other notable sports figures would soon join SportsLine's roster, including Mike Schmidt, Hall of Fame third baseman for the Philadelphia Phillies, and Bob Costas, one of the country's most popular sportscasters. In August 1995 Levy, Namath, Schmidt, and Costas were all present at the Waldorf Astoria in New York when SportsLine officially announced its launch. Said Levy during the ceremony: "Our research showed that no comprehensive online service exists to focus completely on the interest of avid sports fans to the extent we plan to.... We will offer everything a sports fan could ever want."[9]

The path to success would not be easy. ESPN was still the most powerful brand in American sports media, and the company had no desire to relinquish its crown to some flashy Florida-based upstart.

In 1994, as Levy began rallying support for his new site, ESPN was already dipping its toes into the online water, agreeing to a one-year deal with Prodigy. In exchange for $10 million in advertising and a small cut of the revenue, the deal would allow the online service to offer a stripped down ESPN-branded sports section to its customers.[10] At the time Prodigy was doing everything it could to beat back its biggest rival: America Online. Partnering with a brand like ESPN, even if it cost millions, made sense from a competitive perspective. But for ESPN this agreement was nothing more than a brief experiment, a way to buy time before deciding how to proceed in this exciting new world.

When the deal ended, ESPN determined that the best way forward was to launch its own website. Around the same time a technology company named Starwave, led by Microsoft co-founder Paul Allen, was actively looking to collaborate with prominent media partners. Starwave's first sports-related meeting, with the Time Inc.–owned *Sports Illustrated*, didn't go so well. Executives at the magazine were cool to the pitch, leery of internet-based publishing. "They just didn't want to disrupt their existing business model," said the Starwave executive who attended the meeting. Subsequent talks with ESPN were far more productive. Both sides saw the proposed model as mutually beneficial: ESPN would provide the content, and Starwave would provide the technological know-how. "In 10 minutes, they just got it. They understood completely what we wanted to do," said the same Starwave executive after speaking with ESPN.[11]

The two companies soon hashed out an agreement to develop a new site called ESPNet SportsZone. (The name was simplified to just ESPN after a few years.) It went live on April 1, 1995. Upon launch a Starwave executive spoke to the perceived democratic nature of the internet: "In some ways, the Web is the ultimate level playing field. People can come in and judge the content."[12] Of course that wasn't really true. ESPN, with its ability to promote the website to millions of viewers and listeners through its cable networks and radio stations, had a massive advantage. It was the established stalwart, the soon to be Disney-owned eight-hundred-pound gorilla, and if SportsLine ever wanted to compete in this new online space, it had to forge its own unique path.

Levy and his team decided that the athlete was the answer. Building off the momentum it had created through partnerships with Joe Namath and Mike Schmidt, SportsLine began to position itself as the go-to destination for athletes interested in boosting their online presence. Schmidt was an innovator here, using his early relationship with the website to experiment with new forms of fan engagement. In the summer of 1995 Schmidt asked SportsLine users to offer suggestions as to what he should say during his upcoming Hall of Fame induction speech. He ended up receiving 432 emails over the course of a week and a half. One entry suggested that he thank Phillies fans "for always getting on [his] case. They made [him] mad and brought the best out in [him]." Another proposed using the opportunity to announce that he was going to "step into the ring with Mike Tyson for $45 million." The winning entry was a bit more germane: "On this day of honor, you should remind the children out there that through hard work and dedication they, too, may live their dream." The entry came not from a Phillies fan but from a Colorado-based woman who admitted to stumbling upon the contest while randomly browsing the internet. "I'm not real positive of who he is exactly," she said of Mike Schmidt after being chosen as the winner.[13]

Regardless, it was clear that people were excited about connecting with athletes through this new medium. In August 1995 SportsLine announced an official partnership with the largest sports marketing agency in the world, IMG. The agreement provided the website with access to athletes and broadcasters such as John Madden, Wayne Gretzky, and Andre Agassi. In June 1996 SportsLine announced an exclusive relationship with NBA superstar and soon-to-be Olympic gold medal winner Shaquille O'Neal to create Shaq World, "a fully interactive, multimedia universe devoted to the superstar's diverse talents."[14] And in 1997, in the biggest coup of all, the company signed Michael Jordan, the most popular athlete on the planet, to an exclusive ten-year, $10 million agreement.[15] The deal provided Jordan with his very own website, where he would interact with fans, promote his charity work, and, of course, sell merchandise. The earliest iteration of the site included a section devoted to Jordan's record-breaking statistics, links to every song from the *Space Jam* soundtrack, and an interactive forum filled with Michael Jordan's biggest fans. A typical post went like this:

> I am 8 years old. My Mom had to lie for me to get to this web site. Please can I write to you? My mom says that I do no [sic] write well. and writing to you would be good for me as well as helpful. . . . She's typing this because She can type as fast as I can talk. . . . I have ALL your posters. . . . And I even have a bulls [sic] basketball uniform. . . .
>
> thanks
> Nate[16]

As all these deals were announced, SportsLine had to navigate the vagaries of the domain name game. Shaquille O'Neal, who was on his way to the Los Angeles Lakers with a lucrative seven-year deal, had already secured Shaq.com before making a deal with SportsLine. So that one was easy. When the company signed Tiger Woods a few years later, the decision was similarly stress free: TigerWoods.com. But when SportsLine signed Michael Jordan, most of the obvious choices—MichaelJordan.com, MJ.com, Jordan.com—were already taken.[17] Unable to come to an agreement with the owners of those domains, SportsLine ended up going with jordan.sportsline.com, an imperfect solution. Decades later the address that probably made the most sense, MichaelJordan.com, remains in the hands of a small New Jersey-based computer company and provides (for unknown reasons) live feeds of various neighborhoods and marinas around the New Jersey/Philadelphia area.

But Levy knew that merely focusing on the athlete wasn't enough. Even if it provided desirable content, people needed to know the website existed before it could compete with ESPN. In 1997 SportsLine reached an agreement with CBS whereby the broadcast network would provide tens of millions of dollars in promotion and advertising in exchange for a 22 percent stake in the company. Said Levy at the time: "We felt the only way we could compete with ESPN was to have a television partner."[18] The deal came with both a name change—SportsLine became

CBS SportsLine—and millions of eyeballs, as the network could now plaster the CBS SportsLine address across its broadcasts of NFL games, the NCAA basketball tournament, the Daytona 500, and more. While the collaboration reportedly doubled the number of SportsLine visitors, the site still faced an uphill battle for internet sports supremacy. ESPN, for its part, wasn't going anywhere. On the contrary, it seemed to enjoy the battle. A year after the deal was finalized, one ESPN executive even quipped, "When they see ESPN, these guys know we're about sports. When they see CBS, they're asking, 'What are we seeing here, *Murphy Brown* or *60 Minutes*?'"[19]

The battle between CBS SportsLine and ESPN became so competitive that SportsLine began rewarding people for just showing up. In 1999 Levy announced the next iteration of its "SportsLine Rewards" program, in which users could earn points by checking scores, reading news, and playing trivia games. True to the SportsLine model, the potential benefits were player-focused: lunch with former NFL QB Ron Jaworski, the chance to win Michael Jordan's car, and a tailgate party with former NFL running back Tony Dorsett in which Dorsett would "show up at your place on a Sunday afternoon to barbecue on your new grill."[20]

In some ways this was no different from a run-of-the-mill corporate loyalty program, similar to what a hotel or airline might create. But the press release for the initiative indicated that the management team at SportsLine was perhaps laying the foundation for something bigger: "Beyond encouraging consumer loyalty, SportsLine USA's 'SportsLine Rewards' and 'SportsLine Rewards Plus' programs were designed to develop the broadest and deepest database of sports fans anywhere, and to leverage the database to enhance all aspects of SportsLine's revenue model."[21] This model—capturing information about users and using that information to boost revenue—is exactly what companies like Google, Amazon, and Facebook would install to great success over the next few decades. In fact creating the infrastructure to track and subsequently exploit online user behavior would arguably do as much to shape the trajectory of the media business as any idea or concept in history. But to effectively harness this data-heavy strategy, a company needed scale. In other words, SportsLine had to become bigger.

It's at this point that Sports.com once again enters the picture.

How or when the team at SportsLine got its hands on this potentially valuable domain name is unclear. But in 1999 the company rallied its partners in the United States—IMG, Michael Jordan, Shaq—to create a European subsidiary and launch its first venture outside the United States: www.sports.com. By creating a website that prioritized partnerships with entities like Manchester United and Wimbledon, the management team at Sports.com was dutifully following the corporate blueprint laid out by SportsLine over the previous four years. This global expansion continued a year later, when SportsLine joined forces with a company called Asiacontent.com to launch sg.sports.com, an English-language website dedicated to bringing premium sports news and information to Singapore. It was the beginning of what the two companies hoped would be a long, fruitful, and multi-regional relationship. Said the Asiacontent.com CEO: "Whether it's cricket in India, table tennis in China or Manchester United anywhere, Asian audiences are passionate about sport, and together with SportsLine.com and Sports.com, we hope to bring them world class online coverage."[22]

Unfortunately the model being emulated with these international ventures was not a lucrative one, at least from a corporate perspective. According to one financial analyst, SportsLine was "running through cash like a hot knife through butter."[23] Its annual reports to shareholders bore this out.[24] In 2000 the company posted a net loss of $106 million. Over the next two years it lost $61 million and $48 million respectively. Sports.com as a standalone venture didn't do much better, losing $6 million in 1999, $28 million in 2000, and $18 million in 2001.[25] The SportsLine model, predicated on forming relationships with athletes and teams and celebrated so often in various press releases and news articles, was not exactly leading these websites toward profitability. Quite the opposite in fact.

But maybe chasing profitability wasn't the primary objective here. In the swashbuckling days of the late 1990s' internet frenzy a compelling press release was just as valuable (if not more so) to a management team than a well-vetted, long-term business plan. In the first six months of 1997 SportsLine reported a net loss of $14.5 million. Despite that loss and perhaps taking its cue from other cash-hemorrhaging internet startups, the company ploughed ahead with its IPO, going public in November and pricing its stock at $8 per share. Two years later, with its annual net loss reaching $17 million, the stock price hit a high of $63.25, a potential return of nearly 700 percent to anybody lucky enough to have gotten in on the ground floor.[26] Why the increase? For one thing, this was the irrational heyday of the late 1990s dot-com bubble, when anybody with a dollar to spare was hoping to strike it rich with the next paradigm-shifting company. And for another thing, what sports fan wouldn't want to invest in a media company boasting a roster of Michael Jordan, Tiger Woods, and Wayne Gretzky? It's possible, then, that the SportsLine team was simply trying to repeat this success with ventures such as Sports.com, to double- or triple-dip in the lucrative IPO game and to strike it big outside the United States the same way it had been able to find success within it.

Eventually the bubble burst. Investors, no longer seduced by a medium that proved far trickier to monetize than initially thought, ran away as fast as they could. In 2002 SportsLine's stock price sank to under a dollar per share. Rapid global expansion—or any expansion really—no longer made sense. In May the company announced in a financial report that Sports.com had essentially gone bankrupt. As part of the process the domain name Sports.com was sold to "an unrelated third party," a sale reported as "not material" to the company's financial standing. Translation: it didn't get a lot for it.[27] Two years later, in 2004, CBS finally did the inevitable, taking full control of SportsLine.com for a fraction of its original stock price.

As we look back, the saga of SportsLine and Sports.com tells us a lot about what the emergence of the internet would mean for the larger sports media landscape. First, it made clear that competition for the attention of sports fans was about to increase more in the coming years than it had cumulatively in the previous century. Until the internet came around, establishing a new distribution platform had been both logistically and financially cumbersome. To create a new newspaper or magazine you needed a printing press. To create a cable network you needed cameras and a satellite (and lots of other stuff). But to create a website in the late 1990s all you needed was a computer. Suddenly well-funded upstarts like SportsLine or domain-driven ideas like Sports.com were competing not only with industry stalwarts like ESPN and *Sports Illustrated*, but also with NFL message board commentators, college football bloggers, and amateur fantasy baseball podcasters, many of whom created their platforms more as a hobby than as a profit-oriented business.

This leads to the second lesson: all this increased competition would make it that much harder to make money. In 1996 a journalist at *Fortune* magazine questioned the online strategy being pursued by many legacy media companies: "In a rush to do business on the Internet, many media companies have left common sense behind. TV networks and publishers are spending millions of dollars to give away content they ordinarily sell. Few have more than a vague hope of getting a return on their investment. All of which raises a question: Can't anybody here play this game?"[28] He had a point, but what was the alternative? If you were stubborn enough to charge for content in the mid- to late nineties, internet users were simply going to go elsewhere for similar information. And with a rush of money coming in from investors, the focus was far more about building a user base than it was about creating a sound and sustainable business model. Think about this: Levy and the team at SportsLine had a coveted first-mover advantage, the financial backing of the most prestigious and sought-after venture capital firm in the United States, the promotional weight of three of the most popular athletes in the world, and a collaboration with one of the country's original broadcast networks, and it *still* couldn't make money on the internet. Not a good sign.

In that same *Fortune* article mentioned above a representative from USA *Today* talked about how "the Web is really moving toward a broadcast model," to which the author wonders, "But broadcasts need mass audiences to flourish. . . . Can ESPNET SportsZone compete with *Seinfeld* and *Monday Night Football*?"[29] Of course it couldn't—mostly because it would never have to. Instead the internet would come to resemble almost the complete opposite of the broadcast model: a hyper-personalized stream of instantaneous and never-ending information. And the fact that these analysts were even comparing the internet to the traditional broadcast model suggests a fundamental misunderstanding of what kind of medium the internet would become and a severe miscalculation of the changes it would unleash upon the entire media industry.

Last but not least, the SportsLine origin story and its short-lived but intriguing Sports.com side anecdote provided evidence that a clever domain name would rarely be enough to succeed within the ultra-competitive online landscape. Instead the "brand" and its ever-present marketing might would continue to reign supreme. ESPN entered the digital space early *and* had a reputation as the premier sports media brand in the country. The latter proved equally as important as the former, if not more so. In fact when Levy negotiated the deal with CBS to rebrand the site, he admitted as much. As the internet grew through the late 1990s and early 2000s, unique sites and personalities and destinations would continue to emerge, differentiating their brands in myriad ways. Some played off the distinctive voice of a single personality. Others were hyper-targeted to niche interest groups. And some positioned themselves as anti-establishment, edgy alternatives to the corporate stodginess of ESPN or *Sports Illustrated*. But despite the grand ambitions of many of these sites, few if any tried to be all things to all people. In some ways Sports.com represents the very antithesis of the internet, an attempted catch-all site designed for a medium that allows for an almost infinite level of personalization. Viewed this way, Sports.com never really had a chance.

Boom!   **15**

Fantasy Sports, Video Games,
and the NFL's *Yellow Line (1998)*

On October 28, 1992, President George H. W. Bush signed the Professional and Amateur Sports Protection Act (PASPA), prohibiting sports betting in the United States except in the four states where it was already legal. The law had been championed by former-professional-basketball-player-turned-U.S.-senator Bill Bradley, who believed that increased gambling would "turn athletes into roulette chips."[1] For the most part the American public was on his side. A national poll conducted at the time found that nearly three in four Americans thought more sports gambling would lead to fixed games. And over 60 percent of respondents agreed that "the integrity of sports would be severely damaged if we allowed legalized gambling on sports."[2]

Bradley also had broad support from his fellow politicians, including the staunch commitment of Jon Kyl, a congressman from Arizona. Kyl was, at least according to one supporter, as "committed, as devoted, to right-wing principles as any man alive."[3] These principles meant reduced taxes, strong borders, family values, and absolutely no gambling whatsoever. This conservative agenda played well with Kyl's constituents, who elected him to the U.S. Senate a few years after PASPA—commonly referred to as the Bradley Act—was signed into law.

Kyl's appointment to the Senate coincided with the emergence of the early internet providers, such as Prodigy and America Online, and Arizona's newest senator saw it as his duty to keep American law up to date with the technological times. Kyl viewed the internet as a shrewd enabler, allowing children to "wager with mom's credit card, click the mouse and bet the house" (a clever phrase that Kyl used often, although he admitted to stealing it from somebody else).[4] In 1997 Kyl penned the Internet Gambling Prohibition Act, which would do exactly as its name implied: prohibit internet gambling. In a hearing to discuss the act, Kyl laid out his rationale: "[T]here are some new studies that talk about the addictive nature of gambling, particularly gambling on the Internet. It enhances the addictive nature of gambling because it is so easy to do."[5]

Kyl's initial bill was broad, outlawing not just traditional gambling (like casino games and sports gambling), but also fantasy sports, one of the fastest-growing segments of the sports media industry. Fantasy sports—in which participants draft a make-believe team and compete against other make-believe teams in how many stats those teams compile—had once been relegated to pen and paper, requiring hours of work by dedicated league commissioners who had to manually add up all the scores. But the web just made everything so much easier. Statistics could be automated; results popped up instantly; records could be archived. And while both ESPN and SportsLine had jumped into the fray and built sizable fantasy audiences, there were also dozens of smaller competitors trying to gain a foothold in the potentially lucrative market. Most of these new sites cost money, somewhere between $20 and $50 to participate in a year-long contest. And most offered prizes, including occasional cash payouts, to the winners.

If Kyl's act had gone through, the entire business would have come toppling down. So, when details of the proposed law became public, the nascent fantasy sports industry went ballistic. Brian Matthews, CEO of CDM Fantasy Sports Inc., one of the biggest operators in the country, complained to the *New York Times* that the law "just doesn't make sense. It would still be legal to do fantasy sports, you just wouldn't be able to do it over the Internet. That's absurd." He compared fantasy sports to the popular office pool and asked, "What are you going to do, put all of America in jail?"[6] Off the advice of some of its media partners, CDM did what any company trying to save its business from crippling legislation would do: it hired a lobbyist. Described at the time as "the first fantasy-sports lobbyist in history," David Safavian was given $5,000 and promised an additional $60,000 if he could save fantasy sports from this group of anti-gambling politicians.[7]

What many of these legislators didn't understand, however—at least when the bill was first introduced—was that fans hadn't become enamored with fantasy sports because they could win money. Instead fantasy sports were a manifestation of two contradictory human desires: community and individuality. On one hand, like so many places on the internet, fantasy sports became a way for people who otherwise didn't know each other to congregate over a shared interest. CDM co-founder Charlie Wiegert understood this benefit, explaining that his company "caters to the people who like baseball and like the idea of fantasy baseball, but don't have three or four friends that they can create a league with. Now, a guy on a farm in the middle of Nebraska can enjoy the game just as much as a guy in the heart of New York City."[8]

It wasn't all about the competition either. When Prodigy's fantasy baseball unexpectedly went down on May 31, 1992, users from across the country came together to commiserate, vent, and complain. A team of researchers found that over three hundred players posted messages during the outage and that most of them "would not typically be engaging with one another in an extended discussion of a single event: college professors, computer programmers, high school seniors, and twelve-year-old managers like the one who identifies himself as 'Snuffy.'"[9] Some users complained that Prodigy had ruined the best part of their weekend. Others wondered how the stoppage would affect their fake team's season-long performance. When one poster told a fellow participant to stop whining and "get a life," the angry user quipped back, "I have a life, and fantasy baseball is part of my life." Fortunately for those involved, service was restored the next day, and the conversation switched to how fun it had been to complain. One wrote: "This is better than going to a shrink and much cheaper too!"[10]

But beyond community, fantasy sports were also about the individual fan's inherent arrogance, a deep-seated belief that if given the chance, the fan could do better: draft a better team, put together a better lineup, run a better play. As an NFL executive remarked during the fantasy sports explosion, "Fans always talk about what an idiot the Washington Redskins general manager is or how dumb this trade the Jets GM made is. The fans now have a chance to prove it."[11] This confidence, hinted at during the rise of sports talk radio in the late 1980s, had reached a resounding crescendo by the turn of the century. Ever since ESPN had introduced all-day, every-day sports content back in 1979, fans had been unintentionally empowered, saturated with an endless cycle of news and information and statistics to the point that many believed that they could—nay, should—be given control of the entire operation.

Some of them were even running their own franchises. In 1998 Electronic Arts (EA) released *Madden NFL 99*, a landmark iteration of the company's long-running football video game. Developed for the Sony PlayStation, the Nintendo 64, and Microsoft Windows-based computers, *Madden NFL 99* was the first edition in the series to incorporate franchise mode, an option that would become one of the game's most popular features in the years to come. Franchise mode wasn't just about scoring more points than your opponent. It was about drafting the right players, signing the right coaches, and putting together a roster that could succeed year after year. Hardcore football fans ate it up. Reviews were glowing. A writer for *Electronic Gaming Monthly* called *Madden NFL 99* the "most in-depth football game I've ever seen."[12]

The game was the result of close to two decades of incremental sports video game innovation. While there had always been a demand for sports titles, the earliest consoles were hardly equipped to handle the intricacy of football or baseball. Advancements came gradually, not least in terms of graphics, with monochromatic rectangles slowly evolving into shapes sort of resembling human beings. One 1981 advertisement for Mattel's Intellivision console suggests that its system was superior to Atari's partly due to the addition of limbs: "Notice the Intellivision players. They've got arms and legs like real players do."[13] And while nearly every sport presented its own challenges, American football was perhaps the hardest to cram into these early systems. It had too many players, the action was too fast, and the rules were too complicated. Still game developers gave it their best shot. Atari was one of the first to the market, calling its game *Football*. Odyssey, a console created by Magnavox, also had a game. It was named *Football*. Not to be outdone, Bally Astrocade pushed ahead with its own version:

Football. Alas, most of these titles were barely football. Playbooks often involved two options, pass or run. Limited processing power meant there were rarely more than ten or so players on the screen at one time. And kicking was an afterthought, sometimes eliminated all together.

Into this crowded yet nascent sports video game market came a man named Trip Hawkins. He did not arrive surreptitiously. Instead Hawkins came in with shine and swagger and with a desire to jazz up the video game industry, to use the "strategies and tactics from Hollywood, to make a New Hollywood."[14] Hawkins was well-suited to lead this charge. Profiles about the entrepreneur often mention his uncanny wit, his palpable charisma, his contrary-to-the-rest-of-the-video-game-industry handsomeness. Take this introduction in one video game history: "It seems that some people are destined to do great things. Trip Hawkins is one of them."[15] Or this one: "It wasn't just education that set him apart, it was his handsome facial features, his taste in suits, and his polished public demeanor."[16] In 1995 Hawkins even made it onto *People* magazine's list of the world's "50 Most Beautiful People": "With his strong bones and thick, brown hair, electronic entertainment magnate William 'Trip' Hawkins III, 41, cuts a charismatic swath through Silicon Valley." Hawkins, for one, said his good looks were a result of his ample productivity: "When I feel like I'm doing something important and making a contribution, that's when I look my best."[17]

Hawkins's golden boy background certainly contributed to this portrayal. He went to Harvard as an undergraduate and Stanford for graduate school before joining Steve Jobs as one of Apple's first hundred employees. In 1982 Hawkins founded EA with the idea that the video game industry needed an aesthetic overhaul. Hawkins thought creators should be attached to their projects, the same way Steven Spielberg and Martin Scorsese were tethered to Hollywood blockbusters. Packaging needed a facelift as well. Early video games were sold in plastic bags or colorless boxes. Hawkins saw this as a wasted opportunity, vowing to use "the packaging to express our values, to honor the creator, the artist and the creative process that resulted in the product."[18]

In 1983 EA released *Julius Erving and Larry Bird Go One-on-One* for the Apple II computer. The game embodied everything Hawkins had been proselytizing at EA: a respected developer, an innovative game, star power, compelling cover art. An early advertisement even touted Erving (known as Dr. J) and Larry Bird not as paid endorsers but as co-collaborators: "When they talked, we listened. When they criticized, we made big changes. When they gave suggestions, we took them. And it shows. This thing is absolutely uncanny."[19] Erving and Bird were reportedly given $25,000 and a small percentage of sales for their endorsement. And both seemed pleased with the final product. "I specifically remember the cover," Bird once remarked; "it turned out great, really looked like Dr. J. and I just finished working out on a New York City playground."[20] Of course they had done nothing of the sort. They did the shoot in Massachusetts. It was completely staged (they were never going to risk injury for a video game shoot). And the sweat had been sprayed on.

Nevertheless, reviewers were impressed. An article in *Electronic Games* said that *One-on-One* "may not be the best game invented in the last 12 months—though hoop-crazed gamers may dispute the point with you—but it is arguably the most significant."[21] A follow-up article commented on the game's incredible realism, how it was possible to break the backboard with a ferocious dunk, and how the players got tired if they moved around too much. Nobody had ever done that before, making the game a "landmark in the history of computer gaming."[22] That was what Hawkins wanted to hear. He was a sucker for realism and would push for it continuously as the years went on. And he knew the presence of Dr. J and Bird on the cover would help move product.

One-on-One was just a warmup. Hawkins's ultimate goal was to make the perfect football game. By the mid-1980s technology had improved to the point that this dream was becoming possible. The increased power of the personal computer and the promise of new 8-bit systems like the Nintendo Entertainment System and Sega Master System allowed for game developers to think well beyond the limitations of *Football* or *Football* or *Football*. Just as important as the technological foundation, though, was the promotional sheen. And just as Hawkins had tapped Dr. J and Larry Bird as collaborators for his basketball title, EA was going to need a football equivalent, someone the company could lean on for both valuable gameplay input and precious marketing power.

While profiles of Hawkins often focus on his good looks and charisma, profiles of John Madden almost always position the

Hall-of-Fame-NFL-coach-turned-legendary-TV-commentator-and-enthusiastic-Tinactin-spokesperson as the quintessential American everyman. Essential to this persona are a few key anecdotes. Nearly every article about Madden mentions that his shoes were perpetually untied. This observation is often paired with a description of his rarely combed hair (with "rumpled" a preferred adjective). And, of course, it's necessary to mention John Madden's fear of flying, mostly because that phobia forced him to ride across the country in a big bus, where he became one with the people, the American people, who brought him gifts like rhubarb pie and wrote stories for their newspapers about how JOHN MADDEN! had stopped to use the pay phone in their tiny, middle-of-nowhere town.

The most telling John Madden anecdote, though, probably comes from one of his own books (*Hey, Wait a Minute: I Wrote a Book!*). The incident took place at some point during Madden's ten-year coaching tenure with the Oakland Raiders, when his wife mentions that one of their sons was soon going to need his own car. Believing his son to be no more than twelve years old, Madden replies, "He's got a few years." To which his wife responds incredulously, "What do you mean, he's got a few years? He's old enough for his driver's permit. He's sixteen." In other words, Madden had been so consumed by football, so engulfed in blocking schemes and defensive coverage, that he had miscalculated the age of his own child *by four years*.[23]

Sensing that it was time to walk away, John Madden retired from coaching in 1978. He had accomplished his two main goals: to win a Super Bowl and to win a hundred games in ten years. An attractive offer from CBS came next, putting Madden in a booth with play-by-play man Pat Summerall. They would go on to form the country's most popular broadcasting duo. In 1984 Trip Hawkins asked Madden if he'd be willing to follow in the footsteps of Dr. J and Larry Bird and lend his name to a video game. Madden agreed, but only if the game looked and played like real football. That meant eleven-on-eleven, a deep playbook, athletes with different skill sets. Hawkins agreed to all of it. Years later Madden would explain to biographer Bryan Burwell why he got involved with EA. "This is my game," he told the author. "This isn't like one of those deals where it's a game someone else invented and I lent my name to it. . . . We started this before there were video games."[24] That's not true; there were plenty of football games when EA started developing *John Madden Football*. But Madden undoubtedly played a big role. One person involved with the game told ESPN that the developers "spent hours just learning blocking schemes."[25]

The first version of *John Madden Football* came out for the Apple II computer in 1988. Two other computer versions—one for the Commodore and one for MS-DOS—came out the following year. The game was far from a perfect representation of actual football. It was choppy; ran slowly; and could handle only two uniform colors, red and blue. Without an official license from the NFL Players' Association (NFLPA), the game used made-up names. The quarterback on San Francisco was "Joe Idaho" (instead of Joe Montana). The quarterback for Miami was "Danny" (like Dan Marino). On the back cover of the game was John Madden's "Ten Commandments," a list of attributes that would set the game apart from the pack. For instance, the game had realistic gameplay conditions: "Some guys aren't mudders. Some guys can't hold a block on grass. That's real football. That's in the game." Yet despite this attention to detail *John Madden Football* didn't exactly revolutionize the genre. One review said the game had a "bleak, almost remote look that simply does not invite more play."[26]

Over the next few years *John Madden Football* improved. Much of it had to do with better hardware, allowing the team at EA to develop the game they had wanted to develop all along. In 1990 the company released *John Madden Football* for Sega's exciting new 16-bit console, Genesis. Described by EA as "a game as big and tough as the man himself," it was widely praised as groundbreaking. The next few years saw EA reach a licensing agreement with the NFL, which meant it could use real team names, and the NFLPA, which meant it could use real player names. These agreements made an already good game even better, infusing gameplay with a heightened sense of realism. Gamers swooned, snatching up each subsequent version of *Madden* with enthusiasm.

The NFL, meanwhile, was enjoying its own moment in the spotlight. In 1993 Australian media mogul Rupert Murdoch shook up the American media landscape by launching a bidding war for a package of NFL television rights. Following the playbook he had used in Europe—throwing out an absurd number and hoping it stuck—

Murdoch secured the rights for Fox, his seven-year-old, last-in-the-ratings broadcast network. The cost was substantial: $1.6 billion over four years, hundreds of millions more than the incumbent CBS was offering. To spearhead the network's new sports department Murdoch tapped his friend David Hill, veteran of both World Series Cricket and the launch of Sky Sports. And for the broadcasting booth Murdoch got John Madden, luring him over to the struggling network with an annual salary of about $8 million, higher than any player earned in the NFL and three times what Madden had been making at CBS.

Rupert Murdoch and David Hill vowed to add glitz and glamor to American sports, to modernize broadcasts for a generation raised on MTV and video games. Terry Bradshaw, who had come over from CBS to serve as an analyst for Fox's expanded pregame show, explained in a glowing *Chicago Tribune* profile of Hill that the Aussie was the right man for the job. "He has a grasp on the workings of TV," Bradshaw said. "And he's fresh. It's great to get a guy in here who's fresh. . . . That allows for the creativity and the imagination." Veteran anchor James Brown couldn't have agreed more, wondering if Hill "was a charter member of Mensa." Even the reporter for the story played into the David Hill hype, explaining how the Australian was, "a mover. When he was head of Sky Sports, Hill and Murdoch created the Premier Division in English soccer to take the place of the former Division 1."[27] Hill, of course, had little to do with the formation of the English Premier League; his boss, Murdoch, had simply outbid everybody for the inaugural television rights. But if Rupert Murdoch was involved, there had to be a little exaggeration.

Even John Madden, a dyed-in-the-wool football traditionalist, understood the Fox approach to sports broadcasting. "The next generation, growing up with computers and video games, to get those kids, you're going to have to let 'em play along on television," he told one reporter. "Murdoch is committed to this."[28] In another interview Madden remembers a discussion he had with David Hill about his best-selling game: "David Hill, the president of Fox Sports at the time, had a meeting with a bunch of us, and he said, 'What we want to do is make our game on television look like the video game.'"[29]

But first, hockey. When Fox bought a package of television rights to the NHL in 1994, David Hill vowed to make it easier for the average fan to follow the game. He enlisted a group of talented engineers who told him they could make the hockey puck glow, an intriguing proposition for somebody who knew next to nothing about hockey (such as David Hill). When the time came to reveal the results of the year-long, $2 million project—the network had chosen the 1996 NHL All-Star Game for the big reveal—Fox went all in on the promotion. In a commercial for the game a voiceover tells the audience, "On January 20th, you will witness the biggest technological breakthrough in the history of sports."[30]

The technology, called FoxTrax, was indeed remarkable; the reaction, not so much. While the casual fan appreciated being able to better follow the puck around the rink, avid fans balked at an innovation they saw as superfluous, even a bit patronizing. When Fox announced that the glowing puck would return for the 1998 playoffs, one reporter called it "a distressing thought for hockey purists, who are insulted by the video-game look of the Fox productions."[31] He then encouraged fans to boycott the televised games, saying it was the only way Fox was going to eliminate the technology from the broadcast. That kind of passive resistance would prove to be unnecessary. In August 1998 ABC/ESPN secured Fox's package of NHL television rights starting with the following season. As a lame duck hockey broadcaster, Fox saw little reason to keep courting the casual fan and did away with the controversial gimmick, pocketing the tens of thousands of dollars per game it took to run the technology.

Meanwhile, the engineering guru behind FoxTrax, a man named Stan Honey, left the network with two other colleagues, Jerry Gepner and Bill Squadron, to form a company called Sportvision. Dedicated to "adding value for sports fans on TV, the Internet, video games, in arenas, and more," Sportvision had given Fox some equity in its company in order to retain control of the FoxTrax technology. But the glowing puck was old news, and within months of its founding Sportvision had a new product to bring to market. Officially named "1st and Ten" but popularly known as the "yellow line," Honey and his team had figured out a way to superimpose a digital line on a football broadcast to indicate the point to which a team had to advance in order to get a first down. How did they do it? Mostly through a deep understanding of color palettes and shades of green. Since the "stickiness" of the line was dependent on the system's knowing what was and what wasn't grass, Sportvision would "take swatches of grass at different times of day to enhance the color palette in each city." The technology also involved a series of sensors attached to game cameras so that "once inserted, [they] could keep the line in proper perspective as the play proceeded and the cameras panned and zoomed."[32]

When Sportvision was ready to pitch its invention to broadcasters, Fox was the obvious first stop. But when presented with the cost—$25,000 for each game—David Hill balked. Perhaps Hill had become risk averse because of the mixed reaction to the glowing puck. Or maybe the native Australian simply didn't recognize how valuable the technology could be for the football fan. Either way, Hill allowed Sportvision to walk out of the meeting without a deal. CBS and ABC came next; both networks liked the technology but asked for some time to mull it over. Not ESPN. Although last to receive the pitch, the network hammered out a deal with Sportvision within a week. Jed Drake, ESPN's head of remote production, was so excited about the yellow line that he requested full exclusivity for the 1998 NFL season. Sportvision reluctantly agreed.

The yellow line debuted on September 27, 1998, during a Sunday night game between the Baltimore Ravens and the Cincinnati Bengals. The reaction was unanimous: people loved it. Unlike the glowing puck, the technology was deemed neither distracting nor condescending, a seamless and useful broadcast enhancement. The yellow line was so well received that a few months after its debut, a Harris Interactive Poll (admittedly funded by Sportvision) found that 92 percent of football viewers would "like to see the super-imposed first down lines used on all football telecasts." Nearly two-thirds of "casual" viewers though that the line increased their understanding of the game, and over 90 percent thought it would increase understanding for kids.[33] Applauded by industry experts for its groundbreaking, fan-friendly innovation, ESPN and Sportvision would go on to win an Emmy award for the technology.

When the exclusivity clause ran out after the season, Sportvision made the rounds and signed agreements with the other networks. Before long the yellow line was an expected part of all football broadcasts. Proof of this longevity came in 2001, when Fox discontinued the use of the line in an effort to once again cut its budget. Sportvision countered by creating a website (www.LovetheLine.com) where fans could voice their displeasure about the network's unpopular decision. The fans didn't mince words, as evidenced by the following comment: "Fox has shown us that there is nothing they care about more than money. They don't care about the game, they don't care about the fans, it's money money money. What has Fox done about the controversy? They shut down the fan feedback page. That tells you everything you need to know right there."[34] By November Fox and its advertising team had found a sponsor willing to support the cost of the line, returning the technology to the broadcast.

As the years went on, David Hill would subtly attempt to rewrite the history of the yellow line. In a 2010 interview with the *Los Angeles Business Journal*, a reporter follows up a discussion of Hill's long career in Australia and the UK by saying, "You were also responsible for putting the first-down line marker on football broadcasts." Hill responds to the prompt with an anecdote about John Madden: "Yeah. See, I didn't grow up with American football—I had to learn it. What are they trying to do? Well, they're trying to get the first down, so let's show [the viewer] where they've got to get to the first down. I was fiddling around on an early computer program, and if you put an X here and you put an X there, you got a line. And I thought, wow. It was something I talked to John Madden about way back in '94. He said, 'Boom! Let's do it!'"[35] How neat and tidy and fun it would be if all this were true—that is, if John Madden used his catchphrase ("Boom!") in regular conversations around the office and if the football legend synonymous with the greatest football video game series of all time was also the reason that television broadcasts had become more like video games. But while it's possible that this conversation did indeed happen and while it's inarguable that David Hill played a crucial role in the evolution of the sports media industry, the credit for this remarkably useful and universally beloved broadcast enhancement must go to the team at Sportvision.

Regardless of how it all came about, American football fans had it pretty good as the century came to a close. Thanks to advancements like the yellow line, following the action had never been easier. Flat-screen televisions and high-definition broadcasts, soon to be widespread, would make the at-home experience even better. A growing number of fans even had fake teams to root for while watching these increasingly vivid games, where real players played on teams they didn't even know existed. And if these fake teams struggled, no problem. The fan could shut the game off, turn on PlayStation or Nintendo 64, and create *another* fake team—a fake franchise even—thanks to John Madden and his long-running video game. Never before had fans been so utterly immersed and deeply involved in professional football, even if most of their involvement was entirely fictional and totally self-serving.

And yet Senator Jon Kyl held firm on at least one activity the fan craved. He was adamant that there'd be no wagering on games— and *especially* no wagering on games through the internet. In 1999 Kyl presented a new version of his Internet Gambling Prohibition Act to Congress. This version included an exemption for the fantasy sports industry, a change applauded not only by fantasy sites and their lobbyist David Safavian, but also by Marianne McGettigan, the representative of Major League Baseball's Player Association. McGettigan had argued that banning fantasy sports would "be a disservice to many of baseball's most avid fans," especially since the league saw "no countervailing public purpose being served." Unlike with sports gambling, she argued, in fantasy sports "there is no incentive for anyone to attempt to change the outcome of any one game, the performance of any one player."[36] That's because avid fantasy sports participants don't really care who wins any one particular game. They care about their *own* team, the fake one they personally assemble, a team that could potentially contain players from a dozen or more real teams. Thus there would be no under-the-table handouts or point shaving scandals because of fantasy sports.

In fact the fantasy sports exemption wasn't the only one that had found its way into the bill. In an article published in 2000, "Wanna Bet This Bill Is Really Strange?," a reporter at *Fortune* magazine wrote, "If you need further proof that Congress works in weird ways, here it is. Lawmakers are now considering a bill called the Internet Gambling Prohibition Act of 1999 . . . [but] while the bill would ban some forms of Web gambling—mostly casino-style games of chance—it would encourage others. Because of a little-noticed exception in the fine print, the legislation would actually expand parimutuel betting—wagers placed on the outcome of competitions like horse and dog racing and jai alai."[37]

The inclusion of so many contradictions had been the work of lobbyists who had successfully done what lobbyists are paid to do. They had sent targeted political donations with a wink, wink. They had wined and dined people who enjoyed being wined and dined. And they had promised "this" in exchange for "that." On July 17, 2000, whatever was left of the Internet Gambling Prohibition Act was rejected by the U.S. House of Representatives. A subsequent investigation by reporters at the *Washington Post* found that that the impetus for the bill's final defeat had come not from the fantasy sports and horse racing and dog racing and jai alai industries, which were already in the clear with the revised bill, but rather from a small internet-based company called eLottery. Aware that the passage of the act would mean certain bankruptcy for its already struggling brand, executives at eLottery had hired their own lobbyist, who subsequently compiled a team of influential strategists to help defeat it. Chief among this group was the Reverend Louis P. Sheldon, head of the Traditional Values Coalition and author of *The Agenda: The Homosexual Plan to Change America*, who allegedly received tens of thousands of dollars to convince many House Republicans to vote against something they would have otherwise voted for.[38]

While the initial demise of the Internet Gambling Prohibition Act bill (it would be revived and revised a few years later) is only tangentially related to the sports media industry—and while the debate about internet gambling, and sports wagering specifically, was really just getting started—the tale nonetheless serves as a good reminder that power is frequently opaque, often illusory. It's also a reminder as to why things happen in this world, why certain events unfold in unexpected ways, and how control of billion-dollar opportunities can often swing from one group of people to another in the most unexpected ways.

Part 5 / Control

The industry had grown; it was now huge. Who would take control?

There were many contenders. Up first were the media companies, which weren't going to let the arrival of the most disruptive piece of technology in human history topple the corporate empires they had so carefully assembled. Standing close to these conglomerates were the leagues and teams, which had billed these companies millions of dollars for the right to air their games. Sure, they were cashing enormous checks. But was selling their most valuable asset, the live rights, still the best model?

You guys figure it out, thought the players, as long as a fair share of the profits and attention filtered down our way. And maybe throw some love over here, said the politicians, many of whom loved the economic heft of the sports media industry but couldn't help feel left out of all the excitement. And then there were the fans, told in 1979 that they were about to enter sports heaven with the launch of ESPN, only to be ushered into enhanced versions of that paradise every year since. Is it really a surprise that they started to feel a bit, well, entitled?

This battle for control, told over the next five chapters, would take various forms. First, there's a story about a media company trying to start a league (chapter 16) and then about a league trying to start a media company (chapter 17). Not to be ignored, the fan comes barging in, ranting and raving and demanding attention (chapter 18). Down in South America a government attempts a return to an earlier era (chapter 19), while players everywhere, after decades of being shushed, grab the microphone away from the broadcasters and the owners and the fans (chapter 20).

And as the century entered its second decade, the true winner in this battle of control would become clear. The victors would have no qualms about making themselves known: they were loud, confident, and opinionated. For better or for worse everybody else would be forced to pay attention to what they had to say.

Rapidly Converging Media Platforms

16

The Rise and Fall of the WUSA (2001–3)

Despite his prominent role in the groundbreaking satellite broadcast of the 1975 "Thrilla in Manila," Gerald "Jerry" Levin had never really been a sports guy. As a child, Levin was bookish, earning straights A's and graduating second from his high school class. In college Levin became a philosophy guy and spent most of his days pondering life's big questions. By graduation Levin had come to a few grand conclusions: "we impute meaning and purpose to things that are totally adventitious or accidental; that there is no God; that there just is; that there's no life after death."[1] Those convictions led Levin to become a lawyer and then a businessman, eventually landing with Charles Dolan at HBO. In 1980, high off the success of his successful cable television experiment starring Muhammad Ali and Joe Frazier, Levin became head of Time Inc.'s video group, the fastest-growing part of the Henry Luce–founded company. A decade later Time Inc. acquired Warner Communications and became one of the most powerful media conglomerates in the world. Two years after that Levin maneuvered his way to the top of the ladder, blindsiding a colleague with whom he had worked for two decades, and secured the roles of chairman, CEO, and president of the new Time Warner Inc. When asked about his manipulative actions years later, Levin had this to say: "When your existence is up for grabs, you don't know how you are going to react. It's like a Hemingway thing—you know, you're an individual survivor."[2]

By 1999 Levin was still playing survivor. Time Warner's magazines—*Time, Fortune, People, Sports Illustrated*—were still a reliable source of revenue, and cable television remained a profitable business. But everybody was talking about—and, more important, pouring money into—the internet. How could Levin bring the panache and integrity of one of the country's oldest media brands into this new internet-focused era? It was a vexing dilemma. At first Levin tried to keep the innovation in-house. In 1994 Time Warner launched a web portal named Pathfinder, designed to host content from the company's collection of brands. Personalization was important. One reporter explained that "a father can set up a program called 'Dad's News,' for example, which might include the latest international news, weather news and a business update."[3] But Pathfinder was difficult to maintain, terribly unprofitable, and closed down after a few years. In 1999 Time Warner tried again with a site called Entertaindom. It was described as "the most comprehensive effort by a major media company to present on the Web actual entertainment content."[4] It was easier said than done, of course, especially in an era when most people had painfully slow internet connections.

Into the picture came Steve Case, also not really a sports guy and also a survivor. His company, America Online (AOL), had been left for dead multiple times since the middle of the decade. But Case and AOL had always come out ahead; one former executive likened the company to a "New York cockroach."[5] How did Case do it? By appealing to the masses, by making things easy, and by understanding that people on the internet wanted to talk to other people on the internet. By 1999, according to one report, AOL was bringing in more money than the combined revenues of its twenty closest competitors.[6] Investors loved what they saw and valued AOL, a precocious teenager, at almost twice as much as Time Warner, a company that had been around in some form for over seventy years.

In late November 1999 Case and Levin sat down for dinner to discuss the future of their companies, of media, of themselves. They quickly realized that the AOL mission statement put together by Case—"To build a global medium as central to people's lives as the telephone or the television . . . and even more valuable"—synced up well with Levin's own high-minded vision of Time Warner. They both adored the late Henry Luce; they both sort of wanted to be Henry Luce. They drank wine and talked about how great their companies had been and could be. By the end of the night they had agreed that these two amazing companies should become one amazing company. Nobody would stand a chance. They'd control everything. And everybody involved would make lots of money.

The press release announcing the formation of AOL Time Warner came out on January 10, 2000. It introduced the "the world's first fully integrated media and communications company for the Internet Century," with the goal of becoming the "premier global company delivering branded information, entertainment and communications services across rapidly converging media platforms."[7] How would this all play out? Sports provided a blueprint. At the time of the merger Time Warner owned the Atlanta Braves, the cable network on which the Braves played, and one of the main cable providers that distributed that network to individual homes. By incorporating AOL into this chain, the company could now sign people up for AOL at the Braves stadium, sell tickets online, host message boards and fantasy games, and work toward complete monopolization of the Braves fans' attention. This was vertical integration at its very best, a way to maximize the utility of "rapidly converging media platforms." But what if—and in the late 1990s no "what if" was too big a "what if"—the company could own not only the team and the network and the wires and the promotion, but also the very league itself? It couldn't happen with Major League Baseball; the other owners would never have agreed to such an arrangement. But what if the league didn't exist yet?

Women's sports, still sorely underrepresented across the entire media landscape, provided a potential path forward. Despite the efforts of people like Billie Jean King the women's sports media explosion of the 1970s and 1980s had never really materialized. Dozens of studies proved this to be true, quantitatively detailing the sporadic coverage of women's sports across nearly all American media platforms. One 1997 study looked at over a thousand stories on two national sports programs— ESPN's *SportsCenter* and CNN's *Sports Tonight*—and found that less than 5 percent were about women athletes.[8] Another study in 1999 examined sports coverage on three Los Angeles network affiliates and found that a little more than half of the newscasts in the chosen sample "contained no coverage of women's sports whatsoever."[9] And a third investigation found that less than 7 percent of *Sports Illustrated* and ESPN *The Magazine* covers between 1987 and 2009 contained women.[10]

Despite these gloomy findings the prior decades had provided a few glimmers of hope. Much of the optimism came from an entity that didn't even exist until the 1980s yet would quickly evolve into one of the most celebrated sports teams in American history. The first U.S. women's national soccer team was cobbled together in 1985, exactly a hundred years after the creation of its male counterpart. It was formed at the behest of the U.S. Soccer Federation, which decided that it wanted to send a team to compete at the Mundialito (or "Little World Cup") in Italy. Seventeen amateur female players were chosen to represent the United States. They were given a free pair of shoes, ten dollars a day, and old men's uniforms that needed to be hemmed. Once the tournament began, the American squad was manhandled by teams that had been playing together for years. That wasn't a surprise; they weren't expected to win. But the players relished the experience: playing in packed stadiums, against good competition, with all the fanfare and pageantry of an international tournament. It would be a sign of things to come.

Four years later came the first-ever FIFA-sanctioned world championship for women's soccer. China was chosen as host, and twelve teams were invited to participate. While not technically a world cup in name—FIFA wasn't ready to consecrate this experiment with such a hallowed designation (it eventually would, retroactively)—the Americans arrived far more prepared than they had been in Italy. They were considered one of the tournament favorites, having blitzed through their qualifying matches with a cumulative score of 49-0. The dominance continued once the (not) World Cup was under way. Led by prolific scorer Michelle Akers-Stahl, the Americans breezed through the early rounds before defeating a highly regarded Norway team in the final. It was the first time the United States had ever won an international soccer tournament. After the game coach Anson Dorrance told reporters, "I feel what we've done here is proof to the world we are a developing soccer nation."[11]

With FIFA on board it was only a matter of time until the International Olympic Committee followed suit. It did so by installing women's soccer as an official event for the 1996 Summer Olympic Games, just in time for the gold medal favorite U.S. team to serve as host (and sell tons of tickets). The team duly followed the desired narrative, easily advancing out of its group and defeating Norway in the semifinals to reach the finals against China. In front of over seventy thousand people at Sanford Stadium in Athens, Georgia, a group of soon-to-be-American legends—players like Julie Foudy, Mia Hamm, Kristine Lilly, and Brianna Scurry—made history as the first-ever women's soccer team to win a gold medal. Unlike so many historic sporting events, however, this match wouldn't be tethered to a "can-you-believe-it?" television viewership number. Forced to cram an entire Olympics schedule into a single prime-time broadcast window—and perhaps conditioned by decades of broadcast network soccer apathy—NBC declined to show the match in its entirety, choosing instead to offer a series of live look-ins and a post-match celebratory interview with Bob Costas.

It was a missed opportunity, one on which other companies would capitalize. Executives at Nike, for instance, saw the rise of the U.S. women's national team as a way to promote its brand to a historically underserved demographic: women. By the time the 1996 Olympics rolled around, Nike had already signed budding superstar Mia Hamm and released a commercial starring Hamm and her teammates. The significance of the moment wasn't lost on Tisha Venturini, one of the players in the ad. "The biggest thrill is someone's actually doing a big-time commercial about women's soccer," Venturini told a reporter. "It's come such a long way."[12] Yet Hamm remained the undisputed star, using the well-oiled Nike marketing machine to boost her profile. In 1999 Hamm had a year as impressive as any American athlete has ever had: she became the all-time leading international goal scorer; starred in one of the most iconic sports commercials of all time with NBA legend Michael Jordan; began her own foundation, dedicated to raising awareness and funds for bone-marrow and cord-blood transplants *and* to developing opportunities for females in sport; and had the biggest building on Nike's campus named after her. She was an absolute superstar, one of the most recognizable athletes in the country, and she made a ton of money off her unprecedented popularity.

Hamm's teammates weren't so lucky. Playing soccer for the women's national team was part-time work, good for some spending money here and there but hardly enough to live on. And compared to the salaries of their male colleagues, the women's were downright disrespectful. At the 1998 World Cup members of the U.S. men's national team scored a single goal across three games, came in last place in their group, and made $20,000 each. If they had won—which they really had no chance of doing—they would have taken home nearly $400,000 per player. A championship for the women in the 1999 tournament, meanwhile, would net only $12,500 for each player.[13] For Mia Hamm's less famous colleagues this system was hardly sustainable. The most logical solution was the creation of a full-time women's professional league, one that could provide regular work and a reliable salary.

The players knew that a memorable performance at the 1999 Women's World Cup could provide the impetus needed to launch a league. So in the buildup to the tournament they hit the road, agreeing to nearly every media promotion they were offered and executing an exhausting grassroots campaign that had them handing out flyers at soccer camps around the country. "It was the equivalent of being a door-to-door salesperson," goalkeeper Brianna Scurry told writer Caitlin Murray.[14] Nevertheless, the campaign worked: nearly eighty thousand people showed up for the first game at Giants Stadium in New Jersey to watch the Americans defeat Denmark 3–0. That was followed by a crowd of sixty-five thousand at United States vs. Nigeria (7–1) and fifty thousand at United States vs. North Korea (3–0). The Americans then disposed of Germany (3–2) and Brazil (2–0), allowing them to advance to the championship against China.

The World Cup final took place on July 10, 1999. In his book *The Girls of Summer* Jere Longman writes, "The timing for the final could not have been more exquisite, slotted in the test-pattern weeks between the end of professional basketball and the beginning of football."[15] Americans were indeed dialed in, both on television—the match would have an audience comparable to a broadcast of *Friends* or NFL *Monday Night Football*—and in person, with over ninety thousand people filling up the Rose Bowl stands. The match was tense and remained scoreless through regulation and overtime. It came down to penalty kicks. Both teams converted their first two opportunities.

Then China missed, opening the door for the Americans. Successful strikes by both Kristine Lilly and Mia Hamm left the fate of the match to longtime national team member Brandi Chastain. She buried the kick; the crowd erupted. Chastain then ripped off her shirt, swung it in the air, and sank to her knees.

Over the years Chastain's goal would become one of the most celebrated sporting events in U.S. history. The immediate reaction was more mixed, a hodgepodge of awe and mansplaining. Reporter Peter Kerasotis at *Florida Today* explained why he was disappointed in Chastain's actions: "You'd like to think women can be recognized for something truly outstanding and not feel compelled to take off clothes. You'd think winning soccer's World Cup would have been recognition enough. You'd think we wouldn't need anything more than that to discuss at the water cooler. But then Brandi Chastain decided to take off her shirt."[16] Over at the *Denver Post* Mark Kiszla explained what female athletes needed to do to earn his respect moving forward: "If women athletes really want to evolve into winners who do more than ape the look-at-me theatrics of money-grubbing male superstars, the big changes must be left to Chastain. . . . From now on, keep your shirt on. Act like you've been there before. True champions do."[17] And John Eisenberg of the *Baltimore Sun* explained why the 1999 World Cup final, although fun and entertaining, was hardly a harbinger of future success: "No, it's not going to spawn a thriving women's pro league. And no, it doesn't mean millions of women are going to start spending months on the couch, gnawing on chips and numbly watching whatever games show up on cable. Women have more important things to do, such as balancing work, exercise and motherhood. That 30-hours-a-day load doesn't leave a lot of time for a nightly megadose of ESPN2."[18]

At least one prominent media executive, John Hendricks, disagreed with Eisenberg's insulting-on-a-few-levels take. Hendricks was the founder of Discovery, a network that had nothing to do with sports; it was all about science and documentaries and telling the audience how the world worked. But Hendricks was indeed a sports guy, going so far as to devote an entire chapter in his autobiography to his two proudest middle school athletic achievements (a no-hitter and a 70-yard touchdown pass). After attending the 1996 Olympic Games and seeing the reaction when the American women's soccer team won gold, Hendricks began to wonder if a professional league was indeed viable. Three years later, after the 1999 World Cup triumph, Hendricks decided to act on this instinct. He had always considered himself an entrepreneur—the subtitle of his book is "An Entrepreneur's Story"—and has admitted to becoming "intoxicated" with the potential sponsorship opportunities of women's soccer.[19] Hendricks gathered up his rich media friends, including his buddies at the newly formed AOL Time Warner, and pitched the idea of a professional women's soccer league built by, and in some ways built *for*, these rapidly converging media platforms.

In February 2000, just a month after Levin and Case had finalized their historic agreement, Hendricks and his colleagues announced the creation of the Women's United Soccer Association (WUSA). The league, buoyed by an initial investment of $40 million, would begin play in April 2001. It would operate as a single entity, meaning that profits (or losses) would be shared equally among its founding owners. All eight teams would be owned by a cable television company or by somebody connected to a cable television company. In addition to Hendricks and cable television tycoon Amos Hostetter, who together owned three teams, the list included AOL Time Warner (two teams), Comcast (one team), and Cox Communications (two teams). AOL Time Warner would also air twenty-two games across its TNT and CNN/SI cable networks, produce the studio show *Inside WUSA Soccer*, and host the official WUSA website on its CNNSI.com platform. Put it all together and it sure looked like Levin and Case had achieved the holy grail, sports media style: complete and total convergence.

Competing on the field for the WUSA would be the best of the best, not just Mia Hamm and Brandi Chastain, but also Julie Murray (Australia), Sissi (Brazil), and Sun Wen (China). Most important, all the Americans on the 1999 World Cup team were involved, deliberately dispersed throughout the league as "founding players." Other players would be chosen through a draft, with a large pool of potential players as former college players became intrigued by this unique opportunity. One late round pick, Trudi Sharpsteen, a healthcare consultant in Los Angeles, told a reporter that she was taking a pay cut of around $200,000 to participate: "Why not take a couple years off from real work and do something I love?"[20]

In his autobiography Hendricks explains: "There is a vast gap between the *dream*, which is the vision that arises at the confluence of all of those curiosity-driven streams of experience, and the *idea*, which is the road map for the practical implementation of that dream."[21] The vision for the WUSA was exciting. As the league prepped for its launch in early 2001, a reporter at the *Los Angeles Times* wrote that the WUSA "might be the most significant experiment ever in women's sports. Certainly, it is the most far-reaching."[22] The first match reflected this optimism. It featured the BayArea CyberRays, starring Brandi Chastain, against the Washington Freedom, starring Mia Hamm, and it attracted an enthusiastic crowd of over thirty thousand. But an exciting opening night was not indicative of future success. The practical implementation of launching a professional women's soccer league was fraught with obstacles, compounded by the owners' inexperience in a brand new industry. Grant Wahl, a reporter at *Sports Illustrated*, wrote that the league was "woefully disorganized at first."[23] Finding stadiums in which to play proved difficult. Initial response from potential sponsors was tepid. And attendance, while promising at the start, tailed off as the year went on.

By far the most confounding part of the WUSA rollout is how an entity exclusively owned and operated by media companies could so poorly manage that entity's media strategy. Upon launch of the league Hendricks had stressed how important television was to its success. Referring to the gold medal match during the 1996 Olympic Games, Hendricks said, "I just knew in the stands that night that the missing ingredient was television, that if television was added, it would be overwhelming for the country. . . . It was kind of a milestone for me."[24] The initial plan was sound, as the league's first match aired nationally at noon on AOL Time Warner–owned cable network TNT, with the movie *A League of Their Own* serving as an appropriate and relevant lead-in. It would go downhill from there. TNT would continue airing WUSA games for the next few weeks before handing off control to CNN/SI. The all-sports network, also owned by AOL Time Warner, was available in tens of million fewer households than TNT and was so unsuccessful that it would cease operations just a year later. Meanwhile, the AOL Time Warner–produced WUSA studio show, *Inside WUSA Soccer*, was inexplicably buried in the early morning hours, not on

ESPN or even CNN/SI, but on Discovery, often sandwiched between programs with little to no connection to women's soccer. One early morning Discovery schedule in 2001 went like this: infomercial, info-mercial, infomercial, infomercial, *Inside WUSA Soccer*, infomercial.[25]

With such a strategy underwhelming television ratings were all but inevitable. Multiple reports pegged the average rating at a .4. This is both low and misleading since the number doesn't include viewership on CNN/SI (meaning the average was almost certainly even lower than reported). It was also never clear how the television contract actually worked. In 2000 Grant Wahl reported that the WUSA had secured a four-year, $3 million television contract with TNT and CNN/SI.[26] But that report reeked of public relations, a way to boost enthusiasm for a league that had just been announced and using a reporter who worked for an AOL Time Warner company. In 2003 another reporter at CNN wrote that the money had gone the other way, that the WUSA had paid AOL Time Warner for the privilege to get its games on television.[27] Either way, the WUSA abandoned its deal with AOL Time Warner after the first year and decided to go in a different direction, signing a two-year television deal with an entity called PAX-TV.

Again, a strange move. PAX was the creation of John Paxson, the founder of the Home Shopping Network, a free-to-air entity dedicated to getting people to buy stuff via their telephones while watching tele-vision. The strategy was remarkably successful: people bought tons of stuff, and Paxson became very wealthy. After a "spiritual rebirth" on New Year's in Las Vegas in 1986, Paxson threw himself into religion, buying up dozens of radio and television stations in order to form what would become the Worship Network. His goal was now twofold: moral-ity *and* money. As Paxson wrote, "While profit isn't the primary moti-vation behind a business, it is the byproduct of a business that pleases God."[28] In 1998 Paxson executed another pivot, using his vast network of local television stations to launch PAX-TV, a network devoted not to religious programming—"Christian programming stinks," Paxson said at the time—but rather to programming that would be sought out by well-meaning Christian families. That meant "no gratuitous sex, no violence, no obscene language."[29] The network went to market with the slogan "Parental Discretion Unnecessary" and filled its programming schedule with repeats of *Touched by an Angel* and *Dr. Quinn, Medicine Woman*. PAX was safe, family-friendly, and not very popular.

In 2002 the WUSA was inserted into the PAX programming schedule. The league's president and CEO, Lynn Morgan, told reporters that PAX's ability to consistently air games in the mid-afternoon, as opposed to earlier in the day, would help the league attract the type of viewers it was looking for: those who spent their Saturday mornings playing soccer. The network also had a big footprint; at close to ninety million homes, it was in as many homes as TNT. Yet nobody who knew anything about media thought this was a good idea. Sports columnist Johnette Howard wrote that the decision was a "mystifying choice." And she suggested that Morgan's reliance on availability was misguided: "The number of households getting the signal isn't what is important, the number of households watching the signal is. Meaningful cross-promotional ties and marketing opportunities, building personalities, reaping bonuses like the consistent news coverage some rights-holders could provide, also should have mattered a great deal to the WUSA."[30]

Add "appropriate lead-ins," the programming that airs before a show, to Howard's list. A good lead-in strategy provides viewers with a free sample, a way to test content they may not have even known about beforehand. It's the reason network executives often air the program they're most excited about immediately after the Super Bowl; there will always be several million people who just leave the television on and keep watching. Morgan had touted PAX's consistent schedule as a way to create "destination viewing" for WUSA fans. In other words, viewers would know exactly when and where to watch these games on a weekly basis. But new leagues need to have an audience before they can create a destination at which this audience can gather. Good lead-ins help build this awareness. On PAX the WUSA was never blessed with good lead-ins. The first game aired after eight straight hours of infomercials and a half hour of bass fishing. A match two months later aired after nine straight hours of infomercials. If somebody had stuck around after that block of content, it's probably because he or she had simply fallen asleep on the couch.

Five days before the start of the 2003 FIFA Women's World Cup the WUSA announced that it was shutting down. It was a sad day, but nobody was very surprised. Attendance had decreased; television ratings were anemic; payroll had been slashed. The initial team of cable television investors had spent an estimated $100 million trying to find a path toward profitability. That path had proved elusive, and John Hendricks's friends had seemingly run out of patience. They also may have been distracted by more pressing matters, such as the bursting of the dot-com bubble in 2000 and the wretched economy brought on by the attacks on September 11, 2001. The WUSA had been a fun experiment. If it had worked out, Hendricks and his friends would have been thrilled. If not, no big deal. While twenty or thirty million was but a drop in the bucket for these companies, it was also an easy slash once executives and shareholders started demanding cuts.

Executives at AOL Time Warner, in particular, were consumed with things far more important than the WUSA. As even the most causal Wall Street historian knows, the entire company had gone up in flames almost immediately after the merger. There were dozens of reasons why: the economy, insufficient leadership, improper accounting practices, internal culture clashes. In 2001 AOL Time Warner posted a net income loss of nearly $5 billion. In 2002 it posted a now-famous-in-business-schools loss of *$98 billion*, including a $46 billion write down of the value of America Online. The merger had been disastrous, one of the worst decisions in corporate history. Executives at both companies would quickly learn that navigating this evolving media landscape, with more content options than ever before, was going to require more than just getting bigger. Convergence, vertical integration, scale: they're all just buzzwords, far easier to write and talk about than to actually execute, much less make profitable. It's really hard to be really good at one thing. It's almost impossible to be really good at all the things at the same time.

Of course that didn't mean that people wouldn't stop trying. And just as some media companies were trying to start their own sports leagues, some leagues were actually trying to start their own media companies.

Content

17

NBA and Turner Agreement (2007)

In 1983 the men's basketball team at the College of William and Mary received a bid to play in the National Invitation Tournament (NIT). This was big news, the first time the team had ever qualified for a postseason competition. In the days leading up to the game alumni all over the country called the school asking how they could follow along. With no obvious solution assistant athletic director Tom Zawistowski decided to find a way himself, sitting in his office with the radio on so that fans could call in on one of the athletic department's lines and listen over the speaker phone. The game was a bust—William and Mary lost—but the phone broadcast was a rousing success. That got Zawistowski thinking.

Several years later, in the midst of the 1–900 number frenzy, Zawistowski launched TeamLine, a service through which displaced fans could call a number and listen to the local radio broadcast of their favorite teams. Nothing about it was cheap: the infrastructure involved a $21 million call center in Kent, Ohio, and the average cost to listen to a three-hour game was about $30. "What we're doing today couldn't have been done 16 months ago," Zawistowski told a reporter in 1991. "It's scary. We're so far out on the cutting edge."[1] Even more important than the technology, however, was the content. Zawistowski had secured approval to rebroadcast games from every team in the NHL, most of the NFL, and over a hundred colleges. For the teams and leagues the decision was a no-brainer: a quick signature in exchange for a cut of the profits and a bunch of happy out-of-town fans. In its first full year the service logged two million minutes. Zawistowski saw this as just the beginning, suggesting that on-demand, niche content was the future of the media landscape: "We've become so diverse and so fragmented, it's impossible to really have too many things that cater to a national audience."[2]

While Zawistowski had the right idea, the emergence of the internet in the mid-1990s made everything about TeamLine obsolete. Other fans with similar ideas began porting the concept into the digital realm. Cameron "Chris" Jaeb, a Minnesota sports fan living in Texas, was one of the earliest. Jaeb was working his way through a series of start-up companies when he began thinking about fans outside the immediate geographic area of their favorite teams. Those fan bases, thought Jaeb, could be monetized if somebody figured out how to take a piece of localized sports content and make it not localized. In other words, do what Zawistowski did but on the internet. Jaeb pitched his idea to a few hundred investors. They all passed; most had no idea how the internet worked. But then an acquaintance named Todd Wagner encouraged him to pitch the idea to a guy named Mark Cuban. They met at a California Pizza Kitchen in Dallas. After ten minutes Cuban said he was in. It turns out Cuban was also a displaced fan and had been thinking about doing something similar.[3]

Jaeb, Wagner, and Cuban put together a website and went about selling their idea. This was Cuban's expertise; he loves selling, thrives on it. In his series-of-blog-posts-turned-book (*How to Win at the Sport of Business*) Cuban mentions "sales" (thirteen mentions) and "selling" (seventeen) far more often than he does "revenue" (three) or "profit" (zero). Not surprisingly, the three entrepreneurs turned out to be very good at selling. They sold local radio stations on putting their broadcasts on the internet. They sold colleges and leagues on rebroadcasting their games. They sold advertisers on the value of reaching a tech-savvy audience. And they sold their company to the press as a once-in-a-lifetime, industry-disrupting innovation. Jaeb soon departed, leaving Wagner and Cuban as the co-owners. From there what was once Cameron Communications evolved into AudioNet. With visions of moving beyond audio, it soon became Broadcast.com.

As the name of the company evolved, so did its elevator pitch. Early on AudioNet was described as a "connection to salvation" for displaced sports fans, created by two frustrated Indiana University alums— Cuban and Wagner—who lived in Texas.[4] A few years later the vision for the site had grown. "If we do things right, what AudioNet will hopefully be in five years is the next cable company," Wagner explained. "It'll be a cable company with literally hundreds and hundreds of channels—cable as we know it today, only on steroids."[5] While Cuban and Wagner liked to talk up the sports aspect, especially in the early years, the site was really one of the internet's first content aggregators. It had a little bit of everything, which in turn made the platform as a whole about as untargeted as possible. At various points during those early years an AudioNet listener could find snow reports for various U.S. ski mountain areas, live feeds for the NHL playoffs, a link to the Dallas Police Department scanner, a Paul McCartney concert, Intel CEO Andy Grove's keynote address from a technology conference, a discussion of social security reform, and a link through which a child could talk to Santa and his favorite elf, Ernie McFoozel.

Revenue for the site came not from people paying to listen to individual sports events, as Cuban had once suggested, or from monthly subscriptions, as a cable company might work. Instead it came from a mix of advertising and from companies paying AudioNet to stream live events such as corporate shareholder meetings. The site was never profitable, losing around $14 million in 1998 and nearly $8 million in 1999.[6] But those losses were not enough to temper public excitement. In mid-1998 Bloomberg called Broadcast.com the "latest Internet stock superstar," reporting that its value more than tripled on its first day of public trading.[7] A few months later a stock split led to another drastic rise in market capitalization. The company's perplexing valuation was hard to believe even in an era of perplexing valuations. One reporter tried to work through the issue by comparing Broadcast.com—with 250 employees, an office in an old warehouse, and a value of $4.8 billion—with the fast-food restaurant Wendy's—which had 150,000 employees, over 5,000 restaurants, and a value of only $2.8 billion.[8] In early 1999, with consolidation all the rage, internet pioneer Yahoo! agreed to buy Broadcast.com for $5.7 billion in stock. The acquisition, explained one analyst, fed into Yahoo!'s goal of becoming "the only place you need to go for anything and everything you need on the Web."[9] It also made Mark Cuban and Todd Wagner very rich. Even Jaeb got paid, pulling in around $50 million even though he hadn't worked for the company for years.

At first it seemed that Wagner and Cuban would stick around. In an interview in November 1999 Cuban mentioned that he wanted to "combine our digital media leadership with [Yahoo!'s] incredible network to create the dominant 21st Century media company."[10] That same month Cuban attended a Dallas Mavericks game and decided that maybe being a media tycoon wasn't what he really wanted. Instead he wanted to buy a basketball team. In January 2000, while Yahoo!'s stock price hit an all-time high, Cuban was named owner of the Mavericks. Over the next year Yahoo!'s stock price plummeted nearly 90 percent. That was hardly an issue for the Broadcast.com co-owners, though, because they had pulled off a series of financial maneuvers to protect their fortune from that very scenario. "Yahoo could go to zero tomorrow and I'm still going to have a 'B' next to my name," Cuban told one newspaper.[11]

Such protection was a good thing because Cuban was quickly racking up thousands of dollars of fines for berating referees from his courtside seat in Dallas. Many saw the outbursts as part of a bigger plan, a way to insert the once-moribund Mavericks into the public conversation. It worked; everyone was talking about this new, over-the-top billionaire owner. Even the man in charge of issuing the fines, NBA commissioner David Stern, saw the value Cuban was bringing to the league. In one interview he commented that "Mark Cuban is one of the best salesmen I've ever met."[12]

At the time the league needed all the publicity it could get. The retirement of Michael Jordan, a prolonged labor dispute, a shortened season, and an NBA Finals with a historically low television rating meant Stern was getting desperate. Like Cuban, he had never been afraid to tinker with the status quo, to adjust strategy based on the shifting winds of economic trends. In the early 1980s, during another era of reduced ratings and dwindling interest, Stern had even toyed with the idea of moving the NBA off broadcast television. "It's fair to say this could be the very last network deal, from the NBA's choice," Stern told reporter Larry Siddons after the league finalized a four-year, $88 million agreement with CBS set to conclude in 1986. And what then, David? With a "look akin to a child who is asked if he'd like to finish the carton of ice cream," Stern described a potential do-it-yourself broadcasting model for the NBA Finals: "Conservatively, let's say the average customer would pay a total of $10 for the seven games. Again conservatively, let's say we have penetration into 10 percent of the homes. That's 3.1 million homes at $10 each, or $31 million."[13] Or more money than the league was currently making with its entire network deal.

The allure of this simple math, buoyed by the growth of cable television, enticed individual teams as well. The Seattle SuperSonics were the innovators on that front, the first team to provide television access to every exhibition and regular-season game during the 1981–82 season. For $120 Sonics fans would receive broadcasts of all games through a network called the SuperChannel and, if they were willing to leave their couches, an additional $120 worth of tickets.[14] Executives around the league were intrigued yet wary of the team's do-it-yourself approach, skeptical that enough fans would pony up enough cash to justify the $1.2 million the Sonics had invested in the project. The critics would be proven right. The SuperChannel experiment lasted just a few years before the team's performance sagged, attendance dropped, and ownership reverted to a limited broadcast schedule of twenty-five road games for the 1985–86 season.

Stern's idea to move the NBA off network television would have been equally misguided. The league's haul from this arrangement would more than double in its next deal with CBS. It would more than *triple* in the deal after that, when NBC secured the rights with a four-year, $600 million agreement beginning in 1990. More important than the money, however, was the visibility. The first eight years of the "NBA on NBC" partnership would coincide with the league's most popular era. There were big city teams like those of New York, Chicago, and Houston; memorable personalities such as Marv Albert, Ahmad Rashad, and Hannah Storm; and a transcendent superstar in Michael Jordan. It was destination viewing. The "NBA on NBC" even had an anthem: John Tesh's "Roundball Rock!" In 1998 the league enjoyed its highest-rated regular season and finals of all time, with the Chicago Bulls beating the Utah Jazz in six games to win the championship. Over seventy million Americans watched at least part of the final game as Michael Jordan crossed over Bryon Russell to sink the title clinching shot with just over five seconds remaining.

That was peak NBA; the decline came quickly. Jordan's retirement (his second of three) and a protracted labor dispute led to a disjointed 1998–99 season with sloppy play and reduced ratings. As if he didn't have enough to deal with, David Stern was also tasked with figuring out what to do about the internet. He knew the medium brought both opportunities and threats. The web was allowing fans to gather in targeted silos—on websites and blogs and messages boards—where they could geek out about their interests for hours at a time. That was good; the NBA had some of the most dedicated fans in the world. Yet the league made most of its money by selling rights to its games, and companies like Broadcast.com were allowing consumers to access dozens of sporting events (and lots of other stuff) for free with little more than a click of a mouse. That wasn't good. A league-wide memo sent by Stern summarized the challenges at hand: "The 'electronic environment' for experiencing sports is changing dramatically. The increasing multitude and variety of entertainment products now available, together with the new technologies that can deliver them in new and more immediate ways, gives our fans more viewing options than ever before."[15]

In 1999, just as Mark Cuban was exiting the media business and beginning his new life as an NBA rabble-rouser, David Stern decided to act, launching the first full-time television network owned by a professional sports league. With a cost of $10 million NBA.com TV represented "the convergence of the Internet, television and basketball."[16] What did that mean? Nobody was quite sure, which is probably why the description was often repeated verbatim by league employees and put in direct quotes by reporters. Regardless, the NBA was uniquely positioned to launch its own channel because of NBA Entertainment, a revenue-generating extension of the league created by Stern in the early 1980s. Housed in a facility in New Jersey, NBA Entertainment was a basketball content factory, the place where the league edited and produced classic games, halftime features, documentaries, and shows such as NBC's NBA *Inside Stuff*. This content would form the backbone of the new network's programming schedule. There would be endless repeats of "hardwood classics," hours of news and information and statistics, and lots of references to NBA League Pass, the league's pricey package of out-of-town games for the displaced or die-hard fan. One reporter called the network "NBA meets MTV meets WebTV."[17] Another said it was "so graphics and number-intensive that it resembles CNBC on steroids."[18] A third called the network "one of the most important developments in sport business since the creation of the salary cap."[19] Adam Silver, president of NBA Entertainment and future NBA commissioner, acknowledged that the network was unique, noting that unlike other channels, it wasn't a place where a viewer was supposed to linger: "We're programmed to be watched in short bits."[20] Kind of like the internet. But on television. Thus, NBA.com TV.

By 2000 the league had also taken complete control of its audio broadcasts, charging fans $29.95 a season to stream games through its website, NBA.com. Around the same time Stern negotiated a deal with a company called Convera Corp., which helped "safeguard copyrighted material" on the internet, so that its games couldn't be streamed elsewhere. The commissioner saw the network and website as integral to keeping the league's customers engaged and envisioned a future in which the fan would be able to "produce his or her own game feed from multiple cameras."[21] In fact while there were no live games on NBA.com TV, many analysts thought that it was only a matter of time before Stern started putting the league's most valuable asset on its fancy new toy. One writer suggested that NBA.com TV "lays the groundwork for the league to eventually break away from those distribution deals as sports rights fees are squeezed by tighter network finances."[22]

In fact, with the landscape changing so quickly, some believed the NBA would have to settle for less than the $660 million a year it was bringing in with its network and cable agreements. The dip never came. In 2002 the NBA signed a series of deals that increased its annual take to $766 million. NBC, which was reportedly losing at least $100 million on its previous deal, was replaced by ABC and ESPN. AOL Time Warner, a partner in some form since 1984, remained on board and would be airing games on its cable network TNT. It also became an investor in NBA TV (the confusing ".com" was quickly dropped), spending $45 million for a 10 percent stake. And while live games would soon appear on the league-owned net, the premier matchups remained in the hands of the league's two big partners. NBA TV became a landing spot for the leftovers.

The subsequent years brought worse news: the uninspiring return and third retirement of Michael Jordan (2003), a shocking brawl between players and fans in Detroit (2004), and the lowest-rated NBA finals of all time (2007). Yet just a few weeks after the Spurs four-game victory over the Cavaliers in 2007, the league signed eight-year deals that increased its annual television take to nearly a billion dollars. The contracts included provisions for digital rights, with ESPN/ABC securing a package that included the ability to air games on both its website and through mobile devices. Said ESPN's vice president of content John Skipper of the digital component: "It's critical to us, and we increasingly prefer to position it as we are buying content; we are not buying television and distributing it over all the platforms."[23] The Turner Broadcasting side of the deal, announced as an extension of "the longest-running league/network programming partnership in professional sports," was even more interesting. There were multiple components. Nearly every aspect of running NBA TV—from programming and marketing to payroll and human resources—would now be Turner's responsibility. Production for the network would move from the NBA office in New Jersey to a new five-thousand-square-foot studio in Turner's facilities in Atlanta, Georgia. Turner would also assume operations for NBA.com and NBA League Pass and would help sell advertising for these digital extensions.[24]

Those were the details. The big takeaway was this: David Stern was pausing his do-it-yourself experiment. When he launched NBA.com TV as "the convergence of the Internet, television and basketball," the commissioner had dreamed of the league expanding its media operations—after all, shouldn't the NBA distribute its own content in a world where all were starting to distribute their own content? In one article Stern was quoted as saying, "Whether the fight to get into the home is ultimately won by DSL or cable modem or wireless, the issue is content. We think we have content."[25] Stern was right; the issue is *always* content. With the explosion of cable television and the growth of the internet, the amount of available content grew. Some experts predicted that this saturation would lead to decreased viewership and the erosion of the value of sports rights. They were half right. The infusion of more content into the media landscape did decrease viewership for many leagues—the NBA included—but it didn't dilute the value of sports. On the contrary, it made highly sought-after content even more valuable, with networks (and eventually streaming platforms) needing something they could use to compete in a crowded market. And programming that had to be watched live and could be peppered with advertising? Absolute gold. In the 2000s live rights to popular sports became one of the most valuable assets in the entire media industry.

With networks increasingly willing to pay the league more and more money for its content, David Stern's ultimate vision of having the league do things such as produce customized games for the individual fan seemed both logistically and financially unnecessary. In fact why was the league getting intricately involved in the media side at all when it had perfectly capable partners willing to shoulder that load? After the 2007 agreements the NBA could focus on creating the content—the actual basketball games—while Turner Broadcasting could focus on producing and distributing it. Stern explained that it was nothing more than good business: "We think the best way to optimize our suite of digital and television assets in the U.S. is with a media company that can provide us with the scale, expertise and resources to enhance and grow these properties."[26]

This finally brings the story back to Broadcast.com. With Cuban and Wagner gone, the renamed Yahoo! Broadcast Services didn't last very long. In 2002, just three years after the sale, the company more or less pulled the plug on its $5.7 billion acquisition. Many suggested that the service failed because the economy crashed and advertising dried up, crushing the company's business model. There's truth to that. The other part of the story, however, is that Yahoo! never kept up the breakneck content-acquisition pace of the original founders. Sports, so important to Cuban and Wagner's pitch in the early days, pretty much disappeared. On one day in late January 1999, for instance, the sports section of Broadcast.com had links to the Super Bowl press conference, an NHL game between the New York Rangers and Carolina Hurricanes, the Australian Open, and two ACC men's basketball games. That's not bad. Three years later, in late January 2002, the main sports page had only three videos: one about the history of the

University of North Carolina men's basketball team, one about NFL wide receiver Jerry Rice, and one called *Surfing: All Aboard*, which was described as "one of the best, if not the best, surfing videos of 2001." There were zero links to live games.[27]

Mark Cuban understood content was key to the entire operation. In 1999 Cuban told *Fast Company*: "We rarely if ever produce original content. We only use content that has some level of demand. This way we don't have to pay to create demand, which is the hardest and most expensive asset to create."[28] What he didn't tell the magazine, although he may have been thinking it, was that when you don't make the content, you need to constantly be on the search for more of it. That's exhausting. Remember, Mark Cuban was an expert salesman. He convinced many leagues and colleges (and all the other entities that signed on for Broadcast.com) to hand over the audio rights for his new service. When Yahoo! came calling, he said, "Look at all the stuff we have!" And then he cashed out before all the content went its separate ways, fragmented across the tentacles of the expanding internet. Cuban, in essence, went from being a content distributor (Broadcast.com) to a content provider (Dallas Mavericks).

Broadcast.com fizzled because there's always going to be a competitive market for content that delivers a guaranteed audience. That's also one reason why sports leagues and conferences experimented but never went completely all-in with their own media platforms. It's just not worth it. As the traditional media companies—ESPN and Fox and Turner—kept elevating the cost for sports rights, any do-it-yourself effort launched by an individual league would have had to guarantee the league more than it was getting from its partners. Add to that equation the trouble of staffing a network, coordinating production, ensuring distribution, selling advertising, and dealing with angry customers, and suddenly becoming a media company doesn't sound so attractive.

The NFL probably went the furthest of the American professional leagues, launching its own cable network in 2003 and airing an exclusive slate of Thursday night games starting in 2006. Like the NBA, the NFL had significant experience producing its own content. For decades NFL Films had been pumping out over-the-top, slow-motion, music-accompanied highlights of memorable games and seasons, serving as what one *Sports Illustrated* writer has called "the most effective propaganda organ in the history of corporate America."[29] NFL Films was straight from the Pete Rozelle handbook—sugar-coated, shiny, do-no-wrong public relations—and would be installed as the perfect content provider for the new cable network. Upon the launch of NFL Network and recognizing its position of strength, the league demanded a substantial per-subscriber fee from cable companies. The companies balked, distribution slowed, and a series of legal battles ensued. Through it all the NFL made sure not to disrupt its core business: the national broadcast deals. The lucrative result of the 1961 Sports Broadcasting Act, these deals continued to increase unabated.

And what about the in-market broadcast rights to individual teams? Again Mark Cuban provides a good example as to what happened. The man once anointed "the king of streaming" by one magazine never bothered to launch his own streaming service to broadcast Mavericks games.[30] Instead Cuban has maintained a relationship with the same cable network (Fox Sports Southwest, which became Bally Sports Southwest) since purchasing the team. Perhaps the estimated $50 million in annual revenue he receives is more attractive than the allure of creating another cash-bleeding media company.[31] And while individual teams like the Mets and Yankees would get involved in the cable business, most did so by creating partnerships with already established players. Success has varied. Others, like the Mavericks, were quite satisfied to hand broadcasting duty off to others in exchange for tens (or hundreds) of millions of dollars.

Again, it's hard to be good at one thing. It's almost impossible to be really good at all things all at once. That was Cuban's rationale for developing Broadcast.com, as he once explained in response to a question about content creation and content distribution: "Culturally, it's hard to be everything. And then there's the technology aspect of it. It's hard to say, OK, you know, how am I going to stream millions of hours, millions of users? It's not an easy thing to do."[32] What often makes the most sense, then, is a marriage between the entity good at getting the content to the consumer and the entity good at creating the content. That's the reason why, forty years after David Stern fantasized about the NBA selling its championship round directly to consumers, most sport leagues still sell the most valuable chunk of their most valuable asset to other companies for distribution. As Stern would say in 2008: "Developing your own expertise in every aspect of a business will ultimately turn out to be too expensive for us and not avail us of the best opportunity for growth."[33] Once leagues figured this part out, they'd concentrate their energy on their primary revenue source: the live event. They would then do what they could to make sure the internet wouldn't hijack their golden goose.

Everything else, however—all the pregame and postgame and commentary and discussion—turned out to be much harder to protect.

The Sports Guys

18

Leitch vs. Bissinger on Costas Now *(2008)*

By 2000, five years after it had launched its website, ESPN was still trying to figure out how the internet worked. It's not that the company's site wasn't doing well. It was, especially when compared to cash-hemorrhaging competitors like SportsLine. But the executive who had been put in charge of ramping up ESPN's digital strategy, eventual president John Skipper, didn't really know what he was doing: "When I went to run ESPN.com, I am not sure I had ever been on the site," he told author James Andrew Miller years later. "I didn't know the first thing about the Internet; I was not an early adopter of technology." His plan was to keep it simple: "We're not leading a movement; we're coming over there to create great content." Skipper was an unabashed advocate of print, having worked at both *Spin* and *Rolling Stone* before being tapped to launch ESPN *The Magazine*. So his strategy was to take what made magazines great—"feature writers and design and photography"—and translate that style to the internet.[1]

One example of this "old media through new media" approach was the creation of ESPN.com's Page 2. Unveiled on November 6, 2000, Page 2 was described as a "fact-filled, fan-happy, serious and sometimes less-than-serious page that will give sports fans a fresh and different take on the world of sports."[2] The site's first day lived up to this somewhat contradictory introduction. It featured a rambling essay by newspaper reporter Brian Murphy ("Monday musings with the Murph"), a list of University of Tennessee basketball player Michelle Snow's favorite dunkers, and point spreads for upcoming NFL games. Fluff, mostly.[3]

But tucked away in the corner was something else entirely: an article from celebrated American writer Hunter S. Thompson. Never one to be bound by traditional editorial standards or buttoned-up journalistic tact, the *Fear and Loathing in Las Vegas* author used his space on Page 2 to rail not only against American politics and the hypocrisy of the NFL, but also both topics at the same time. The convoluted ellipse- and ampersand-riddled rant began as a diatribe about the recent U.S. presidential election between Al Gore and George W. Bush: "The whole Presidential election, in fact, was rigged and fixed from the start. . . . It was a gigantic Media Event, scripted & staged for TV. It happens every four years, at an ever-increasing cost & 90 percent of the money always goes for TV commercials. Of course, nobody would give a damn except politics is beginning to smell like professional football, Dank & Nasty. And that's a problem that could haunt America a lot longer than four years, folks."[4]

But hold on; didn't Thompson enjoy football? Wasn't that a require- ment to work at the world's most famous sports media brand? Maybe not. The NFL, according to Thompson, was a shell of its former self. Just like politics. "The teams change names & locations every year," Thompson wrote. "Even winning coaches go crazy with angst or get fired on the whim of a new owner. Players come & go like substitute teachers or half-bright fashion models. They took to beating their wives in public & and getting arrested for Murder. But the games go on like clockwork and the money keeps pouring in. . . . Most stadiums are sold out every Sunday. But only rich people can afford to attend the games in person. It's not much different from getting involved in National Politics."[5]

Perhaps Thompson was ahead of his time. As internet commenta- tors would learn over the next few decades, political tirades are one of the most effective ways to engage (and enrage) an online audience blessed with almost infinite options. But they weren't the *only* way, as Thompson's contemporaries would soon figure out. Over at AOL, for instance, an aspiring sportswriter named Bill Simmons—who went by the nickname "Sports Guy"—was quickly building an audience by writing about the Celtics, the Patriots, the Red Sox, movies, drinking, porn, and (most of all) himself. Cognizant of his growing anti-establishment persona, Simmons openly eschewed the press box, which he claimed was "artificial and weird and you can't cheer or experience a game the way typical sports fans experience things." (This quote came from an interview in which Bill Simmons interviewed himself.) Even then differentiation was tough: "The other biggest problem is an identity thing—since so many people have home pages or homemade sites on the 'Net, some people might mistakenly believe that I'm just some yahoo fan who loves sports and started a home page that people liked."[6] But Simmons, according to Simmons, was not that at all. Instead he was a diligent worker who had dedicated significant time and effort to develop a robust audience.

In that same "interview" Simmons revealed what he believed had been his two most popular pieces up to that point. The first was a three-thousand-word, play-by-play recap of an "epic" gambling trip he took with some of his buddies to Las Vegas. Employing a Simmons-favorite "running diary" format, the article includes a roundup of his wacky friends (like Bish and Hopper and the Doctor); his goals for the excursion (the big one: don't cheat on his girlfriend); an O. J. Simpson joke ("I feel like Ron Goldman as he was handing over Nicole's glasses outside her condo. . . . In other words, I am suddenly and inexplicably getting K-I-L-L-E-D"); and a recap of a conversation he and his friends had about the porn star Rocco Siffredi. The article contains a couple of sports analogies—"a hot craps table is like Game Six of the 1975 World Series"—and a few random sports anecdotes, but it's mostly about Bill Simmons and how much Bill Simmons liked to gamble and how much money Bill Simmons lost.[7]

The other popular piece, "Grading the Wimbledon Babes," was written in response to a reader poll Simmons had conducted about a potential topic for an upcoming column. The idea had been included as a joke but had garnered nearly half the votes. Forever beholden to his readers, Simmons plowed ahead with the column but not without a few disclaimers: "If you're a female reader, just do yourself a favor and stop reading right now. I'm not kidding. Just stop." This was an apt warning, mostly because of what Simmons had to say about Venus and Serena Williams: "Call me crazy, but I think they're cute in an

Amazon kinda way. . . . Any man who hasn't thought about being in the middle of a Williams sister sandwich is lying." And what he had to say about Monica Seles: "Always looks like she hasn't showered in about five days. . . . Used to be much cuter a few years ago, before she was stabbed in the back." And what he had to say about Jennifer Capriati: "One of my buddies in the know swears that Capriati had a breast reduction, so we're going to have to dock her grade just on rumor alone."[8] This was the kind of content Simmons's readers craved. And because he kept churning it out, his readership kept growing. A year or so after this column was written, Simmons was hired by ESPN as part of the company's attempt to expand its online offerings, specifically on its new Page 2 extension. He quickly became the company's most popular columnist.

That Simmons used booze and boobs to boost his readership was hardly groundbreaking. Media moguls like Rupert Murdoch had deployed such an attention-grabbing shortcut for decades, even if Rupert could never quite figure out how to do it on the internet. And Simmons was hardly alone in those early internet days. Other digital "sports guys" (and they were indeed mostly guys) were doing similar things with this exciting new medium. One of them, a former broadcaster and radio personality named Brooks Melchior, carved out a digital niche by combining sports news and analysis with pictures of scantily clad young women. He called it "SportsByBrooks" (SBB), even though the blog was as much about women as it was about sports. As one colleague told journalist Jeff Pearlman years later, "[Melchior] knew what brought people to the site. Girls with comic-book sized breasts."[9] Melchior also knew how to stretch the brand, hosting dozens of live in-person "gigs" where fans of the blog would come together to eat and drink and take pictures with girls in tight clothes.

Sports + women = young male audience. Young male audience = advertisers. These were simple formulas. And creators soon figured out that the recipe could be enhanced even further with the addition of a critical ingredient, the most alluring content category of all: gossip. One of the best at putting it all together was a blogger named Will Leitch. Leitch began his online writing career on a website called *The Black Table*, where he penned a column called "Life as a Loser." One column describes an unusual encounter with a man on a subway.

Another details Leitch's reaction when he finds out he needs to take a drug test. But what Leitch really wanted to do was stick it to the man, to challenge the sports media establishment. In the mid-2000s he reached out to executives at the gossip site Gawker and pitched his idea of a sports extension: "The Internet and sports are made for each other. But what has really been missing has been a strong, askew voice from outside the circle jerk of buffet-addled sportswriters interviewing naked athletes. Independent sports blogs are everywhere, but they don't have any passion. They're mostly just stat nerds." The founder of Gawker, Nick Denton, thought all that was fine, but what he liked most of all in Leitch's proposal was that the site would come with an entrenched archrival, a powerful entity to poke and prod until that entity was forced to respond: "What decided me on Deadspin [the site Denton and Leitch would eventually create] was the existence of a clear enemy. It was arranged not so much around one singular passion as one singular jihad against the cozy cartel of ESPN and the managers."[10]

Yet this "jihad" was hardly singular. The voices emerging from the blogosphere enjoyed having an enemy—a classic "us vs. them" strategy—and the established sports media companies were easy marks. Sometimes the targets were oddly specific. One popular blog was launched with the explicit purpose of getting Hall of Fame second baseman Joe Morgan fired from his job as an ESPN baseball analyst. It was called, naturally, FireJoeMorgan.com (FJM). The site's writers soon discovered that there was a healthy market for instant mockery of all sports punditry, something that the blogosphere was well equipped to handle. FJM writers would watch or read about sports, absorb the analysis, and then ridicule that analysis with additional analysis. Nobody was safe; everybody was fair game. Some of it was quick—a joke or two about some inane color commentary during a regular-season baseball game. But often it was quite detailed, such as the time one of the site's founders, a writer who called himself "Ken Tremendous," wrote six thousand words about twelve minutes of content from radio host Colin Cowherd: "I wish I could convey his strained, howling voice . . . the condescending way he makes his points, as if he were speaking to a four year-old . . . the way his arrogance and self-assuredness positively oozes through one's car speakers as he blathers on."[11]

In October 2005 FJM published a self-congratulatory post called "Are We Responsible? I Think Definitely." Here's what FJM writer Matthew Murbles had to say about a recent discovery: "Guess which fat idiot's name is no longer listed in the ESPN.com list of baseball contributors? Does this mean he has been fired? Or did they just ban him from approaching a keyboard? I think either represents a huge victory. Good work, everybody."[12] Nevertheless, the site continued for three more years until FJM announced that it was shutting down in late 2008. The writer explained that the shutdown came because "the realities of our professional and personal lives make FJM a time/work luxury we can no longer afford."[13] Indeed, it would have been difficult for one to maintain FJM while producing, writing for, and occasionally acting in NBC's *The Office*, as FJM founder "Ken Tremendous," a.k.a. Dwight Schrute's cousin Mose, a.k.a. soon-to-be-major-Hollywood-power-player Michael Schur would have been forced to do.

In 2008 the tension among all these up-and-comers—Deadspin, SBB, FJM—and the old guard exploded into the open on *Costas Now*, an HBO talk show hosted by longtime broadcaster Bob Costas. It was designed as a panel discussion; it turned into a pissing match. Representing the old timers was Pulitzer Prize–winning journalist Buzz Bissinger. Representing the new kids was Will Leitch, founding editor of Deadspin. And representing the athlete was star NFL wide receiver Braylon Edwards. Costas began the segment with a voiceover: "The wild west of the internet—the blogosphere. A virtual bulletin board where anyone can post anything. Opinions, photos, videos. All blurring the lines between news and gossip, truth and rumor, commentary and insult."[14] As the pre-edited portion ended and the camera revealed the four men sitting on stage in front of a live audience, Costas, who clearly had his mind made up about the "wild west" before the panel had even begun, turned to Leitch and said, "The way this was framed by you and Michael Schur is, 'Hey, what's the problem with having more information and quicker access to it? What's the problem with somebody being able to voice their opinion? Instead of just hearing it from a cab driver, now that cab driver can go on the internet, he can blog, he can be on a site, he can express his opinion.'" But this access, Costas argued, wasn't the problem. Instead the problem was the "tone of gratuitous potshots and mean-spirited abuse."

At this point Leitch began his defense: "You know, it's not news to say that people are different online than they are in person." But he didn't get very far because Buzz Bissinger was fired up and ready to go: "I'm just gonna interject because I feel very strongly about this. I really think you're full of shit. Because I think blogs are dedicated to cruelty. They're dedicated to journalistic dishonesty. They're dedicated to speed." Bissinger then asked Leitch if he had ever read the work of W. C. Heinz, a mid-century American journalist considered by many as one of the greatest sports columnists of all time. Leitch said yes. But Bissinger didn't care. He had used the Heinz reference only in order to compare the journalist to a Deadspin writer named "Balls Deep." Bissinger then looked at Leitch and asked, "How can you be proud of that stuff?"

Hoping to defuse the situation, Costas took control and conceded that not everything on the internet was terrible: "There are a number of sports blogs that are well written, make good points, are insightful and are funny. But there is a very large percentage where the quality is poor and the tone is abusive." Given the chance to respond to this point, Leitch made the fan-centric point that the internet allowed for competition, and competition was a good thing: "The nice thing about the web is that it's a meritocracy. Sure, anyone *can* start a blog. But to get a readership, you have to be serious, you have to be consistent, it's hard goddamn work doing a blog." Fair enough, said Costas, before he read a series of comments made by Deadspin readers in response to analyst Sean Salisbury's being let go by ESPN: "Good riddance fuckface" and "So long you fetus-faced windbag" and "Good luck managing a Denny's, douchebag."

At this point Leitch laughed and pleaded with the audience to understand the difference between the writers and the commenters. Bissinger didn't buy it: "What does it add? What does it contribute?" he asked of these random commentators. Nevertheless, the segment ended with Bissinger conceding that the industry to which he'd devoted his life's work had been overrun: "This guy, whether we like it or not, is the future. I'm not the future." He then turned to Leitch and made a prediction: "I think the future in the hands of guys like you is really, really going to dumb us down to a degree that I don't know we can recover from."

Two hours after the segment aired, Leitch took to Deadspin to discuss the show. He wrote: "It was obvious that Bissinger had been building up to this for a long time, those dark nights wondering what the kids were searching online, those terrifying moments when the world seemed to be spasming out of his control. . . . They all built up to this." Leitch, however, maintained that he had come out on top during the confrontation, that Bissinger's breakdown had invalidated his argument, and that the relentless vitriol thrown his way was simply the last gasp of sports media's old guard: "We just watched a man immolate on national television. To have piled on the carnage would have been discourteous. The future is obvious to anyone even slightly interested in looking. We just stand aside, as he, as they, watch the light shrink, then fade, then vanish."[15]

A few months before the airing of the *Costas Now* episode, Will Leitch had published a book called *God Save the Fan*. It was one of the reasons he had agreed to be on the show. Touted by its publisher as a "manifesto" for fans "suffering from a sense of listless dissatisfaction brought on by the leagues and networks," the book covers a variety of subjects. One chapter is called "Willie McGee: My Sister's First Black Man." Another looks at the "Ten Most Loathsome ESPN Personalities and Their Worst Moments." A year later, fresh off the most talked-about media appearance of his career, Leitch released a paperback version with a new three-thousand word chapter about the *Costas Now* encounter. The new material sparked even more discussion, including a piece in the *Village Voice* in which the reporter questioned why Leitch continued to bring up the incident: "Is it possible that someone who has dished out such major league sass to corporations like ESPN can't take a little tough talk from Buzz Bissinger without whining, particularly when it brings him national attention?"[16] What we had here, then, was an article about a book chapter about a television appearance—a debate about a debate about a debate—none of which *actually* had to do with sports. The entire charade, thousands of words of bluster and bravado and cheap shots, was about the people who watched or listened to or wrote about sports. It was sports guys arguing with other sports guys. There would never be a winner. Maybe that was the point. And viewed from that angle, perhaps the most memorable part of the *Costas Now* encounter was the mostly forgettable contributions of Braylon Edwards, who had sat quietly on a stage next to two guys angrily debating how best to write about and discuss a sport that he played for a living.

The rise of the new sports guys at the expense of the former sports guys was evidence of two important if not surprising revelations. The first was that the average sports fan sure had a lot to say. And with the internet he or she finally had a chance to say it. Talk radio had teased this shift toward sports punditry democracy, providing fans with the opportunity to call up and voice their opinions live, on-air. But the nature of talk radio also allowed the often cantankerous hosts—and nobody was more cantankerous than these hosts—to cut the fans off mid-sentence, to silence them, to put them in their place and return the microphone to the so-called experts. The internet took away this muzzle; it was impossible to hang up on somebody online. Here was a place where the fan could rant and ramble freely, a place that would gladly host six-thousand word soliloquys not only about Notre Dame football or New York Yankees baseball, but also about somebody *talking* about Notre Dame football or New York Yankees baseball. This wasn't inside baseball. This was inside, inside baseball. The creation of podcasts, talk radio that broke free of any temporal restrictions, only increased these opportunities, places where fans could ramble without having to write anything down. The sports guys had been unshackled; content would follow—lots and lots and lots of content. Some of it would be good, smart, and insightful. A lot of it would be jokes about porn.

The second revelation from the rise of the new sports guys was even more important than the first: what Simmons and his ilk had made clear with their writing was that maybe sports fans didn't want to just talk about their favorite players and teams. Maybe what sports fans really wanted to talk about was themselves: whom they rooted for and why, how their fantasy teams were doing, how hung over they were when they saw this game or that match, how they handled being verbally accosted by Buzz Bissinger. Maybe that was the allure of some of this early sports guy-ish content. Less "Hey, I could be friends with this guy" and more "Hey, that guy is me!" Perhaps Simmons hadn't built an audience because he had an interesting friend named Sully, gambled on the NFL, and found it difficult to not cheat on his girlfriend. Instead maybe Simmons had built an audience because all those reading his columns also had a friend named Sully and gambled on the NFL and found it difficult to not cheat on their girlfriends. For all those sports guys Simmons was simply a mirror. And his readers liked what they saw: themselves.

An Essential Good   **19**

Fútbol para Todos (2009)

In August 2009 ESPN sent Bill Simmons to a World Cup qualifying match between the United States and Mexico at the Estadio Azteca (Aztec Stadium) in Mexico City. If the article he wrote about the experience was any indication, Simmons was scared the entire time. He rode through the city in "SUVs with bulletproof windows and security guards." Once at the stadium, he chose not to sit not in the stands, an atmosphere that came to resemble a "prison riot," but rather in a suite with some ESPN and American soccer executives. Yet even that arrangement was daunting as he "got trapped in one of Azteca's oppressively hot elevators and saw [his] life briefly flash before [his] eyes." Luckily Bill Simmons survived, churning out a few thousand words about the ordeal. In addition to the harrowing details the piece contained the usual Sports Guy jokes. One about alcohol: "I drank enough tequila to kill Salma Hayek." Another about dog fighting: "Michael Vick could crash a PETA rally and get a friendlier reception than the Americans did at Azteca." There was some rudimentary soccer analysis and gushing praise for young American forward Jozy Altidore. And there was a brief attempt at a grand conclusion, one that came to Simmons as he rode home from the game (in the car with bulletproof glass of course) and saw a lone fan standing on a bridge enthusiastically waving a Mexican flag: "I remember thinking to myself, 'Nobody in America will ever care about a sport that much.' And we won't."[1]

Unfortunately that was the extent of the analysis. More concerned with adhering to the let's-talk-about-me Sports Guy brand, Simmons made little attempt to understand *why* Mexicans, or Latin Americans as a whole, might care so much about soccer. It seemed like a wasted opportunity, especially for a guy who enjoyed breaking things down into their component parts. (Simmons once wrote over two thousand words comparing the 1990s show *Beverly Hills 90210* to the 2000s show *The O.C.*) And the discussion would have been particularly timely, as just a few days after this match, the president of Argentina went on television and did exactly what Simmons had failed to do: she explained why soccer meant so much to Latin Americans. Then she announced a new sports media–related policy, one so unusual and so contrary to the trajectory of the industry over the prior thirty years that it demands its own discussion.

We'll get to that. But first the issue at hand: why do Mexicans care so much about soccer? For that we turn to Benedict Anderson's *Imagined Communities*, a book many first-year sociology or political science students know well. In this well-cited treatise Anderson suggests that the breakdown of traditional monarchies and religious communities hundreds of years ago forced humans to find a new way to understand who they were and what space they occupied in the world. The idea of the planet as a collection of autonomous nations, a world made up of different countries, fit the bill. Anderson goes on to define each of these nations as "an imagined political community" in which "the members of even the smallest nation will never know most of their fellow-members, meet them, or even hear of them, yet in the minds of each lives the image of their communion."[2] Other scholars went on to call these communities "fictions" or "social constructs" or "myths." The main point is this: there are no lines on the earth to properly delineate Argentina from Chile or Mexico from Guatemala. If human beings were somehow wiped off the face of the earth, countries would immediately cease to exist. In other words, a country is only a country because we humans say that it's a country.

And because these entities exist only in our minds, we must constantly find ways to keep them alive. We do so, Anderson suggests, by employing a variety of rituals and artifacts. Newspapers allow people in different locations to wake up and read stories about their fellow citizens. Censuses reinforce the fact that "everyone has one—and only one—extremely clear place" in the world.[3] Maps create a visual image of how the world is broken up and where each nation fits into the larger puzzle. And national anthems offer a linguistic unifier across both space and time.

Sports help too. Take Mexico as a prime example. For the first hundred or so years of its existence Mexico behaved less like a country and more like a collection of distinct regions, unable or unwilling to develop a coherent identity. Then in the early twentieth century the Mexican Revolution shook up the status quo. The fighting went on for decades; a series of leaders came and went. The revolution altered the nation's trajectory, although historians rarely agree as to how and to what extent. Regardless, the lengthy conflict necessitated a complementary unifying influence. It was around this time that soccer became useful. As historian Joshua Nadel has argued, "While it would be a stretch to say that soccer alone brought the nation back together after ten years of internecine struggle, it definitely played a role."[4] The government did what it could to promote the sport. It exempted equipment from foreign tariffs, promoted a national system of physical education, and created the Mexican Federation of Association Football. In short the government hoped that soccer would be an outlet through which Mexicans of all regions and backgrounds could be Mexican together. Decades later Bill Simmons would witness this phenomenon firsthand.

The sport's unifying influence was even stronger elsewhere in Latin America, especially in Argentina. Soccer arrived at a time when Argentines were seeking a way to distinguish their country from both their European colonists and their South American neighbors. Together with another of Anderson's artifacts, the media industry, the sport helped Argentina define what it meant to be Argentinian. Newspapers and radio stations and movies suggested that the country's players were "more beautiful, more artistic, more precise" than their English counterparts.[5] The sports magazine *El Gráfico* was at the forefront of this discussion, suggesting that this inimitable Argentinian flair was a product of the country's unique playing conditions. One historian summarizes this theory as follows: "The wastelands and open spaces of the city provided the physical canvas on which the *pibe*'s [young, poor boy's] imagination and energy could be expressed."[6] Success on the global stage gave credence to the idea that this style was not only distinct, but also effective: a series of wins by the country's most popular club team in Europe in 1925, a silver medal at the 1928 Amsterdam Olympics, second place at the first-ever World Cup in 1930. Coupled with the *pibe* mythology, these victories created an "epic narrative, in which soccer contributed, in an important way, to the 'invention of a nation.'"[7]

Once this powerful connection among soccer, media, and Argentinian identity was established, it was only a matter of time until politicians decided they needed to control it. Sometimes it was to protect their country's "epic narrative" from an unexpected deviation. The administration of President Juan Perón, for instance, prevented Argentina's men's national team from participating in three international tournaments—the 1949 Copa America and both the 1950 and 1954 World Cups—out of fear that the team would lose, the press would pounce, and the country would slip into a deep depression. These fears were only heightened when Brazil lost to Uruguay in the 1950 World Cup final in front of an estimated two hundred thousand fans at the Maracanã Stadium in Rio de Janeiro. The magnitude of the loss on the Brazilian psyche is difficult to overstate; it reverberated throughout the country for decades. Some argue the pain has never gone away. A Brazilian anthropologist has called the match "perhaps the greatest tragedy in contemporary Brazilian history."[8] A prominent playwright has compared the loss to the bombing of Hiroshima.[9] It created the kind of deep national wound Perón was trying to avoid.

A shift in the political winds forced Perón to flee the country in 1955, and the national team soon resumed play. Two disappointing World Cups (1958 and 1962) were followed by the country's reaching the 1966 quarterfinals and losing to eventual champion England. That same year Argentina received a valuable consolation prize when it was named host of the 1978 World Cup. Celebration ensued. There was hope that Argentina, like England in 1966, could become one of the few countries to hoist the championship trophy on its own turf. But politics complicated this optimistic outlook. By the mid-1970s Argentina was being governed by a ruthless military junta. Most citizens lived in constant fear. Led by General Jorge Videla, those in charge had opponents detained, tortured, and often killed. Some of the tactics used were unfathomably cruel, such as the revelation years later that babies of captured women were stolen and given to families loyal to the regime. Videla and his allies also maintained control of the country's media, establishing onerous jail terms for anyone who dared mention the opposition or say anything negative about the people in charge. Dozens of journalists were rounded up and murdered; hundreds more were jailed.

With Argentina set to host one of the most visible sporting events in the world, Videla set about trying to figure out why the world had such a negative view of his country. To help with this inquiry Videla paid the U.S. public relations firm Burson Marsteller (BM) a million dollars to investigate and then improve Argentina's international image. In its initial report back to the general BM laid out some obvious hurdles: "The matter of terrorism and human rights, the alleged anti-Semitism and repression and isolationism must all be put to rest if Argentina is to assume its rightful place in the world."[10] Nonetheless, Burson Marsteller was up for the task, outlining a three-pronged public relations strategy by which it would approach influencers in the press, in business, and in the travel industry in order to change Argentina's global image.

The government knew that the most important component to this rehabilitation strategy was the 1978 World Cup. Taking a page from Adolf Hitler's use of the 1936 Olympics, Videla and his administration saw the tournament as an event that could get everybody to stop talking about all the people disappearing. In an interview with the *New York Times* in 1978 an official subtly laid out the strategy as follows: "If it were necessary to make some correction in our image which exists abroad, the 1978 World Cup will be just the occasion to show the world our real way of life."[11] But not everybody was on board with the strategy. The country's most famous writer, Jorge Luis Borges, had no interest in using soccer as an antidote for what he believed were deeply ingrained societal woes: "I am a fervent patriot and, I hope, a good citizen, but I emphatically do not hold the uncanonical belief, now voiced by the press, and by the radio, of salvation through football. . . . I abhor or hate Communists, Nationalists and Fascists impartially, and I think the cult of football is hardly a remedy for these ailments."[12]

Nonsense, said the government, who saw soccer as the perfect distraction. Videla and his cronies went to work preparing Argentina for the tournament. They built state-of-the-art color television facilities, banned criticism of the national team, and encouraged the country's newspapers to print stories about the intricate preparations. Foreign journalists, identified by BM as one of the more stubborn yet promising groups of potential ambassadors, were invited to Argentina on all-expense-paid trips to interview a curated group of government officials. Despite these efforts many reporters remained suspicious of the junta's intent. Just a few weeks before kickoff the British National Union of Journalists (NUJ) sent every British reporter who planned on traveling to Argentina a pamphlet that was meant "to draw the attention of the sportswriters to the obliteration of press freedom and trade union rights by the military junta which now rules Argentina." The handbook not only encouraged journalists to look beyond the pitch for "stories worth pursuing," but also provided a few tips in terms of navigating the dicey social and political environment. It suggested that reporters do their best to not look "subversive" (because the organization had evidence that an international photo journalist had been shot because he did "look subversive") and offered some Spanish phrases that might be useful in a pinch. For example: "Dejen de torturarme, por favor" (Please stop torturing me). And: "Por favor entregen mi corpo a mi familia" (Please deliver my body to my family).[13]

Of course all this preparation would have been for naught had Argentina's national team not lived up to expectations. But a crisis was averted as the team followed the junta's desired script, defeating the Netherlands in the final to become the fifth host to win a World Cup. The international press fell in line too, equating the victory with a rousing national rebrand. Here's a section from the Associated Press story printed in hundreds of newspapers across the United States the next day: "The win meant more to Argentina than just a sports title. Through four years of efforts, $700 million in stadium investments, and a vibrant young team, Argentina changed part of its image abroad not only as a soccer power but as a developing nation."[14]

The momentum wouldn't last. A few years later, with a faulty economy diminishing the junta's already tenuous popularity, the government tried another tactic to rile up some nationalistic fervor.

This time the approach was war rather than sport as the government authorized an invasion of the British-controlled Falkland Islands (Argentina calls the islands Islas Malvinas). But if the 1978 World Cup was a meticulously planned triumph, the 1982 war was the complete opposite: a hastily designed follow-up act. Ten weeks and hundreds of deaths later, Argentina was forced to surrender. The next year the junta lost power. Democratic elections resumed soon after.

The next two decades saw a rapid acceleration of Argentina's media industry. The government, which for decades had played a critical role in the development of print, radio, and television, mostly stepped aside, allowing for new investment by both national and international companies. As far as sports media was concerned, many of the usual suspects got involved. ESPN, intent on fulfilling its "Worldwide Leader in Sports" moniker, entered Latin America in 1989. Fox followed a few years later. In 2000 the U.S. investment firm Hicks Muse Tate & Furst poured hundreds of millions of dollars into its Pan-American Sports Network (PSN), a twenty-four-hour Spanish/Portuguese language network focused on Latin American sport. But it had terrible timing. Faced with a trifecta of bad news—the dot-com bust, 9/11, and a massive financial collapse in Argentina—the network lasted only two years.

PSN got at least one thing right: its emphasis on soccer. The network launched with a broadcast of the opening match of Copa Libertadores, a tournament made up of the best South American club teams (similar to the UEFA Champions League in Europe). PSN executives, in fact, said that over half of all the network's programming would be soccer-based: live events, replays, news programs. ESPN had followed a similar strategy, beaming broadcasts of English and Spanish soccer into the region from Bristol, Connecticut, before opening offices across Latin America. Perhaps most indicative of the region's obsession with soccer, however, was a Fox Sports show airing in Argentina called *Minuto a Minuto*. With the Argentina Premier Division airing exclusively on a different pay network, the show was developed as a more affordable alternative, covering matches not through live video footage on the field but rather through "the celebration and anguish of coaches and fans in packed stadiums." These shots were accompanied by narration that resembled a radio broadcast. Called "quirky but successful" by one media outlet, the show became the second-highest-rated show on Fox Sports.[15]

Minuto a Minuto was produced by Torneos y Competencias, a sport production firm launched in the early 1980s by the Paraguayan businessman Carlos Ávila. Together with Argentina's largest media conglomerate, Grupo Clarín, Torneos had significant control over the country's sports media market. The two companies had owned the rights to Argentina's Premier Division since 1991, airing the matches on a pay-television network named TyC Sport since 1994. For Clarín soccer rights were a lucrative if relatively minor component of a much larger media empire. By the late 2000s the company controlled not only these rights, but also Argentina's most popular daily newspaper, its most popular broadcast network, its most popular twenty-four-hour cable news channel, and its two largest cable television providers. It was like AOL Time Warner, only way more successful.

The election of President Cristina Kirchner in 2008 threatened to disrupt Clarín's good fortune. Dispute over an agricultural tax, combined with a concerted legislative focus on diversifying Argentina's media industry (never good for a giant conglomerate), led to "warlike escalation" between the Kirchner camp and Grupo Clarín.[16] Two other factors, a drudging in a congressional election and the realization that most top-flight soccer clubs were in significant debt, pushed Kirchner into a political power play, one that she thought could boost the national sport, placate the masses, and deal a blow to her political nemesis. She named the initiative Fútbol para Todos (FPT): "Soccer for All."

The policy was announced in August 2009. Standing between the president of the Asociación del Fútbol Argentino (AFA—Argentina's soccer federation) and Diego Maradona, the most popular Argentinean player of all time, Kirchner went on television and announced that her administration would be purchasing the television rights to the Argentina Premier Division. The games, which had aired on the Torneos and Clarín–owned TyC Sport for the past fifteen years, would subsequently be broadcast on free-to-air television. "I am 56 years old and I joined politics very young, when there [was] no opportunity to vote, when there was no democracy," Kirchner said to the cameras, "but believe me that democracy is still incomplete to the extent that we cannot guarantee each and every one of the Argentines the access to essential goods." Although she couldn't guarantee everything for everybody, she was happy to announce that her administration could at least provide one very important, very essential good: "What we are guaranteeing today is . . . the right to recreation, the right to sports, the right to be treated as equal to the citizen who has greater purchasing power. It is part of the democratization that we Argentines owe ourselves."[17] Translation: Kirchner was providing free soccer on television.

Kirchner also stressed her administration's role as a counterweight, both financially and culturally, to an increasingly powerful corporate system (wink, wink, Clarín): "When these corporations become monopolies, when these corporations seek to take over the life, opinion, heritage and honor of Argentines, we live in a less democratic society, we live in a more extortive society, more subject to the pressure of what they are going to say or what are they going to put on me if I say or do this or that." But—and this was an important but—Kirchner stressed that the state was *not* subsidizing soccer. Ignoring the fact that the government was paying more than double what incumbent TyC Sport had paid, Kirchner dismissed the critics who viewed the arrangement as little more than a politically motivated handout. The league didn't need help, she said; it could clearly make money on its own (even though it hadn't been doing that for quite some time). In fact once the government got its sponsorship system up and running, enough money would start pouring in not only to cover the fees for the television rights, but also to fund the further development of all sports across all of Argentina.

This never happened; there were never any profits. Instead Kirchner used the games as proprietary billboards, a place to advertise her administration in a manner not unlike the way Hitler had used the 1936 Olympics and the military junta had used the 1978 World Cup. The campaign didn't come cheap. During the eight years of FPT the government spent approximately $10 billion pesos (or $1.4 billion dollars) on the initiative.[18] The significant outlay was fodder for critics, including *La Nación* journalist Alejandro Catterberg, who complained in 2013 that the money "could have been used to renovate the transportation system, improve routes, build homes or make other productive investments." Yet even the critics understood that fixed potholes and better compensated teachers wouldn't have provided Kirchner the kind of boost she received from free soccer: "Rich, poor, young, old, from the Capital or the interior, educated or not: those who watch a lot of matches have, on average, an image of Cristina Kirchner twenty points higher than those who don't."[19]

Besides benefitting the Kirchner administration and bolstering a cash-strapped and poorly run national soccer league, FPT was supposed to help bring Argentina together, to unify a fractured country through the collective appeal of the national sport. But Jonathan Wilson suggests that the program may have actually done the exact opposite. As Wilson explains, in the 1980s and 1990s, Argentinean soccer had been plagued by the incursion of the *barras bravas*, violent gangs propped up by corrupt politicians and complicit club administrators. These groups had even wriggled their way into club finances, often pilfering money through ticket sales and parking schemes. Fighting between the groups was common, almost expected. David Goldblatt explains the evolution of soccer fandom in Argentina as follows: "While under Perón football had served to integrate urban barrios and the wider nation, football in the 1990s deepened local, neighbourhood and tribal affiliations to clubs. It did so at the price of exacerbating the opposition and hostility between cities and neighbourhoods in an Argentina that was increasingly divided and in which, for most, trust and loyalties accrued to an ever-diminishing circle of people and institutions."[20] Soccer was no longer bringing Argentina together. On the contrary, it was breaking the country apart.

After decades of mismanagement and the financial calamity of 2001 the resources to fund the activities of the *barras* had dried up. Many of those involved had moved onto other pursuits. Then came Kirchner's announcement and an influx of money, allowing these gangs to reemerge from the shadows. In some ways the situation was even worse than before. With their having more resources than ever, Wilson has written how the animosity among groups in the FPT era "ceased to be soccer violence in any meaningful sense and became simply gang warfare."[21] In 2013 things got so bad that the government permanently banned fans of the visiting team from attending live matches.

With FPT Kirchner was about eighty years too late. As we saw in the first half of this book, the purpose of the sports media industry had once been fiercely debated. During the early parts of the twentieth century there were plenty of prominent people who argued for the industry as a means to achieve social cohesion, nation building, and collective unity. Those ideals were quickly consumed by capitalism, swallowed up by runaway growth. The industry had become all about money, deliberately designed to be squeezed for as much profit as possible. But Kirchner probably didn't care that much about all those ideals anyway. To many, FPT was nothing more than a political stunt masked by nationalistic rhetoric and designed to curry favor with an increasingly angry electorate. In the end it's telling that the government actually paid a premium for the rights rather than receiving a discount. That detail, more than any other, made apparent that while the government wanted to project an image that it was indeed in charge of this industry, it most certainly was not. And probably never would be again.

20

#Jeah

Ryan Lochte at the Summer
Olympic Games (2012)

When Cristina Kirchner went on television to announce "Fútbol para Todos," few were surprised to see national soccer legend Diego Maradona by her side, a living prop brought along to help sway public opinion. Born into poverty in the outskirts of Buenos Aires, Maradona turned professional at fifteen, the youngest player in Argentina Premier Division history. It didn't take long for the country to realize that he embodied the unique national playing style championed by *El Gráfico*, a street kid with uncanny agility and skill. After six years with two clubs Maradona transferred to FC Barcelona in Spain, where he clashed with management before moving on to Napoli in Italy, where he helped the club capture its first-ever Italian championship. At the 1986 World Cup in Mexico, Maradona was the catalyst for Argentina's triumph. The Diego legend was codified not in the final but during a quarterfinal match against England when he scored two of the most famous goals in soccer history within a five-minute span.

Despite all this success and adoration Maradona's relationship with the press had always been frayed. As he moved from Argentina to Spain to Italy and then back to Argentina, Maradona was trailed by opportunistic reporters ready to pounce on the next great Diego story. There were many. Drugs, parties, extramarital affairs, the Italian Mafia; Maradona's life was both sordid and fascinating. In 1994 the press was handed what many believed to be the perfect coda to the Diego Maradona story: an expulsion from the World Cup in the United States after the Argentinean legend tested positive for performance-enhancing drugs. As expected, the international press jumped all over the news. Rob Hughes, writing in London for *The Times*, was introspective: "How could we explain to the children, to the future generation, that this was the finest and also one of the most corrupt footballers of his or any other lifetime?"[1] Filip Bondy of the *New York Daily News* (back page headline: "MARA-DONE-A") was less charitable, calling Diego "a one-man circus to the end, a sad clown in full makeup."[2]

This sort of backlash, along with an inability to control his life's ongoing narrative, had always frustrated Diego Maradona. His biographer, Jimmy Burns, recounts a moment in Italy when Maradona went to the office of a newspaper, crumpled up a recently published article, and stuffed it into the mouth of the reporter who had written it. The animosity never wilted, remaining in place even decades after Maradona's playing career had ended. In 2009, upon securing a bid to the upcoming World Cup as coach of Argentina's national team, Maradona stood in front of the gathered media and said: "To all of you who did not believe in us, and I apologize to all the women here, you can suck my dick and keep sucking it. I am black or white, I'll never be grey in my life. You can take it up your ass."[3] He was suspended for two months and fined $15,000.

Perhaps it's a good thing that Maradona's career preceded the digital age. One can only imagine what a twenty-five-year-old Diego, strung out on cocaine and surrounded by a team of leech-like enablers, would have tweeted in the middle of the night from his villa in Naples. The end of Maradona's career, in fact, coincided almost perfectly with the rise of the internet in the mid-1990s. For athletes the new medium was both a blessing and a curse. On one hand, there were now thousands of additional critics ready to offer their opinions, judgments, and suggestions. Newspapers and magazines had always operated with limited real estate and minimal interactivity. But the internet was infinite, allowing the most irrelevant plays or comments to become fodder for debate. On the other hand, the medium also brought a host of benefits, such as the ability of athletes to sidestep the traditional gatekeepers, to speak directly to fans, and to say what they'd always wanted to say without being misquoted or misinterpreted by a self-serving reporter or editor.

Many saw great potential in this new tool, including Cleveland Indians outfielder Albert Belle. Like Maradona, Belle had never gotten along with reporters. In 1994, after a journalist asked Belle about the index cards he used to take notes on opposing pitchers, he angrily accused the writer of rummaging through his locker without permission, even though the index card anecdote had come from his own manager. The next year, before Game 3 of the World Series, Belle charged through the locker room and unleashed a "four-minute, expletive-filled tirade" aimed specifically at NBC reporter Hannah Storm.[4] The league fined Belle $50,000 and forced him to apologize.

A few years later Belle took his reputation into his own hands, partnering with a company called Athlete Direct to create his own website. The site promised to forego the usual channels (that is, journalists) to offer a behind-the-scenes peek into the life of the real Albert Belle, now a member of the Baltimore Orioles. As the president of Athlete Direct explained it, "Everyone knows Albert on the field . . . but not many people have had the chance to learn about Albert off the field."[5] The site also sold Albert Belle's Slugger Cereal, offered daily crossword puzzles (of which Belle was reportedly a fan), and gave unsolicited financial advice via a section called "Bank on Belle." Here's one example: "As you proceed up the pyramid, bond funds are the next alternative."[6] Even more important was the following disclaimer from Belle: "I'm not a financial guru or anything."[7]

Albert Belle was one of many athletes experimenting with their own sites in the early days of the World Wide Web. As mentioned above, SportsLine had helped several superstars create their own internet portals, with Michael Jordan and Shaquille O'Neal being two of the company's most prominent partners. Athlete Direct was an even bigger player, signing up close to three hundred athletes. Its roster was impressive, with superstars like Kobe Bryant, Ken Griffey Jr., Mia Hamm, Martina Hingis, and Alex Rodriguez. Many posted mundane updates about life on the road, answered fan mail, and sold merchandise. Others were more innovative. Dennis Rodman of the Chicago Bulls put together a poll asking fans what his new haircut should look like. Reggie Miller of the Indiana Pacers ran a contest looking for the best haiku. And Bryon Russell of the Utah Jazz used his site to sell his 1994 Toyota Land Cruiser.[8]

And then there were the no-filter athletes, for whom the internet was seemingly built. NBA star Charles Barkley, who once donned slave chains for a controversial *Sports Illustrated* cover, used his new website to riff on any and all topics. About Dennis Rodman: "I am a lot better than Dennis Rodman :) But nobody in the world gets better strippers than Dennis, he's the stripper magnet of civilization!" About college basketball: "I think that college basketball is in trouble, it's been in trouble and is getting worse. . . . The colleges making money on these kids have to find a way to give these kids some money." And about politics: "When it comes to politics they make you choose between being Republican, Democrat, Liberal, Conservative and that's unfair. If you're a Republican you don't want bad to happen to Democrats and vice versa. If you're rich you don't want bad to happen to poor and vice versa. They're supposed to do what's best for the majority of people and we lose that because the media tells you what to think."[9]

A few dedicated athletes eschewed the turnkey solutions offered by SportsLine and Athlete Direct in order to do it themselves. C. J. Nitkowski, a pitcher for the Detroit Tigers, was one of them, creating www.cjbaseball.com "to humanize professional athletes, to show that I'm a regular guy."[10] The site had a calendar with Nitkowski's schedule (November 24, 2000, was "Have Baby!"); journal entries throughout the season; and entertaining reviews for golf courses and restaurants. A Streetcar Named Desire in Kansas City received a score of 2.5 out of 5, mostly because "refills for a soda were $1.25 each, that was annoying." Kantaro Sushi in San Francisco received a similar score because it was "small and smelled like gerbils or hamsters or something." Neither compared to California Pizza Kitchen in Boston, which scored a 4.25 because "the salad is awesome, they shred the lettuce, and it's always cold."[11]

John Amaechi, a British-American Penn State graduate who had a five-year NBA career, was similarly willing to venture into non-basketball topics. He wrote poetry—"People are very much like stars, their very existence is a source of wonderment, joy, superstition and fear"—and included sections on his likes (cars, music, his house in Arizona) and dislikes (narrow-mindedness, bigots, liars). In early 2000

Amaechi even waded into the never-ending American gun debate, arguing that the Second Amendment was "written in a time when the 'new' nature of the country and the many different elements vying for power meant anarchy was a lingering possibility. It's worth noting that people were a lot more likely to be mauled by a bear as they hung the laundry out than shot by a sixth grader."[12] Amaechi soon discovered that controversial internet opinions rarely went unnoticed. The next month he posted the following email from a reader: "I read your comments about our right to keep and bear arms. May I remind you that we Americans have used our 'guns' to kick your British asses twice and to save your asses twice. If you don't like our constitutional rights as set forth by our founding fathers—GO HOME (you aren't that good of a basketball player anyway)."[13]

The birth of the internet meant that athletes had a powerful new bullhorn and could now speak directly to their fans. The fans had the same tool and planned on speaking right back. Both had so much to say. As the big digital platforms began to emerge—Facebook came out in 2004, YouTube in 2005, Twitter in 2008—it would only get easier. Custom websites were supplanted by individual social media profiles. At the same time, the proliferation of smartphones—the first iPhone was announced by Steve Jobs in 2007—meant that the athlete was constantly connected: on the road, at home, in the gym, at the club. Lengthy, well-edited blog posts were replaced by short Twitter updates. And as the number of gatekeepers slowly melted away, athletes were suddenly faced with a truly glorious and truly frightening proposition: they could now say whatever they wanted, whenever they wanted, about every possible topic.

Advice from coaches and commissioners and general managers was uniform: be careful. While social media allowed for an unprecedented level of access and interactivity, the potential pitfalls were plentiful. A poorly worded Facebook post might cause backlash; an ill-timed tweet could sink a career. Daryl Morey, general manager of the Houston Rockets, explained how the new media landscape would affect athletes of all levels: "For the players, it will eliminate any illusion that they're not public figures. They'll know that everything they do they've got to pay attention to and watch what they say." Morey himself wasn't too interested in social media. Official team matters? Sure. But Rockets fans shouldn't expect him to be tweeting out anything personal anytime soon. "I guess you're supposed to tweet your ham sandwich or something. I don't have time for that. But whenever I've got inside info that we're comfortable sharing, I'll use [a tweet] for that."[14] Of course a decade after offering this advice, Morey would find himself embroiled in his own Twitter controversy, one that would cost the NBA billions of dollars and put Morey—a public figure!—squarely in the international political spotlight. That story will get its due in chapter 23.

For now, back to the emerging social media landscape, where no athlete embodied the shift from the old internet (websites) to the new internet (social media) more than NBA Hall of Famer Shaquille O'Neal. The man known as Shaq—or Shaq Daddy or Shaq Fu or Shaq Diesel—had a presence on the internet from the very beginning. In 1995 O'Neal signed a deal with Bill Gates and Microsoft and became, at least according to one source, "the first person to have a site on an online service exclusively devoted to one celebrity."[15] Ever the self-promoter, Shaq released the following statement about the agreement: "Computers are definitely the wave of the future. We want to be part of that explosion and offer kids and fans a ride in the Shaqmobile up the infohighway."[16]

A year later Shaq ditched Microsoft to team up with Michael Levy and SportsLine. Together they created Shaq World (www.shaq.com), a "fully interactive, multimedia universe devoted to the superstar's diverse talents."[17] Shaq World had a lot of content—news, videos, photos, game recaps—but it was hardly indicative of one of the world's most charismatic athletes, a seven-foot, three-hundred-pound unicorn who shattered backboards with his dunks, played a genie in a Hollywood movie, and once wrote a rap with the lyrics, "You don't like Shaq, frankly I don't give a damn, I know I got skills man, I know I got skills man."[18] Shaq's website was the complete opposite of the man himself, so safe and mundane that it even had a section called "Fun Center," as if the rest of the content was anything but. Touted as a forum through which Shaq could connect with his fans, the site was mostly written from a third-person perspective: Shaq did this and Shaq did that. It was clear that the one thing Shaq didn't do was work on his own website.

In 2008 Shaquille O'Neal decided to join a new social media service called Twitter, a platform where individuals could update their "status." It was short, instant, and immediate. It was also easy, requiring little more than a few words and the click of a button. Shaq loved it and posted often. "I'm standing at the Oklahoma city national memorial" was one early update. "Dam i smell lousiana gumbo and jumbalaya" was another. Shaq took the idea of connecting with his fans quite literally, often tweeting out his location so that fans could find him and get an autograph: "Hint. Between 15th and 1st eating lunch, outside."[19] By May 2009 Shaq's follower count was up to a million.

The platform became Shaq's playground. He was clearly having a blast, commenting on other NBA players, telling followers what he was eating, and making a bunch of "your mama" jokes aimed at comedian Kevin Hart ("@kevinhart Yo Mama so fat Her cereal bowl came with a lifeguard").[20] In June 2011 Shaq tweeted that his playing career was coming to an end. The retirement sparked a bidding frenzy, with both Turner and ABC/ESPN hoping the four-time NBA champion and future Hall of Famer would be interested in joining their NBA coverage. A month later Shaq announced that he'd be joining TNT's *Inside the NBA*, one of the most celebrated sports studio shows of all time. For Turner it was a calculated risk. The show was often lauded as the best in the business, and the enviable chemistry among host Ernie Johnson and analysts Kenny Smith and Charles Barkley was often cited as the reason why. Would the show survive the intrusion of a spotlight-seeking NBA legend?

Yet for the show's executives it was a worthy gamble. Shaq was a once-in-a-lifetime get, a household superstar who carried a lot of clout across NBA circles, both online and off. The idea of clout, in fact, was all the rage. It was even being measured, at least within the social media world. One of the main authorities on clout was Klout, a company created to measure the effectiveness of digital persuasion: "Our friendships and professional connections have moved online, making influence measurable for the first time in history." A person's Klout score was measured by "a killer team of scientists and engineers" and based on three things: the number of people a user influences; how much the user gets people to respond to a message or spread it further; and the influence of the people each user was influencing.[21]

The Klout scale ranged from 0 (no influence) to 100 (so much influence), with an average score of 20. In mid-2012 the only human being in the world with a perfect Klout score was eighteen-year-old singer Justin Bieber. U.S. president Barack Obama was just behind, with a 94. Talk show pioneer Oprah Winfrey had an 85, former vice presidential candidate Sarah Palin was at 72, and the duck from the Aflac insurance commercials was at 47.[22] In the sports world Shaq had a decent amount of Klout, with a score of 77. That was on par with fellow NBA superstar Dwight Howard (also 77) and a bit higher than cycling legend Lance Armstrong (73) but still well behind global soccer icons such as Portugal's Cristiano Ronaldo (84) and England's Wayne Rooney (86).[23]

Klout helped usher the advertising world into the influencer era. In 2010 the company partnered with Virgin America Airlines to award people with high Klout scores a free flight to Toronto, the airline's newest destination. According to an article at the time, "Those who accept the offer aren't required to tweet, blog, or otherwise publicize the experience—though Virgin, of course, hopes that they will."[24] This model—giving free stuff to people with lots of social media followers—would become standard practice over the next decade, forever changing the way brands would approach marketing. It also meant that the early days of social media—the random thoughts and lunch updates and "Yo Mama" jokes—would soon be overwhelmed by carefully curated profiles designed to gain influence and attention. The hope was that compensation, in some fashion, would follow. Athlete profiles would become similarly scripted, with agents and managers warning players that too much unfiltered content could affect their ability to bring in multimillion dollar endorsement deals. Yet every so often there emerged a profile that embodied both the off-the-cuff unpredictability of early social media and the meticulously prepared branding of a later era. And in 2012 the world was blessed with one of these hybrids: a truly unique voice, candid and amusing, without shame, amplified by the world's premier amateur athletic competition.

Ryan Lochte was a natural talent in the pool, the son of two coaches, but he didn't start to take swimming seriously until he made the Junior Olympics as a fourteen-year-old. From there he became a star, receiving an athletic scholarship to swim at the University of Florida and then an invitation to compete at the 2004 Summer Olympics in Athens. He won two medals in Greece and then promptly misplaced them. "They could be in a drawer somewhere," Lochte told *Florida Today*. "Could be on e-bay, too, I don't know."[25] No problem; there'd be more. Four years later in Beijing, while teammate Michael Phelps won an Olympic-record eight gold medals, Lochte held his own with two silvers and two golds. While Phelps became a global superstar, Lochte carved out his own niche: a decorated champion who never took himself too seriously. As he told one reporter, "Swimming is so disciplined that you hardly ever see anyone's personality. I love to race, and when I'm in the water that's all I'm thinking about, but afterwards I'm smiling and giggling and having a good time. I think if I'm myself then people will be able to relate to that."[26]

Twitter was perfect for this philosophy, a way for Lochte to express his unfiltered thoughts to a growing audience. Lochte even developed his own catchphrase: Jeah. He would say it often as a greeting or celebration. Take this tweet from 2009: "The meet is finally done. I got one word for that . . . . JJJJJJJJJJEEEEEEEEEEAAAAAAAAAAH-HHHHHH!" During one interview Lochte was asked to explain what "Jeah" meant: "It means, like almost like everything. Like, happy. Like if you have a good swim you say 'Jeah!' Like, it's good. Like, so I guess it means good."[27]

Over the next few years Lochte's profile would grow, both in and out of the pool. At the 2011 World Championships Lochte won five gold medals and beat Phelps in two head-to-head races. As his performance improved, so did his social media savvy. Lochte became hyper-focused on connecting with his fans—the so-called "Lochte Nation"—utilizing a growing Twitter feed, an active Facebook profile, and a custom website (www.ryanlochte.com) to do so. In June 2012 *Vogue* put Lochte on its cover alongside U.S. goalkeeper Hope Solo and tennis champion Serena Williams. He was only the fourth man to appear of the magazine's cover, joining Richard Gere, George Clooney, and LeBron James. The accomplishment was both tweet-worthy and Jeah-worthy: "Thanks to Anna Wintour for her belief in me and for the honor of being the 4th man on the cover of Vogue. #Jeah! @ voguemagazine."

As the 2012 Summer Olympics approached, it was starting to seem as if the summer was going to belong to Ryan Lochte. Not only was the swimmer in peak physical condition, but the London games were also shaping up to be the first Olympics to fully take advantage of the new social media platforms. While Twitter had been around in 2008, the platform hadn't yet reached mass adoption; more tweets were actually sent during the few hours of the 2012 opening ceremony than during the entire two weeks of the 2008 competition in Beijing.[28] Reporters used social media to pass along results. Players used the platforms to update their fans on their conditioning. And countries used them to brag about medal counts. The International Olympic Committee embraced the new platforms, encouraging athletes to engage with fans and issuing guidelines on how to do so effectively. Many took note of the best practices. A handful did not. Voula Papahristou, a Greek triple jumper, was expelled from London for posting a racist message on Twitter: "With so many Africans in Greece, the West Nile mosquitoes will be getting home food!!!" Swiss soccer play Michel Morganella came next, sent home for describing the South Korean team as a "bunch of mongoloids [who] can go burn." One reporter explained the situation by musing, "It used to be drugs that got you kicked out of the Olympics. Now it's the most intoxicating drug of all: The ability to let the world know your thoughts in 140 characters or less."[29] Another put the visibility of social media into historical context: "The ancient Greek Olympians competed in the nude, but none of them, from Orsippus of Megara to Leonidas of Rhodes, were any more bare to the world than someone in 2012 using a Twitter account."[30]

Ryan Lochte wasn't concerned. He was like Shaq circa 2008, just trying to have some fun with it all. Lochte's fan-friendly approach was never more apparent than a week before the start of the Olympics, when Phelps used Twitter to express frustration with the new Olympic swim caps: "We used to be able to have front and back side with flags, but for some reason there are rules that tell us we cant do that anymore? Smh [shaking my head] gotta love an organizing committee telling us we can't do that anymore." Lochte, meanwhile, ignored that controversy in favor of the following: "LOCHTE NATION!! I want to talk to a fan of mine today! Who wants a call from me? It's going to happen sometime this morn so be ready!" The prize went to a teenage girl with the username @jeahlochte. The audio from the subsequent four-minute phone call was then posted to YouTube for all of Lochte Nation to hear.[31]

Lochte didn't have a coherent social media strategy so much as a free-flowing stream of consciousness. There was a lot of fan interactivity, some simple observations, tons of typos. Here are some posts from the weeks leading up to the Olympics (all presented exactly as written):

JULY 8: "The Lochte Nation LOCHTENATORS!!! #Lochtenation #Jeah!"

JULY 15: "Cold weather in France. There goes my tan, no #Jeah"

JULY 17: "If u choose one path to get to where u wanna be in life, doesn't mean u have to abandon all the other paths"

And some posts during the Olympic Games:

JULY 24: "Rocks, paper, siccor . . ."

JULY 30: "everyone is selling dreams until u can buy one"

JULY 31: "Always reach for the moon cuz if u slip up u will still be a star!! #Jeah"[32]

Lochte ended up having a decent Olympics—five total medals, including two golds—but didn't dominate the way some experts had expected. He was also once again overshadowed by Phelps, who took home four golds and two silvers. Upon conclusion of the games Lochte began working on the other part of his career. He filed an application to trademark the phrase "Jeah," saying he was going to put it on sunglasses, key chains, trading cards, and more. Lochte then made cameos on both NBC's *30 Rock*—in which he played a "sex idiot"—and Fox's *90210*. In November Lochte signed with Creative Artists Agency (CAA), one of the most prominent talent representation firms in the world. Soon after, his team announced the launch of a reality show on the cable television network E! named "What Would Ryan Lochte

Do?" (WWRLD). Said Lochte's agent at the time: "He is an incredibly endearing personality who is sexy, entertaining and fun. Watching this show, I believe people will fall into three categories: they want to be him, sleep with him or mother him."[33] Despite an advantageous lead-in—it doesn't get much bigger than Ryan Seacrest interviewing the Kardashian family—the first episode struggled to find an audience, pulling in around eight hundred thousand viewers and ranking 27 out of the 33 Nielsen-rated primetime cable shows in the United States that night.[34] The show fell off even further from there, with WWRLD placing second to last in weeks two and three. It continued for ten total episodes and was promptly canceled.

The tweeting would endure. By 2014 Lochte had over a million followers. The typos had gone down, the product placements had gone up, but the #Jeahs had remained steady. Two years later, at the Summer Olympics in Brazil, Lochte found himself at the center of a major controversy involving a vandalized bathroom, a security guard, and a taxi cab. The press spent several days trying to unravel what had happened since Lochte had manufactured his own version of the events. It eventually came out that Lochte and three other American swimmers had gotten drunk and caused a ruckus at a gas station. When he returned to the United States, Lochte turned to social media to issue an apology. On Instagram Lochte wrote a long post with nary a #Jeah in sight: "I want to apologize for my behavior last weekend—for not being more careful and candid in how I described the events of that early morning and for my role in taking the focus away from the many athletes fulfilling their dreams of participating in the Olympics."[35]

Things would never be the same for Ryan Lochte. He lost all his sponsors and was ridiculed online. The sports world—and the social media world—would move on to the next distraction. And the Ryan Lochte saga, from rising stardom to peak fame to apology video, would go down as a perfect example of what can happen in a media environment where anybody can say anything about any topic at any moment. For the individual athletes, whose legacies have traditionally been shaped by sportswriters and broadcasters, the internet was a gift. It allowed them to build their own brands and craft their own images, exactly as Diego Maradona and Albert Belle had hoped would happen. But the maintenance of those brands necessitates a captive audience, an attentive crowd. When the sports fan is presented with almost infinite content, it becomes harder to pay attention to any one thing for longer than is absolutely necessary. #Jeah was fun. Then it wasn't. Fans moved on. So while it might seem as though the athlete had been given an unprecedented level of control, it was really the person on the other side of the screen, the person hitting the PLAY and LIKE and FOLLOW and COMMENT buttons, who was now calling the shots.

Everybody else would simply have to adapt.

Part 6 / The Fan

Let's take a quick detour to the music industry, which was undergoing its own seismic transformation. For decades record companies had made most of their money by selling albums, bundles of songs available for a single price. While some of these albums were masterpieces from beginning to end, many contained filler, a throwaway song or two (or more) tacked on so that buyers felt that they got their money's worth.

Everything was going great until the MP3 arrived in the 1990s. A digital file format capable of efficiently storing an individual song, the MP3 allowed people to bypass the filler and to seek out only the hits. At first it was all illegal. Then Apple rolled out iTunes, a legal alternative. And finally the streaming services arrived, with their monthly subscriptions and fully customizable playlists.

Album sales plummeted, as did total music industry revenue. Artists began focusing on the live performance, a perishable product that couldn't be copied. New business models were invented. New expectations were set. The album never went away; it remains the primary vehicle through which artists release music. But it's been relegated to a bench role, at least financially. The winners? The listeners, who had not only a seemingly endless catalog at their disposable, but also the means by which to sort through that music, song by song. And thus the music industry's great unbundling was complete.

What can music teach us about sports? A lot. Because just as the listener was unbundling, so was the fan. No longer confined to weekly issues of *Sports Illustrated* (a bundle), morning episodes of ESPN's

SportsCenter (a bundle), or nightly local news broadcasts (a bundle), sports fans became increasingly interested in shaping their own routines. They hopped from site to site to read the morning news, followed their favorite athletes and teams through social media, and went to YouTube to create their own highlight reels. Sure, they came back together to watch the live event. But even those were becoming customized, with more and more fans "second-screening": staring at their phones or tablets while watching the game to check on their fantasy teams, place bets, and chat with their friends (and enemies) on Twitter.

The great unbundling would turn into an epic showdown among the old stalwarts, who wanted to save their revenue streams; the new upstarts, who wanted to create revenue streams; and the fans, who couldn't care less about revenue streams. And nobody was more affected by the great unbundling than a thirty-year-old sports media behemoth, seemingly invincible for decades, one of the most valuable media brands of all time, who now faced a multitude of dangers. While ESPN dug its heels into its old way of doing business, the company nonetheless remained beholden to its mission statement: "To serve sports fans. Anytime. Anywhere." That meant adapting to new expectations, new mediums, and new opportunities. And it meant finding out what each one of the fans wanted from this new, almost impossibly cluttered industry. It would not be easy.

On-Demand   **21**

*ESPN's College Football Playoff
Championship Megacast (2015)*

It's 2014. You just graduated from the University of Oregon. Congratulations! It was a fun four years. You studied hard, completed three internships, and went to nearly every football game. As a writer for the campus newspaper, you even got to sit in the press box. In your senior year the Ducks went 12–1 and beat Kansas State in the Fiesta Bowl. That was awesome. After the game head coach Chip Kelly bolted to the NFL. That wasn't ideal. But you're not worried. The team's quarterback, Marcus Mariota, has two more years of eligibility. The team's offensive coordinator, Mark Helfrich, was promoted to replace Kelly. He'll do a great job. This is a stable team, a team built to last. A national title remains a real possibility.

All that right there—analyzing and discussing college football—that's your favorite activity. It's what you hope to do with your life, to become a sports reporter. Of course the internet has sort of changed what that means. Newspapers, once the landing place for aspiring journalists, are struggling. Total advertising revenue has been cut in half over the past six years. Jobs are disappearing. You tell your aunt and uncle you want to be a sportswriter, and they laugh: "You should go into engineering," they say. But they don't even watch college football. They don't understand.

One thing that hasn't changed is the industry leader: ESPN. You grew up wanting to work for ESPN. You still do. And from everything you read, the self-proclaimed "Worldwide Leader in Sports" has never been stronger. Its cable business is thriving: both ESPN and ESPN2 are in nearly one hundred million American homes, bringing the company an estimated six dollars per subscriber per month. That's billions of dollars every year before a single ad is sold. On the internet ESPN is king, with an audience one and a half times bigger than its closest competitor.[1] Its mobile application is dominating too, the most popular choice in the sports category. The company is both global, airing across all seven continents (yep, even Antarctica), and local, with a growing emphasis on city-specific sites in New York, Los Angeles, Boston, Chicago, and Dallas. ESPN is also doubling down on its commitment to women, rolling out a redesigned espnw.com and a series of documentaries focusing on the fortieth anniversary of Title IX. Worth somewhere in the neighborhood of $50 billion, ESPN is likely, at least according to one pundit, "the most valuable media property in the United States."[2]

Yet even though ESPN has seven thousand employees, you find it hard to break through. You apply for a couple of jobs and hear nothing. No worries; you get a temporary job at an advertising agency in New York and decide to wait it out. You even get your own apartment, a small (very small) studio downtown. The rent immediately means half your paycheck is spoken for. And this leads to a major dilemma: do you sacrifice even more of your hard-earned salary for cable television? ESPN airs more college football than any other network; you can't imagine life without it. How else would you start your Saturday if not with Kirk Herbstreit and Lee Corso and ESPN *College Gameday*, the company's legendary on-site pregame show? How else would you end your day if not with offensive-heavy Pac-12 showdowns that run into the early morning hours? But you also can't stomach the idea of shelling out more than a hundred dollars every month for a cable television bundle that includes dozens of channels you'll never watch. You're not sure what to do.

Why can't you just pay for ESPN on its own? That's frustrating. You do some research and discover an unlikely ally: U.S. Senator John McCain. The ex-Marine and 2008 presidential candidate describes himself, just like you do, as a "certifiable sports nut and ESPN fanatic."[3] And yet McCain is sick and tired of paying for cable television. He wants ESPN, sure, but he has no interest in all the other stuff: Comedy Central, MTV, Discovery. It's like he's living in your head. He even feels bad for all those people who *don't* watch ESPN: "Whether you watch ESPN or not, and admittedly I do all the time, all cable subscribers are forced to absorb this cost."[4]

You find out that McCain has actually gone down this road before. In 2006 he introduced the Consumers Having Options in Cable Entertainment Act (the CHOICE Act). Silly name, yeah, but the intentions were good: to try to persuade companies to sell channels à la carte (that is, unbundled). Unfortunately the act went nowhere. So McCain tried again seven years later. In May 2013, as you wrapped up your junior year in Oregon, he had this to say: "Services such as iTunes and Netflix have led a revolution in how consumers purchase and experience music and video entertainment. They have upended entire industries to allow consumers to buy digital content where they want, when they want."[5]

Exactly, John McCain! You're a millennial, part of the on-demand, social media generation. A seemingly infinite amount of content— music, movies, photos, articles—has been readily accessible for as long as you can remember. If you want to listen to a specific song, you can. If you want to watch a particular music video, no problem. Sometimes you went the legal route. As McCain suggested, iTunes was good for that. So was Netflix. But for the harder to access content, there were other options. The Pirate Bay, an online depository of stolen content, almost always had what you needed. You didn't use it *that* much. When you did, it felt like you were cheating the system a bit. But what was the alternative? Not watching the movie you wanted to watch that day? Come on.

You laugh at your parents, who sit down to watch shows at specific times on specific days. You'll never do that. Instead you're convinced that you're in complete control of your media intake, that you watch and listen and read what you want when you want to. You're half right. Because while you were living it up in Eugene over the past few years, there were thousands of really smart people trying to figure out what you wanted to read or listen to or watch next. They wanted to know *you*—your likes, your dislikes, your guilty pleasures—better than you know them yourself. They collected data; that information was used to create algorithms; those algorithms became recommendation systems. And those recommendation systems became the foundation for Facebook and Twitter and Instagram and YouTube. They fed you recommendations. You consumed more content. Within that content were ads. That's how most of these companies made their money.

Sports is no different. While the big games remained the big games—nobody had to recommend that you watch Oregon vs. USC—all the other stuff, the recaps and the analysis and the opinion columns, became part of the digital recommendation ecosystem. You know that world well, having been introduced to it through your side gig at Bleacher Report. Launched when you were in middle school, Bleacher Report began as a place where aspiring sports columnists could hone their craft. An introduction to the "About Us" section on an early version of the brand's website explained that "the real experts aren't the stiffs with the journalism degrees and the empty catch phrases. . . . They're the fans who've been following their teams since age four, painting their faces since age five, and holding onto their old Topps cards for longer than they care to admit."[6] The part of the website that really caught your eye was this: "Q: Who is eligible to become a writer for Bleacher Report? A: Everyone."

Bleacher Report was also completely free, with a business model built off advertising. That meant the company had to cut some corners. You remember reading that only 1 percent of the site's seven thousand contributors actually got paid, with compensation ranging from "a few hundred to a couple thousand dollars per month."[7] That made sense; you never got paid. But you wrote for Bleacher Report because you enjoyed it and because you thought it was cool that people wanted to hear your thoughts about the Oregon Ducks' wide receivers. Only much later did you realize that you were contributing free content to a site whose success would threaten the dominance of the companies you hoped to work for in the future (like ESPN). In 2012 Bleacher Report was purchased by Turner Broadcasting for $200 million. Turner saw young people like you gravitating to these kinds of sites to consume gobs of personalized information about their favorite teams and players. Turner had decided that it was easier to just buy the company rather than develop its own extension. Such big companies always just want to get bigger, don't they?

ESPN went in a different direction. In 2006 it launched MyESPN, a way for online users to create a personalized home page with news from specific teams and leagues. You were just getting on the internet at that time and asked your parents if you could create a profile. Sure, they said; it was better than being on MySpace. The first team you picked? Easy: the Oregon Ducks. A few years later, in 2009, ESPN launched a studio show called *SportsNation*. At the time, the producer explained that fans would have "unprecedented input in the show's daily rundown."[8] That had sounded great to you, an aspiring sportswriter and somebody who felt that *SportsCenter* had grown stale. You became a dedicated fan, voting in all the *SportsNation* polls.

Around the same time, all your favorite personalities started joining a new social media app called Twitter. Your favorite fantasy football analyst, former Hollywood screenwriter Matthew Berry, joined the service in February 2009. Long time baseball writer Peter Gammons came on in March. Up and coming NFL reporter Adam Schefter joined ESPN in April and created a Twitter profile a few months later. Soon you had a highly curated Twitter feed of all your people: Gammons, your Uncle Todd, Berry, the old lady from your town who went to every Super Bowl. It was clear what ESPN was trying to do: create a personalized sports experience for every single fan. You were all for it.

Today, in 2014, there's so much stuff, so much content. And so much of it is free. Still, as you sit in your new apartment, you can't help but feel a void. Your entire life has been dedicated to the full ESPN experience, top to bottom, soup to nuts. You soon realize that you need the mothership—ESPN proper, the cable television network—to truly be a part of the ESPN universe. All this hype about the first four-team college football playoff in history (airing exclusively on ESPN) isn't helping. Then ESPN announces that *College Gameday* is heading to Eugene, Oregon, on September 6, 2014, for a matchup between the Ducks and the Michigan State Spartans. You're not going to miss a minute of that. Not a chance. You break down and sign up for cable. The bundle you get is expensive but extensive. It provides access not only to ESPN, but also ESPN2 (dedicated to stuff not airing on ESPN), ESPNU (dedicated to college sports), ESPN Classic (dedicated to things that happened a while ago), and ESPNEWS (dedicated to things that just happened or are currently happening). You also get some other sports networks with your bundle, such as the Pac-12 Network and Fox Sports 1, as well as the usual lineup of broadcast nets: ABC, CBS, FOX, and NBC.

It's game day. Then *Gameday*. Herbstreit picks the Ducks to win. So does Lee Corso, who proceeds to don the head of the Ducks mascot. Students whoop and holler. You start yelling in your apartment. ESPN pans to shots of Oregon's campus. There's your dorm! There's the building where your astronomy course was! The nostalgia is real. A few hours later (this West Coast/East Coast thing is annoying) it's time for kickoff. The game happens to be on FOX, not ESPN, which is fine since you've got all the networks now. It goes well. Mariota throws for over 300 yards and 3 touchdowns. Royce Freeman punches it in twice. A shaky first half is followed by a dominant second half. The Ducks roll, beating the Spartans 46–27. It's going to be a good year.

Even better: you're going to be able to watch all the games from the comfort of your apartment in New York City, thousands of miles from Oregon. It's a modern miracle, all thanks to the plethora of choices on your cable television package. Besides one hiccup against Arizona (available on ESPN), the Ducks begin to cruise, taking out Washington (Fox Sports 1), California (Fox Sports 1), Stanford (FOX), Utah (ESPN), Colorado (Pac-12 Network), and Oregon State (ABC). Victories against Arizona in the Pac-12 championship game (back to FOX) and Florida State in the playoff semifinals (ESPN) give the Ducks a spot in the national championship against the Ohio State Buckeyes (ESPN).

After weeks of waiting, finally, it's January 12, 2015. Ohio State vs. Oregon: the most important college football game in history. You think so anyway. ESPN seems to agree; it's going all out, providing fans with more than twelve ways to watch the championship across all of ESPN's platforms. Man, does it take its mission seriously—to serve sports fans, anytime, anywhere. Here's how it will shake out. Fans who prefer the traditional broadcast, with limited bells and whistles, will be served by the main cable network, ESPN. ESPN2, airing a broadcast with a collection of coaches breaking down film and talking strategy, will be the destination for the football nerds. The broadcast on ESPNU will be for the casual fans, with people like Jay Bilas (an NBA announcer) and Julie Foudy (who analyzes women's soccer) discussing the matchup in "a specially-created viewing theatre." ESPNEWS will focus on plays away from the ball, including an in-depth look at the offensive and defensive lines, while ESPN Classic will cater to the minimalists, with a broadcast that uses nothing but the "natural sounds of the game." And ESPN3 will be for the home fans, with radio calls from each school and "isolated cameras on their home team's head coach and marquee players."[9]

Should you flip around, testing all the broadcasts? Seems too distracting. You need to concentrate. In the end you decide on a muted ESPN broadcast on your television and the ESPN3 Oregon radio feed on your laptop. You also log into Twitter so that you can discuss the game in real time with your friends and pull up the website of one of your favorite bloggers, who is doing a "live diary" of the game. You're hoping that's a sufficient amount of content. If not, you'll adjust.

The game starts off well, with Marcus Mariota finding wide receiver Keanon Lowe for a touchdown. The Ducks lead 7–0. The Buckeyes counter with three straight touchdowns before Oregon hits a field goal right before halftime to make it 21–10. A 70-yard bomb at the beginning of the third quarter (21–17) and a short field goal a few minutes later (21–20) have you thinking comeback. That is, until Ohio State running back Ezekiel Elliott takes over, scoring 3 touchdowns over the final fifteen minutes to hand the Buckeyes the first-ever College Football Playoff championship trophy. You close your laptop, silence your phone, and turn off your television.

The game was good for ESPN. The megacast got rave reviews, and the matchup delivered the largest cable television audience of all time. This was the future, everybody said: customizable live events catering to the whims of the individual fan. But the game wasn't so good for you. Weeks of waiting and dozens of hours of your life for this, an unmitigated disaster. You're sad. But wait . . . you just remembered something. A few hours ago you called your bookie and made a $200 wager on the total number of points to be scored. You took the under, the savvy move. It hit. And as the memory of the Ezekiel Elliott takeover fades into the background, you can't help but think about what you're going to do with your money. Maybe continue your cable subscription for another few months?

Nah, it's not worth it, especially since you can find most of the stuff you need in the dark trenches of the internet. Instead you decide to let your winnings ride. The NBA is in full swing. The Blazers look like they're undervalued this week. Dame Lillard is scorching hot. They'll win by twenty, easy. And the NFL playoffs? Even better. Patriots vs. Colts and Seahawks vs. Packers are coming up. You download an episode of your favorite podcast. They're trying to guess the point spreads for each of the games. You play along before calling up your bookie to bet on the games. Screw it; you throw in a parlay, meaning you'll win even more if you choose the correct side in both games. Go big or go home, right?

By the next day you've completely forgotten about the championship game. Instead you've become a Colts and Seahawks fan. You just need the former to lose by less than a touchdown and the latter to win by more than a touchdown. It's a lock. You jump on Twitter and share a screenshot of your upcoming bets. Things are looking up. Tough losses sting, but there's always a shot at redemption. Especially when you can just pick a new team.

Now, if only all of this were legal . . .

Millionaire Makers

22

Murphy vs. NCAA (2018)

On May 14, 2018, the U.S. Supreme Court struck down the Professional and Amateur Sports Protection Act (PASPA), the federal law that prohibited all but a few states from legalizing sports gambling. When PASPA was enacted in 1992, it had overwhelming support from the American public. Yet over the next few decades sentiment toward sports betting would shift. While that happened, cash-strapped politicians began eyeing the activity as a potential revenue generator. Leading the charge was New Jersey governor Chris Christie, whose push to legalize sports gambling came from his goal of resuscitating Atlantic City, the state's quickly deteriorating gambling mecca. When thinking about the tens of billions that Americans bet illegally on sports every year, Christie didn't see addiction or corruption or scandal. Instead he saw dollar signs: "Even if the states only get a piece of that illegal activity, you're talking about a significant amount of revenue that will be coming in."[1]

In 2012 Christie signed legislation that would allow New Jersey casinos to offer sports wagering. That same year the NCAA joined four professional sports leagues in a lawsuit to stop the state from going ahead with its plan. By the time the issue made its way to the Supreme Court, Christie's term as governor had ended. In his place was Phil Murphy, a former Goldman Sachs executive and U.S. ambassador to Germany whose surname will forever be associated not with finance or politics but with point spreads, parlays, and moneylines. The case commonly referred to as *Murphy vs.* NCAA wasn't about whether sports gambling *should* be legal. Instead it was a classic American political showdown: federal power versus states' rights. In other words, did PASPA overstep the federal government's authority? In the end the court said that it had: "The legalization of sports gambling requires an important policy choice, but the choice is not ours to make. . . . Our job is to interpret the law Congress has enacted and decide whether it is consistent with the Constitution. PASPA is not."[2]

The defeat of PASPA opened the door to billions of dollars in new revenue while also changing the way sporting events were packaged and produced. It was an industry-defining moment, one without real precedent. And for many the decision was long past due, especially considering the state of sports gambling elsewhere. Over in the United Kingdom betting shops—physical locations where British sports fans could go and place a wager—had been around since the 1960s. In the beginning the shops were quite gloomy, with proprietors required to keep the windows dark so as not to tempt the average citizen strolling by. Loitering was also prohibited: the patron was expected to enter, place a bet, and leave. Nonetheless, money poured in. Powerful brands like William Hill and Ladbrokes emerged, and the government cashed in, steadily increasing its take from taxes. New rules in the 1980s brought a more comfortable experience as shops were allowed to install televisions, offer food, and serve drinks. The emergence of the English Premier League in 1992 and the elimination of a rule requiring bettors to wager on no fewer than three soccer games at once, conceived as a way to limit match fixing, provided additional sparks. Around the same time, the Australian government followed suit and went all in on legalized sports betting. When it did, Aussies came out in droves, betting enough on their favorite sports—rugby, cricket, Australian rules football—to deliver a boost to both local and national administrative coffers. By the end of the century sports betting was firmly entrenched across both the British and Australian sports landscapes. It was legal, popular, and profitable.

That wasn't the case in the United States, where sports wagering was similarly prevalent yet illegal nearly everywhere. In 1986 *Sports Illustrated* published a thirty-page report with the headline "Gambling: America's National Pastime?" The article began with the admission that nobody really knew how much Americans wagered on sports. One federal investigator estimated that the Mafia alone grossed $40 billion annually from sports wagering. Another expert called that an exaggeration, suggesting that the *total* market was closer to $30 billion. And what were Americans betting on? Here's how one bookie explained it: "It used to be that 85 percent of my customers made bets on horses. Now it's just the opposite—90 percent of their bets are on [team] sports, with football way ahead, then basketball and baseball."[3]

Accessibility and availability were the drivers here. For many sports fans gambling is about the minute-by-minute juice, watching the action unfold while having a financial stake in whoever comes out on top. As the sports media industry expanded—cable television, more local options, the 1984 NCAA Supreme Court case—the fan was given the opportunity to consume more and more games. And more games meant more juice. "Television has done wonderful things for gambling in America," one bookie told *SI*.[4] Many media outlets were happy to support this growing interest, providing fans with the information they needed (or at least information they thought they needed) to become what they all aspired to be: sharps, wise guys, pros. Newspapers printed moneylines and injury lists; broadcasters discussed point spreads; magazines hired "experts" like Jimmy the Greek.

On August 23, 1989, sports gambling became a front-page story in the United States when Cincinnati Reds manager and all-time hits leader Pete Rose was banned for life from Major League Baseball for allegedly betting on games. The scandal spurred lots of talk about integrity, about the sanctity of fair competition, and about saving amateur and professional sports from the incursion of this destructive vice. With the Rose scandal still fresh in the public's mind New Jersey senator and former professional basketball player Bill Bradley began rallying his fellow politicians, insisting that legislation was needed to "preserve the opportunity for all young people who desire to participate in sports to regard the game as theirs and not the gamblers."[5] In 1992, as legalized sports gambling proliferated throughout the United Kingdom and Australia, PASPA was brought to a vote. It was barely debated and passed easily.

Then came the internet, sending both the legal and illegal parts of the sports gambling world into a frenzy. On January 17, 1996, a

Finnish man named Jukka Honkavaara made the first-ever online sports wager through an online sportsbook called Intertops. "It was an electric moment," former Intertops executive Simon Noble said about watching Honkavaara's $50 bet on English soccer club Tottenham Hotspur come through the system.[6] Tottenham won the game, Honkavaara banked $2 (the Spurs were heavy favorites), and Intertops made a small commission. Two years later Noble told the *Washington Post* that the company had grown to over three hundred thousand customers, many of them "young professionals or college students." Noble chalked it up to the ease afforded by the internet: "It's a whole new class of people who are betting because it's convenient."[7]

The company's growth was also a product of Noble's marketing prowess. While his primary tactic—getting quoted in the popular press as an online gambling expert—was textbook public relations, some of his other techniques were more unorthodox. In 2001 Intertops launched Moolette.com, a live game where bettors watched a cow roam through a field painted with red and black squares containing different numbers. Winners were determined by the square over which the cow decided to take care of business. Here's how it was promoted: "Combining the glamour and excitement of the world's most sophisticated casino game, with the bowel movements of a large heifer, Moolette.com has taken the county fair game of Cow Patty Bingo into the 21st century."[8]

Dozens, if not hundreds, of competitors would soon emerge. Most of the sites followed a familiar script: they were launched by a man, operated from the lax regulatory environment of the Caribbean, and saddled by poor customer service. But not all. The most prominent of the outliers was Bet365, which was run by a woman named Denise Coates, operated from the English city Stoke-on-Trent, and treated its customers with respect. Thanks to a comprehensive menu of available wagers and timely payouts, Bet365 soon grew a reputation for legitimacy and trust in an industry lacking both. Users increased, revenues swelled, and profits rolled in. In time Denise Coates would be described as "the country's most successful self-made businesswoman."[9]

As business boomed, Denise Coates laid low and gave few interviews. Not so for many of her competitors, many of whom wanted to generate as much attention as possible. Calvin Ayre, founder of the gambling site Bodog, was a prime example. Ayre gave interviews to anybody willing to talk, inserted himself into nearly all of Bodog's marketing, and repeatedly vowed to turn the company into a thriving multimedia empire. Marketing was paramount, and Ayre soon embarked on a series of maneuvers designed to chisel some glamour onto the Bodog name. In one interview Ayre explained that Bodog customers "don't dream of being boring—that's not who they want to be. I think of it like James Bond. You're soaking up a little of it. You're a voyeur. There's a bunch of people who know they'll never be me—but that doesn't mean they don't dream about it."[10]

In 2003 Ayre collaborated with a gambling news website to spread provocative tales about the supposed Bodog CEO, a fictional character named Cole Turner. On his blog Ayre says he got the idea from watching the ABC sitcom *Home Improvement*, a show in which the neighbor Wilson "is often in scenes but you never actually see his entire face and don't know what he looks like."[11] When Calvin Ayre went on vacation to Southeast Asia, he used the time to concoct a ridiculous story about Turner's traveling into the jungle to confront drug dealers and search for abandoned ruins. One 2003 dispatch reported the following: "Bodog Expedition stumbling across a lost city deep in the jungles of Northern Cambodia. Since there were no trails where they were they were hacking their way through virgin jungle so it's highly unlikely that this has ever been discovered before."[12] In reality "Cole Turner" was really Calvin Ayre, and the "lost city" was the popular tourist destination of Angkor Wat. Yet the absurd marketing stunt got people talking about Bodog, which was exactly what it was designed to do. By 2006 one estimate pegged Bodog's revenue at over $7 billion, "enough to make it the seventh-largest online gambling operation in the world."[13] That same year Ayre made it onto the cover of *Forbes* magazine as one of "the richest people in the world." The title of the article was "Catch Me If You Can."[14]

This braggadocio was simply too much for some American politicians, especially those who had fought for years to keep gambling illegal. In 2006 the crackdown began. It started with arrests. David Carruthers, CEO of Betonsports, was detained as he was changing planes in Dallas, Texas. A few months later Peter Dicks, the chairman of Sportingbet, was arrested while getting off a plane in New York

City. Both companies had pulled in billions of (tax-free!) revenue from American gamblers, putting them squarely in the crosshairs of publicity-seeking politicians. Once the United States decided to crack down on internet gambling, these globe-trotting executives made easy marks, often flying through the United States on their way to company offices in Central or South America. While Dicks was eventually allowed to fly back to England, Carruthers would end up being sentenced to nearly three years in jail. Both would lose their jobs.

Then, in October 2006, the U.S. government passed the Unlawful Internet Gambling Enforcement Act (UIGEA). Designed to buttress existing legislation, the act prohibited companies from knowingly accepting payments from parties involved in online wagering. And since it became illegal to move money around, there was no way for gamblers to pay or be paid. Combined with the arrests of Carruthers and Dicks, the passing of UIGEA sent ripples through a once prosperous yet shady industry. For some, doing business in the United States just wasn't worth it anymore. Several sites simply stopped serving American customers.

While gambling sites sputtered toward an uncertain future, it was business as usual for fantasy sports. Similar to previously proposed bills, UIGEA contained a "carve out" for the fantasy sports industry, specifying that "bets" or "wagers" were allowed as long as the contest included players from different teams, offered prizes unrelated to the number of participants, and had outcomes that reflected "knowledge and skill." Meant as a way to placate both the fantasy sports industry and the professional leagues, the exemption nonetheless left the sports gambling door slightly ajar, just wide enough for clever entrepreneurs to peek through and recognize the potential millions, or perhaps billions, that remained on the table.

Here's why. The new legislation specified that taking a $10 bet that the Bears would beat the Packers by more than six points was illegal. Taking a bet that the Bears would win a game straight up was also illegal. But taking a $100 entry fee for a chance to win $500,000 (as long as that prize was determined beforehand) in a contest where the participant had to pick the best performing players from teams across the NFL—say, the Bears' quarterback and the Packers' wide receiver and the Seahawks' running back—fell outside the parameters of the law. That's fantasy sports, right? Kind of. But in 2006 fantasy sports was still mostly seen as a season-long affair, a long slog with your friends or co-workers where you might take home a couple hundred bucks at the end of the year. After the passage of UIGEA some innovators begin thinking: what if you could play fantasy sports every single day? And what if—and this part was even more important—you could win money? What emerged was the daily fantasy sports industry (DFS), a collection of websites allowing fantasy sports enthusiasts to partake in daily games for cash prizes. Three questions from an early FAQ for Fantasy Sports Live—one of the first sites to enter the industry—illustrate the tenuous gray area in which these DFS sites operated: (1) "Is this service legal?"; (2) "Isn't this gambling?"; and (3) "Is my money safe?"[15] The answers, according to the team at Fantasy Sports Live, were yes, no, and of course!

The get-rich-quick stories came next. In 2011 a junior at Elon University in North Carolina became one of the first DFS celebrities when he turned sixty bucks into several thousand dollars on a site called DraftStreet. Knowing the appeal of this classic rags-to-riches story, DraftStreet went into public relations mode, pitching the tale of user "Hixville Hunk" to Barstool Sports, a popular sports blog catering to a young male demographic. A few days later, tucked in among stories like "Kid Gets Detention for Farting on Bus" and "Dude Gets Foot and Face Stuck in Escalator at Penn Station," was an article with the following headline: "Does Turning 60 Bucks into $9,000 on DraftStreet Get This Dude Laid?"[16] The stunt worked, increasing awareness of daily fantasy sports and persuading thousands of Barstool bros to sign up on DraftStreet to try their luck at picking a winning team.

Fast forward to December 8, 2013. The Denver Broncos, led by future NFL Hall of Famer quarterback Peyton Manning, were hosting the Tennessee Titans, led by journeyman Ryan Fitzpatrick. It was cold—about 18 degrees at kickoff—and there was debate about whether a thirty-seven-year-old Manning could succeed in such frigid conditions. It was a silly conversation, it turns out, as Manning threw for nearly 400 yards and 4 touchdowns. With just over three minutes left in the game, the Broncos, up 44–28, had the ball at the Titans' 5-yard line. For nearly everybody—the owners, the players, the coaches, most of the fans—the game was essentially over. For everybody, that is, except for another thirty-seven-year-old: Travis Spieth from Dakota Dunes, South Dakota. Spieth was participating in the first-ever, one-day $1 million DFS contest on a site called FanDuel. He was doing well, set to make at least $100,000 from his $10 entry. But then Manning handed the ball to Broncos running back Montee Ball, whom Spieth had on his daily fantasy team. Ball barreled into the endzone, making the blowout an even bigger blowout, and pushing Spieth's team up to first place in the contest. When the game ended, Spieth found himself the winner of a million dollars. "Off of 10 dollars, this is like the American dream," Spieth told one reporter.[17]

Thus began an intense marketing war to convince sports fans that the American dream could be theirs. By the summer of 2015 two power players in the daily fantasy industry had emerged: FanDuel and DraftKings. Both companies were worth over $1 billion, and both were hyper-focused on growing their user base. That fall the two companies saturated sports television with ads, becoming the two highest-spending brands in the country. ESPN alone aired over five thousand ads from each over the first month of the NFL season. Most of the spots played to the aspirations of the individual sports fan, such as the DraftKings promo that promised an easy path toward success: "It's the simplest way to win life-changing piles of cash every week."[18] The biggest DraftKings contests also had the perfect name: the Millionaire Maker. Because what average, run-of-the-mill sports fans didn't dream of becoming millionaires by proving that they knew more about sports than their friends?

To many politicians, including those who had helped pass the UIGEA, this sure seemed like gambling. The constant advertising, with messages of easy access and instant riches, didn't help. Nor did the controversy that erupted when a DraftKings employee with access to valuable inside information won $350,000 on FanDuel, his company's main competitor. The FBI and Department of Justice started sniffing around. State prosecutors took steps to shutter the sites in their jurisdictions. DraftKings and FanDuel poured money into their own legal strategies, trying to justify their existence using the loopholes granted by UIGEA. Perhaps swayed by a public largely unconcerned with the "dangers" posed by daily fantasy, state legislators began to cave. In March 2016 Virginia passed a law legalizing and regulating daily fantasy. Others followed. This gradual legalization set the table for the 2018 *Murphy vs. NCAA* Supreme Court ruling. No, daily fantasy wasn't gambling, at least according to the law. But the discussion surrounding the industry suggested that most Americans were finally ready to legalize an activity that had been prevalent for years, even while it was technically illegal. *Murphy vs. NCAA* was discussed, debated, and then decided. Legalized sports gambling, on a state-by-state basis, would follow.

And yet even with billions of dollars of potential revenue, success wasn't going to be easy. The products offered by these sites—point spreads and moneylines and proposition bets—differ little from platform to platform. Customers hop around, driven less by loyalty to a particular brand than by getting the best possible odds. This reality is best demonstrated by the ups and downs of DraftKings, one of the biggest players in the space. With its history of daily fantasy, the company was well positioned to offer traditional sports betting in any state where it became legal. After the company went public in 2019, its stock jumped sevenfold, a return far outpacing the overall market. Even during this ascent, however, massive marketing, research, and legal expenditures meant the underlying numbers weren't pretty. In 2018 DraftKings reported a net loss of $76 million. In 2019 that loss doubled, to $142 million. And in 2020, as legalized sports gambling continued to spread around the United States, DraftKings reported a net loss of over $1 billion.[19]

But enough about the companies; what about the fans? The benefit of hindsight allows us to see the legalization of sports gambling in the United States as the next step in a gradual process through which fans were given more voice, more control, and more power. It started in the late 1980s with the birth of sports talk radio. Fans loved having an outlet; they'd call up to vent and rant and complain. But the hosts—people like Mike and the Mad Dog—were still the ones in charge: they could hang up whenever they wanted. Then came the internet, an open and limitless forum for esoteric thoughts on relief pitcher usage and MVP voting. Message boards blossomed and blogs flourished. Around the same time, fantasy sports and video games evolved, providing fans the means to become not only coaches of their favorite teams, but general managers and owners as well. Franchises were built; plays were called; fake championships were celebrated. Social media and podcasts extended the fans' voices to new platforms and new mediums. They could now be both pithy or verbose, depending on what the situation called for. Twitter was good for "The Ravens suck!" Podcasts excelled at "Here's sixty minutes about why the Ravens suck!" And YouTube was great at "Here's twenty minutes about that guy's sixty-minute rant about why the Ravens suck!" There was no shortage of opinions, no dearth of confidence. One big evolution remained: allowing average fans—such as had happened with owners and players and leagues and media networks—to make a ton of money. While DFS had teased this possibility, the fall of PASPA made it a reality. It was time to make some millionaires.

Was this progress? It depends on whom you ask. Despite the influx of money there's been resistance to the rapid spread of legalized sports wagering. It's come from politicians alarmed at the speed at which a once illegal activity has taken hold, purists concerned about the integrity of the games, and fans who see their favorite sports being inundated by inane stats and meaningless outcomes. In 2021 an Australian sportswriter living in New York gave a firsthand preview of what he believed was coming. The United States was entering a "world in which sports betting is a permanent fixture of conversation, a slow-moving magmatic sludge that eventually takes over every space, every interaction, every friendship in which sport plays an important role." Forget social gatherings, he warned; those were about to be overtaken by gambling zombies: "Things became even worse once sports gambling went fully digital; betting friends would turn up at social gatherings with a glazed-over, half-absent expression on their faces, then quickly become engrossed in the betting apps on their phones or excuse themselves to 'go have a flutter.'" Giving fans the ability to place a wager, he concluded, is "part of the package of 'innovations' that the corporate controllers of global sport have engineered to increase fans' emotional and financial investment in teams, while diminishing our collective representation in those teams' direction. It's the exemplar of a sporting economy that promises global connection while delivering universal distraction, in which sport's governing bodies give us more and shinier toys to play with, even as we all sink deeper into the depression of empty engagement and meaningless expenditure." Finally, the warning: "And it's coming to America soon."[20]

Superfine Market Segmentation **23**

NBA *Global Games (2019)*

While sports fans were trying to make millions, sports teams and leagues had their sights on billions. Domestic growth was fine; in most places it showed no signs of stopping anytime soon. But international expansion was the golden goose. During the early 2000s European soccer leagues such as the English Premier League and Spain's La Liga began to see increased interest from the American sports fan because clever television executives began inserting games into weekend morning television windows—football as an appetizer to football, if you will. Meanwhile, American leagues like the NFL and NBA looked to Mexico and Europe for some easy wins. They hosted international games, promoted foreign players, sold jerseys, and added new languages to their social media portfolios.

But no region was more compelling than Asia, where over a third of the world's population lived in just two countries. Of course neither China nor India is a monolith. Languages and customs vary, as do cable systems and internet availability. Opaque political and regulatory issues add further complexity in both places. Yet together the two countries offer an irresistible prize: the combined potential of nearly *three billion* new fans. So teams and leagues began to stubbornly chip away, convinced that slow but steady progress would forge a profitable path forward. By 2019 it seemed that the NBA had cracked the code. Its Chinese business was flourishing; there was exciting progress in

India. In October of that year the league embarked on a series of pre-season games on the other side of the world, incorporating both Asian giants into its schedule for the first time. The teams left the United States with sunny optimism. They returned dejected and confused, the unwilling participants in a global diplomacy case study, all thanks to a single person and seven words. Here's how it happened.

The story begins in China, where an overview of the media landscape boils down to this: the government decides what's allowed and what isn't. This system of control began with radio and Mao Zedong, the leader of China's Communist revolution in 1949. According to media scholar Ying Zhu, Mao and his team used radio to disseminate their Communist agenda, to "promote every aspect of the greatest social engineering show on earth, designed literally to change people's minds about how to live and co-exist."[1] It worked; loyalty to Mao, to the party, and to China grew. A television extension, Beijing Television, arrived in 1958, subsidized entirely by the state. The programs had purpose. China's first drama, *A Mouthful of Vegetable Pancakes*, was created to encourage "frugal food habits."[2] Color television arrived in 1973, along with a second government-led channel. In 1978 Beijing Television was renamed China Central Television (CCTV) and started selling ads. The hope was that CCTV—soon to expand into even more networks—could one day pay for itself. This shift brought some tension. In order to sell ads CCTV needed to air programs that people wanted to watch. Dry state-driven propaganda wouldn't work. Livelier fare was needed.

In 1985 the American broadcast network CBS began sending CCTV two football games a year as part of a larger programming package. The games aired on Chinese television months after being played. Viewers liked them but were never quite sure what they were watching. Said one CBS executive: "They saw all those people running up and down the field trying to hit each other and thought it was the most hilarious thing they'd ever seen."[3] While one of the games was chosen at random, the Chinese always requested that the Cotton Bowl be included in the package. Why? Nobody knew, although a reporter at the time facetiously quipped that it was because the Chinese wanted "to show the dangers of capitalist corruption, and a Southwest Conference school is the best example college football has to offer."[4] In 1986 another American staple arrived when Walt Disney CEO Michael

Eisner convinced CCTV to air a cartoon starring Mickey Mouse and Donald Duck. The program would air once a week and was expected to reach around thirty million people. CCTV's deputy director explained the agreement as an investment in the country's future: "Chinese children need to absorb various kinds of good nourishment."[5]

Professional basketball came next. In 1987 NBA commissioner David Stern traveled to CCTV headquarters with a proposal: would the network be interested in showing some NBA content in exchange for a cut of advertising revenues? The two parties agreed on a deal, and the NBA soon became a staple on Chinese television. The maneuver was part of Stern's grand strategy to internationalize the sport, a tactic he hoped would eventually lead to a "world series of basketball."[6] He also no doubt saw the potential of the Chinese market: a billion people and growing. In 1995 CCTV launched a channel specifically devoted to sports—kind of like a state-run ESPN—allowing for even more basketball coverage. The network soon became the second-highest grossing entity within the CCTV empire.[7] By the end of the decade Michael Jordan would be named the "most admired American in China."[8] Stern's foresight was paying off.

China's subsequent shift toward "state capitalism"—a model that allowed non-Chinese entrants into the media landscape as long as they adhered to the government's strict regulations—brought interest from nearly every major international media conglomerate. Who can resist a billion consumers with increasing levels of disposable income? Certainly not Rupert Murdoch, who tiptoed into the country through a stake in a satellite network. Jerry Levin and Steve Case, in their quest for the world's preeminent media platform, showed up as well. In 2001 AOL Time Warner signed a deal to become the first foreign broadcaster to distribute its content through Chinese cable television.[9] Meanwhile, the NBA kept plodding along, signing content deals with over a dozen additional Chinese networks.

In 2002 a gift from the basketball heavens: a seven-foot, six-inch unicorn named Yao Ming. Drafted first overall by the Houston Rockets, Yao quickly became the most famous Chinese athlete on the planet. In 2005 he received the most votes in All-Star Game history and was named starting center for the Western Conference team. Three years later, at the 2008 Summer Olympic Games in Beijing, he was asked to carry the torch for the Chinese delegation through Tiananmen Square. It was one of the most important roles at one of the most important national sites during one of the most important international events in modern Chinese history. Everything was lining up for the NBA to establish itself as the county's most popular professional sports league. Millions of fans and billions of dollars were expected to follow.

In 2006 the league reached a deal with a Beijing internet company to offer its games on-demand, for free, a day after they were played. Two years later ESPN joined four other investors to secure an 11 percent stake in the league's new subsidiary, NBA China. That entity went on to secure a merchandise deal with Alibaba, China's most popular e-commerce site, and a streaming deal with Tencent, the country's multimedia giant. So one part of the scene is set: a significant NBA presence in a growing market with tight government regulations, buoyed by the brief yet impressive run of a once-in-a-generation Chinese player playing for the Houston Rockets. Time to bring in the protagonist.

Daryl Morey's ascent to the top of the basketball food chain was fast. It began with a computer science degree from Northwestern University and an MBA from MIT's Sloan School of Management. After a brief stint in the consulting world Morey took a job with the Boston Celtics, where he was soon named senior vice president of operations and information. Proximity to his alma mater allowed him to moonlight as a professor, and he proselytized on the use of analytics—Morey was one of the first statisticians to promote the idea that points scored and points allowed were better predictors of future success than wins and losses—and the importance of business fundamentals while running a professional sports franchise. Don't do anything rash; firm over individual; follow the data. Things like that. Here's what Morey had to say about his managing philosophy: "The new ownership of teams comes from venture capital and management consulting backgrounds. They are analytical people and that is how they are going to run sports teams. . . . Whether you're running [the team] as a business or a championship team, the goals are the same: maximize profits."[10]

All that sounded great to Houston Rockets owner Leslie Alexander, who hired Morey away from the Celtics in 2006 and installed him as general manager the following season. With the MIT grad in control the Rockets had a few solid years, followed by a few mediocre ones. In 2012 Morey decided to shake things up, trading a handful of role players and some draft picks to the Oklahoma City Thunder for a promising young guard named James Harden. Harden would evolve into one of the league's best players; Morey, into one of its most celebrated executives. Many described the Rockets' GM as an innovator, a data-driven disrupter trying to reinvent the way a basketball team was put together. The press labeled him a geek, a nerd. It was all complimentary. There was talk, some of it coming from Morey himself, that other executives didn't like doing business with him. He became something of a folk hero within the basketball analytics crowd, and the conference that he co-founded, the MIT Sloan Sports Analytics Conference, became an industry darling.

The fact that the Rockets kept winning, at least in the regular season, certainly helped. In 2017–18 Houston won sixty-five games and broke the record for most three-pointers made in a season. The barrage of threes was deliberate, the result of a philosophy championed by both Morey and head coach Mike D'Antoni. (That philosophy: three points is worth more than two points, so shoot more three-pointers.) The Rockets made it all the way to Game 7 of the Western Conference Finals, where, despite an injury to point guard Chris Paul, they stuck to their regular season philosophy, shot a ton of threes, missed a ton of threes (twenty-seven in a row at one point), and bowed out to the eventual champion, the Golden State Warriors.

NBA Twitter, an always lively and often ruthless corner of the internet, quickly swarmed, mocking the team's tendency to rack up wins during the regular season yet falter in the playoffs. There were the usual provocations: terse one-liners and sarcastic memes. Daryl Morey no doubt saw much of it. He was a prolific social media user and had sent out close to eight thousand tweets since signing up for Twitter a decade earlier. His regular usage belied a previous attitude, one dismissive of the platform's value. Back in 2009 Morey had downplayed Twitter's appeal, telling one reporter, "I guess you're supposed to tweet your ham sandwich or something. I don't have time for that." He also hoped that the players understood what they were getting themselves into if they chose to partake in social media shenanigans:

"They'll know that everything they do they've got to pay attention to and watch what they say."[11]

That comment was prescient, as we'll soon see. During the 2018–19 season the Rockets won fewer games and once again lost to the Warriors in the playoffs. Time to move on, thought Morey. In the offseason the team shipped the popular Chris Paul (and lots of draft picks) out of town for the enigmatic yet talented Russell Westbrook. It was a divisive trade, a risky gambit, a bet on the present in exchange for the future. Some said it was orchestrated by Harden, not Morey. Others claimed Chris Paul wanted out of Houston. Regardless, it seemed like it would be the most controversial thing Daryl Morey would ever do as general manager of the Houston Rockets. It would not be so.

In October 2019 the NBA scheduled two games between the Houston Rockets and the Toronto Raptors in Japan as part of the league's annual preseason Global Games initiative. During his first morning abroad Morey sent out a tweet of the sun rising over the city from his room at the Ritz-Carlton. The caption: "Tokyo wakes up." That message was little more than a "look-where-I-am-right-now" post, repeated by thousands of others across the internet every day. Harmless. Then a few more finger taps and a click of the send button: "Fight for Freedom, Stand with Hong Kong."[12] That message was a professed political position on the autonomy of Hong Kong, one of the most controversial and complicated issues in modern China. And it was exactly the type of content the Chinese government prohibits.

Morey wasn't in China. Nor was he Chinese. But he was an executive of the Houston Rockets, one of China's most popular professional sports teams. People in China followed what Daryl Morey had to say, were interested in what he had to say. And wait, hold on, what did Daryl Morey just say? The message was screenshotted. It was shared. It was put into articles and news reports. Everybody associated with professional basketball started talking about it. Those seven words would go on to become the most famous tweet in NBA history, embroiling the league in an entirely unexpected and costly geopolitical affair that would take years to untangle.

Morey quickly deleted the initial message. He then holed up in his hotel for a few days before sending two additional tweets. The first: "I did not intend my tweet to cause any offense to Rockets fans and friends of mine in China. I was merely voicing one thought, based on one interpretation, of one complicated event. I have had a lot of opportunity since that tweet to hear and consider other perspectives."[13] And the second: "I have always appreciated the significant support our Chinese fans and sponsors have provided and I would hope that those who are upset will know that offending or misunderstanding them was not my intention. My tweets are my own and in no way represent the Rockets or the NBA."[14]

Nope, they didn't represent the Rockets or the NBA, as suggested by nearly everybody else's statements in the tweet's aftermath. Standing at a press conference with his teammate Russell Westbrook, Houston Rockets superstar James Harden said: "We apologize, you know, we love China, we love playing here. For both of us, individually, we go there once or twice a year, they show us the most support and love."[15] Rockets owner Tilman Fertitta sent out his own tweet, saying, "Listen . . . @dmorey does NOT speak for the @HoustonRockets. Our presence in Tokyo is all about the promotion of the @NBA internationally and we are NOT a political organization."[16] LeBron James, the most famous player in the NBA, had this to say: "I don't want to get into a word or sentence feud with Daryl Morey, but I believe he wasn't educated on the situation at hand, and he spoke, and so many people could have been harmed, not only financially, but physically. Emotionally. Spiritually. So just be careful what we tweet and what we say, and what we do. Even though yes, we do have freedom of speech, but there can be a lot of negative that comes with that too."[17]

And then there was Brooklyn Nets owner Joe Tsai. Tsai had been a majority NBA owner for only two months at that point but nonetheless felt compelled to speak out about a topic he was uniquely qualified to discuss. Born in Taiwan, educated in the United States, and holding both Canadian and Hong Kong passports, Tsai made his billions as co-founder of Alibaba, the sprawling Chinese e-commerce giant and one of the biggest companies in the country. In an open letter posted to his Facebook profile, Tsai responded to a single person expressing his thoughts on a complex situation by issuing a statement meant to represent the collective opinion of over a billion people: "The one thing that is terribly misunderstood, and often ignored, by the western press and those critical of China is that 1.4 billion Chinese citizens stand united when it comes to the territorial integrity of China and the country's sovereignty over her homeland. This issue is non-negotiable."[18]

The fallout came quickly. NBA games were taken off CCTV and Tencent. Player appearances were canceled, Alibaba stopped selling Rockets gear, and Chinese sneaker companies paused negotiations with NBA players. By mid-October Adam Silver admitted that "the losses have already been substantial. . . . I felt we had made enormous progress in building cultural exchanges with the Chinese people and I have to regret that much of that is lost."[19] A few months later Silver announced that Morey's tweet had probably cost the league "hundreds of millions of dollars."[20]

Morey would explain to a fellow league executive that the sentiment for the message came from his time at MIT, where the Hong Kong–China relationship had been a frequent topic of discussion. The specific timing of the tweet, meanwhile, "coincided with the implementation of a new law in Hong Kong prohibiting protesters from wearing masks."[21] Asked months later if he regretted sending the message, Morey told ESPN's Jackie MacMullan that he was "very comfortable with what [he] did." But Morey also admitted that he became "extremely concerned" after the message drew so much attention: "You don't want the second-most powerful government on Earth mad at you, if you can avoid it. In this case, I couldn't." And Morey definitely didn't want to lose his job. A year after sending the tweet he said, "In the last 12 months, I had moments where I thought I might never work in the NBA again, for reasons I was willing to go down for. . . . But I love working, I love what I do, and I didn't want that to happen." Maybe Morey would have indeed been okay if he had lost his job for the tweet. But he certainly didn't feel that way at the time, evidenced by how quickly he removed the tweet and how willing he was to send two additional tweets explaining that it wasn't his intention to "offend" or "misunderstand" Chinese fans or sponsors. And the 76ers paying Morey a reported $10 million a year after he left the Rockets—making him one of the few people to emerge financially better off from the whole situation—no doubt contributed to his being "very comfortable" with his actions upon reflection a year later.[22]

While reactions to Morey's tweet were varied and came from every angle, one of the most unexpected was a letter co-authored by eight

American politicians, including two—Republican senator Ted Cruz (Texas) and Democratic representative Alexandria Ocasio-Cortez (New York)—who couldn't be further apart on the American political spectrum. In the letter, addressed to Commissioner Silver, the group questioned why one of the world's most progressive sports leagues, made up of players who "have a rich history of speaking out on sensitive topics of social justice and human rights inside the United States" might capitulate to the demands of a "repressive single party government." The letter claimed that the Chinese Communist Party (CCP) was "using its economic power to suppress the speech of Americans inside the United States." How dare the NBA not unequivocally support Morey's right to say whatever he wanted. By issuing a wishy-washy response and encouraging Morey to back down, the league put profit over pride, something these politicians would never, ever, ever do: "While it is easy to defend freedom of speech when it costs you nothing, equivocating when profits are at stake is a betrayal of fundamental American values."[23]

A similar narrative was percolating over in India, a country that had just hosted its first-ever professional basketball games—two matchups between the Indiana Pacers and the Sacramento Kings in Mumbai—as another stop on the NBA's 2019 preseason global tour. With basketball fresh on the country's mind India's lively press was more than willing to offer its opinion on the NBA's latest controversy. An editorial in the *Hindu Business Line* followed the same script as the letter from the politicians, accusing the NBA of "kowtowing to China while defending free speech and progressive values in the U.S., and even the rights of players to 'take the knee' during the national anthem as a form of protest."[24] The *Economic Times* went the satirical route, posting a faux advice column written by "LeBron James" that mocked James's own response: "I can barely type this out; the tears are streaming down, and the pain is unbearable. The things that I have to face in my life, Doc. The misery and the trauma. . . . The thing is that so many people could have been harmed, not only financially, but physically, emotionally, spiritually. But the opprobrium I have faced for this! What have I done to deserve it?" To which the fake adviser responds, "You are not alone in putting your billions ahead of the rights, courage and lives of the Hong Kong Chinese. Even Apple is doing it. It was said of an empire that it ruled the waves, but for itself, it waived the rules. So true for America today."[25]

One person who remained silent on the topic was Vivek Ranadivé, the Mumbai-born owner of the Sacramento Kings and the man most responsible for convincing Adam Silver to bring the NBA to India. Ranadivé had always respected Morey and admired his unique approach to building a basketball team. Like Morey, Ranadivé was a data guy—loved it; lived by it. That's how he had made his billions, by turning real-time data across various industries into useful and actionable insights. Ranadivé told anybody who would listen that the key to a successful business was to get "the right information to the right people at the right time in the right context."[26] In his book *The Power of Now*, Ranadivé referred to this concept as "superfine market segmentation," suggesting that the massive increase in global information would allow companies to "define and serve a new, superfine market of one individual or less than one (the many markets within one customer), fulfilling the dream of mass customization."[27]

In 2010 Ranadivé used his fortune to become part owner of the NBA's Golden State Warriors. Three years later he became the majority owner of the Sacramento Kings. Ranadivé then embarked on a quest toward what he called NBA 3.0, a vision of the future where the Kings were a global brand, basketball was the second most popular sport in the world, and data ruled everything. Both China and India were integral to this plan. In the past the two countries were seen by international sports and media giants as two untapped markets with unlimited potential. Companies like ESPN and Fox came in with business models ported over from other regions. They started cable networks, aired live games, and had highlight shows. But they were stymied by language differences, local competition, strict government controls, and complex regulatory barriers. Digital technology alleviated some of these issues, making the distribution of sports content, often via mobile devices, much easier and more scalable. People like Ranadivé began seeing these countries not so much as two big untapped markets but rather as billions of untapped individual markets: "the needs of individual customers as opposed to generalized market segments."[28] It was no longer "How do we reach the Indian sports fan?" but rather "How do we reach Rahul in New Delhi, the guy who really likes the

Los Angeles Lakers and hopes to visit California next year?" If you're going to pursue "superfine market segmentation," why not do so in the two countries that make up a third of the world's population?

By 2019, while basketball fandom was still in its infancy in India, the personalization of sports media was already in motion. The social media industry was thriving. Fantasy sports had taken off. People were wagering on games, although it was still mostly illegal. A few years later the streaming rights to the country's most popular sports league—the Indian Premier League, a competition involving a style of cricket called Twenty20—would go to Viacom18, a company jointly owned by one of India's most powerful corporate conglomerates, Reliance Industries, and an investment group that included Rupert Murdoch's son James. After the deal was announced, a Reliance executive explained that the company hoped to provide cricket fans with more control of their viewing experience. Speaking to stakeholders at an annual meeting, a Reliance executive noted that "we can now deliver not just one video stream, but multiple video streams, showing multiple camera angles at the same time, and that too in ultra-high definition. . . . This makes every game truly immersive, even better than the real-match experience, as well as personalized to suit preferences of each and every viewer."[29] There it was, superfine market segmentation. In a country with 1.3 billion superfine segments.

And China? Well, as Daryl Morey proved, things were a bit more complicated over there. Superfine market segmentation in China isn't impossible. It's already been achieved, with Joe Tsai's Alibaba as one of the best examples. Similar to the multifaceted Amazon in the United States, Alibaba does it all, with one author noting the company is "what you get if you take all functions associated with retail and coordinate them online into a sprawling, data-driven network of sellers, marketers, service providers, logistics companies, and manufacturers."[30] In other words, Alibaba excels at getting the right *stuff* to the right people at the right time in the right context.

So just take this system and turn *stuff* into *information*, right? Not quite. In China that's the government's job. And when a company interferes with the CCP's role of controlling the flow of information, it's a problem. That's what Daryl Morey did; the entire league would pay the price. Superfine market segmentation, then, is possible only if all levels of the media industry are working in concert, from the government to the media companies all the way down to the individual consumer. If the spigot is turned off from the top, by an autocratic administration hell-bent on distributing a single, unified message of collectivity and cohesion, then the great unbundling of the media industry discussed above is logistically impossible. Instead all those superfine market segments—the individual consumers—revert to "generalized market segments." In this case China once again becomes China, a single entity—basically the polar opposite of superfine.

It would be years before CCTV resumed airing NBA games on a consistent basis. And as Chinese basketball fans waited for a resolution, the onset of the global COVID-19 pandemic pushed the league's international ambitions onto the back burner. With a couple of oversized hurdles complicating the path forward, the ultimate goal of Adam Silver and Vivek Ranadivé and Joe Tsai—taking the two biggest markets on the planet and breaking them down into their three billion component parts—would have to wait.

Epilogue

Sports Heaven

We've come full circle, back to 2021 and the boxing match that started this entire narrative. Nearly a hundred years after Jack Dempsey squared off against Georges Carpentier, former Major League Baseball (MLB) superstar Jose Canseco stood in the ring across from Barstool Sports intern Billy Football. Fifteen seconds later Canseco was cowering on the ground, pleading with the referee to blow the whistle while he nursed his supposedly injured shoulder. Canseco's request was granted, and Billy Football was declared the winner. It was a ridiculous spectacle, a pointless endeavor. Unparalleled absurdity. And yet it's helpful for our purposes here, an apt conclusion to a hundred years of sports media evolution. Why? For the final time let's follow the money—or, better yet, the moneyline.

A few months before Rough N' Rowdy 13—that is, the Jose Canseco–Billy Football fight—an American company named Penn National Gaming (soon to change its name to Penn Entertainment) purchased a third of Barstool Sports. Two years later Penn exercised an option to eventually take full control of the brand, valuing Barstool at over half a billion dollars. The rationale for a company primarily involved with racetracks and casinos to invest and then acquire Barstool was obvious: it provided access to a gambling-crazed, sports-addicted demographic right around the time that the U.S. Supreme Court was opening the path toward legalized sports wagering. An online sportsbook, named Barstool Sportsbook, arrived soon after, allowing Stoolies to wager on events in states where gambling was legal and where Penn Entertainment had a license.

But setting it all up proved difficult. By the time Jose Canseco vs. Billy Football came around, the only Barstool Sportsbook through which Stoolies could wager on the fight was in Michigan. For the rest of the country BetOnline, one of the offshore books, provided another option. Yet despite the limited options, having the ability to wager on this match was important. It layered intrigue onto a boxing match between two guys who didn't really know how to box. As one blogger wrote before the fight, "Place a bet on whoever the hell you want. Crack a few beers. Sit back on your couch. Enjoy the show. Then brag to your friends the next day that you made $20 on this fight. Or laugh with your friends that you lost $20 betting on an intern or a retired ball player. Either way just have fun and don't forget the beers."[1] In other words, make sure the fight becomes about *you* rather than the two people in the ring.

The Penn/Barstool partnership wouldn't last long. Just a few months after purchasing Barstool outright, Penn Entertainment was presented with an even bigger opportunity: the chance to partner with the most prolific brand in sports media history. Barstool was quickly sold back to its founder (for a reported $1 and a cut of future revenue) while a multibillion, decade-long deal with ESPN was hammered out. In November 2023 the companies launched ESPN BET, a collaborative sportsbook running on Penn's established betting platform and promoted through the vast ESPN multimedia machine.

All of this dealmaking was in response to the biggest question facing the modern sports media industry: how do you keep the sports fan's attention in an era of seemingly infinite content choices? Many solutions have been suggested. Some platforms have tried more highlights and fewer hot takes. Others have gone with fewer highlights and more hot takes. Maybe the fan wants more in-depth analysis: the speed at which the ball comes off the bat and the shooting percentage of a player from every spot on the floor. Or maybe the fan, as Roone Arledge would have argued, just wants to see more shots of the cheerleaders. There's also been plenty of debate about whether sports media platforms should simply double down on the stars. Should they increase the number of stories about Lionel Messi and Patrick Mahomes? Or have sports fans reached Lionel Messi and Patrick Mahomes saturation? The data would suggest the former—that is, that the big stars sell; anecdotal social media sentiment would probably suggest the latter. But while all these strategies have been attempted, the tactic that almost everybody agrees works the best is the customization and personalization of the sports media experience: the transformation of *our team* into *my team*. Season-long fantasy sports were a great building block, giving fans the ability to create their own customized squad. Video games fit the mold as well: Want to know what would happen if LeBron James and Kevin Durant were on the same team for a whole season? Go ahead and try it. The increased accessibility and visibility of daily fantasy and gambling have only continued this trend, allowing fans to create dozens of their own "teams" easily and often. These activities make sports *personal*.

The shift toward personalization has now evolved well beyond fantasy, video games, and gambling. In 2017, for instance, Spanish soccer club Real Madrid announced a partnership with global technology giant Microsoft to "generate a detailed user profile of each fan" in order to build personalized experiences. Custom highlights, virtual stadium tours, deals on merchandise—those sorts of things. According to Real Madrid CEO José Ángel Sánchez, the partnership was a brand new way of thinking about (and monetizing) the club's fan base, "a complete disruption of the business model that football [soccer] has had over the past 15 to 20 years."[2]

Other teams and leagues around the world are heading down similar paths. In 2020 NBA commissioner and sports media prognosticator Adam Silver explained that "the next generation not only expects the product to conform to their schedule. They want to mold the product to conform to what it is they want to consume."[3] Two years later the NBA announced the launch of its own redesigned mobile application. The app had fantasy games where fans could win prizes, voting campaigns where they could voice their opinions, and a "social-like vertical video experience" with a never-ending feed of algorithmically chosen content. In other words: TikTok, basketball style. "What makes this app unique in the sports world," said Chris Benyarko, the league's executive vice president of direct to consumer, "is that it's both a deeply personalized experience and an all-in-one destination."[4] Everything for everybody, only different everythings for everybody.

The global pandemic, beginning in March 2020, only accelerated this shift toward customization. As fans were forced out of stadiums and arenas and into their living rooms, there was plenty of talk about using digital tools to recreate the in-person community. In an interview in early 2021 an executive at MLB explained that baseball "is a connection vehicle for people, it brings people together." Because of that the league was focusing on "building tools, products, and a digital ecosystem that allows our fans to connect with each other." But many of the tools this executive went on to mention were less about creating community and more about serving the needs of the individual fan. One product, called Rally, allowed baseball fans to "log in, follow the game, try to predict what's going to happen, score points, and redeem those points for merchandise." Another was Film Room, a place where the league was "democratizing access to highlights," allowing its fans to "to search for whatever they want to create their own highlight reels."[5] My games, my team, my highlights. Perfect for a situation where fans were on their own, trapped in their apartments or houses, watching games played in empty stadiums.

The personalization strategy being pursued by Real Madrid and the NBA is hardly limited to sports. Instead it's an appropriate reflection of the modern media landscape, a place where we consume what we want when we want it. No longer a function of newspaper editors and network programming teams, as they were in the 1960s and 1970s, our content choices are now governed by our own wants, our own desires. It's all right there, just a click (and often a credit card) away. Choices abound: hundreds of cable and satellite stations; dozens of streaming and social media services; billions of websites. Sure, the blockbusters still exist. Netflix's hit show *Squid Game* was watched for nearly two billion cumulative hours in the month after its release in 2021. But viewings of that particular show were preceded and followed by an infinite number of content combinations. Some ran to Facebook to state their opinions, others logged onto TikTok to post reaction videos, and still others just stayed put for whatever personalized, algorithmically chosen content Netflix had lined up next: "If you liked this, you may also like this . . ."

It's difficult to untangle the intricacies of this evolution: is the media landscape more customizable because we want more personalization, or do we want more personalization because the media landscape is more customizable? It's a good question, one endlessly discussed by people who study such things. And there's probably a little bit of truth to both sides. When ESPN launched in 1979, the network began the telecast with this statement: "If you love sports, if you really love sports, you'll think you've died and gone to sports heaven." But then the anchors went on to talk endlessly about Notre Dame or the Yankees when lots of people weren't fans of Notre Dame or the Yankees, and some viewers thought, "This isn't *my* sports heaven." So personalization became hard to resist, both for the media companies who saw new revenue streams through superfine market segmentation and for the modern sports fan, whose allegiances often run the gamut from family loyalty to hometown team to local team to college affiliation to season-long fantasy team to daily fantasy team to current three-team parlay. That's a lot to keep up with. Given the choice to have it all laid out neatly in front of them, what fans could possibly say no to that?

As we've seen, the purposes of sports and media and sports media have been a matter of discussion for years. In the 1930s two early radio researchers suggested that "Radio is perhaps our chief potential bulwark of social solidarity."[6] In the 1940s Eurovision was conceived as part of a solution whereby "many problems would be resolved if every European could be made conscious of his status as a European—a member of a nation within a group of nations."[7] In the 1950s Henry Luce, the founder of *Sports Illustrated*, believed that his magazines "have been outstanding, and often pioneers, in showing to Americans what American life is like," and he believed a sport-specific publication could enhance this objective.[8] In the 1980s with the advent of sports talk radio, one media researcher explained that "in an age when communication is expected to do something, sports talk demonstrates an older function of communication, that of concretizing social rather than economic communities."[9] And in the 1990s one well-known historian maintained that sports remained a tool through which "the individual, even the one who only cheers, becomes a symbol of his nation himself."[10]

All this sentiment exists within the same overarching and some-what optimistic notion: sports, media, and sports media bring people together, promote social cohesion, and build community. And yet the palpable shift toward personalization and customization, where each fan's experience is increasingly tailored to meet individual needs and desires, ostensibly pushes against this purpose, prioritizing the individual over the group. Some executives try to have it both ways, issuing grand statements about community building and togetherness while rolling out their new fan-centric initiatives. In response to Real Madrid's personalization efforts mentioned above, José Ángel Sánchez had this to say: "We can create a one-to-one relationship with fans around the planet with the Microsoft solution, connecting this huge community of people and making the experience of being a supporter of Real Madrid much better."[11] Yet there are inherent contradictions within that very sentence, an illogical bridge that starts with "one-to-one" relationships and ends with a "huge community of people." How one leads to the other is unclear: if you make the experience all about the individual fan, which these teams and leagues seem to be doing, then it's going to be all about the fan. All that other stuff—the community, the cohesion, the togetherness—takes a back seat.

The obvious counterargument to this suggestion is that the foun-dation of sport's community-building function, the live event, still reigns supreme. The world's greatest matchups—Barcelona vs. Real Madrid at Camp Nou, India vs. Pakistan at Eden Gardens, Auburn vs. Alabama at Bryant-Denny Stadium, Hawthorn vs. Geelong at the Melbourne Cricket Ground—remain some of humanity's most impres-sive demonstrations of social solidarity, moments where individuals become part of something greater than themselves. But pay attention to what's happening at these events. Don't focus on what's happening on the field or court or pitch but rather in the stands. If you do, you'll see thousands of individuals holding up their phones, taking videos of whatever's happening in front of them. A replay of the official broadcast is hardly sufficient; these fans need proof of their own involvement, their own experience. It has to be custom. It has to be shareable. And it has to be personal.

In fact, as owners around the world look to increase revenue, many new arenas and stadiums are being redesigned not with the purpose of bringing people closer together but rather with the hope of moving them further apart. Money, making its final appearance in this story, is again the motivating factor. Bleachers have been replaced with seats, increasing prices and comfort while decreasing capacity. Stand-alone bars and restaurants dot newly built concourses, serving as escape hatches for small contingents of bored attendees. Specific areas for e-gaming, fantasy sports, and gambling have been constructed for fans who attend one game but have immediate interests in other games. And in-stadium museums have evolved to include not only rows of trophies and walls of famous jerseys, but also interactive stations where fans can post social media selfies, don virtual reality glasses, and test their skills with carnival-like attractions ("Are you faster than Neymar? Prove it!").

There's also the increased focus on the premium experience as new stadiums carve out space for a carefully curated group of VIPs. Take Chase Center, the sparkling home of the NBA's Golden State Warriors. While attendees of the 1921 Dempsey vs. Carpentier match sat on bleachers at a makeshift boxing ring constructed on a farm in Jersey City, attendees of the 2022 NBA Finals had the option (if their wallets would allow it) of watching the Warriors battle for a championship from one of the arena's exclusive courtside lounges. Just steps from the court—but with no actual view of the court—these lounges reflect the aesthetics of Napa Valley and were inspired by "the interior of a wine barrel." As they relax in these fancy hideaways, attendees are welcomed to spend the game sampling finger foods from the lounge's "complete harvest table." There's even an "oversized media wall" looming over the festivities, so fans who care about the actual game rather than the appetizers won't miss a minute of the action.[12] Such lounges cost over a million dollars per game.

But while the Chase Center's courtside lounges are contenders, of all the gimmicks and gadgets and innovations to emerge from the past hundred years of our watching, listening to, or reading about sports, the one I believe best exemplifies the evolution of the sports media industry is a relatively inconsequential piece of technology called Fancam. Founded back in 2010, Fancam works with stadiums and arenas to install cameras that capture high-resolution photos, sortable by seat number, of every fan in attendance. This basically means that after a century of progress, during which the entire sports media experience has been enhanced and altered and molded in a variety of ways, sports teams are now paying thousands of dollars so that fans can buy a ticket, attend the live event, leave the stadium, go home, and look at pictures of themselves on the internet.

Perhaps this is finally it: sports heaven.

Notes

Prologue

1. Jose Canseco (@JoseCanseco), Twitter, December 19, 2020; https://twitter.com/josecanseco/status/1340383711326572544?lang=da.
2. Billy Football (@Billyhottakes), Twitter, December 19, 2020; https://twitter.com/Billyhottakes/status/1340386089396297728.
3. Dave Portnoy (@stoolpresidente), Twitter, December 19, 2020; https://twitter.com/stoolpresidente/status/1340387485420056580.
4. "Rough N' Rowdy 13"; https://web.archive.org/web/20210203172649/https://www.roughnrowdybrawl.com/.
5. "I'm gonna destroy Jose Canseco," TMZ, February 5, 2021; https://www.tmz.com/2021/02/05/billy-football-barstool-sports-intern-vows-to-destroy-jose-canseco-shock-the-world/.
6. Jose Canseco (@JoseCanseco), Twitter, January 14, 2021; https://twitter.com/JoseCanseco/status/1349761194438127619?ref_src=twsrc%5Etfw.
7. Jose Canseco (@JoseCanseco), Twitter, January 21, 2021; https://twitter.com/josecanseco/status/1352264059731767298.
8. Jose Canseco (@JoseCanseco), "Jose Canseco," Twitter, February 5, 2021; https://twitter.com/josecanseco/status/1357723824838557697.
9. Jose Canseco (@JoseCanseco), Twitter, February 5, 2021; https://twitter.com/josecanseco/status/1357891596876931074.
10. Jose Canseco (@JoseCanseco), Twitter, February 8, 2021; https://twitter.com/josecanseco/status/1358993190406283267.

1. The Fight of the Century

1. Quoted in "Jeffries Won't Fight Johnson," *Philadelphia Inquirer*, February 6, 1904.

2. Jack London, "Fight of the Century," *Philadelphia Inquirer* (New York Herald Company), July 2, 1910.

3. H. E. K., "Fighters Await Tap of the Gong," *Chicago Tribune*, July 4, 1910.

4. John L. Sullivan, "Johnson Wins in 15 Rounds; Jeffries Weak," *New York Times*, July 5, 1910.

5. *San Francisco Examiner*, July 5, 1910.

6. Rex Beach, "Johnson and Age Defeat Jeffries," *Chicago Tribune*, July 5, 1910.

7. Samuels, *The Magnificent Rube*, 236.

8. Samuels, *The Magnificent Rube*, 251.

9. Edward B. Moss, "In the Ring for a Million," *Harper's Weekly*, May 14, 1910.

10. Ramsaye, *A Million and One Nights*, 110.

11. "1894 Boxing Match—Corbett and Courtney before the Kinetograph—HD Version," Victorian & Edwardian Martial & Exercise Films, May 18, 2017, YouTube video; https://www.youtube.com/watch?v=9jlgSJtNkWI&ab_channel=Victorian%26EdwardianMartial%26ExerciseFilms.

12. Orbach, "Prizefighting," 259.

13. Ramsaye, *A Million and One Nights*, 110.

14. "Eight Killed in Fight Riots," *New York Times*, July 5, 1910.

15. "Twenty-One Deaths as Result of Riots after Reno Battle," *Washington Times*, July 5, 1910.

16. "Cities Prohibit Fight Pictures," *Chicago Tribune*, July 6, 1910.

17. Quoted in Orbach, "The Johnson-Jeffries Fight," 340.

18. Quoted in Orbach, "The Johnson-Jeffries Fight," 341.

19. Quoted in Grieveson, "Fighting Films," 45.

20. "Crowd Is Saddened When Johnson Wins," *New York Times*, July 5, 1910.

21. "Bulletin Machine Fascinates Crowds," *New York Times*, April 25, 1911.

22. R. A. Smith, *Play-by-Play*, 13.

23. "David Sarnoff," *Radio Hall of Fame*; https://www.radiohalloffame.com/david-sarnoff.

24. Samuels, *The Magnificent Rube*, 82.

25. Associated Press, "Dempsey Sends Prize Milch Cow to Mother," *St. Louis Globe-Democrat*, July 1, 1921.

26. "Dempsey to Wear 3-Day Beard as Armor for Jaw," *New York Evening World*, July 1, 1921.

27. *Akron Beacon Journal*, July 1, 1921.

28. Dr. William Brady, "Carpentier's Mental Reaction Faster Than Dempsey's," *Lancaster News Journal*, June 27, 1921.

29. "San Diego Vets Score Dempsey; 'With' George," *Saskatoon Daily Star*, June 23, 1921.

30. Genevieve Forbes, "What of Women? Easy! Georges Is an Adonis: Hence the Fair Ones Hope He'll Whale Dempsey," *Chicago Tribune*, July 2, 1921.

31. "Parisians to Get News from Planes," *New York Times*, July 2, 1921.

32. *Arkansas Daily Gazette*, July 2, 1921.

33. "Voice-Broadcasting the Stirring Progress of the 'Battle of the Century,'" *Wireless Age*, August 1921.

34. Spalding, "1928," 36.

35. Quoted in "Dempsey Proves Prowess," *New York Times*, July 3, 1921.

36. "Voice-Broadcasting the Stirring Progress of the 'Battle of the Century.'"

37. J. Andrew White, "The First Big Radio Broadcast," *Reader's Digest* (UK edition), January 1956.

38. Quoted in May, "Meet J. Andrew White," 448.

39. Thomas H. White, "Battle of the Century: The WJY Story," January 1, 2000; https://web.archive.org/web/20190917193728/https://earlyradiohistory.us/WJY.htm.

40. White, "The First Big Radio Broadcast."

41. Quoted in White, "The First Big Radio Broadcast."

42. "Fight News Heard by Wireless Phone," *Scranton Republican*, July 4, 1921.

43. "Maine Man Gets Fight Reports by Wireless," *Boston Globe*, July 3, 1921.

44. "Wireless Telephone Spreads Fight News over 120,000 Miles," *New York Times*, July 3, 1921.

45. Craig, "Daniel Starch's 1928 Survey."

46. "Facts about the Fight," *Chicago Tribune*, September 23, 1927.

47. "Millions 'See' Fight in Radio Ringside Seats," *Chicago Tribune*, September 23, 1927.

48. Jack Steele, "Was Jack Dempsey Robbed by the 'Long Count'?," *Sports Illustrated*, September 28, 1987; Earl Gutsky, "Dempsey-Tunney II: The Long Count Fight," *Los Angeles Times*, September 22, 1987.

2. A Dangerous Precedent

1. "The Dempsey-Tunney Fight—A Dangerous Precedent," *Radio Broadcast*, December 1926.

2. Quoted in "Big Bout Unlikely to Go on the Air," *New York Times*, September 18, 1926.

3. Associated Press, "Fight Broadcast to Cover Most of U.S.," *Boston Globe*, September 21, 1926.

4. "The Dempsey-Tunney Fight—A Dangerous Precedent."

5. Carl H. Butman, "Radio Advertising Privilege Granted," *Evening Star*, October 3, 1926, 38.

6. Cantril and Allport, *The Psychology of Radio*, 24.

7. "The Decision in the 'Who Is to Pay for Broadcasting?' Contest," *Radio Broadcast*, February 1925.

8. Zeh Bouck, "Can We Solve the Broadcast Riddle?" *Radio Broadcast*, April 1925.

9. Bouck, "Can We Solve the Broadcast Riddle?"

10. H. D. Kellogg, "Who Is to Pay for Broadcasting—and How," *Radio Broadcast*, March 1925.

11. Bouck, "Can We Solve the Broadcast Riddle?"

12. "$100,000 Demand Bars Broadcast of Olympics," *Broadcasting*, August 15, 1932.

13. Hamilton Fyfe, "The Way They Have in America," *Radio Times*, November 26, 1926.

14. Hamilton Fyfe, "The Way They Have in America," *Radio Times*, January 21, 1927.

15. Hamilton Fyfe, "The Way They Have in America," *Radio Times*, January 7, 1927.

16. "BBC Royal Charter Archive"; https://www.bbc.com/historyofthebbc/research/royal-charter; accessed February 2021.

17. Huggins, "BBC Radio and Sport 1922–39."

18. "Commercial Football," *The Times*, April 2, 1930.

19. *Radio Times*, April 17, 1931.

20. von Saldern, "Volk and Heimat Culture."

21. Hadamovsky, *Propaganda and National Power*, 68.

22. Hadamovsky, *Propaganda and National Power*, 83.

23. Hadamovsky, *Propaganda and National Power*, 69.

24. Hadamovsky, *Propaganda and National Power*, 100.

25. Hobsbawm, *Nations and Nationalism since 1780*, 143.

26. The most comprehensive overview of the media setup for the 1936 Olympic Games is in Socolow, *Six Minutes in Berlin*.

27. George Lilley, "Tuning the 'Thrill' Bands," *Philadelphia Inquirer*, August 9, 1936.

28. Braven Dyer, "The Sports Parade," *Los Angeles Times*, June 28, 1936.

29. Associated Press, "Television Picture Shakes Like Jelly," *Palm Beach Post*, August 10, 1936.

30. *Baltimore Sun*, August 20, 1936.

31. Guttmann, "Berlin 1936," 73.

32. Krüger, "Germany," 27.

33. "Reich Radio to Link Nations for Games," *New York Times*, July 19, 1936.

3. Made for Television

1. Capouya, *Gorgeous George*, 49.

2. One estimate can be found at https://www.earlytelevision.org/us_tv_sets.html; accessed March 2021.

3. Red Smith, "Sport Cameos," *St. Louis Post Dispatch*, February 27, 1949.

4. Jimmy Cannon, "Pity the Wrestlers . . . and Their Fans," *New York Post*, February 2, 2003 (reprint).

5. Quoted in Capouya, *Gorgeous George*, 2.

6. Quoted in Godfrey, *Philo T. Farnsworth*, 186.

7. "Tennis Stars Act in New Television," *New York Times*, August 25, 1934.

8. Quoted in Associated Press, "Sarnoff Opens RCA Television at World Fair," *Meriden Daily Journal*, April 20, 1939.

9. Walker and Bellamy, *Center Field Shot*, 26.

10. P. G. Parker to John Royal, September 19, 1932; NBC Archives, Wisconsin Historical Society, Madison WI (cited in Walker, *Crack of the Bat*, 78).

11. Niles Trammell to L. R. Lohr, NBC president, August 29, 1938; NBC Archives, Wisconsin Historical Society, Madison WI (cited in Walker, *Crack of the Bat*, 76).

12. Walker, *Crack of the Bat*, 82.

13. Jack Gould, "The News of Radio," *New York Times*, September 4, 1947.

14. Jack Gould, "World Series May Not Be Televised, High Cost Being the Principal Deterrent," *New York Times*, September 10, 1947.

15. Walter Winchell, "Man about Town," *Times Dispatch*, September 17, 1947.

16. Advertisement, *News Journal*, September 30, 1947.

17. Advertisement, *Herald-News*, September 23, 1947.

18. "Series to Be Televised," *New York Times*, September 27, 1947.

19. "Dodger Bean Soup!," *Brooklyn Daily Eagle*, October 1, 1947.

20. "Court Adjourns to See Big Game on Television Set," *Brooklyn Daily Eagle*, October 1, 1947.

21. "All-Night Line at Bleachers Noisy, Happy," *Brooklyn Daily Eagle*, October 4, 1947.

22. H. I. Phillips, "The Once Over: The Terrors of Television," *Evening News* (Associated Newspapers), October 7, 1947.

23. "Stratovision Plan for Series Bright," *Broadcasting*, October 11, 1948.

24. J. Frank Beatty, "TV Pitches Curve," *Broadcasting*, October 18, 1948.

25. J. Frank Beatty, "Stratovision's Debut," *Broadcasting*, June 28, 1948.

26. Walker and Bellamy, *Center Field Shot*, 81.

27. Jeane Hoffman, "Gorgeous George, Pride of Beauty Parlors, Gets Dough from Turkeys," *Los Angeles Times*, March 23, 1952.

4. Gee Whiz

1. Grantland Rice, "Yankees Cop Series, Downing Dodgers, 5–2," *Atlanta Constitution* (North American Newspaper Alliance), October 7, 1947.

2. Grantland Rice, "Casey Brooks' Only Pitcher among Hurlers," *Birmingham News* (North American Newspaper Alliance), October 7, 1947.

3. Grantland Rice, "The Sportlight," *Harrisburg Telegraph*, October 7, 1947.

4. Grantland Rice, "The Call of the Curfew," *Boston Globe* (North American Newspaper Alliance), October 7, 1947.

5. Rice, *The Tumult and the Shouting*; the calculation came from Fountain, *Sportswriter*, 4.

6. Quoted in "Grantland Rice Joins the *Tribune*," *New York Tribune*, January 3, 1915.

7. Rice, *The Tumult and the Shouting*, Loc 1592.

8. Rice, *The Tumult and the Shouting*, Loc 1849.

9. Grantland Rice, "Notre Dame Again Trims West Point," *Boston Globe*, October 19, 1924.

10. "Sport," *Time*, October 27, 1924.

11. Brinkley, *The Publisher*, 137.

12. Quoted in Brinkley, *The Publisher*, 285.

13. Henry Luce, "The American Century," *Life*, February 1941.

14. Peterson, *Magazines in the Twentieth Century*, 25.

15. Quoted in MacCambridge, *The Franchise*, 38.

16. "Soundtrack," *Sports Illustrated*, August 16, 1954, 24.

17. Quoted in MacCambridge, *The Franchise*, 68.

18. William Faulkner, "An Innocent at Rinkside," *Sports Illustrated*, January 24, 1955.

19. Harry Phillips, "Memo from the Publisher," *Sports Illustrated*, January 5, 1959.

5. The Greatest Game Ever Played

1. Quoted in David Harris, "Pete Rozelle," *New York Times Magazine*, January 15, 1984.

2. Quoted in Harris, "Pete Rozelle."

3. Bowden, *The Best Game Ever*, Loc 89.

4. Tex Maule, "The Best Game Ever Played," *Sports Illustrated*, January 5, 1959.

5. George R. R. Martin, "NFL Championship—'The Greatest Game Ever Played'"; www.nfl.com/100/originals/100-greatest/games-1; accessed April 2021.

6. Bowden, *The Best Game Ever*, Loc 38.

7. Ben Strauss, "Sixty Years Ago, Maury Povich Played a Bit Part in the 'Greatest Game Ever Played,'" *Washington Post*, December 26, 2018.

8. Eisenberg, *The League*, 326.

9. "Latest Ratings," *Broadcasting*, February 16, 1959.

10. "Latest Ratings," *Broadcasting*, February 10, 1958; "Latest Ratings," *Broadcasting*, February 8, 1960. (The game actually doesn't show up in the Top Ten in 1960, meaning it had a reach smaller than the previous year's game.)

11. "NFL Dismissal Report," *Broadcasting*, July 20, 1953.

12. United States v. National Football League, 116 F. Supp. 319 (E.D. Pa. 1953); decision available at https://law.justia.com/cases/federal/district-courts/FSupp/116/319/1902662; accessed April 2021.

13. Celler, *You Never Leave Brooklyn*, 153.

14. Celler, *You Never Leave Brooklyn*, 153.

15. "ABC-TV Gets Game," *Broadcasting*, June 13, 1960.

16. Table (NFL television deals), *Broadcasting*, August 28, 1961.
17. "CBS and NFL Sign New Contract," *Broadcasting*, January, 15, 1962.
18. "$9.3 Million CBS Football Pact Held Illegal," *Broadcasting*, July 24, 1961.
19. Quoted in "Justice Throws a Block," *Broadcasting*, September 4, 1961.
20. Quoted in Harris, *The League*, 13–14.
21. Harris, *The League*, 14.
22. MacCambridge, *America's Game*, 19.
23. Quoted in Steadman, *The Greatest Football Game Ever Played*, 10.

6. Our World

1. Lommers, *Europe—On Air*, 188.
2. The acronym was based on the organization's name in French.
3. Lommers, *Europe—On Air*, 195.
4. Translation is from Lommers, *Europe—On Air*, 186.
5. "Real International Broadcasting: Proposals for a European Alliance," *Wireless World*, August 1944.
6. "French Enthusiasm," *The Times*, June 3, 1953.
7. Henrich-Franke, "Creating Transnationality through an International Organization?," 71.
8. John Hytch, "Looking at Europe," *The Times*, August 22, 1956.
9. John Hytch, "How Europe Is Coming to View Itself," *The Times*, August 28, 1957.
10. Quoted in Hytch, "Looking at Europe."
11. Henrich-Franke, "Creating Transnationality through an International Organization?," 73.
12. "World Cup Finance," *The Times*, July 1, 1958.
13. Goldblatt, *The Ball Is Round*, 403.
14. "British Football Geared to Club Strength," *The Times*, December 23, 1955.
15. "Softer Conditions Than Usual for Kick-Off," *The Times*, August 18, 1956.
16. *Daily Record*, May 19, 1960 (cited in Hare, "Football and the European Collective Memory in Britain," 112).
17. Chisari, "When Football Went Global."
18. Alastair Reid, "The World Cup," *New Yorker*, September 10, 1966.
19. "The Game Itself's the Thing," *The Times*, May 21, 1966.
20. "Babel Corner at Broadcasting House," *The Times*, June 30, 1966.
21. Torin Douglas, "Tracking 30 Years of TV's Most Watched Programmes," BBC.com, January 22, 2012; https://www.bbc.com/news/entertainment-arts-16671101.
22. Mason, "England 1966," 94.
23. Henrich-Franke, "Creating Transnationality through an International Organization?," 68.
24. Henrich-Franke, "Creating Transnationality through an International Organization?," 79.

25. Quoted in "Conflict Splits World Telecast," *Broadcasting*, June 26, 1967.

26. "Conflict Splits World Telecast."

27. "Our World 1967 Full Broadcast," Ryan Baker, January 2, 2020, YouTube video; https://www.youtube.com/watch?v=s3LmQFt4pQc&t=192s&ab _channel=RyanBaker.

28. Michael Billington, "Notable Feat of Organization," *The Times*, June 26, 1967.

29. Arledge, *Roone*, 41.

30. Vogan, *ABC Sports*, p. 34.

31. Arledge, *Roone*, 140.

7. Libber vs. Lobber

1. Reid and Soley, "*Sports Illustrated*'s Coverage of Women in Sports."

2. Joe David Brown, "Beauty on the Bars," *Sports Illustrated*, July 18, 1960. Quote about Annie Famose is from Bob Ottum, "Annie Doesn't Ski Here Anymore," *Sports Illustrated*, February 10, 1969.

3. Bil Gilbert and Nancy Williamson, "Sport Is Unfair to Women," *Sports Illustrated*, May 28, 1973.

4. This quote is in the promotional material of Roberts, *A Necessary Spectacle*.

5. Quoted in LeCompte, *The Last Sure Thing*, 260.

6. King, Howard, and Vollers, *All In*, 160.

7. King, Howard, and Vollers, *All In*, 186.

8. Jerry Kirshenbaum, "Sport's $5 Million Payday," *Sports Illustrated*, January 25, 1971.

9. Quoted in Don Van Natta, "The Match Maker," ESPN.com, March 26, 2020; http://www.espn.com/espn/feature/story/_/id/9589625/the-match -maker.

10. Nancy Woodhull, "She Says: Jocks Miss 'Old Days,'" *Orlando Sentinel* (Knight News Service), September 20, 1973.

11. George Puscas, "Riggs Has Fun with Other Half of King Family," *Detroit Free Press*, September 20, 1973.

12. Dan Nelson, "Female Chauvinist," *Bismarck Tribune*, September 21, 1973.

13. Vince DiPaolo, "Riggs Psyche Will Win over King Talent," *Belvidere Daily Republican*, September 20, 1973.

14. Edwin Pope, "Step Right Up for the Big Con," *Miami Herald*, September 20, 1973.

15. "Tennis Battle of the Sexes special (September 20, 1973)," YouTube; https://www.youtube.com/watch?v=qqB3yi8MVbQ&t=373s&ab channel= pannoni14.

16. Ratings for this week are available in *Broadcasting*, October 8, 1973. While these ratings include only the "share" metric, an average audience was estimated by an AP article written on September 21, 1973, and published

in, among other places, the *Journal Times* in Racine, Wisconsin. It gives the average audience number as forty-eight million.

17. This number seems to have taken on a life of its own. Here are just two examples: King, Howard, and Vollers, *All In*, 5; Rebecca Sun, "How the Real Battle of the Sexes Match Broke TV Records and Inspired Trump," *Hollywood Reporter*, January 9, 2018.
18. Quoted in Associated Press, "Outside U.S. Match Flopped," *Leader-Post*, September 21, 1973.
19. Associated Press, "Gals Ecstatic over Billie," *Lancaster New Era*, September 21, 1973.
20. John Underwood, "Now Everybody Has the Bug," *Sports Illustrated*, November 11, 1974.
21. Wind, *Game, Set, and Match*.
22. Douglas Kreutz, *Arizona Daily Star*, March 9, 1993.
23. Gary Deeb, "Chastain's Humiliation Over," *Miami Herald* (*Chicago Tribune* Service), June 22, 1977.
24. Deeb, "Chastain's Humiliation Over."
25. D. Wilson, *The World Was Our Stage*, Loc 2081; emphasis in original.
26. Quoted in Britni de la Cretaz, "An Audience of Athletes: The Rise and Fall of Feminist Sports," *Longreads*, May 22, 2019; https://longreads.com/2019/05/22/an-audience-of-athletes-the-rise-and-fall-of-feminist-sports.
27. Quoted in Grace Lichtenstein, "Woman Producing TV Sport Special," *New York Times*, January 8, 1974.
28. Cooky, Messner, and Hextrum, "Women Play Sport, but Not on TV," 225.
29. Arledge, *Roone*, 140.

8. Another Fight of the Century

1. "Cup Soccer, at $10 to $20, Upsets TV Viewers Here," *New York Times*, July 7, 1974.
2. Quoted in "Cup Soccer at $10 to $20, Upsets TV Viewers Here."
3. Edwin McDowell, "TV Network Lifts World Cup Goal," *New York Times*, June 1, 1978.
4. McDowell, "TV Network Lifts World Cup Goal."
5. Quoted in "Cup Soccer at $10 to $20, Upsets TV Viewers Here."
6. Vogan, "Exhibiting Ali's Super Fights"; "Theatre TV Continues Strong Second Telecast," *Box Office*, June 30, 1951; "Theatre TV Fight Showings a Sensation at Boxoffice," *Box Office*, June 23, 1951.
7. James M. Jerauld, "Rush for Television Projectors Is On," *Box Office*, June 30, 1951.
8. "Theatre TV Continues Strong Second Telecast."
9. McCarthy, "Like an Earthquake!," 313.
10. Wilfrid Sheed, "Boxing's Loyalists Now Gather in Theaters to Shout Their Affections for the Game," *Sports Illustrated*, March 9, 1970.

11. "Liston-Clay Championship Sets Closed TV Record," *Box Office*, March 2, 1964.

12. Quoted in Leonard Koppett, "Fight TV Facing Integration Snag," *New York Times*, February 24, 1964.

13. Leonard Koppett, "All the World's a Stage, via TV, for Title Fight," *New York Times*, February 23, 1964.

14. "Opponents of Boxoffice Television Marshall Forces for an Attack," *Box Office*, June 30, 1951.

15. Licklider and Taylor, "The Computer as a Communications Device," 21.

16. Licklider, "Televistas," 212.

17. John Walson interview, *Cable Center*, https://www.cablecenter.org/the -barco-library/the-hauser-oral-history-project/w-z-listings/john-walson -program-penn-state-collection; accessed July 2020.

18. Sam Kennedy, "Cable TV Invented in Mahanoy City," *Allentown Morning Call*, March 4, 2007.

19. Arthur Unger, "Chuck Dolan: The Reluctant Gatekeeper," *Television Quarterly* 24, no. 4, 1990.

20. Mair, *Inside HBO*, 3.

21. Quoted in "Wiring Manhattan: Sterling Communications and Cable Television in New York City," *New York Historical Society*, June 6, 2018; http:// blog.nyhistory.org/wiring-manhattan-sterling-communications-and -cable-television-in-new-york-city.

22. Both quotes are from Kram, *Ghosts of Manila*, 27, 130.

23. Dave Anderson, "Ali and Frazier Make It Official," *New York Times*, December 31, 1970.

24. "Bull v. Butterfly: A Clash of Champions," *Time*, March 8, 1971.

25. Dave Anderson, "The Marcos 'Thrilla,'" *New York Times*, March 10, 1986.

26. "A New Voice in Asia," *Time*, October 21, 1966.

27. John Sharkey, "The Marcos Mystery: Did the Philippine Leader Really Win the U.S. Medals for Valor?" *Washington Post*, December 18, 1983.

28. Quoted in Mark Kram, "For Blood and for Money," *Sports Illustrated*, September 29, 1975.

29. "Bird Is in Hand for Pay Cable," *Broadcasting*, October 6, 1975.

30. Quoted in Kram, *Ghosts of Manila*, p. 169.

31. Quoted in "Ali-Frazier III: 'Thrilla in Manila,'" *Sports Illustrated*, October 1, 2012; https://www.si.com/boxing/2012/10/01/01ali-frazier-iii-the -thrilla-in-manila.

32. Many have made this mistake, including *Marketplace* (https://www .marketplace.org/2017/08/25/why-do-we-pay-100-watch-fight-pay -per-view-mayweather-mcgregor/) and *Bleacher Report* (https:// bleacherreport.com/articles/1164237-floyd-mayweather-and-the-10 -biggest-boxing-pay-per-view-events-of-all-time).

33. Les Brown, "TV Notes: Who Jockeyed ABC into First Place?," *New York Times*, November 2, 1975.

34. Quoted in Jonathan Lemire, "Original Cable Guy," *Columbia College Today*, January 2005.

35. Mark Kram, "'Lawdy, Lawdy, He's Great,'" *Sports Illustrated*, October 13, 1975.

36. Kram, *Ghosts of Manila*, 108, 44, 3.

37. Kram, *Ghosts of Manila*, 63, 30.

38. Paul F. Kagan, "Clearer Picture: Home Box-Office Helps Brighten Outlook for Cable TV," *Barron's National Business*, November 24, 1975.

39. Gershon and Wirth, "Home Box Office," 116.

9. An Arid Spectacle

1. Hogan and Murphy, *The Tap-Dancing Knife Thrower*, 85.

2. Hogan and Murphy, *The Tap-Dancing Knife Thrower*, 90.

3. Griffen-Foley, *Sir Frank Packer*, Loc 1043.

4. Griffen-Foley, *Sir Frank Packer*, Loc 4761.

5. Quoted in Griffen-Foley, *Sir Frank Packer*, Loc 5276.

6. Haigh, *The Cricket War*, 29–30.

7. Bill O'Reilly, "Case for Some Wise 'Umpiring,'" *Sydney Morning Herald*, May 10, 1977.

8. John Arlott, "The Big Bumper from Down Under," *The Guardian*, May 10, 1977.

9. "Not Cricket?" *Sydney Morning Herald*, May 11, 1977.

10. John Woodcock, "Tests Have Nothing to Fear from the Circus," *The Times*, May 10, 1977.

11. Ian Peebles, "No One-Eyed Hatred at the Circus," *The Guardian*, July 6, 1977.

12. Quoted in Quick, *World Series Cricket*, 113.

13. Eric Beecher, Nigel Wilson, and Peter McFarline, "The Balance Sheet at Stumps," *The Age*, February 20, 1978.

14. Michael Davie, "View from the Top," *The Age*, February 18, 1978.

15. Quoted in Eric Beecher, Nigel Wilson, and Peter McFarline, "Packer Is Batting on Regardless of Cost," *The Age*, February 22, 1978.

16. Quoted in Haigh, *The Cricket War*, 128.

17. Quoted in Haigh, *The Cricket War*, 88.

18. "Packer Circus Scores Best with the Young," *The Age*, May 31, 1978.

19. Bill O'Reilly, "Chappell, Lillee the Destroyers," *Sydney Morning Herald*, November 29, 1978.

20. John Woodcock, "A New Day Dawns in the Sydney Light," *The Times*, November 29, 1978.

21. Haigh, *The Cricket War*, 165.

22. Hogan and Murphy, *The Tap-Dancing Knife Thrower*, 163.

23. Richard Gulliatt, "The Man Who Sold Hollywood on 'Crocodile Dundee,'" *New York Times*, August 21, 1988.

24. Quoted in Gulliatt, "The Man Who Sold Hollywood on 'Crocodile Dundee.'"

PART 4. GROWTH

1. Tony Kornheiser, "A Dash for the Cash," *Washington Post*, February 11, 1994.

10. How to Be Rich

1. Getty, *How to Be Rich*, 36.

2. Getty, *As I See It*, 20.

3. Getty, *As I See It*, 33.

4. Getty, *How to Be Rich*, 36.

5. Quoted in Clyde H. Farnsworth, "Richest Man Label Irks Getty; 'How Can Anybody Be Sure?,'" *New York Times*, July 30, 1964.

6. Getty, *How to Be Rich*, 52.

7. Evey and Broughton, ESPN, 30.

8. "George F. Getty 2d, Oldest Son Of Oil Billionaire, Dies on Coast," *New York Times*, June 7, 1973.

9. Evey and Broughton, ESPN, 43.

10. Evey and Broughton, ESPN, 12.

11. Getty, *How to Be Rich*, 24.

12. Rasmussen, *Sports Junkies, Rejoice!*, 87.

13. Evey and Broughton, ESPN, 83.

14. Freeman, ESPN, 68.

15. Getty, *How to Be Rich*, 30.

16. Evey and Broughton, ESPN, 118.

11. A Classic Cartel

1. "Late Literary Cullings," *Nebraska State Journal*, January 10, 1892.

2. "Literary Notes," *Quad-City Times*, January 24, 1892; "At the Baptist Church," *Vermont Phoenix*, August 19, 1982; "Flying Wedge," *Boston Globe*, November 24, 1892.

3. Quoted in "Flying Wedge."

4. J. H. Sears, "A Football Scientist," *Harper's Weekly*, December 2, 1893.

5. "Flying Wedge."

6. "Deaths from Football Playing," *Washington Post*, October 15, 1905.

7. "Yale's Football Wrecks," *New York Times*, October 1, 1893.

8. "Hears Football Men," *Washington Post*, October 10, 1905.

9. Quoted in "Remarks at the Alumni Dinner of Harvard University in Cambridge, Massachusetts," *American Presidency Project*; https://www

.presidency.ucsb.edu/documents/remarks-the-alumni-dinner-harvard
-university-cambridge-massachusetts; accessed September 2021.

10. Savage et al., *American College Athletics*, vi.

11. Savage et al., *American College Athletics*, 189, 265, 158.

12. Savage et al., *American College Athletics*, xvi.

13. Sperber, *Shake Down the Thunder*, 177.

14. Savage et al., *American College Athletics*, 95.

15. R. A. Smith, *Play-by-Play*, 36.

16. Quoted in R. A. Smith, *Play-by-Play*, 62.

17. Sperber, *Onward to Victory*, 388.

18. Sperber, *Onward to Victory*, 388.

19. Quoted in Sperber, *Onward to Victory*, 401.

20. Quoted in Sperber, *Onward to Victory*, 401.

21. Quoted in International News Service, "Krause, Hesburgh Flail NCAA Video Control," *South Bend Tribune*, January 4, 1953.

22. Philip Taubman, "Oklahoma Football: A Powerhouse That Barry Built," *Esquire*, December 5, 1978.

23. Taubman, "Oklahoma Football."

24. Quoted in John Dreyfuss, "Bill Banowsky: He's a Man at the Crossroads," *Los Angeles Times*, February 18, 1975.

25. Associated Press, "Judge Rules NCAA Violated Antitrust Rules," *Alexandria Daily Town Talk*, September 16, 1982.

26. Philip Hager, "Supreme Court Hears NCAA's TV Dispute," *Los Angeles Times*, March 21, 1984.

27. Quoted in Jerry McConnell, "Banowsky: Ruling No Automatic Goldmine," *Daily Oklahoman*, June 28, 1984.

28. Quoted in "Supreme Court's NCAA Ruling," *Miami Herald*, June 28, 1984.

29. William Taaffe, "Too Much of a Good Thing," *Sports Illustrated*, October 15, 1984.

30. Jim Laise, "Supreme Court Television Decision Raises Questions," *Fort Worth–Star Telegram*, July 1, 1984.

31. William F. Reed, "We're Notre Dame—And You're Not," *Sports Illustrated*, February 19, 1990.

12. 1-800-SPORTS

1. N. R. Kleinfield, "Business Dials 1-900-PROFITS," *New York Times*, May 8, 1988.

2. Glen Macnow, "Celebrities and Hucksters Cashing In on 1-900 Lines," *Philadelphia Inquirer*, February 10, 1991.

3. Macnow, "Celebrities and Hucksters Cashing In on 1-900 Lines."

4. Kleinfield, "Business Dials 1-900-PROFITS."

5. Phil Jackson, "Think Skins Game Is Fun Viewing Now? How 'bout If Players Put Up the Bucks?," *Baltimore Sun*, November 27, 1992.

6. Macnow, "Celebrities and Hucksters Cashing In on 1-900 Lines."
7. Quoted in "Gary Carter and Keith Hernendez [sic]—Spanning the World," MyInnerEyeSports, August 31, 2011, YouTube video; https://www .youtube.com/watch?v=Xm7LjKgERXs&ab_channel=MyInnerEyeSports.
8. Quoted in Macnow, "Celebrities and Hucksters Cashing In on 1-900 Lines."
9. Quoted in Macnow, "Celebrities and Hucksters Cashing In on 1-900 Lines."
10. Neil Best, "Bill Mazer, Sports Talk Radio Pioneer, Dies at 92," *Newsday*, October 23, 2013.
11. "Bill Mazer Sports Talk Show after Game 2 of 1966 World Series (WNBC Radio)," epaddon, March 5, 2017, *YouTube* video; https://www.youtube .com/watch?v=xo4aRmXmHpc&ab_channel=epaddon.
12. Quoted in Herman Weiskopf, "See No Evil, Hear No Evil . . . Ha!," *Sports Illustrated*, September 4, 1972.
13. Weiskopf, *On Three*, 87.
14. Birchard, *Jock around the Clock*, 22.
15. Andrew Feinberg, "The Return of the Radio Network," *New York Times*, April 12, 1981.
16. Quoted in Birchard, *Jock around the Clock*, 31.
17. Quoted in Birchard, *Jock around the Clock*, 27.
18. Birchard, *Jock around the Clock*, 57.
19. Quoted in Rushworth M. Kidder, "FCC's Fowler: Free-Market 'Ideologue' or Free-Speech Champion?," *Christian Science Monitor*, May 20, 1985.
20. Fowler and Brenner, "Marketplace Approach to Broadcast Regulation."
21. "Emmis Broadcasting in Biggest Challenge," *New York Times*, February 26, 1986.
22. Quoted in Sullivan, *Imus, Mike and the Mad Dog, & Doris from Rego Park*, 8.
23. David J. Halberstam, "Ex-CBS Radio CEO Joel Hollander Recalls the Birth and Growth of the USA's First All-Sports Station, WFAN," *Sports Broadcast Journal*, June 28, 2019; https://www.sportsbroadcastjournal.com/ex-cbs -radio-ceo-joel-hollander-recalls-the-birth-and-growth-of-the-usas-first -all-sports-station-wfan.
24. Halberstam, "Ex-CBS Radio CEO Joel Hollander Recalls the Birth and Growth of the USA's First All-Sports Station, WFAN."
25. Quoted in Sullivan, *Imus, Mike and the Mad Dog, & Doris from Rego Park*, 13.
26. Nick Paumgarten, "The Boys," *New Yorker*, August 30, 2004.
27. Quoted in Sullivan, *Imus, Mike and the Mad Dog, & Doris from Rego Park*, 45.
28. Chandrani Ghosh, "A Guy Thing," *Forbes*, February 22, 1999; https://www .forbes.com/forbes/1999/0222/6304055a.html?sh=d8dce13e2f0e.
29. Paumgarten, "The Boys."

30. Frank Ahrens, "For All-Sports Radio, Fans Are All Ears," *Washington Post*, February 11, 1993.
31. Quoted in Halberstam, *Sports on New York Radio*, 328.
32. Bob Kravitz, "Radio Gab Spewing Inanities," *Capital Times* (Scripps-Howard News Service), January 28, 1994.
33. Rick Reilly, "Look Out for the Bull!" *Sports Illustrated*, March 14, 1994.
34. Haag, "'The 50,000-Watt Sports Bar,'" 456.
35. Quoted in Daniel H. Forer, *Mike and the Mad Dog* (documentary), ESPN Films: 30 for 30, 2017.
36. Haag, "'The 50,000-Watt Sports Bar,'" 466.
37. Halberstam, *Sports on New York Radio*, 327.
38. Quoted in Sullivan, *Imus, Mike and the Mad Dog, & Doris from Rego Park*, 51.
39. Quoted in Forer, *Mike and the Mad Dog*.
40. Quoted in Austin Murphy, "Calls of the Wild," *Sports Illustrated*, September 16, 1996.

13. A Whole New Ballgame

1. "Premier League Launch," Sky Sports Retro, April 18, 2020, YouTube video; https://www.youtube.com/watch?v=-EFiPldOq9s&ab_channel=SkySportsRetro.
2. "Margaret Thatcher—1985 Statement on the Heysel Stadium Tragedy," May 25, 2019; https://www.ukpol.co.uk/margaret-thatcher-1985-statement-on-the-heysel-stadium-tragedy/.
3. Craig R. Whitney, "Disaster Throws the Spotlight on Nation's 'Slum Stadiums,'" *New York Times*, April 17, 1989.
4. Lord Justice Taylor, "The Hillsborough Stadium Disaster—Interim Report"; https://commons.wikimedia.org/wiki/File:Hillsborough_Taylor_Interim_Report_Cm765.pdf; accessed October 2020.
5. Lord Justice Taylor, "The Hillsborough Stadium Disaster—Final Report," 5; https://www.jesip.org.uk/wp-content/uploads/2022/03/Hillsborough-Stadium-Disaster-final-report.pdf; accessed October 2020.
6. Lord Justice Taylor, "Final Report," 5.
7. Lord Justice Taylor, "Final Report," 7.
8. Lord Justice Taylor, "Final Report," 7.
9. Lord Justice Taylor, "Final Report," 23.
10. Quoted in *The Night Football Changed Forever* (documentary), ITV, 2016.
11. Robinson and Clegg, *The Club*, 10.
12. *The Night Football Changed Forever*.
13. Quoted in *The Night Football Changed Forever*.
14. "There They Go, There They Go," *The Economist*, January 18, 1992.
15. Andrew Walker, "Rupert Murdoch: Bigger Than Kane," BBC News, July 31, 2002; http://news.bbc.co.uk/2/hi/uk_news/2162658.stm.

16. Chenoweth, *Rupert Murdoch*, 34.
17. Torin Douglas, "Forty Years of *The Sun*," BBC *News*, September 14, 2004, http://news.bbc.co.uk/2/hi/uk_news/magazine/3654446.stm.
18. Chenoweth, *Rupert Murdoch*, 42.
19. Quoted in William Shawcross, "Murdoch's New Life," *Variety*, October 1999.
20. Melnick, "The Mythology of Football Hooliganism," 3.
21. Hall, "The Treatment of 'Football Hooliganism' in the Press," 25.
22. *Daily Mirror*, April 4, 1977 (as cited by Hall, "The Treatment of 'Football Hooliganism' in the Press").
23. "The Truth," *The Sun*, April 19, 1989.
24. "The Final Whistle," *Sunday Times*, April 16, 1989.
25. Laurence Hooper, "Nature of British Televised Soccer to Change Following BSkyB Deal," *Wall Street Journal*, May 20, 1992.
26. Nicholas Hills, "Tainted TV Deal Shows Elite League Soccer Not Played on Level Field," *Ottawa Citizen*, May 25, 1992.
27. David Lacey, "Future Sold for Pie in the Sky," *The Guardian*, May 20, 1992.
28. Quoted in "Liverpool to Refund Monday Matches," *The Times*, June 9, 1992.
29. Quoted in Clive White, "QPR Pull Plug on BSkyB," *The Times*, August 15, 1992.
30. Robinson and Clegg, *The Club*, 40.
31. Quoted in "First Sky TV 'Monday Night Football'—Pre Match— Manchester City v. Queen's Park Rangers (retroQPR)," *YouTube*; https://www.youtube.com/watch?v=HLI3R9z97NQ&ab_channel=retroqpr.
32. Quoted in "First Sky TV 'Monday Night Football'—Pre Match— Manchester City v. Queen's Park Rangers (retroQPR)," YouTube; https://www.youtube.com/watch?v=HLI3R9z97NQ&ab_channel=retroqpr.
33. Quoted in "Manchester City v. Queens Park Rangers 1992/93," *CityTilIDie*, December 17, 2010; https://www.citytilidie.com/latest/qpr-home-199293/.
34. Quoted in "Manchester City v. Queens Park Rangers 1992/93," *CityTilIDie*, December 17, 2010; https://www.citytilidie.com/latest/qpr-home-199293/.
35. Adrian Langford and Richard Hunt, "How Sky Scored an Own Goal," *The Guardian*, December 14, 1992.
36. Adrian Langford and Richard Hunt, "The Fans' Verdict," *The Guardian*, December 15, 1992.
37. Quoted in Ken Auletta, "The Pirate," *New Yorker*, November 13, 1995.
38. Michael Wolff, "Rupert to Internet: It's War!" *Variety*, November 2009.

14. Sports.com

1. Mark Gibbs, "No More freelunch.com on the 'Net," *Network World*, September 25, 1995.

2. "Visionary in Obscurity: Charles Stack," *Smart Business*, July 22, 2002; https://sbnonline.com/article/visionary-in-obscurity-charles-stack -operates-in-two-business-communities-151-cleveland-and-the-internet -151-and-isn-146-t-well-known-in-either-this-time-around-that-146-s -going-to-change-he-hopes/.

3. "Sports.com Completes $52.5 Million Second Round of Funding," Bloomberg News, January 12, 2000; https://www.bloomberg.com/press -releases/2000-01-12/sports-com-completes-52-5-million-second-round -of-funding.

4. David Kirkpatrick, "Is Net Investing a Sucker's Game?" *Fortune*, October 11, 1999.

5. "Prodigy commercial," jacky9br, February 1, 2011, YouTube video; https://www.youtube.com/watch?v=gMIsTOZxVOO&ab_channel=jacky9br.

6. Glenn Rifkin, "At Age 9, Prodigy On-Line Reboots," *New York Times*, November 8, 1993.

7. Quoted in Robert D. Shapiro, "This Is Not Your Father's Prodigy," *Wired*, June 1, 1993.

8. Scott Newman, "SportsLine Investors Can Put 'W' in Win Column," *Journal Record* (Bloomberg News), May 21, 1998.

9. Quoted in "Joe Namath, Mike Schmidt and Bob Costas Introduce SportsLine USA"; https://www.cbssports.com/info/aboutus/press/1995 /kickoff; accessed June 2020 (no longer active).

10. Eric Fisher, "ESPN.com, Engine of Innovation," *Sports Business Journal*, March 30, 2015; https://www.sportsbusinessjournal.com/Journal/Issues /2015/03/30/Media/ESPNcom.aspx?hl=Eric+Fisher&sc=0.

11. Quoted in Fisher, "ESPN.com, Engine of Innovation."

12. Quoted in John Evan Frook, "SportsLine USA, ESPNet SportsZone Armed with Ad Strategies," *Communications Week*, September 25, 1995.

13. Quoted in George Puro, "A Hall of Fame Idea," *Sporting News*, July 24, 1995.

14. "Shaquille O'Neal Takes His Game to the World Wide Web", June 26, 1996; https://www.cbssports.com/info/aboutus/press/1996/shaq.

15. Brad Stone, "Jock-Fight on the Net," *Newsweek*, July 20, 1997.

16. Forums, SportsLine.com; https://web.archive.org/web/19990225155347 /http:/ww1.sportsline.com/u/jordan/chat/mjforum.html; accessed June 2020.

17. George Mannes, "Jordan Hoping to Net Big Winner at Web Site," *Daily News*, June 26, 1997.

18. Quoted in L. A. Lorek, "How Michael Levy Hit It Big with SportsLine," *Sun-Sentinel*, October 18, 1998.

19. Quoted in Newman, "SportsLine investors Can Put 'W' in Win Column."

20. "SportsLine USA, Inc. Launches Second Phase of SportsLine Rewards Program"; https://www.cbssports.com/info/aboutus/press/1999 /newrewards; accessed June 2020 (no longer active).

21. "SportsLine USA, Inc. Launches Second Phase of SportsLine Rewards Program"; https://www.cbssports.com/info/aboutus/press/1999/newrewards; accessed June 2020 (no longer active).

22. Quoted in "SportsLine.com, Inc., Sports.com Limited and Asiacontent .com Limited Join Forces to Create Asian Sports Internet Joint Venture"; https://www.cbssports.com/info/aboutus/press/2000/asia; accessed June 2020 (no longer active).

23. Quoted in "Flirting with Disaster," *Forbes*, December 3, 1997.

24. SportsLine.com, Inc. annual reports; available at http://getfilings.com /comp/k0000945688.html; accessed July 2020.

25. SportsLine.com Form 10-K, 2003; http://getfilings.com/o0001193125-04 -052106.html; accessed July 2020.

26. SportsLine.com Form 10-K, 2000; http://getfilings.com/o0000950170-01 -000438.html; accessed July 2020.

27. SportsLine.com annual report, 2002.

28. Marc Gunther, "Web + Sports = Profit. Right?" *Fortune*, March 4, 1996.

29. Gunther, "Web + Sports = Profit. Right?"

15. Boom!

1. Kate McKenna, "Bill to Ban New Sports Betting Sweeps through U.S. Senate," *Asbury Park Press* (States News Service), June 3, 1992.

2. Steve Wilstein, "Survey Shows America Hedging on Betting Issue," *Lexington Herald-Leader* (Associated Press), January 21, 1993.

3. Darrin Hostetler, "Bland Ambition," *Phoenix New Times*, August 11, 1994; https://www.phoenixnewtimes.com/news/bland-ambition-6425236 ?showFullText=true.

4. Neil Reisner, "Is On-line Gambling Hot? You Bet," *Miami Herald*, October 3, 1999.

5. Internet gambling hearing, March 23, 1999; https://www.govinfo.gov /content/pkg/CHRG-106shrg59677/html/CHRG-106shrg59677.htm.

6. Quoted in Jeri Clausing, "Gambling Bill Would Outlaw Online Fantasy Sports Games," *New York Times*, June 23, 1998.

7. Scott Newman, "NFL Players Union Seeking Profit from Fantasy Football Leagues," *Corpus Christi Caller-Times* (Bloomberg News), August 25, 1998.

8. Glenn Gamboa, "Fantasy Leagues Move beyond the Office," *Tallahassee Democrat (Akron Beacon Journal)*, May 4, 1997.

9. Hiltner and Walker, "Super Frustration Sunday," 105.

10. Hiltner and Walker, "Super Frustration Sunday," 112.

11. Newman, "NFL Players Union Seeking Profit from Fantasy Football Leagues."

12. "Madden 99 Review," *Electronic Gaming Monthly*, October 1999.

13. Advertisement, *Electronic Games*, Winter 1981.

14. Trip Hawkins AMA, *Reddit*, 2020; https://www.reddit.com/r/Madden

/comments/ih50ff/hi_reddit_my_name_is_trip_hawkins_and_i_am
_the/.

15. DeMaria and Wilson, *High Score!*, 164.

16. Kent, *The Ultimate History of Video Games*, 261.

17. *People*, May 8, 1995.

18. Colin Campbell, "How Electronic Arts Lost Its Soul," *Polygon*, issue 8;
    https://www.polygon.com/a/how-ea-lost-its-soul; accessed February 2022.

19. *Electronic Games*, January 1984.

20. Quoted in Patrick Sauer, "How Dr. J and Larry Bird Helped Build a Video
    Game Empire," *Vice*, May 25, 2017; https://www.vice.com/en/article
    /wje9kq/how-dr-j-and-larry-bird-helped-build-a-video-game-empire.

21. Software preview, *Electronic Games*, May 1984.

22. Annie Katz, "Electronic Pressbox," *Electronic Games*, July 1984.

23. Madden, *Hey, Wait a Minute*, 9.

24. Burwell, *Madden*, 179.

25. Patrick Hruby, "The Franchise," *ESPN*, October 8, 2005; http://www.espn
    .com/espn/eticket/story?page=100805/madden.

26. *Video Games and Computer Entertainment*, February 1990 (as cited in
    [YouTube] "John Madden Football," *Vault 1541*, February 3, 2019; https://
    www.vault1541.com/2019/02/youtube-john-madden-football.html).

27. Quoted in Steve Nidetz, "Fox Boss Learns Football—and Success," *Chicago Tribune*, November 27, 1994.

28. Quoted in Sean Mitchell, "Gridiron John," *Los Angeles Times Magazine*,
    September 4, 1994.

29. Quoted in Tom Bissell, "Kickoff: Madden NFL and the Future of Video
    Game Sports," *Grantland*, January 26, 2012; https://grantland.com
    /features/tom-bissell-making-madden-nfl.

30. "NHL Glowing Puck Advertisement [engineering history]," YouTube,
    February 11, 2014; https://www.youtube.com/watch?v=J5xXKTCoWMc&
    ab_channel=engineeringhistory.

31. Dan Caesar, "To Derail 'FoxTrax,' Fans Might Have to Boycott," *St. Louis
    Post-Dispatch*, April 24, 1998.

32. Bill Squadron, "The Story behind Football's Innovative Yellow First Down
    Line," *Sports Illustrated*, July 18, 2013; https://www.si.com/nfl/2013/07
    /18/nfl-birth-yellow-line.

33. "Sportvision's '1st & Ten' Technology a Huge Hit with Sports Fans,"
    March 31, 1999; https://web.archive.org/web/20011013043336/http://
    www.lovetheline.com/harris.htm.

34. LovetheLine.com; https://web.archive.org/web/20011221092627/http://
    www.lovetheline.com/display.asp; accessed February 2022.

35. Quoted in Richard Clough, "David Hill: Inside the Box," *Los Angeles Business Journal*, December 5, 2010; https://labusinessjournal.com/media
    /sports-media/inside-box/.

36. Internet gambling hearing, March 23, 1999.
37. Jeffrey Brinbaum, "Wanna Bet This Bill Is Really Strange?," *Fortune*, June 12, 2000.
38. Susan Schmidt and James V. Grimaldi, "How a Lobbyist Stacked the Deck," *Washington Post*, October 16, 2005.

16. Rapidly Converging Media Platforms

1. Quoted in Munk, *Fools Rush In*, 22.
2. Quoted in Munk, *Fools Rush In*, 42.
3. Deirdre Carmody, "Time Inc. Raises Its Multimedia Profile with an Internet Test," *New York Times*, October 24, 1994.
4. Michael A. Hiltzik, "Time Warner Site Is Purely for Entertainment," *Los Angeles Times*, November 29, 1999.
5. Chip Bayers, "Over 17 Million Served," *Wired*, October 1, 1999.
6. Saul Hansell, "Now, AOL Everywhere," *New York Times*, July 4, 1999.
7. Paul Murphy, "From $350bn to . . . ," *Financial Times*, May 12, 2015.
8. Tuggle, "Differences in Television Sports Reporting of Men's and Women's Athletics."
9. Messner, Duncan, and Cooky, "Silence, Sports Bras, and Wrestling Porn," 40.
10. Martin and McDonald, "Covering Women's Sport?"
11. Quoted in Barbara Basler, "U.S. Women Beat Norway to Capture World Cup," *New York Times*, December 1, 1991.
12. Quoted in Brian Clark, "Nike to Modesto Soccer Player: Just Do It!" *Modesto Bee*, Tuesday, March 28, 1995.
13. Jere Longman, "Pride in Their Play, and in Their Bodies," *New York Times*, July 8, 1999.
14. Quoted in Murray, "The National Team," Loc 483.
15. Longman, *The Girls of Summer*, 15.
16. Peter Kerasotis, "Chastain Ruins Great Moment," *Florida Today*, July 13, 1999.
17. Mark Kiszla, "Now Comes Tough Part for Women," *Denver Post*, July 15, 1999.
18. John Eisenberg, "A Priceless Point from Cup Women," *Baltimore Sun*, July 18, 1999.
19. Jere Longman, "Women's Soccer League Folds on World Cup's Eve," *New York Times*, September 16, 2003.
20. Quoted in Grant Wahl, "Inside Soccer," *Sports Illustrated*, March 12, 2001.
21. Hendricks, *A Curious Discovery*, 95.
22. Grahame L. Jones, "Women Ready to Kick-Start Soccer League of Their Own," *Los Angeles Times*, April 1, 2001.
23. Grant Wahl, "Strong Finishing Kick," *Sports Illustrated*, September 3, 2001.

24. Quoted in "sa Q&A with John Hendricks," *Soccer America*, January 19, 2001; https://www.socceramerica.com/publications/article/13208/sa-qa-with-john-hendricks-were-able-to-invest.html.

25. Television schedule, *Albany-Democrat Herald*, August 12, 2001.

26. Grant Wahl, "Battle of the Sexes," *Sports Illustrated*, May 1, 2000.

27. Chris Isidore, "Cup No Kick for Women's Soccer," cnn, September 19, 2003; https://money.cnn.com/2003/09/19/commentary/column_sportsbiz/sportsbiz/.

28. Paxson, *Threading the Needle*, 161.

29. Matt Schudel, "Lowell W. Paxson, Home Shopping Network Co-Founder and tv Mogul, Dies at 79," *Washington Post*, January 18, 2015.

30. Johnette Howard, "wusa Hopes Success Breeds Success," *Concord Monitor* (*Newsday*), April 8, 2002.

17. Content

1. Quoted in Brett McMurphy, "TeamLine Answers Call for Telephone Broadcasts," *Tampa Tribune*, February 13, 1991.

2. Quoted in Pete Wickham, "Dial $$$ for Feast," *Ottawa Citizen*, November 10, 1991.

3. "The Unknown Founder Who Got 10% of Broadcast.com," *Mixergy*; https://mixergy.com/interviews/chris-jaeb-broadcast-interview; accessed June 2022.

4. David Wilkison, "Alums Keep Tabs on Teams with Cyberspace Broadcasts," *Hawaii Tribune-Herald* (Associated Press), October 13, 1996.

5. Quoted in Terry Wallace, "It's How They Play the Game," *Journal and Courier* (Associated Press), March 16, 1998.

6. Yahoo! Form 10-k, 2000; http://getfilings.com/o0000912057-01-007693.html; accessed June 2022.

7. "Broadcast.com Latest Internet Stock Superstar," *Democrat and Chronicle* (Bloomberg News), July 18, 1998.

8. Dan Piller, "Broadcast.com Stock Soars after Split Is Announced," *Fort Worth Star-Telegram*, January 12, 1999.

9. Mylene Mangalindan and John Shinal, "One-Stop Web-ing," *Town Talk* (Bloomberg News), April 4, 1999.

10. Quoted in Julie Piotrowski, "Broadcast.com (Now Yahoo! Broadcast Services)," *Fast Company*, November 30, 1999; https://www.fastcompany.com/61848/broadcastcom-now-yahoo-broadcast-services.

11. Quoted in Mitchell Schnurman, "Collaring Their Gains," *Fort Worth Star-Telegram*, March 4, 2001.

12. Quoted in Jeff D'Alessio, "nba's Stern Standing Tall," *Florida Today*, September 30, 2002.

13. Larry Siddons, "nba Eye Profits to Be Gained from Cable Television Networks," *Marshall News Messenger* (Associated Press), January 14, 1982.

14. Joe McGuff, "Battle's on for Fortunes in Cable TV," *Kansas City Star*, February 11, 1981.

15. Quoted in Bob Raissman, "NBA Coaches' Wires Crossed," *New York Daily News*, March 12, 2000.

16. Associated Press, "NBA to Launch 24-Hour TV Network," *Daily Oklahoman*, September 24, 1999.

17. Daniel Roth, "The NBA's Next Shot," *Fortune*, February 21, 2000.

18. Bart Hubbuch, "Cameras in Locker Room Have Coaches Wired Up," *Orlando Sentinel (Dallas Morning News)*, March 12, 2000.

19. Schuyler Baehman, "All NBA Channel Heralds New Sports-TV Partnership," *Post-Crescent*, October 4, 1999.

20. Quoted in Ed Sherman, "Fantastic: All NBA, All the Time," *Chicago Tribune*, December 16, 1999.

21. Greg Johnson, "NBA Teaming with Intel on Net Venture," *Los Angeles Times*, September 14, 2000.

22. Richard Tedesco, "NBA Drives Direct to Fans," *Broadcasting & Cable*, September 27, 1998.

23. Quoted in Paul J. Gough, "Follow the Bouncing Ball: NBA Deal Goes beyond TV," *Hollywood Reporter*, June 28, 2007; https://www.hollywoodreporter.com/business/business-news/follow-bouncing-ball-nba-deal-141039/.

24. "Turner Broadcasting and the National Basketball Association Broaden Partnership with Digital Rights Agreement," *Webwire*, January 18, 2008; https://www.webwire.com/ViewPressRel.asp?aId=56966.

25. Roth, "The NBA's Next Shot."

26. Quoted in "Turner Broadcasting and the National Basketball Association Broaden Partnership with Digital Rights Agreement."

27. Pages accessed via Internet Archive's Wayback Machine; https://archive.org/web/.

28. Quoted in Piotrowski, "Broadcast.com (Now Yahoo! Broadcast Services)."

29. Douglas Martin, "Ed Sabol, Who Elevated Football Founding NFL Films, Dies at 98," *New York Times*, February 9, 2015.

30. "A Talk with the King of Streaming: Mark Cuban," *Internet World*, October 1, 1999.

31. John Ourand, "Another NBA Club Strikes RSN Deal," *Sports Business Journal*, November 23, 2015.

32. Quoted in "A Talk," *Internet World*.

33. Quoted in Paul J. Gough, "NBA's Digital Pass-Off Puts TNT Expertise on the Point," *Hollywood Reporter*, January 18–20, 2008.

18. The Sports Guys

1. Quoted in Miller and Shales, *Those Guys Have All the Fun*, 646.

2. Greg Auman, "ESPN.com Unveiling Page 2," *Tampa Bay Times*, October 27, 2000.

3. "ESPN.com Page 2," ESPN.com, November 6, 2000; http://www.espn.com /page2/001106.html.

4. Hunter S. Thompson, "The Fix Is In," ESPN.com, November 6, 2000; https://proxy.espn.com/espn/page2/story?id=906189.

5. Thompson, "The Fix Is In."

6. Sports Guy's Bio Page, *Digital City Boston,* September, 1999; https://web .archive.org/web/19991202020230/http:/home.digitalcity.com/boston /sportsguy/main.dci?page=sgbio.

7. Bill Simmons, "Viva Las Vegas," *Digital City Boston*; https://web.archive .org/web/19991204012745/http://home.digitalcity.com/boston/sportsguy /main.dci?page=vegas1; accessed December 2021.

8. A re-post of this article can be found at https://www.reddit.com/r /billsimmons/comments/8cwcmk/bs_classic_grading_the_wimbledon _babes; accessed December 2021.

9. Quoted in Jeff Pearlman, "The Yang Slinger: Vol. III," October 25, 2021; https://pearlman.substack.com/p/the-yang-slinger-vol-iii.

10. Quoted in Charlie Warzel, "Deadspin: An Oral History," *AdWeek*, January 28, 2013; https://www.adweek.com/performance-marketing/deadspin -oral-history-146794.

11. "12 Minutes of Hell, with Colin Cowherd," FireJoeMorgan.com, January 13, 2006; https://web.archive.org/web/20060419004929/http:// firejoemorgan.blogspot.com/2006/01/12-minutes-of-hell-with-colin -cowherd.html.

12. "Are We Responsible? I Think Definitely," FireJoeMorgan.com, October 1, 2005; https://web.archive.org/web/20060221103426/http:// firejoemorgan.blogspot.com/2005_10_01_firejoemorgan_archive.html.

13. "The Relatively Short Goodbye," FireJoeMorgan.com, November 13, 2008; https://web.archive.org/web/20081202170711/http://www.firejoemorgan .com:80/.

14. Quoted in "Leitch vs. Bissinger on HBO," Craig Fehrman, September 1, 2017, YouTube video; https://www.youtube.com/watch?v=tQrrcwMMKl4 &ab_channel=CraigFehrman. All quotes in this and the next four paragraphs are from this online video.

15. Will Leitch, "Of Jimmy Olson, Spittle and the Dying of the Light," *Deadspin*, April 30, 2008; https://deadspin.com/of-jimmy-olson-spittle-and -the-dying-of-the-light-385513.

16. Allen Barra, "Jockbeat: Will Leitch Not Done Milking Buzz," *Village Voice*, February 9, 2009; https://www.villagevoice.com/2009/02/09/jockbeat -will-leitch-not-done-milking-buzz.

19. An Essential Good

1. Bill Simmons, "Sporting Emotions at the Highest Pitch," ESPN.com, August 17, 2009; http://www.espn.com/espn/page2/story?page=simmons/090817.
2. Anderson, *Imagined Communities*, 6.
3. Anderson, *Imagined Communities*, 170.
4. Nadel, *Fútbol!*, 188.
5. J. Wilson, *Angels with Dirty Faces*, 27.
6. Goldblatt, *The Ball Is Round*, 204.
7. Alabarces and Rodríguez, "Football and Fatherland," 118.
8. Bellos, *Futebol*, 45.
9. Bellos, *Futebol*, 43.
10. Quoted in Andrea Fishman and Richard Alan White, "The Selling of Argentina: Madison Ave. Packages Repression," *Los Angeles Times*, June 11, 1978.
11. Quoted in Lowell Miller, "World Cup—or World War?" *New York Times*, May 21, 1978.
12. Quoted in Brian Glanville, "World Cup Soccer Madness in Argentina," *Washington Post*, June 12, 1978.
13. Quoted in John Groser, "Warning to Journalists of World Cup 'Dangers,'" *The Times*, May 20, 1978.
14. Dennis Redmont, "More Than a Title: Argentina Wins World Cup, New Image," *State Journal* (Associated Press), June 26, 1978.
15. Charles Newberry, "It's a Goal . . . but Viewers Can't See It," *Variety*, May 23, 2004.
16. Mastrini, Becerra, and Bizberge, *Grupo Clarín*, 44.
17. The Spanish version of the speech is available at https://es.wikisource.org/wiki/Discurso_de_Cristina_Fern%C3%A1ndez_en_el_acto_de_firma_de_convenio_entre_la_AFA_y_el_SNMP; accessed June 2022. The quote in the following paragraph is also from Kirchner's speech. My translations.
18. Bernardo Vázquez, "El fin de Fútbol para Todos: Al Gobierno le costó $5 millones por día en 2016," *Cronista*, March 1, 2017; https://www.cronista.com/economia-politica/El-fin-de-Futbol-para-Todos-al-Gobierno-le-costo-5-millones-por-dia-en-2016-20170103-0041.html.
19. Alejandro Catterberg, "Una poderosa herramienta de propaganda al servicio del Gobierno," *La Nación*, January 27, 2013; https://www.lanacion.com.ar/politica/una-poderosa-herramienta-de-propaganda-al-servicio-del-gobierno-nid1549460/.
20. J. Wilson, *Angels with Dirty Faces*, 301; Goldblatt, *The Ball Is Round*, 801.
21. J. Wilson, *Angels with Dirty Faces*, 355.

20. #Jeah

1. Rob Hughes, "No Hiding Place Left for Flawed Genius Maradona," *The Times*, July 1, 1994.
2. Filip Bondy, "A Big Kick in the Head," *New York Daily News*, July 1, 1994.
3. Quoted in Burns, *Maradona*, Loc 4951.
4. Associated Press, "Belle Fires Away at Media before Game," *Times Herald*, October 25, 1995.
5. Quoted in Noah Liberman, "If Belle Blows Up Again, His Web Site Could Be a Hot Spot," *Sports Business Journal*, April 19, 1999.
6. Liberman, "If Belle Blows Up Again."
7. Scott Newman, "Belle Setting Site on Financial Advice," *Arizona Republic* (Bloomberg News), June 6, 1999.
8. Chris Tomasson, "Nothing but Net," *Akron Beacon Journal*, May 23, 2000.
9. Quoted in "AthleteNow Exclusive," *AthleteNow*, July 8, 2001; https://web.archive.org/web/20010708043505/http://www.athletenow.com/charles_barkley_chat.shtml.
10. Jerry Crasnick, "'Net Result: Nitkowski Makes His Pitch," *Sunday Record* (Bloomberg News), April 23, 2000.
11. Restaurant reviews, cjbaseball.com, October 13, 1999; https://web.archive.org/web/19991013070832/http://cjbaseball.com/restaurants.htm.
12. Quoted in "Basketball Diaries," Meech.org, March 21, 2000; https://web.archive.org/web/20000510124815/http://www.meech.org:80/index1.html.
13. Quoted in "Basketball Diaries," Meech.org, April 11–14, 2000; https://web.archive.org/web/20000510124815/http://www.meech.org:80/index1.html.
14. Quoted in Shira Springer, "Keeping You Posted," *Boston Globe*, July 3, 2009.
15. "Shaq Seeks Unique Deal with Microsoft," *Orlando Sentinel*, June 6, 1995.
16. Quoted in Gene Yasuda, "Shaq to Be a Microsoft Starter," *Orlando Sentinel*, July 19, 1995.
17. "Shaquille O'Neal Takes His Game to the World Wide Web," *CBS Sports*, June 26, 1996; https://www.cbssports.com/info/aboutus/press/1996/shaq.
18. "(I Know I Got) Skillz," *Genius*, September 7, 1993; https://genius.com/Shaquille-oneal-i-know-i-got-skillz-lyrics.
19. All tweets are from Shaq's old Twitter handle, which was @The_Real_Shaq. The Oklahoma tweet was on November 25, 2007. The gumbo tweet was December 2, 2008. The lunch tweet was March 5, 2009.
20. Tweet from @The_Real_Shaq, June 30, 2009.
21. "About Klout," *Klout*, February 6, 2012; https://web.archive.org/web/20120206140859/http://klout.com/corp/about.
22. Seth Stevenson, "What Your Klout Score Really Means," *Wired*, April 24, 2012; https://www.wired.com/2012/04/ff-klout/#:~:text=The%20scores

%20are%20calculated%20using,shares%20that%20your%20updates %20receive.

23. Stuart Thomas, "How Do 11 of the Most Popular Athletes on Twitter Rank on Klout?" *Yahoo!*, March 5, 2012; https://www.yahoo.com/news/11-most -popular-athletes-twitter-rank-klout-043023408.html.

24. Laurie Segall, "Measure Your Social Networking Klout," CNN, June 25, 2010; https://money.cnn.com/2010/06/25/technology/klout/index.htm.

25. Quoted in David Jones, "Gators' Golden Child," *Florida Today*, June 22, 2008.

26. Quoted in Jessica Salter, "London 2012 Olympics: Can the Laidback Ryan Lochte Record Nine Golds?" *The Telegraph*, March 23, 2012; https://www .telegraph.co.uk/sport/olympics/swimming/9156170/London-2012 -Olympics-Can-the-laidback-Ryan-Lochte-win-a-record-nine-golds.html.

27. Quoted in "Ryan Lochte Explains 'Jeah,'" The Daily Reezy, July 30, 2009, YouTube video; https://www.youtube.com/watch?v=w6par1NTH5g&ab _channel=TheDailyReezy.

28. THR Staff, "London 2012: Social Media Takes Its Toll on Olympics," *Hollywood Reporter*, August 1, 2012; https://www.hollywoodreporter.com /news/general-news/london-2012-social-media-olympics-356538/.

29. Tim Dahlberg, "Athletes, Fans Won't Win Gold for Tacky Tweets," *Desert Sun* (Associated Press), August 1, 2012. Athletes' quotes are from this article.

30. Mike Lopresti, "From Greece, We Have First Twitter Casualty of the Olympics," *News Herald* (USA Today), July 26, 2012.

31. Erin Quinn, "Michael Phelps and Ryan Lochte: Creating Twitter Traffic," *Bleacher Report*, July 19, 2012; https://bleacherreport.com/articles /1265765-michael-phelps-ryan-lochte-creating-twitter-traffic-from-us -olympic-swim-camp.

32. Quoted in Sally Holmes, "Deep Thoughts from Ryan Lochte," *New York*, August 2, 2012; https://www.thecut.com/2012/08/deep-thoughts-from -ryan-lochte.html.

33. Quoted in "Ryan Lochte Gets His Own E! Reality TV Show," CBSNews, January 8, 2013; https://www.cbsnews.com/news/ryan-lochte-gets-his-own -e-reality-tv-show/.

34. "Ratings," *The Futon Critic*, April 23, 2013; http://thefutoncritic.com /ratings/2013/04/23/sundays-cable-ratings-game-of-thrones-nba -playoffs-top-charts-336513/cable_20130421/.

35. Ryan Lochte (@ryanlochte), "I want to apologize for my behavior . . . ," Instagram, August 19, 2016; https://www.instagram.com/p /BJSwyLJBoSH/?taken-by=ryanlochte&hl=en.

21. On-Demand

1. David Scott, "ESPN by the Numbers, March 2013," ESPN *Front Row*, March 4, 2013; https://www.espnfrontrow.com/2013/03/espn-by-the-numbers -march-2013/.

2. Derek Thompson, "The Global Dominance of ESPN," *The Atlantic*, September 2013; https://www.theatlantic.com/magazine/archive/2013/09/the-most-valuable-network/309433/.

3. John McCain, "Cable TV, the Right Way," *Los Angeles Times*, May 23, 2013.

4. Quoted in Joe Flint, "McCain Targets Cable Channel Bundling," *Los Angeles Times*, May 10, 2013.

5. McCain, "Cable TV, the Right Way."

6. "About Us," *Bleacher Report*, February 5, 2007; https://web.archive.org/web/20070205024048/http://www.bleacherreport.com/about-us/.

7. Jeff Bercovici, "To Pay or Not to Pay? Bleacher Report Finds a Third Way," *Forbes*, August 22, 2011; https://www.forbes.com/sites/jeffbercovici/2011/08/22/to-pay-or-not-to-pay-bleacher-report-finds-a-third-way/?sh=2b5330191efe.

8. George Szalai, "ESPN: Digital Front and (Sports) Center," *Hollywood Reporter* (Associated Press), May 20, 2009; https://www.hollywoodreporter.com/business/business-news/espn-digital-front-sports-center-84320/.

9. Mike Humes, "ESPN 'CFP Megacast': More Than 12 Ways to Follow National Championship across ESPN Platforms," *ESPN Press Room*, January 8, 2015; https://espnpressroom.com/us/press-releases/2015/01/espn-cfp-megacast-more-than-12-ways-to-follow-national-championship-across-espn-platforms/.

22. Millionaire Makers

1. Quoted in Phil Rosenthal, "Details Remain, but Illinois Ready to Get in Game," *Chicago Tribune*, May 15, 2018.

2. Tim Hackett, "Sports World Reacts to the Supreme Court's Sports Betting Decision," *Sports Illustrated*, May 14, 2018; https://www.si.com/more-sports/2018/05/14/sports-betting-supreme-court-decision-reactions.

3. Quoted in "Gambling: America's National Pastime?" *Sports Illustrated*, March 10, 1986.

4. Quoted in "Gambling: America's National Pastime?" *Sports Illustrated*, March 10, 1986.

5. Quoted in Steve Wilstein, "Survey Shows America Hedging on Betting Issue," *Lexington Herald-Leader* (Associated Press), January 21, 1993.

6. Quoted in Mike Johnson, "Simon Noble: A Deep Dive with the Man Who Witnessed the First Online Wager," *Gambling News*, February 4, 2021; https://www.gamblingnews.com/news/simon-noble-a-deep-dive-with-the-man-who-witnessed-the-first-online-wager/.

7. Quoted in Mark Asher, "On-line Bettors Take Their Chances, Reap the Rewards," *Washington Post*, January 24, 1998.

8. "Why Do You Think They Call It 'Craps'?" *News and Observer*, December 26, 2001.

9. Simon Bowers, "Denise Coates: The Hidden 24/7 Woman behind Bet365," *The Guardian*, June 8, 2012.
10. Quoted in Josh Dean, "The Personality behind Online Gaming Site Bodog," *Fast Company*, July 1, 2008; https://www.fastcompany.com /898669/personality-behind-online-gaming-site-bodog.
11. "Cole Turner Is an Asshole," *MyLegacyKit—Medium*, February 16, 2022; https://mylegacykit.medium.com/cole-turner-is-an-asshole-a1b592db2502.
12. "Cole Turner Is an Asshole."
13. David Baines, "Vancouver's Other Billionaire," *Vancouver Sun*, September 22, 2006.
14. Matthew Miller, "Catch Me If You Can," *Forbes*, March 11, 2006; https:// www.forbes.com/forbes/2006/0327/112.html?sh=210078301514.
15. FAQ, FantasySportsLive.com, November 23, 2010; https://web.archive.org /web/20101123072537/https://fantasysportslive.com/faq.html.
16. Quoted in Chen, *Billion Dollar Fantasy*, 24.
17. Quoted in Tom Savage, "Meet the Million-Dollar Fantasy Owner," *Argus Leader*, December 20, 2013; https://www.argusleader.com/story/news /2013/12/20/meet-the-million-dollar-fantasy-owner/4139375.
18. "DraftKings Fantasy Football TV Spot, 'Real People, Real Winning,'" iSpot .tv, August 14, 2015; https://www.ispot.tv/ad/7U9V/draftkings-fantasy -football-real-people-real-winnings.
19. DraftKings Holdings Inc., *Stock Analysis*; https://stockanalysis.com /stocks/dkng/financials/; accessed November 2022.
20. Aaron Timms, "I Saw Betting's Toxic Sludge," *The Guardian*, September 21, 2021; https://www.theguardian.com/sport/2021/sep/21/us-sports -betting-legal-adverts.

23. Superfine Market Segmentation

1. Zhu, *Two Billion Eyes*, 13.
2. Scotton and Hachten, *New Media for a New China*, 85.
3. Quoted in David Whitley, "Football May Be Getting a Few Million New Fans," *Tallahassee Democrat*, May 18, 1988.
4. Whitley, "Football May Be Getting a Few Million New Fans."
5. Quoted in "Mickey Mouse Makes His TV Debut in China," *Ledger-Enquirer* (Associated Press), October 27, 1986.
6. "World Series of Hoops?" *New York Daily News* (Associated Press), October 24, 1987.
7. Zhu, *Two Billion Eyes*, 241.
8. Li, *Chinese Media, Global Contexts*, 12.
9. Mark Landler, "AOL Gains Cable Rights in China by Omitting News, Sex, and Violence," *New York Times*, October 29, 2001.
10. Quoted in Melanie Nayer, "Programs Teaching the Business of Sports Are a Hit," *Boston Globe*, October 16, 2005.

11. Quoted in Shira Springer, "Keeping You Posted," *Boston Globe*, July 3, 2009.

12. Daryl Morey (@dmorey), Twitter, October 4, 2019; (post deleted).

13. Daryl Morey (@dmorey), "I did not intend my tweet . . . ," Twitter, October 6, 2019; https://twitter.com/dmorey/status/1181000808399114240.

14. Daryl Morey (@dmorey), "I have always appreciated the significant support . . . ," Twitter, October 6, 2019; https://twitter.com/dmorey/status/1181000809363857409.

15. Quoted in Reuters, "'We Love China,' James Harden Says after Houston General Manager's Tweet Backing Hong Kong Protesters," *New York Times*, October 7, 2019.

16. Tilman Fertitta (@TilmanJFertitta), "Listen. . . . @dmorey does NOT speak for the @HoustonRockets . . . ," Twitter, October 4, 2019; https://twitter.com/TilmanJFertitta/status/1180330287957495809.

17. Quoted in Ohm Youngmisuk, "LeBron James: Daryl Morey Was 'Misinformed' before Sending Tweet about China and Hong Kong," ESPN, October 14, 2019; https://www.espn.com/nba/story/_/id/27847951/daryl-morey-was-misinformed-sending-tweet-china-hong-kong.

18. Joe Tsai, "Open Letter to All NBA Fans," Facebook, October 6, 2019; https://www.facebook.com/joe.tsai.3781/posts/2653378931391524.

19. Quoted in Anjalee Khemlani, "NBA's Silver Says Financial Losses from China Crisis Are 'Fairly Dramatic,'" *Yahoo! Money*, October 17, 2019; https://money.yahoo.com/nbas-losses-from-spat-with-china-substantial-adam-silver-says-161828430.html.

20. Jabari Young, "NBA Will Lose Hundreds of Millions of Dollars Due to Rift with China, Commissioner Says," CNBC, February 16, 2020; https://www.cnbc.com/2020/02/16/nba-will-lose-hundreds-of-millions-of-dollars-due-to-rift-with-china-commissioner-says.html.

21. Kevin Arnovitz, "Inside the NBA's Silent Tension Surrounding Daryl Morey," ABC13 (ESPN), November 12, 2019; https://abc13.com/sports/inside-the-nbas-silent-tension-surrounding-daryl-morey/5691814/.

22. Jackie MacMullan, "Philadelphia 76ers' Daryl Morey Was Worried Hong Kong Tweet Might End NBA Career," ESPN, December 23, 2020; https://www.espn.com/nba/story/_/id/30587457/philadelphia-76ers-daryl-morey-was-worried-hong-kong-tweet-end-nba-career.

23. The full letter was available at https://gallagher.house.gov/sites/gallagher.house.gov/files/NBA%20China%20Letter.pdf; accessed November 2022 (post deleted).

24. Venky Vembu, "Free Speech Makes for Dirty Business," *Hindu Business Line*, October 10, 2019; https://www.thehindubusinessline.com/opinion/columns/the-cheat-sheet/free-speech-makes-for-dirty-business-just-ask-nba/article29628024.ece.

25. "Dr D's Column: Does LeBron James's Concern about Daryl Morey's Misinformed Tweet Reflect True American-ness?," *Economic Times*, October

23, 2019; https://economictimes.indiatimes.com/magazines/panache
/dr-ds-column-does-lebron-jamess-concern-about-daryl-moreys
-misinformed-tweet-reflect-true-american-ness/articleshow/71715379
.cms?from=mdr.

26. Quoted in Ryan D'Agostino, "The Man Who Knows Everything," *Esquire*, January 19, 2012.

27. Ranadivé, *The Power of Now*, 15.

28. Ranadivé, *The Power of Now*, 15.

29. Quoted in Express News Service, "IPL Telecast Will Have Multiple Streams, Viewers Can Choose Personalised Camera Angle to Watch Game," *Indian Express*, August 30, 2022; https://indianexpress.com /article/sports/cricket/jio-5g-ipl-telecast-will-have-multiple-streams -viewers-can-choose-personalised-camera-angle-to-watch-game -8120104/.

30. Ming Zeng, "Alibaba and the Future of Business," *Harvard Business Review*, September/October 2018.

Epilogue

1. Quoted in "Where to Bet Jose Canseco vs. Billy Football," *WhereToBet*; https://www.wheretobet.net/boxing/jose-canseco-vs-billy-football; accessed November 2022.

2. Quoted in "The Transformation of Real Madrid," *Microsoft*, October 24, 2017; https://news.microsoft.com/europe/features/the-transformation -of-real-madrid/.

3. Quoted in Bruce Schoenfeld, "L.A. Clippers Owner Steve Ballmer Wants to Save Sports by Reinventing the Way We Watch Them," *Fast Company*, May 4, 2020; https://www.fastcompany.com/90490917/l-a-clippers -owner-steve-ballmer-wants-to-save-sports-by-reinventing-the-way-we -watch-them.

4. Quoted in "The NBA Launches a First-of-Its-Kind New App Experience for Fans, Driven by the Power of Data," *Microsoft*, September 27, 2022; https://news.microsoft.com/transform/the-nba-launches-a-first-of-its -kind-new-app-experience-for-fans-driven-by-the-power-of-data/.

5. Jeff Beer, "MLB's Chris Marinak on How COVID-19 Is Changing the Fan Experience," *Fast Company*, April 1, 2021; https://www.fastcompany.com /90620931/the-mlbs-chris-marinak-on-how-covid-19-is-changing-the -fan-experience.

6. Cantril and Allport, *The Psychology of Radio*, 24.

7. "Real International Broadcasting: Proposals for a European Alliance," *Wireless World*, August 1944.

8. Quoted in Brinkley, *The Publisher*, 285.

9. Haag, "'The 50,000-Watt Sports Bar,'" 466.

10. Hobsbawm, *Nations and Nationalism since 1780*, 143.

11. Quoted in "Real Madrid Brings the Stadium Closer to 450 Million Fans around the Globe, with the Microsoft Cloud," *Microsoft*, June 7, 2019; https://customers.microsoft.com/es-es/story/729437-real-madrid-brings-the-stadium-closer-to-450-million-f.
12. "Courtside Lounges," *Chase Center*, https://www.chasecenter.com/courtside; accessed November 2022.

Selected Bibliography

Alabarces, Pablo, and María Graciela Rodríguez. "Football and Fatherland: The Crisis of National Representation in Argentinian Soccer." *Culture, Sport, Society* 2, no. 3 (1999): 118–33.

Anderson, Benedict. *Imagined Communities: Reflections on the Origin and Spread of Nationalism.* London: Verso, 2006.

Arledge, Roone. *Roone: A Memoir.* New York: HarperCollins, 2002.

Athique, Adrian. *Indian Media: Global Approaches.* Cambridge: Polity, 2012.

Banowsky, William Slater. *It's a Playboy World.* Old Tappan NJ: Fleming H. Revell, 1969.

Bellos, Alex. *Futebol: The Brazilian Way of Life* (Kindle edition). New York: Bloomsbury USA, 2014.

Birchard, John. *Jock around the Clock: The Story of History's First All-Sports Radio Network* (Kindle edition). Bloomington IN: Xlibris, 2010.

Bonifer, Michael, and L. G. Weaver. *Out of Bounds: An Anecdotal History of Notre Dame Football.* First ed. New York: Piper Publishing, 1978.

Bosa, Mihir. *Game Changer: How the English Premier League Came to Dominate the World* (Kindle edition). Singapore: Marshall Cavendish International Asia Pte Lte, 2012.

Boutilier, Mary A., and Lucinda San Giovanni. *The Sporting Woman.* Champaign IL: Human Kinetics, 1983.

Bowden, Mark. *The Best Game Ever: Giants vs. Colts, 1958, and the Birth of the Modern NFL* (Kindle edition). New York: Atlantic Monthly Press, 2008.

Brinkley, Alan. *The Publisher: Henry Luce and His American Century.* New York: Knopf, 2010.

Budin, Steve, and Bob Schaller. *Bets, Drugs, and Rock & Roll: The Rise and Fall of the World's First Offshore Sports Gambling Empire.* New York: Skyhorse Publishing, 2007.

Burns, Jimmy. *Maradona: The Hand of God* (Kindle edition). London: Bloomsbury, 2010.

Burwell, Bryan. *Madden: A Biography*. Chicago: Triumph Books, 2011.

Butcher, Melissa. *Transnational Television, Cultural Identity and Change: When Star Came to India*. New Delhi: Sage Publications, 2003.

Cantril, Hadley, and Gordon W. Allport. *The Psychology of Radio*. New York and London: Harper and Brothers Publishers, 1935.

Capouya, John. *Gorgeous George: The Outrageous Bad-Boy Wrestler Who Created American Pop Culture* (Kindle edition). New York: HarperCollins e-books, 2008.

Celler, Emanuel. *You Never Leave Brooklyn*. New York: John Day Company, 1953.

Chen, Albert. *Billion Dollar Fantasy: The High-Stakes Game between Fanduel and DraftKings That Upended Sports in America*. Boston: Houghton Mifflin Harcourt, 2019.

Chenoweth, Neil. *Rupert Murdoch: The Untold Story of the World's Greatest Media Wizard*. New York: Crown Business, 2001.

Chisari, Fabio. "When Football Went Global: Televising the 1966 World Cup." *Historical Social Research/Historische Sozialforschung* (2006): 42–54.

Cooky, Cheryl, Michael A. Messner, and Robin H. Hextrum. "Women Play Sport, but Not on TV: A Longitudinal Study of Televised News Media." *Communication & Sport* 1, no. 3 (2013): 203–30.

Craig, Steve. "Daniel Starch's 1928 Survey: A First Glimpse of the US Radio Audience." *Journal of Radio & Audio Media* 17, no. 2 (2010): 182–94.

Cuban, Mark. *How to Win at the Sport of Business: If I Can Do It, You Can Do It*. New York: Diversion Books, 2013.

DeMaria, Rusel, and Johnny L. Wilson. *High Score!: The Illustrated History of Electronic Games*. New York: McGraw-Hill/Osborne, 2004.

Domeneghetti, Roger. *From the Back Page to the Front Room: Football's Journey through the English Media*. West Yorkshire: Ockley Books, 2014.

Douglas, Susan J. *Listening In: Radio and the American Imagination, from Amos 'n' Andy and Edward R. Murrow to Wolfman Jack and Howard Stern*. New York: Times Books, 1999.

Eisenberg, John. *The League: How Five Rivals Created the NFL and Launched a Sports Empire*. New York: Basic Books, 2018.

Eisenstock, Alan. *Sports Talk: A Fan's Journey to the Heart and Soul of Sports Talk Radio*. New York: Pocket Books, 2001.

Evey, Stuart, and Irv Broughton. *ESPN: The No-Holds-Barred Story of Power, Ego, Money, and Vision That Transformed a Culture*. Chicago: Triumph Books, 2004.

Fountain, Charles. *Sportswriter: The Life and Times of Grantland Rice*. New York: Oxford University Press, 1993.

Fowler, Mark S., and Daniel L. Brenner. "Marketplace Approach to Broadcast Regulation." *Texas Law Review* 60 (1981): 207–57.

Fox, Elizabeth. *Latin American Broadcasting: From Tango to Telenovela.* Luton: University of Luton Press, 1997.

——— . *Media and Politics in Latin America: The Struggle for Democracy.* Newbury Park, CA: Sage Publications, 1988.

Freeman, Michael. *ESPN: The Uncensored History.* Dallas TX: Taylor Publishing, 2000.

Getty, J. Paul. *As I See It : The Autobiography of J. Paul Getty.* Revised edition. Los Angeles: J. Paul Getty Museum, 2003.

——— . *How to Be Rich.* New York: Jove Books, 1986.

Gershon, Richard A., and Michael O. Wirth. "Home Box Office." In *The Cable Networks Handbook*, edited by Robert Picard, 114–22. Riverside CA: Carpelan, 1993.

Godfrey, Donald G. *Philo T. Farnsworth: The Father of Television.* Salt Lake City: University of Utah Press, 2001.

Goldblatt, David. *The Ball Is Round: A Global History of Soccer.* New York: Riverhead Books, 2008.

Grieveson, Lee. "Fighting Films: Race, Morality, and the Governing of Cinema, 1912–1915." *Cinema Journal* 38, no. 1 (Fall 1998): 40–72.

Griffen-Foley, Bridget. *Sir Frank Packer: A Biography* (Kindle edition). Sydney: Sydney University Press, 2014.

Guttmann, Allen. "Berlin 1936: The Most Controversial Olympics." In *National Identity and Global Sports Events: Culture, Politics, and Spectacle in the Olympics and the Football World Cup*, edited by Alan Tomlinson and Christopher Young, 65–81. Albany: SUNY Press, 2012.

Haag, Pamela. "'The 50,000-Watt Sports Bar': Talk Radio and the Ethic of the Fan." *South Atlantic Quarterly* 95, no. 2 (1996): 453–70.

Hadamovsky, Eugen. *Propaganda and National Power.* New York: Arno Press, 1972.

Haigh, Gideon. *The Cricket War: The Story of Kerry Packer's World Series Cricket.* London: Bloomsbury, 2017.

Halberstam, David J. *Sports on New York Radio: A Play-by-Play History.* Lincolnwood IL: Masters Press, 1999.

Hall, Stuart. "The Treatment of 'Football Hooliganism' in the Press." In *Football Hooliganism: The Wider Context*, edited by Roger Ingham, Stuart Hall, John Clarke, Peter Marsh, and Jim Donovan, 15–36. London: Inter-Action Imprint, 1978.

Hare, Geoff. "Football and the European Collective Memory in Britain: The Case of the 1960 European Cup Final." In *European Football and Collective Memory*, edited by Wolfram Pyta and Nils Havemann, 101–18. London: Palgrave Macmillan, 2015.

Harris, David. *The League: The Rise and Decline of the* NFL. Toronto: Bantam Books, 1986.

Hauser, Thomas. *Muhammad Ali: His Life and Times.* New York: Simon & Schuster, 2006.

Hendricks, John. *A Curious Discovery: An Entrepreneur's Story.* New York: Harper Business, 2013.

Henrich-Franke, Christian. "Creating Transnationality through an International Organization? The European Broadcasting Union's (EBU) Television Programme Activities." *Media History* 16 (2010): 67–81.

Hesburgh, Theodore M., and Jerry Reedy. *God, Country, Notre Dame: The Autobiography of Theodore M. Hesburgh.* Notre Dame IN: University of Notre Dame Press, 2018.

Hiltner, Judith R., and James R. Walker. "Super Frustration Sunday: The Day Prodigy's Fantasy Baseball Died: An Analysis of the Dynamics of Electronic Communication." *Journal of Popular Culture* 30, no. 3 (Winter 1996): 103–17.

Hobsbawm, Eric. *Nations and Nationalism since 1780: Programme, Myth, Reality.* Cambridge: Cambridge University Press, 1990.

Hogan, Paul, and Dean Murphy. *The Tap-Dancing Knife Thrower.* Sydney NSW: HarperCollins, 2021.

Huggins, Mike. "BBC Radio and Sport 1922–39." *Contemporary British History* 21, no. 4 (2007): 491–515.

Izenberg, Jerry. *Rozelle: A Biography.* Lincoln: University of Nebraska Press, 2014.

Jordan, Jerry N. *The Long-Range Effect of Television and Other Factors on Sports Attendance.* Washington DC: Radio-Television Manufacturers Association, 1951.

Kane, Mary Jo. "Media Coverage of the Female Athlete before, during, and after Title IX: *Sports Illustrated* Revisited." *Journal of Sport Management* 2, no. 2 (1988): 87–99.

Kent, Steven L. *The Ultimate History of Video Games: From Pong to Pokémon and Beyond—The Story behind the Crazy That Touched Our Lives and Changed the World.* New York: Three Rivers Press, 2001.

King, Billie Jean, Johnette Howard, and Maryanne Vollers. *All In: An Autobiography.* New York: Alfred A. Knopf, 2021.

Kisseloff, Jeff. *The Box: An Oral History of Television, 1920–1961.* New York: Penguin, 1995.

Kohli-Khandekar, Vanita. *The Indian Media Business.* Fourth ed. New Delhi: Sage Publications, 2013.

Kram, Mark. *Ghosts of Manila: The Fateful Blood Feud between Muhammad Ali and Joe Frazier.* New York: HarperCollins, 2001.

Krüger, Arnd. "Germany: The Propaganda Machine." In *The Nazi Olympics: Sport, Politics, and Appeasement in the 1930s*, edited by Arnd Krüger and William Murray, 17–43. Urbana: University of Illinois Press, 2003.

Lawrence, Paul R. *Unsportsmanlike Conduct: The National Collegiate Athletic Association and the Business of College Football.* New York: Praeger, 1987.

LeCompte, Tom. *The Last Sure Thing: The Life and Times of Bobby Riggs.* Easthampton MA: Black Squirrel Publishing, 2003.

Li, Jinquan. *Chinese Media, Global Contexts.* London: Routledge Curzon, 2003.

Licklider, J. C. R. "Televistas: Looking Ahead through Side Windows." In *Public Television, A Program for Action*, 201–25. New York: Harper & Row, 1967.

Licklider, J. C. R., and Robert W. Taylor, "The Computer as a Communications Device." *Science and Technology*, April 1968.

Lillee, Dennis. *Lillee: An Autobiography.* London: Hodder, 2003.

Lipsyte, Robert. *Sportsworld: An American Dreamland.* New York: Quadrangle/New York Times Book, 1975.

Lommers, Suzanne. *Europe—On Air: Interwar Projects for Radio Broadcasting.* Amsterdam: Amsterdam University Press, 2013. Technology and European History, vol. 7.

Longman, Jere. *The Girls of Summer: The U.S. Women's Soccer Team and How It Changed the World.* New York: HarperCollins, 2000.

Lumpkin, Angela, and Linda D. Williams. "An Analysis of *Sports Illustrated* Feature Articles, 1954–1987." *Sociology of Sport Journal* 8, no. 1 (1991): 16–32.

Lyons, Eugene. *David Sarnoff: A Biography.* New York: Harper & Row, 1966.

MacCambridge, Michael. *America's Game: The Epic Story of How Pro Football Captured a Nation (Kindle edition).* New York: Anchor Books, 2005.

——— . *The Franchise: A History of Sports Illustrated Magazine.* New York: Hyperion, 1997.

Madden, John. *Hey, Wait a Minute: I Wrote a Book.* New York: Ballantine Books, 1984.

Mair, George. *Inside HBO: The Billion Dollar War between HBO, Hollywood, and the Home Video Revolution.* New York: Dodd, Mead & Company, 1988.

Martin, Adam, and Mary G. McDonald. "Covering Women's Sport? An Analysis of *Sports Illustrated* Covers from 1987–2009 and ESPN The Magazine Covers from 1998–2009." *Graduate Journal of Sport, Exercise & Physical Education Research* 1 (2012): 81–97.

Mason, Tony. "England 1966: Traditional and Modern?" In *National Identity and Global Sports Events: Culture, Politics, and Spectacle in the Olympics and the Football World Cup*, edited by Alan Tomlinson and Christopher Young, 83–98. Albany: SUNY Press, 2006.

Mastrini, Guillermo, Martín Becerra, and Ana Bizberge. *Grupo Clarín: From Argentine Newspaper to Convergent Media Conglomerate*. London: Routledge, 2021.

May, Myra. "Meet J. Andrew White, the Most Famous Announcer in Radio." *Radio Broadcast* 5, no. 6 (October 1924): 447–53.

McCarthy, Anna. ""Like an Earthquake!"" Theater, Television, Boxing, and the Black Public Sphere." *Quarterly Review of Film & Video* 16, nos. 3–4 (1997): 307–23.

McCullough, Brian. *How the Internet Happened: From Netscape to the iPhone*. New York: Liveright Publishing, 2018.

McQuilkin, Scott A., and Ronald A. Smith. "The Rise and Fall of the Flying Wedge: Football's Most Controversial Play." *Journal of Sport History* 20, no. 1 (1993): 57–64.

Melnick, Merrill J. "The Mythology of Football Hooliganism: A Closer Look at the British Experience." *International Review for the Sociology of Sport* 21, no. 1 (1986): 1–21.

Messner, Michael A., Margaret Carlisle Duncan, and Cheryl Cooky. "Silence, Sports Bras, and Wrestling Porn: Women in Televised Sports News and Highlights Shows." *Journal of Sport and Social Issues* 27, no. 1 (2003): 38–51.

Miller, James A., and Tom Shales. *Those Guys Have All the Fun: Inside the World of ESPN*. New York: Little, Brown, 2011.

Miller, Russell. *The House of Getty*. New York: Henry Holt, 1985.

Munk, Nina. *Fools Rush In: Steve Case, Jerry Levin, and the Unmaking of AOL Time Warner*. New York: Harper Business, 2004.

Murray, Caitlin. *The National Team: The Inside Story of the Women Who Changed Soccer* (Kindle edition). New York: Abrams Press, 2019.

Nadel, Joshua H. *Fútbol! Why Soccer Matters in Latin America*. Gainesville: University Press of Florida, 2014.

Nylund, David, and Eric Anderson. *Beer, Babes, and Balls: Masculinity and Sports Talk Radio*. Albany: SUNY Press, 2007. SUNY Series on Sport, Culture, and Social Relations.

Orbach, Barak Y. "The Johnson-Jeffries Fight 100 Years Thence: The Johnson-Jeffries Fight and Censorship of Black Supremacy." *New York University Journal of Law & Liberty* 5 (2010): 270–346.

——— . "Prizefighting and the Birth of Movie Censorship." *Yale Journal of Law and the Humanities* 21 (2009): 251–304.

Parsons, Patrick R. *Blue Skies: A History of Cable Television*. Philadelphia: Temple University Press, 2008.

——— . "The Evolution of the Cable-Satellite Distribution System." *Journal of Broadcasting & Electronic Media* 47, no. 1 (2003): 1–17.

Paxson, Lowell. *Threading the Needle: The Pax Net Story*. New York: Harper Business, 1999.

Pearson, John. *Painfully Rich: The Outrageous Fortune and Misfortunes of the Heirs of J. Paul Getty*. New York: St. Martin's Press, 1995.

Pelé. *Why Soccer Matters: A Look at More Than Sixty Years of International Soccer*. New York: Celebra, 2014.

Peterson, Theodore. *Magazines in the Twentieth Century*. Urbana: University of Illinois Press, 1956.

Poe, Alison. "Active Women in Ads." *Journal of Communication* 26, no. 4 (1976): 185–92.

Powers, Ron. *Supertube: The Rise of Television Sports*. New York: Coward-McCann, 1983.

Quick, Shayne Pearce. *World Series Cricket, Television and Australian Culture*. PhD dissertation, Ohio State University, 1990.

Ramsaye, Terry. *A Million and One Nights: A History of the Motion Picture through 1925*. New York: Simon & Schuster, 1926.

Ranadivé, Vivek. *The Power of Now: How Winning Companies Sense and Respond to Change Using Real-Time Technology*. New York: McGraw Hill, 1999.

Rasmussen, Bill. *Sports Junkies Rejoice! The Birth of ESPN*. Hartsdale NY: QV Publishing, 1983.

Reid, Leonard N., and Lawrence C. Soley. "*Sports Illustrated*'s Coverage of Women in Sports." *Journalism Quarterly* 56, no. 4 (1979): 861–63.

Rice, Grantland. *The Tumult and the Shouting: My Life in Sport* (Kindle edition). New York: A. S. Barnes, 1954.

Riggs, Bobby, and George McGann. *Court Hustler*. Philadelphia: J. B. Lippincott, 1973.

Roberts, Selena. *A Necessary Spectacle: Billie Jean King, Bobby Riggs, and the Tennis Match That Leveled the Game*. New York: Crown, 2005.

Robinson, Joshua, and Jonathan Clegg. *The Club: How the English Premier League Became the Wildest, Richest, Most Disruptive Business in Sport*. London: John Murray, 2018.

Rudel, Anthony J. *Hello, Everybody! The Dawn of American Radio*. Orlando: Houghton Mifflin Harcourt, 2008.

Samuels, Charles. *The Magnificent Rube: The Life and Gaudy Times of Tex Rickard*. New York: McGraw-Hill, 1957.

Savage, Howard J., Harold W. Bentley, John T. McGovern, and Dean F. Smiley. *American College Athletics*. New York: Carnegie Foundation for the Advancement of Teaching, 1929.

Schatzkin, Paul. *The Boy Who Invented Television: A Story of Inspiration, Persistence, and Quiet Passion*. Silver Spring MD: TeamCom Books, 2002.

Scotton, James Francis, and William A Hachten. *New Media for a New China*. Malden MA: Wiley-Blackwell, 2010.

Sinclair, John. *Latin American Television: A Global View*. London: Oxford University Press, 1998.

Smith, Bill L. "The Argentinian Junta and the Press in the Run-up to the 1978 World Cup." *Soccer & Society* 3, no. 1 (2002): 69–78.

Smith, Ronald A. *Play-by-Play: Radio, Television, and Big-Time College Sport.* Baltimore: Johns Hopkins University Press, 2001.

Smulyan, Susan. *Selling Radio : The Commercialization of American Broadcasting, 1920–1934.* Washington DC: Smithsonian Institution Press, 1994.

Socolow, Michael J. *Six Minutes in Berlin: Broadcast Spectacle and Rowing Gold at the Nazi Olympics.* Urbana: University of Illinois Press, 2016.

Spalding, John W. "1928: Radio Becomes a Mass Advertising Medium." *Journal of Broadcasting & Electronic Media* 8, no. 1 (1963): 31–44.

Sperber, Murray A. *Onward to Victory: The Crises That Shaped College Sports.* New York: Henry Holt, 1998.

———. *Shake Down the Thunder: The Creation of Notre Dame Football.* Bloomington: Indiana University Press, 2002.

Steadman, John. *The Greatest Football Game Ever Played: When the Baltimore Colts and the New York Giants Faced Sudden Death.* Baltimore: Press Box, 1988.

Stockmann, Daniela. *Media Commercialization and Authoritarian Rule in China.* New York: Cambridge University Press, 2013.

Stoddart, Brian. *Saturday Afternoon Fever: Sport in the Australian Culture.* North Ryde NSW, Australia: Angus & Robertson, 1986.

Streible, Dan. "A History of the Boxing Film, 1894–1915: Social Control and Social Reform in the Progressive Era." *Film History,* 1989: 235–57.

Sullivan, Tim. *Imus, Mike and the Mad Dog, & Doris from Rego Park: The Groundbreaking History of WFAN.* Chicago: Triumph, 2013.

Tuggle, Charles A. "Differences in Television Sports Reporting of Men's and Women's Athletics: ESPN *SportsCenter* and CNN *Sports Tonight.*" *Journal of Broadcasting & Electronic Media* 41, no. 1 (1997): 14–24.

Vogan, Travis. *ABC Sports: The Rise and Fall of Network Sports Television.* Oakland CA: University of California Press, 2018. Sport in World History, 4.

———. *ESPN: The Making of a Sports Media Empire.* Urbana: University of Illinois Press, 2015.

———. "Exhibiting Ali's Super Fights: The Contested Politics and Brief History of Closed-Circuit Boxing Broadcasts." *Film History* 30, no. 3 (2018): 1–31.

von Saldern, Adelheid. "Volk and Heimat Culture in Radio Broadcasting during the Period of Transition from Weimar to Nazi Germany." *Journal of Modern History* 76, no. 2 (2004): 312–46.

Waisbord, Silvio R. "Leviathan Dreams: State and Broadcasting in South America." *Communication Review* 1, no. 2 (1995): 201–26.

Walker, James Robert. *Crack of the Bat: A History of Baseball on the Radio.* Lincoln: University of Nebraska Press, 2015.

Walker, James Robert, and Robert V Bellamy. *Center Field Shot: A History of Baseball on Television*. Lincoln: University of Nebraska Press, 2008.

Waltzer, Jim. *The Battle of the Century: Dempsey, Carpentier, and the Birth of Modern Promotion*. Santa Barbara CA: Praeger, 2011.

Ware, Susan. *Game, Set, Match: Billie Jean King and the Revolution in Women's Sports*. Chapel Hill: University of North Carolina Press, 2011.

Weiskopf, Herman. *On Three: Inside the Sports Huddle*. Boston: Little, Brown, 1975.

Whannel, Garry. *Fields in Vision: Television Sport and Cultural Transformation*. London: Routledge, 1992. Communication and Society series.

Wilson, Doug, and Jody Cohan. *The World Was Our Stage: Spanning the Globe with ABC Sports* (Kindle edition). North Charleston SC: CreateSpace Independent Publishing Platform, 2013.

Wilson, Jonathan. *Angels with Dirty Faces: How Argentinian Soccer Defined a Nation and Changed the Game forever* (Kindle edition). New York: Bold Type Books, 2016.

Wind, Herbert Warren. *Game, Set, and Match: The Tennis Boom of the 1960's and 70's*. New York: Dutton, 1979.

Wolff, Michael, Bryan Burrough, James Wolcott, Graydon Carter, and Sarah Ellison. *Rupert Murdoch: The Master Mogul of Fleet Street: 24 Tales from the Pages of Vanity Fair* (Kindle edition). New York: Vanity Fair, 2012.

Yergin, Daniel. *The Prize: The Epic Quest for Oil, Money, and Power*. New York: Simon & Schuster, 1991.

Zhao, Yuezhi. *Communication in China: Political Economy, Power, and Conflict*. Lanham MD: Rowman & Littlefield, 2008.

Zhu, Ying. *Two Billion Eyes: The Story of China Central Television*. New York: New Press, 2012.

Index

Morey, Daryl, 250–51, 282–88, 289–90
Morgan, Joe, 229
Morgan, Lynn, 211
Morganella, Michel, 255
Morning Call, 101
Morse code, 15
A Mouthful of Vegetable Pancakes, 280
Movies.com, 173
Mozart Theatre, 21
MP3, 259
Ms., 84
Mundialito, 204
Murbles, Matthew, 230
Murder, 56
Murdoch, James, 289
Murdoch, Rupert, 165–68, 169, 170–72, 192–93, 228, 281
Murphy, Bob, 96–97
Murphy, Brian, 225–26
Murphy, Phil, 269–70
Murphy vs. NCAA (2018), 269–70, 276–77
Murray, Caitlin, 206
Murray, Julie, 208
music, sports compared to, 259–60
Muslims and Islam, 98, 108
MyESPN, 265

Nadel, Joshua, 237
Namath, Joe, 176, 178
narrowcasting, 100, 102, 121–22
National Amateur Wireless Association, 20
National Collegiate Athletic Association. *See* NCAA (National Collegiate Athletic Association)
National Educational Television, 80
National Enquirer, 165
National Football League. *See* NFL (National Football League)
National Hockey League, 127, 171, 193–94, 213

national identity, 33–34, 54, 236–38, 240–41, 244–45, 295
National Invitation Tournament, 213
National Union of Journalists, 240
Navy Club, 21
NAWA (National Amateur Wireless Association), 20
Nazis, 32–36, 41
NBA (National Basketball Association): and basketball stars, 252; and content, 220–21; and controversy, 284–88, 290; distribution of, 216–20; and fictional viewer, 268; internationalization of, 279–80, 281–82, 284–86, 287, 288, 290; personalization by, 293–94; publicity for, 216; and Twitter, 251, 283–85; on websites, 174
NBA China, 282
NBA.com TV, 218, 219–20
NBA Entertainment, 218–19
NBA *Inside Stuff*, 218
NBA League Pass, 219, 220
NBA 3.0, 288
NBC: ABC compared with, 79–80; and baseball, 44, 47; and basketball, 217, 218–19; beginnings of, 30; and broadcasting experiments, 41; and call-in sports shows, 147; and fictional viewer, 266; and football, 139, 143; and soccer, 95, 205
NCAA (National Collegiate Athletic Association): beginnings of, 135; as content provider, 127–28; in court proceedings, 132, 141–42, 269–70, 277; as network partner, 128–29; and television, 137–39, 140, 141–42; websites on, 174
NCAA Television Committee, 137–38
Nelson, Dan, 89
Netflix, 263, 294
Netscape Navigator, 173

TikTok, 294
Time, 53–54, 104, 105–6, 202
Time, Inc., 54, 201
Time Life, Inc., 102, 103
The Times, 76, 115, 247
Times Square, 14–15
Time Warner Inc., 201–3
Title IX, 84
TMZ (website), 2
TNT, 208, 209–10, 219, 252
Torneos y Competencias, 242
Toronto Raptors, 284
Tottenham Hotspur, 272
Trade Practices Commission (Australia), 119
Trammell, Niles, 43
Trout, Jack, 152
Truman, Harry S., 66
Trusky, Ed "Peanuts," 101
Tsai, Joe, 285–86, 289–90
Tunney, Gene, 23–24, 27–28
Turner, Ted, 109
Turner Broadcasting, 109, 143, 220, 221, 222, 252, 264–65
Twenty20, 289
Twitter: and baseball, 1, 2; and basketball, 251, 252, 283–84, 284–87; beginnings of, 250; growth of, 265; during Olympics, 255–56, 257; as pastime, 267, 268; pithiness of, 278; recommendations of, 264; and swimmers, 254
TyC Sport, 242–43

UA-Columbia, 106
UEFA (Union of European Football Associations), 74
UIGEA (Unlawful Internet Gambling Enforcement Act), 274–75, 276
Underwood, John, 59
Union of European Football Associations, 74
Unitas, Johnny, 62–63, 64–65, 70

United Kingdom, 77, 270
United Society for Christian Endeavor, 12
unity and peace, media promoting, 71–73, 77–79
University of Georgia, 132, 141–42
University of Notre Dame, 52–53, 136–39, 143
University of Oklahoma, 132, 140–42
Unlawful Internet Gambling Enforcement Act, 274–75, 276
USA Network, 109
USA Today, 89, 183
U.S. Congress, 197–98
U.S. Department of Justice, 65, 276
U.S. House of Representatives, 198
U.S. Justice Department, 88
U.S. Navy, 20
U.S. Olympic Committee, 30
U.S. Soccer Federation, 204
U.S. Supreme Court, 84, 105, 132, 141, 142, 151, 269–70, 277, 291–92
Utah Jazz, 217–18

Valentino, Rudolph, 124
Valley Parade stadium, 160
Vancouver Canucks, 103
Venturini, Tisha, 205
vertical integration, 171, 203, 212
Viacom18, 289
Videla, Jorge, 238–40
video games: development of, 188–90, 191–92; and gambling, 197; influence of, 193–97
Village Voice, 232
Virgin America Airlines, 253
Virginia, gambling in, 276
Virginia Slims Circuit, 86
Vogue, 254
Volksempfänger, 33

Waddle, Chris, 169
wagering. *See* gambling

Wagner, Betty, 38–39

Wagner, George. *See* Gorgeous
George

Wagner, Todd, 214–15, 216, 221

Wahl, Grant, 209, 210

Waldman, Suzyn, 151

Walker, James R., 43, 44

Wall Street Journal, 128, 168

Walsh, Jimmy, 176

Walson, John, 101, 103

Ward, Charlie, 176

Warner Communications, 201

Warren, W. Harold, 21

Washington Freedom, 209

Washington Post, 63–64, 198, 272

Waskilewski, Vincent, 68

websites: beginnings of, 173; of businessmen, 214–15; domain names of, 183–84; and fictional viewer, 264–65; finances of, 181–83; for gambling, 274–75; for general sports, 174–75; of news companies, 225–26; for specialized sports, 175–80; of sports celebrities, 248–51; target audiences of, 228–30

Weiskopf, Herman, *Sports Huddle*, 148–49

Welker, H.J., 23

Wells, H.G., 15

Wen, Sun, 208

Wendy's, 215

Westbrook, Russell, 284, 285

West Germany, 77, 95

WFAN (radio station), 151–53, 154, 155–56

"What Would Ryan Lochte Do?" 256–57

White, J. Andrew, 20, 21–23, 29

whites, 9–10, 12, 14, 16, 24

WHN 1050, 151

Wide World of Sports, 79–80

Wiegert, Charlie, 187

Willard, Jess, 16

William Hill (gambling company), 270

Williams, Andy, 90

Williams, Serena, 227–28, 254

Williams, Venus, 227–28

Wilson (sitcom character), 273

Wilson, Doug, 93

Wilson, Jonathan, 244

Wind, Herbert Warren, 92

Winfrey, Oprah, 253

Wireless Age, 20, 22

wireless technology, 22–23, 32

Wireless World, 73

Wishmeyer, Florence, 148

Witkin, Mark, 147–48

WNBC, 147

women, in sports: attitudes toward, 89; encouragement of, 84; media covering, 83–84, 92, 93, 203–4, 209–10, 211–12, 227–28, 262; and soccer, 204–9. *See also* King, Billie Jean

womenSports, 93

Women's United Soccer Association, 208–10, 211–12

Women's Weekly, 112

Women's World Cups, 206–7, 211–12

Woodcock, John, 115, 119

Woodhull, Nancy, 89

Woods, Tiger, 174, 179, 182

World Championships (2011), 254

World Cups, 74, 75–77, 95–96, 206, 238, 239, 246–47. *See also* Women's World Cups

World Hockey Association, 127

World Series, 43–48, 49–50, 147, 248

World Series Cricket, 116–19

The World Series Cricket Story, 118

World War I, 16, 17–18, 19, 28, 51, 72

World War II, 42, 48, 61, 72–73, 100, 105–6

World Wide Web, 175

Worship Network, 210